01/26/14

#301294

ADVANCE PRAISE FOR *EUROSHOCK*

"Charles Dallara's *Euroshock* is a remarkable achievement. Remarkable in its authoritative and detailed insider's account of what did (and did not) happen. Remarkable in the way it weaves "small picture" details (like dealing with collective action clauses) with "big picture" issues (like the survival of the Eurozone). Remarkable in interspersing fascinating bits of Greek history—not to mention the author's personal history. And, not least, remarkably well written. *Euroshock* is and will remain the definitive account of a singular episode of financial history."
— **Alan S. Blinder, former vice chairman of the Federal Reserve Board and author of the *New York Times* best seller *After the Music Stopped: The Financial Crisis, the Response, and the Work Ahead***

"There can be no-one better placed than Charles Dallara to give the inside story of the biggest crisis the Eurozone has experienced so far. As head of the Institute of International Finance, he was very close to the banks, and has a rare understanding, for an outsider, of the mysterious dynamics of European policy-making. He also has an eye for the personalities and the drama, which make this a compelling read."
— **Sir Howard Davies, chairman of NatWest Group, former director The London School of Economics, and author of *The Chancellors: Steering the British Economy in Crisis Times***

"A unique case in international financial history; it was the private creditors who initiated a restructuring of Greece's debt, not the public sector. This masterpiece shows that a sense of responsibility and commitment to the common good, and the long-term stability of the international system, inspired the private players in this unprecedented negotiation."
— **Jacques de Larosiere, former managing director of the International Monetary Fund and governor of the Banque de France**

"Charles Dallara, a former naval officer who once navigated a destroyer in the Mediterranean, led a group of creditors in one of the most complicated, tumultuous negotiations in modern economic history. Operating under intense market pressures and facing global, regional, and national political forces, his team in the end successfully completed the largest debt restructuring in history, strengthening Greece and stabilizing the Eurozone. This is a gripping story. It portrays a fascinating case of crisis leadership at its best, and I would highly recommend it to those interested in Greece, Europe, and the art of leadership."
— **James G. Stavridis, PhD, former Supreme Allied Commander Europe at NATO; former dean of The Fletcher School of Law and Diplomacy; vice chair, Global Affairs of The Carlyle Group**

"Charles Dallara has created a captivating personal account about one of the world's most complicated and dangerous sovereign debt crises in modern times. He demonstrates in stark detail the human misery and economic chaos that can be generated by debt crises, underscoring the threat that they can pose not just to a country in trouble, in this case Greece, but to neighboring countries and the world at large. The United States is potentially on a path to an even more catastrophic debt crisis, and this book represents a clarion call to both politicians and economists to take action to avoid this calamity. A must-read."

— Nouriel Roubini, distinguished economist; professor emeritus, New York University; and author of *Mega Threats: Ten Dangerous Trends That Imperil Our Future, and How to Survive Them,* and *Crisis Economics: A Crash Course in the Future of Finance*

"In the summer of 2011, Charles Dallara led a small group of economists and bankers called upon to play a pivotal role in determining the fate of a people teetering on the edge of financial collapse. This was not just any society, but the Greek people, whose ancestors had given us most of the ideas that guided much of the modern world including democracy, individual rights, equal justice under law, and the word 'economics.' In a riveting narrative supported with irrefutable documentation, Dallara reveals in *Euroshock* how such a smart people got into such dire straits, and how they were prodded, pressed, and pushed to find the wherewithal to save themselves."

— Nicholas Gage, author of the best-selling book *Eleni*

"A fascinating insider's story of the great Greek debt crisis and unprecedented debt restructuring that helped Greece and the Eurozone survive."

— Graham T. Allison, professor at Harvard University and author of the best-selling book *Destined for War: Can America and China Escape Thucydides's Trap?*

"The story of the Greek sovereign debt crisis, up-front and personal, told by a leading economist who experienced it at the sharp end—and never lost his affection for the Greek people, who had most to lose. A riveting read."

— Roderick Beaton, emeritus professor of Modern Greek and Byzantine History, Language and Literature at King's College London; author of *Greece: Biography of a Modern Nation* and *The Greeks: A Global History*

"This is a remarkable work describing one of the most turbulent periods of economic history in modern Europe. Dallara makes the story highly accessible, transporting the reader directly into the negotiating room, capturing both events and personalities with a keen eye for detail. He helps a layman understand why this episode of high economic drama is so important for all of us."
— **Gay Talese, author of** *Frank Sinatra Has a Cold* **and** *Unto the Sons*

"Charles Dallara charmingly narrates, sparing no detail, the entire course of negotiations that would lead to the haircut of the Greek public debt but also to Greece's return to a path that could save it from the impasse it had fallen into. Participating in these processes himself, Dallara seems more able than anyone to recount and illuminate them."
— **Kostas Kostis, professor of Economic and Social History at National and Kapodistrian University of Athens; author of** *History's Spoiled Children: The Story of Modern Greece*

"Charles Dallara, the right man at the right place, takes us along through his long journey of negotiations inside the perplexing corridors of modern Eurozone politics. He provides an eloquent and convincing description of how a few bankers, under the IIF umbrella, voluntarily initiated and concluded the largest sovereign debt restructuring in history despite the big loss they suffered. The book is a personal story of perseverance and eventual triumph, with vivid descriptions of private discussions with economists, bankers, central bankers, and many key international political figures, and with frequent flashbacks to the earlier Brady Plan for Latin America and to various critical historical episodes that formed the modern Greek nation."
— **Gikas Hardouvelis, chairman of the National Bank of Greece and former minister of finance of Greece**

"This new book by Charles Dallara is a fascinating insider story about the European debt crisis. A great read!"
— **Axel Weber, former chairman of UBS and former president of Bundesbank**

€UROSHOCK

How the Largest Debt Restructuring in History
Helped Save Greece and Preserve the Eurozone

CHARLES H. DALLARA

RODIN
BOOKS™

Hardcover ISBN: 978-1-957588-13-1
eBook ISBN: 978-1-957588-15-5

PUBLISHED BY RODIN BOOKS INC.
666 Old Country Road
Suite 510
Garden City, New York 11530
www.rodinbooks.com

Book and cover design by Alexia Garaventa
Book production by Booktrix

IIF Staff Note, Appendix 6 © 2012 Institute of International Finance, Inc.

Manufactured in Canada

RODIN
BOOKS™

For Peixin

TABLE OF CONTENTS

PREFACE

In 2010 and 2011 Europe was enveloped in a severe economic crisis. The global economy had begun to recover from the upheaval precipitated by the global financial crisis of 2008 and 2009, but now Europe threatened to pull the world back into another period of economic turbulence and misery.

Ireland, Italy, Spain, and Portugal were each caught up in their own web of volatility and job destruction, throwing their economies asunder. They were not, however, moving independently, but in a vortex that fed on the weakness of each country and magnified the risks to Europe as a whole through multiple channels of contagion. The entirety of the European economy came under a dark cloud as doubts grew about the ability of the Eurozone to hold together. A currency union had been created a mere decade before—the crown jewel in the more than half-century-long effort to create a unified Europe—and profound questions were now being raised about the sustainability of the common currency in this tempest.

At the center of this upheaval was Greece. With an economy that was barely 12% the size of Italy's GDP and only 20% of Spain's, Greece had somehow taken center stage in this European calamity. The global markets had abruptly severed the flow of funds to Greece in late 2009, and the Greek economy was being kept afloat by the International Monetary Fund (IMF) and other Eurozone member countries as Greek leaders strove to stanch the bleeding. Efforts to stabilize Greece and bring calm to broader European waters were, however, flagging, as global markets were increasingly infected by the drama playing out in Greece and in other corners of Europe.

The frantic search for solutions began to circle around an exceedingly vexing question: would Greece's debt to private creditors need to be reduced and restructured—as an essential complement to economic reform—in order to bring stability to Greece and ease the virulent spread of market pessimism surrounding Europe?

There were two camps: those who thought that such a move was anathema to the basic concepts underlying Europe's common currency and could lead to a domino effect of other Eurozone countries restructuring their own sovereign debt, thus undermining the euro; and those who felt that a restructuring was the only way to "lance the boil," diminish the spread of contagion, and put Greece on a sustainable path to recovery.

It is no exaggeration to say that at that moment the future of the European economy hung in the balance, as did the potential risk of round two in the global financial crisis.

This book is the story of how that dilemma was eventually resolved, culminating in the largest debt restructuring in history. Greece has now emerged from a decade-long nightmare to recover its independence, and has begun to follow a path of economic renewal and revitalization. But the decisions made along the way had enormous consequences for the citizens of Greece and Europe, as well as for the world economy. This book elaborates on those consequences, as the Greek economy underwent a severe depression, and the livelihoods of millions of Greek citizens were upended.

This is a highly personal perspective, as I was one of the protagonists in this brief but tumultuous phase of European and Greek history. As the Managing Director of the Institute of International Finance (IIF), I, along with a few other brave souls, stepped into a vacuum to initiate the negotiations and the restructuring and to seek to bring it to resolution. Naturally, I view this entire episode through my own personal prism; it is likely that others also intimately involved would characterize events, personalities, and forces rather differently. There is also the challenge of writing about a period of history that occurred a decade ago; memories falter, and they can also play tricks. I have relied upon copious notes and reams of documentation to underpin this book, and I have also consulted with colleagues about my version of what took place. Nevertheless, this is solely my story, and my colleagues bear no responsibility for errors, omissions, and mischaracterizations.

I have appended to this book a number of documents that will provide additional insight into the negotiations. They may be especially valuable to those who want to research the details of the process as it developed. For anyone who still doubts that "Grexit" (a Greek exit from the euro) would have been catastrophic for Europe, I suggest you read Appendix 6.

The narrative opens in Chapter 1 with one of the more dramatic moments of the early phase of the negotiations—a midnight meeting with then Chancellor Angela Merkel of Germany and then President Nicolas Sarkozy of France. The book also provides background on how Greece ended up in this predicament, and how four representatives of the private creditors ended up in that negotiating room. From there, the story unfolds as negotiations intensified over the next year.

I have also laced into the chronicle some of my own background, which, although in some cases not directly related to the Greek debt problem, sheds light on how I first discovered Greece and approached various issues, while also placing the Greek crisis in the broader context of sovereign debt restructurings since the 1980s.

With every painful experience of this scale there are lessons learned for individuals, institutions, and nation-states. My hope is that this book will contribute to those lessons learned as we continue to search for better ways to manage the global economy. Economics is an inexact science at its best, and the challenge of sound economic policymaking is exceptionally difficult when the environment is highly politicized and institutional roles are ill defined and underdeveloped. The disciplines of macroeconomics and international political economy have advanced our understanding of how these forces intersect, but much remains to be learned about how crises such as that faced by Greece can best be avoided, or be better managed when they do manifest themselves.

That is the responsibility that all of us involved in these issues carry to the citizens of Greece, Europe, and the world as we seek to process the lessons learned from this turbulent period in modern European history.

CHAPTER 1

LATE NIGHT WITH MERKEL AND SARKOZY

"Know the right time."

Pittacus of Mytilene, circa 650–670 BC

"Europe on edge as rescue talks stall," read the headline in the *Financial Times* on October 21, 2011.[1] Indeed, European and global markets were both very anxious. A market strategist speculated that "Greece is going to play the role of Lehman Brothers."[2] "Stocks stumble as Europe clouds the market" provided another typical depressing headline on October 25 as the Dow dropped 1.7%.[3] To add to the gloom, an unnamed senior European official was quoted as saying, "We lost the main parachute and we're on the reserve chute and we're not sure that will work."[4] President Sarkozy of France, Chancellor Merkel of Germany, UK's Prime Minister David Cameron, and US President Barack Obama tried to provide a lift by holding a video conference to discuss the situation, but nothing concrete emerged. Merkel, following the lead of Jean-Claude Trichet, President of the European Central Bank, spoke of the worst crisis in Europe since World War II and warned that what was at stake was not just the future of the euro, but of Europe itself.[5]

In the midst of this swirl of market turbulence and political distress, Europe's most senior leaders, the European Commission (EC), and the

International Monetary Fund came together with Greece and its private creditors on the night of October 25, 2011, to search for a way out of Greece's monumental debt problem and Europe's crisis.

It was, in fact, past midnight on October 25–26, 2011, and we were in a small, drab, fluorescent-lit conference room in the basement of the Justus Lipsius building in Brussels, the headquarters of the Council of the European Union. A modern, supposedly functional building, it was built in the early 1990s by a mix of architects, engineers, and construction companies from all over Europe. It certainly felt like an uninspired setting that night to me, but probably any building would have at that dark hour. The subject was Greece—how to pull it out from under the mountain of sovereign debt while at the same time stabilizing an increasingly fragile Eurozone. Lipsius was a sixteenth-century Flemish philosopher best known for his attempt to combine stoicism with Christianity. Somehow, I doubted that his "bear the misfortunes of life with a stiff upper lip" philosophy would appeal too much to the Greek people that night. They had already been through a lot, with the economy shrinking by 5 percent in 2010 and the unemployment rate at 20 percent. But the pain unfortunately was only beginning.

We were faced that night with what seemed like a phalanx of high-ranking European and global civil servants. It may have worked for the ancient Greeks, amassing heavily armed soldiers in a tight formation to overcome the enemy. But it was not working that night for Europe or Greece. Greece was certainly not advancing with the confidence that their forerunners had at the Battle of Marathon in 490 BC. Somehow two and a half millennia of mankind's development had seemingly left Greece on the side of the road. How? When? It was a question I pondered often as I struggled with the grotesque economic realities of Greece in 2011.

Negotiations that night had, in fact, ground to a halt. As the headlines had screamed, global markets were on edge, but Greece's representatives and their Eurozone counterparts still had "no mandate" to search for a solution.

Fueled only by a sandwich and coffee through the night, my patience—and that of my three stalwart colleagues—was wearing thin. I was joined that night by Jean Lemierre of BNP Paribas and Hung Tran and Mikis Hadjimichael of the Institute of International Finance (IIF).

Jean was Senior Advisor to the Chairman of BNP Paribas, one of Europe's largest banks. He was a veteran of both European and global economic and financial negotiations, having risen in the ranks of the French

Treasury to the Director du Trésor position, the leading civil servant in France's Finance Ministry. From there he moved to the presidency of the European Bank for Reconstruction and Development (EBRD), Europe's private sector–oriented development bank, created in the aftermath of the fall of the Iron Curtain. He knew all the players in the European financial landscape, the strengths and the weaknesses of the institutions, and the proclivities of each government. All of this was extremely valuable throughout our negotiations. His presence gave us instant credibility in many official circles even when the officials did not like our position. A product of the best schools of France, he had about him the air of a silver-haired patrician, but was at heart a public servant.

Hung Tran was the Counselor and Senior Director of the Global Capital Markets Department at the IIF. He possessed a highly diversified background in global finance, having spent many years in private markets with Merrill Lynch, Deutsche Bank, and Rabobank. He then moved to the International Monetary Fund (IMF), where he had been Deputy Director of the Monetary and Capital Markets Department. He had a very quick mind in analyzing complex financial problems, and his knowledge of market dynamics was critical as we grappled with the vicissitudes of the markets. A self-made man who escaped Vietnam with his family, Hung exuded a sense of competence and energy.

Mikis Hadjimichael rounded out our quartet. He was another highly trained economist, with a PhD from the London School of Economics. Mikis had spent over two and a half decades on the staff of the IMF in several senior positions, with a vast experience in assessing economic performance and designing reform programs for tons of developing, emerging market, and advanced economies. He joined us just in time at the IIF, in August 2010, as Deputy Director of the Global Capital Markets Department, as Greece's debt was becoming more and more intractable. His inside knowledge of the IMF proved vital time and again as we tried to keep up with the twists and turns of the IMF's negotiating positions. Mikis was a Cypriot, and his detailed understanding of Greek culture, the Greek economy, and of course the Greek language gave him insights that none of the rest of us could possibly match. His bushy eyebrows and goatee created the impression of a professor, and his economic strengths did not belie that.

We had already become a tightly knit group by late October 2011, and we had to be. We were outnumbered from the outset. Four of us representing the major private holders of over $200 billion in Greece's outstanding bonds, versus at least twenty representing European and global officialdom, including the European Central Bank (ECB); the EC; the new European Financial Stability Facility (EFSF); Germany and France as the leading countries of the Eurozone; the ever-present IMF; and the somewhat forlorn representatives of Greece—the country at the center of this uniquely convoluted set of negotiations.

Of course, we had guidance from the top of the world of private finance. In particular, after we had formally organized ourselves as a Creditor Committee for Greece, we had a deep bench of legal and financial advisers. Furthermore, we had additional key staff of the IIF such as Phil Suttle, our Chief Economist, and Jeff Anderson, the head of the European Department. Beyond this reservoir of technical expertise, we had the members of the Creditor Committee and the Board of the IIF, which was led by Joe Ackermann, who were often helping to shape our response at each difficult turn in the road. And yet, in the room that night in Brussels, there were just the four of us.

Greece was at the table, but only barely. They were hardly in charge of their own destiny. This had been like no other sovereign debt negotiation in modern history—certainly none that I had been involved in over four decades in global finance. Greece, represented by two competent public servants, Petros Christodoulou and George Zanias, clearly understood they were not calling the shots. Petros, the Director of Greece's Public Debt Management Agency (PDMA), was an energetic man, fifty-two years of age and without a single hair on his head. He was anxious to defend Greece's interests, but at times was prevented from doing exactly that by the armada of other interests on "his" side of the table—and by the perilous state of the Greek economy. George Zanias, the Chief Economic Advisor at the Ministry of Finance, was older at fifty-seven, an established and respected academic economist. But he was worn down by the grueling process, by the long days and nights, by Greece's failing credibility, and by what must have seemed at times the banality of it all.

But it was neither Petros nor George who led the debtors' side of the table that night. It was Vittorio Grilli, Italy's Deputy Finance Minister. How, you may ask, did an *Italian* official come to represent Greece in these negotiations, which were so critical to the future of the Eurozone? One Eurozone country in dire straits represented by another that was also struggling mightily for credibility in global markets? How indeed? The media headlines would alternate—"Greek Debt Crisis Threatens Eurozone" would scream across one day's tickers, only to be replaced the next day by "Italian Fears Rattle Global Investors." Grilli was a rather handsome Milanese and carried with him a sense of style. At the same time, his furrowed brow conveyed a tinge of perpetual concern—perhaps inevitable given his job.

Grilli was an experienced technocrat who held the somewhat inscrutable title of Head of the Working Group of the Eurogroup. The Eurogroup, in turn, consisted of the Finance Ministers of the Eurozone member countries. In effect, Grilli was in charge of the Deputy Finance Ministers of the Eurozone. His was the unenviable task of heading the negotiations with Greece's private creditors to restructure Greece's debt. Europe had developed a dizzying array of committees, groups, organizations, councils, and funds to guide, orchestrate, and occasionally obfuscate its multilayered activities and operations. Decision-making was exceptionally complicated, replete with opportunities for waste or evasion of accountability by any individual or group. Hot potatoes abounded in Euroland, and no potato was hotter in 2011 than Greece.

Representing Greece was the last place Vittorio Grilli wanted to be. His greatest fear was that Greece's severe malaise could infect Italy and pull both countries into the vortex. Both had deep-seated economic problems, high levels of debt, bloated government bureaucracies, pervasive corruption, and economies riddled with patronage.

The big difference between Greece and Italy on October 25, 2011, was that global markets had already slammed the door on Greece—not one more dollar for the Greek government, they had effectively said. Aside from modest rollovers of Greek government debt financed largely by the Greek banks in the local Greek markets, the Greek government had no access to private capital. Italy, however, was continuing to raise money from private capital markets—although at rising costs due to its deteriorating creditworthiness—and while in a triage state, was not broadly perceived as a lost cause, as Greece was.

But Italy did have one albatross that Greece did not: Silvio Berlusconi. In his third term as Prime Minister, Berlusconi—amazingly, Italy's longest-serving Prime Minister in the postwar period—had become known for his earlier convictions of tax fraud and his frequent need to defend himself against multiple criminal charges. Grilli had to live—and function—with the knowledge that Berlusconi had the potential to torpedo the Italian economy at any moment, whether through his personal shenanigans or his intemperate policy statements.

In June 2011, after the opening session between the private creditors and the entourage representing Greece at the Italian Treasury, Grilli and I had retreated to his office to consider what, if any, progress we had made that day. As we walked down the long corridor of this impressive but somewhat weathered edifice, Grilli was approached hurriedly by one his staff members; Italian Minister of Finance Giulio Tremonti wanted him on the phone urgently.

Grilli was whisked into his nearby office, while I waited in his anteroom, keeping company with a few sixteenth-century pieces of Italian art. After ten minutes, he walked into the anteroom, slumped in his chair and said with a weary voice, "This is why I am so concerned about the Greek negotiations." He explained that Berlusconi had just attacked Tremonti for suggesting that Italy might need a further round of budget cuts. The effect of Berlusconi's attack on the markets was predictable—Italian government bonds came under severe pressure, pushing the yields up to over 4 percent. "I understand that Greece may need its debt restructured and reduced," Grilli stated plaintively. "But I am the Deputy Finance Minister for Italy, and I have to look out for my own country. If Greece restructures, markets may well convince themselves that Italy is next in line. And our debt is five times the size of Greece! It will destroy our bonds, destroy the euro, and take us back to a world of endless instability!"

Even in his dapper double-breasted dark-blue suit, he looked forlorn that day. "I understand, Vittorio, but we cannot procrastinate with Greece," I responded. "If we do, the risk is high that this could pull the euro itself apart. If we fail to reduce Greece's debt in an orderly fashion and put it on a more sustainable path, Greece could simply be the first of the Eurozone countries to be ripped out of this currency union. Italy, and possibly others, could follow. And Italy must deal with the Berlusconi problem, regardless of what happens to Greece." Grilli knew that the markets were once again losing their sense of gravity, doubting whether the euro could be preserved. Greece on one hand, or Berlusconi on the other, could pull Italy under.

Nearly twenty-seven centuries after Homer's *Odysseus*, Grilli was trying to navigate through his own Scylla and Charybdis. Was Berlusconi the six-headed monster, and Greece the whirlpool that could pull Italy into the deep waters of the Mediterranean? When the markets saw Greece and Italy through the same prism, as they often did that summer, it was easy to imagine that Grilli's fears were well founded.

But who was Grilli representing in his negotiations with the private sector—Greece? Italy? All of the Eurozone? There were simply not enough sides of the table on which Grilli could sit. As we moved deeper into the night of October 25, and in the wee hours of October 26, we were getting nowhere. Grilli's ambivalence toward the whole project and his conflict over who he represented was compounded by the fact that he "had no mandate." For five months, we had heard this mantra so often that it seemed like a sick joke—the euro was crumbling, but no one was given the explicit task—or authority—of rescuing it. It seemed impossible to locate a person or an institution who was accountable for those negotiations. Our attempt to focus on Greece was also undermined by the fact that Italy was nearly in chaos, both Ireland and Portugal were in deep trouble as well, and Spain was sliding into recession.

Earlier on the day of October 25, there had been twenty-seven heads of state, presidents or prime ministers, each leading one of the twenty-seven members of the European Union. But sometime in the early morning of Wednesday, October 26, European Council President Herman van Rompuy "invited" ten heads of state to leave the room, to head home, or to "skedaddle," as we would have said in South Carolina, where I grew up. I never could figure out exactly where they went at that time of night—I guess they just headed home to London, to Stockholm, to Budapest, to Prague, and so on. But it seemed a bit like inviting the audience to leave a boxing ring before the main event of the night. Would anyone have left Araneta Coliseum before the "Thrilla in Manila" between Muhammad Ali and Joe Frazier? Greece had still not been sorted—at all—but the EU member states who were not part of the Eurozone apparently had no "legitimate" reason to be present while Greece was resolved—one way or the other.

Extraordinarily heavy rains had spawned damaging floods in Italy earlier that week. As reported in the English language version of *Der Spiegel*,[6] "torrents of water surged through villages in the wine-growing region of Tuscany, carrying away cars, bridges and baby carriages . . .

Monterosso and Vernazza, two of the five world-famous villages that make up Cinque Terre, a popular tourist attraction, were rendered unrecognizable . . . But the catastrophe on the Gulf of Genoa was not a purely natural disaster. The flood damage was also a result of 1.3 million houses that were built illegally, of a countryside recklessly covered in concrete and of poorly fortified dams."

And what was happening in Rome to cope with this disaster? Fisticuffs in parliament. Northern League leader Umberto Bossi's followers got into a scuffle with supporters of Gianfranco Fini, a former Berlusconi ally turned opponent. Parliament was suspended until order could be restored. The dispute was over pension reform, with animosities apparently having flared due to an accusation that Bossi's wife had taken early retirement with full benefits from her teaching job at the age of thirty-nine. Hmm . . .

So who could blame Grilli for not being able to concentrate on Greece's problems? Not I, but our sympathies were more than offset by the need to get something done before the Greek crisis exploded the entire structure of the Eurozone.

We needed a package of measures that would constitute a new deal for Greece, for its private creditors, and for Europe. We were at a Euro Summit with seventeen heads of state sitting above us somewhere in the stratosphere of this enormous bastion of bureaucracy. What were they doing? Certainly, they had other business, but the pressing business of the day—or night, as it were—was Greece. Markets were anxiously looking for a breakthrough, and every politician in Europe knew it. And here we were spinning our wheels.

As the clock moved past midnight, I was approaching my wit's end. We were focusing on three issues crucial to a new deal:

· How much of a haircut, or loss, would the creditors accept?

· How much money would the Eurozone countries contribute to the creditors to cushion the blow of a haircut, and in what form?

· What would be a sustainable level of debt for Greece in the future?

A fourth issue, looming behind all of these, was how much additional money Greece would need from the Eurozone. On each question, potential progress would dance across the table as our discussions meandered. Fine lines on an autumn evening, only to disappear quickly. Why? No mandate. No authority.

But there comes a moment in every negotiation when words need to stop merely circulating like wisps of smoke and instead start to mean something, or people become dispirited, and discussions crumble. This was such a moment.

As Grilli, sitting at the head of the rectangular table in our cramped conference room, once again uttered the words "I am sorry, but I have no mandate," I stood up and spoke directly to him: "Find someone with a mandate." My three colleagues—Jean, Hung, and Mikis—and I picked up our papers, our various electronic gadgetry, and walked out of the room. We sought refuge in a smaller, deserted room across the hall. Grilli followed us out of the room, somewhere between perplexity and comprehension. He then walked down the hall toward the elevators with a purposeful stride in his walk that I had not noticed before. We turned the lights on and settled into the empty room, wondering if anything would happen that night.

After a short while, I wandered down to the vending machine at the end of the corridor, borrowing a euro or two from Jean to pull some coffee out of the machine. I decided to wake Joe Ackermann, the CEO of Deutsche Bank and our Chairman of the Board at the IIF. I wanted to brief him on the situation and to seek his guidance. He was in Russia on a business trip, and after a few attempts to track him down, I woke him at his hotel and told him where things stood. He recognized how much was on the line, since his own bank was a substantial creditor to Greece, but more importantly, he had a special perspective from his leadership role on the IIF board. While he had no interest in giving more ground that would mean larger losses for the creditors, he also had a clear sense of how vulnerable the entire global financial markets were to a failure of these negotiations.

He had lived through the fall of 2008, as we all had, when global markets had been plummeting. He had stepped in to help save Hypo Real Estate, Germany's second-largest mortgage lender, in mid-October 2008, when the German banking system came under severe pressure as a result of the bank's collapse. This was only a week after Lehman had failed, and Chancellor Merkel had asked Joe to coordinate commercial bank support for a rescue effort to prevent the German banking system from coming apart.

He also understood that we were spinning our wheels with Grilli and company. Standing in a dark corner of the corridor, I discussed with

Joe the parameters of a possible agreement, how much ground we would be willing to give in terms of losses for the creditors—or how large of a haircut—and the need for clarity on Europe's financial commitment not only to Greece, but to the banks. He hesitated, but after considerable discussion with him that night, he decided to support our move to halt negotiations. He concluded, however, with a final bit of advice: "You are right to elevate the discussion to someone with authority, but I hope your negotiations don't collapse. It could be a bloodbath in the markets." I hung up, pulled my small, hot, precious cup of coffee out of the machine, and walked back slowly to our holding pen.

While I was on the phone with Joe, Jean had called his CEO, Baudouin Prot, for consultation. We compared notes with our two colleagues, Hung and Mikis. We all agreed that what we did was necessary, but we nevertheless were somewhat concerned as the night moved on. Would there be no resumption of negotiations that evening? Would we be exposed to widespread criticism for withdrawing—a move that could spark a further sell-off in Greek and Italian debt and another round of volatility in global markets?

I then called another of my IIF Board members, Marcus Wallenberg, Chairman of SEB, a midsize Swedish bank. Marcus's bank had no direct exposure to Greece, but he was a Vice Chairman of the Board of the Institute and an astute and experienced businessman, and I often found his advice and judgment very helpful. Sometimes I just needed to bounce ideas off of someone else. He gave additional support for our move, despite the risks.

Finally, Grilli returned with a curious look of accomplishment on his face. "I found someone with a mandate—with authority to negotiate," he said proudly. He regally motioned toward the door. Jean and I searched for our suit jackets, straightened our crumpled ties, grabbed our papers, and followed him down the corridor. He seemed to have a bounce to his step. We turned a corner, found an elevator, and rode it up seven flights.

As soon as we arrived, two security guards greeted us. Now we had three escorts, with Grilli in the vanguard. Suddenly we entered a brightly lit anteroom with posh royal-blue carpet—the color of the European Union flag. It would have been impressive had it not been nearly 2 a.m.

After a sharp right turn, we entered a room full of white furniture. There were six people, all standing to greet us: the most powerful statesmen—and stateswomen—of Europe, lit up under the glow of sparkling chandeliers. We found Herman van Rompuy, the somewhat stiff but capable President of the European Council; Jose Manuel Barroso, a former Prime Minister of Portugal, who served as President of the European Commission; Jean-Claude Juncker, the cordial and skillful Prime Minister and Finance Minister of Luxembourg and Chairman of the Eurogroup; Christine Lagarde, Managing Director of the International Monetary Fund; at the end of the room, the colorful Nicolas Sarkozy, President of France; and slightly beyond him, Angela Merkel, Chancellor of Germany, poised and stately. Grilli then sat down quietly at the other end of the room. It was quickly noticeable as I glanced about that Greek Prime Minister George Papandreou was nowhere to be seen—he had been left behind in the main meeting room, with all of the other Eurozone leaders. I was not surprised by his absence, but slightly saddened. It was, after all, Greece's fate that was being weighed.

Handshakes, greetings, and somewhat forced smiles were exchanged all around. Merkel invited us to sit as we began our search for a formula to achieve the elusive point of sustainability of Greece's debt, while stabilizing the Eurozone.

Thus began the most pivotal moment in months of intense negotiations over Greece's debt, a moment that would lead to the largest debt restructuring in history.

CHAPTER 2

NAVIGATING TO GREECE

"Happy is the man, I thought, who, before dying, has the good fortune to sail the Aegean Sea."

—Nikos Kazantzakis, *Zorba the Greek*

My experience with Greece dates from decades before my involvement in the debt negotiations of 2011. In 1970, following a brief but eye-opening tour in Vietnam as a US Navy midshipman, I was commissioned as an officer and assigned to a guided missile destroyer, the USS *William T. Sampson* (DDG-10), homeported in Charleston, South Carolina. My first position was as gunnery assistant, responsible for two 5-inch 54 guns—the projectiles were 5 inches in diameter, and the barrel was 54 calibers long (22 feet, 6 inches)—designed to help protect a fleet or to attack by firing on other surface warships or aircraft.

Six weeks after reporting for duty, we sailed to the Mediterranean on two days' notice as part of an effort to stabilize Jordan during what became known as "Black September," a battle for control of Jordan between the King of Jordan and the Palestine Liberation Organization (PLO). After transiting the Atlantic Ocean, we headed straight for the eastern Mediterranean, from which we monitored the situation from a stretch of water close to Jordan's coastline for three weeks of "port and starboard duty" (twelve hours on, twelve hours off). After a total of five weeks at sea, we were existing on powdered milk and potatoes, and little else. We needed a break, and came into port in Soudha Bay, Crete, where

The USS Sampson *(DDG-10). This guided missile destroyer was the ship on which I served in the Atlantic, the Mediterranean, and the Black Sea for two and a half years. Pound for pound, one of the best fighting ships of its era.* Photo courtesy of the author

I had my first taste of Greece. Soudha Bay is a deep, natural harbor on the northwestern end of the island. We anchored out, and I was eager to get off the ship after so much time at sea. As the sun set and we had the *Sampson* securely anchored a few hundred yards from shore, I jumped in the ship's motor whaleboat to go ashore.

After even two weeks of sailing, one is used to the continuous movement of the sea, often gliding, at times cutting, and occasionally thrashing through the water. On this occasion, we had been afloat for five weeks, and our "sea legs" were well developed. I stepped ashore at Soudha Bay and stumbled around, searching for the sway of the ship underneath my feet. The land stubbornly refused to move—not even a hint of the pitch or roll to which my feet and whole body were accustomed to responding. Only 30 feet onto Greek soil for the first time, and I was careening around as if I had downed six shots of ouzo, the powerful Greek anise-based drink that many sailors found to their liking.

Finally I sat down on a bench, as a young Greek woman who was dusting the front steps of what appeared to be a coffee shop looked at me with a decided air of disapproval. After I regained my balance, I approached her and asked where one could find a good meal. I was joined by another young officer, David Eckstrom, with whom I had agreed to go ashore on "liberty." Without saying a word, she motioned us inside with her broom handle. It turned out to be a tavern with four or five small

Seeing the Parthenon for the first time, November 1970. Photo courtesy of the author

Seeing the Caryatids on the Erechtheion up close, November 1970. Photo courtesy of the author

wooden tables, each surrounded by a collection of rather frail-looking chairs. We chose a table near the kitchen and were treated to what tasted to us like a feast, highlighted by a delicious moussaka, which brought a warmth to our stomachs that we had almost forgotten.

We decided to call it a night and venture out early the next day to Heraklion, which is considered by many to be Europe's oldest city. Heraklion is near the ruins of the Palace of Knossos, which was the center of the Minoan Empire, dating from roughly 3500 BC and preceding the Athenian age. That was my first direct exposure to classical Greece, and it certainly outdid the history books. David and I endured the dusty, bumpy bus ride across the island along narrow, circuitous roads through the mountains to Heraklion, but our level of anxiety rose when we noticed the multitude of "kandylakia," roadside shrines marking what we assumed to be a terrible tragedy that had occurred. Indeed, many of these rather amazing shrines, erected by the family of the deceased and which include icons and votive candles, do mark an unfortunate accident and a life lost. We weren't terribly reassured when the bus driver informed us that the shrines also marked near-death incidents, where someone miraculously survived an accident.

The Palace of Knossos, residence of the mythical King Midas, is an archaeological wonder, representing the height of European civilization from the period of 2600 to 1400 BC, a full millennium before the Athenians reached their zenith. The Minoans were traders, and they extended their influence far beyond Crete to other Greek islands as well as to Egypt, Cypress, the Levantine coast, Israel, and as far as Anatolia, which is now part of Turkey.

Later on this cruise, we had our first stop in Athens. I took a rare day off to scramble up the side of the Acropolis, enjoying the precious moment when I could walk inside the Parthenon, touch its magnificent Doric columns, even caress the feet of the Caryatids, the magical maidens of the amazing piece of architecture that is the Erechtheion. A few years later this privilege came to an end, understandably, when these historic temples gained protection from the meanderings of tourists like me who were captivated by these wondrous creations.

Of course, this visit to Athens was not to be my last. The *Sampson's* home port was shifted from Charleston to Athens in September 1972, and I was about to become a resident of Greece. I had been promoted to the position of navigator, where I was responsible for charting our voyages, monitoring the ship's position every minute we were at sea, and ensuring its safety from all hazards, especially running aground. Nothing can end a naval officer's career more quickly than running a ship aground. It is a concern that a commanding officer and a navigator always keep foremost with them while at sea. And I mean always—you sleep with your uniform on, so as to be able to bound to the bridge instantly if needed. You never sleep for more than four hours at a time, generally much less. But navigating is a beautiful endeavor, and it especially was in those days. The relocation of the *Sampson* and five other destroyers to Greece was called Operation Pegasus. I did not think much about it at the time, but as I settled into the responsibilities of being the navigator, I realized that Pegasus was not only the divine winged horse of Greek mythology, but also had been transformed by Zeus into a constellation of stars. After that realization, I took special delight in charting stars from the constellation Pegasus.

Much of our time was spent either navigating across the Atlantic or patrolling the Mediterranean, before satellite navigation or GPS, figuring out exactly where we were in a vast and ever-changing sea. We were often far from shore without landmarks or buoys to guide us at night amidst a blackness only slightly eased by starlight, if at all.

Celestial navigation is an art first practiced in the same Mediterranean by the ancient Greeks in their triremes, as noted by the historian Thucydides. It involves a sextant, an archaic instrument that employs a tiny telescope to locate a star or another heavenly body. After reading the body's angle above the horizon, some extensive math by the quartermaster or me would allow us to convert a star's position in the sky to our possible location on the water. The more stars I could "fix," the more precisely we would know where we were.

At night I would climb up onto the side of the bridge, usually a quarter hour or so after sunset so that the stars shone brightly while there was still a visible horizon, brace myself as the ship plowed through the waves, and crane my neck to peer up into the night sky. I'd position the sextant into my eye socket, trying to pick out stars to take readings for our quartermaster. Quartermaster Chief Peters was, like many of the Chiefs in the Navy, able to take orders from an inexperienced officer like me while simultaneously teaching me his craft. Quite a skill combining the two.

"Sixty-one Sygni!" I'd shout out, referring to the bright white dot skimming through the clouds overhead. It was nicknamed the "Flying Star" because of its apparent rapid motion, and I had come to rely upon it as I searched the sky twice a night during this mission in the

Mediterranean. "Forty-seven degrees, twenty-two point five minutes" was its angle over the horizon. The quartermaster would make a note. "Antares!" I'd yell excitedly, with more readings of its angle above the horizon. "Got that, Peters?" I shouted to the quartermaster. "Now I have Scorpio—no, wait! Damn! Lost it!" Most of the constellations had disappeared into the clouds. On I would go, touring the heavens star by star—some hits, many misses. Once I had as many hits—or readings— as I could manage, the quartermaster and I would run the math with the help of celestial tables. No handheld computers in this ancient era of the early 1970s. One good reading would give us only a very rough idea of our location, while another would narrow down the possibilities further. A third reading and we were getting close, and with a fourth good sighting we could often determine our position within a nautical mile or two.

One cold and windy November night in 1972, as we were returning to Athens from a trip to the Black Sea, I "bagged" (took sightings on) Venus, the moon, and four stars. Remarkably, as we made our calculations and converted our "fixes" to lines on the chart, we got six clean lines, all of them crossing at one exact point on the chart. I had never done that before, nor would I ever do it again. Six! I gave the quartermaster a slap on the back, and all he said was, "Helluva job, Mr. Dallara." In the perilous darkness around the ship sailing south in the Aegean Sea, we had figured out exactly where in the world we were, and we also knew where we were headed—the ancient port of Piraeus, Athens's harbor.

It was from this harbor in 480 BC that the Greek fleet had sailed to fight the Persians in the Battle of Salamis, and to repulse them from Europe—permanently, as it turned out. We were traveling across the water, but under the moonlight it also seemed we were traveling back to a time when Athens was the center of the Western world and the source of so much of what constitutes civilization today. Sure enough, in the early morning light, the USS *Sampson* slid smoothly into the Port of Piraeus, jolting us back to the modern world. It was 1972, not 480 BC, but perhaps that was the beginning of everything right there. A perfect alignment of stars had guided me to Athens.

Almost forty years later after my time living in Athens, I was back there frequently in 2011, but this time the stars did not seem so well aligned and the journey seemed more perilous—for me, for Greece, for Europe, and for the world economy.

CHAPTER 3

LIVING IN GREECE AND SAILING THE MEDITERRANEAN DURING THE COLD WAR

"The superpowers often behave like two heavily armed blind men feeling their way around a room, each believing himself in mortal peril from the other, whom he assumes to have perfect vision."

—Henry Kissinger, 1979

My time living in Athens in 1972 and 1973 involved an engrossing mixture of exposure to daily life in Greece, Greek culture, Greek politics, and life aboard a fast-moving Navy combatant. When we initially arrived, the facilities in Piraeus were not ready for six ships (an entire squadron was being transferred to Greece), and so for our first few months of being "homeported" in Athens we were actually based in Eleusis Bay, some twelve miles northwest of Athens. Soon after the USS *Sampson* arrived in Greece, I found a small apartment in Nea Smyrni, a neighborhood in downtown Athens populated mostly by Greeks who had been forcibly removed from Smyrni, Turkey, following Greece's defeat in 1922 by Turkish troops under Mustafa Kemal Atatürk. Unfortunately for me, it was a major project each day we were in port to commute from this neighborhood to the ship's temporary base in Eleusis Bay. Nevertheless, I did not protest.

Eleusis was situated just north of the Strait of Salamis, where perhaps the most important naval battle in history had been fought in 480 BC. My course in naval history as a Naval Reserve Officers Training Corps (NROTC) student at the University of South Carolina had left me intrigued about this epic battle. Led by the brilliant strategist Themistocles and with the full support of the Spartans and other Greek city-states, the Athenians vanquished a much larger navy of the Persian king Xerxes, thus protecting the nascent democracy of Athens and allowing it to flourish. My interest in this battle deepened as a result of a course I took during my senior year at Carolina, "The History of Warfare," which featured the Battle of Salamis. As I settled into an early bus before sunrise each morning, traveling over the bumpy roads that connected Athens to Eleusis, I took some vague satisfaction in knowing that I would be sailing the same waters as the Greek sailors in their triremes, both of us seeking to defend democracy, separated only by two and a half millennia. The *Sampson* sailed every corner of the Mediterranean, chasing Russian submarines, engaging in various NATO military exercises, and monitoring the movements of Russian frigates.

We also sailed through the Bosporus into the Black Sea, a harrowing experience for a navigator, as I feared that at any moment we might collide with a small fishing boat or a ferry. While in the Black Sea, we successfully challenged the Soviet claim to a twelve-mile limit for their territorial waters. In those days, a three-mile limit was still the convention, and we did not want to concede the twelve-mile perimeter in this highly strategic body of water. We therefore sailed as close to three miles off the coast of Odessa and other Soviet ports as we could without causing an international incident. It was the height of the Cold War, and given the sensitivity of the exercise, we had to report our precise position home to the Joint Chiefs of Staff in Washington every four hours. After two sleepless weeks we had managed to accomplish our mission while avoiding a collision with Soviet ships that were trailing us very closely. As we entered the Bosporus to sail back to the Sea of Marmara and the Dardanelles Straits, the Soviet sailors lined the rails of their frigate and saluted us. In a Cold War sign of mutual respect, we returned their salute. Hard to imagine today.

When not sailing the Aegean, I was learning my way around Athens. I discovered there was really nothing that matches a Greek salad in the summer served in a Greek taverna on the waterfront, that Greek buses belched horrific exhaust that lingered in the air for what seemed like an eternity, and that the view of the Parthenon from the rooftop of my apartment building was incomparable. I also discovered that the politics in Greece were particularly complicated at that time, especially for Americans living there.

On April 21, 1967, five years before my arrival, Greek military officers had exercised a coup d'état in Greece amidst what initially seemed like yet another instance of eternal scuffling and squabbling between Greece's two leading postwar political families, the Papandreous and the Karamanlises. Georgios Papandreou was the founder of the Papandreou political dynasty. His political exploits dated back to World War I, when he supported Greece's pro-Western leader, Eleftherios Venizelos. In 1965, however, it was not just a tussle for leadership between Georgios Papandreou and Constantinos Karamanlis. Coming at a time of rising tension and conflict with Turkey over Cyprus, Papandreou also found himself in conflict with the deeply entrenched Greek right wing and its principal supporter, the new Greek king, Constantine II. Only one year on the throne at age twenty-five, the King challenged Papandreou when he sought to become Defense Minister in addition to Prime Minister.

Amidst a tense campaign over new elections, on April 21 a group of military officers executed a coup and the King fled into exile. Greece had, in fact, experienced several coups in the interwar years. But this was the first since World War II, and the first—and still the only one—in Western Europe since the end of the war. Georgios' son, Andreas, wrote a gripping account of his experience while in exile in Canada in 1970, *Democracy at Gunpoint: The Greek Front.*[1]

The junta was never able to establish its legitimacy, either at home or abroad. In the first months of 1973, tensions with Turkey were high as the new junta leadership adopted an aggressive approach toward the President of Cyprus, staging a military coup against him in July 1974. This prompted Turkey to invade Cyprus, and the junta collapsed overnight under its actions and its incompetence, allowing the path for restoring democracy to be reopened.[2]

"Students took the lead in opposing the regime, and in March occupied the Law Faculty of the University of Athens."[3] Those actions were followed by much larger demonstrations on November 17, 1973, at the

Athens Polytechnic, a day still celebrated by Greeks as the day that helped restore democracy to Greece. The political tensions of this era spilled over in the attitude toward the American military presence in Athens, including the officers on the USS *Sampson*. A small but active contingent of anti-American Greek citizens demonstrated against the US Navy presence in Athens. The officers, sailors, and their families were, at times, met with verbal attacks, especially when we were in uniform. On at least one occasion the attacks became violent, and a fellow officer's car was bombed. It took some years, until I was writing this book and discussing the era with Greek friends, that I fully appreciated the reasons that lay behind the negative sentiments toward those of us in our naval outpost in the Eastern Mediterranean. Some perceived our presence there as a statement of support for the junta, and there was also a view that the US may have been involved in the 1967 coup. More on that later in this book, but at that time it was beyond the grasp of young sailors serving their country and NATO interests in the Mediterranean.

Looking beyond our own parochial world of the US Navy, political developments in Greece during this period would plant the seeds of many of the difficulties that beset Greece's economy and the period leading up to the debt crisis of 2009 and 2010. A brief look at this crucial slice of Greece's modern history is in order.

After the demise of the junta, things started on a positive note. By July 1974, democracy was back in Greece as Karamanlis was welcomed back from exile and invited to serve as the Prime Minister, ushering in three and a half decades of generally populist governments, often alternating between those led by Karamanlis and his New Democracy Party and Andreas Papandreou's newly formed Panhellenic Socialist Movement (PASOK). Andreas's father, Georgios, had passed away in November 1968 under house arrest by the junta. Polarizing politics, and frequent changes of government, were often accompanied by clientelist economic policies that bred inefficiencies and distortions for many sectors of the economy. PASOK began with a Marxist philosophy, while Karamanlis's economic policies, largely subservient to foreign policy, were in theory more market-oriented. Nevertheless, under Karamanlis, banks and other enterprises were nationalized, including Olympic Airways, sewage and water supply companies, and city transportation, among other businesses.[4] A pattern developed, whose origins dated back to the times of Ottoman rule of widespread patronage, of growing regulation of the private sector, and a bloated public sector. These policies, which particularly gained ground under the Papandreou government that took office in 1981, undeniably helped lay the groundwork for the debt crisis of 2010.

In 1980, government expenditure was 27% of GDP. Over the years, government expenditure continued to increase, reaching 51% of GDP in 1995 and peaking at 54% in 2011.[5] And an increasing part of the growth in government spending was the cost of civil servant salaries. Between 1971 and 2008, the average annual growth rate of the public sector wage of Greece was 14.2%, the highest among Eurozone countries. During the same period, the average growth of public sector wages among all Eurozone countries was only 5.8%.[6] The Greek civil service expanded at an alarming pace; people employed in the public sector grew from 743,300 in 1985 to 1,022,100 in 2008, an increase of 37.5% in just over two decades.*

Another step was taken in the late 1970s that would have enormous implications for Greece in the decade leading up to the debt crisis: Greece was admitted into the European Community. This had been a major ambition of Constantinos Karamanlis when he returned from an eleven-year exile in France in 1974 to assume the leadership of a newly formed government to replace the junta, a process the Greeks called "metapolitefsi." Karamanlis saw this as an opportunity to consolidate support for Greece's democratic institutions. And as Richard Clogg astutely observes, "membership would somehow place the seal of legitimacy on their country's somewhat uncertain European identity."[7]

This was a historic moment for Greece and for Europe, as it cemented Greece's proper place back in the European community of states. On May 20, 1979, Greece signed the official accession agreement to become a member of the European Economic Community, as it was called at the time, and was officially "back in the family." Constantinos Karamanlis had achieved a long-sought goal, which he believed would integrate Greece fully into the fabric of European values and institutions. After all, Greece's Hellenistic period had laid the foundations for so much of today's modern civilization. In more recent history, Greece had been the only Balkan country to escape the clutches of communism after World

---

* The earliest year for which data are available at the International Labor Organization (ILO) is 1985.

War II, and after a brutal civil war it had established a democracy and began building—or in some respects, rebuilding—the institutions of democracy. But Greece's nearly four centuries under the yoke of the Ottomans weighed heavily on Greece's "Europeanness" at that time. "Ottoman rule had the effect of isolating the Greek world from the great historical movements such as the Renaissance, the Reformation . . . the scientific revolution, the Enlightenment, and the Industrial Revolution," argues Richard Clogg.[8] In his view, this would have a profound effect on the lack of certain institutional developments in Greece during this period. As Francis Fukuyama points out in *Political Order and Political Decay*, "the real division between Northern Europe and Southern Europe is not a cultural one . . . it is between a clientelistic and non-clientelistic Europe." As he observes, "both Greece and Italy used public employment as a source of political patronage, leading to bloated and inefficient public service and ballooning budget deficits."[9] In the case of Greece, some aspects of Greece's "low-trust society," as Fukuyama describes it, have their roots in the Ottoman period and the early years of independence in the nineteenth century. As Clogg notes in his work, "The capriciousness of Ottoman rule and the weakness of the idea of the rule of law helped to shape the underlying states of Greek society and to determine the attitudes to the state and to authority that have persisted up to the present."[10]

The distrust of government extended to the tax system. Businesses often kept two sets of books: an accurate one for the family, and another for the tax collector. Indeed, the Ottoman tax collector was often among those officials whom the average Greek citizen would most often encounter. It was considered a family obligation by many to evade taxes. Regrettably, those habits had not changed very much by 2011. In 2010–2012, when the "Troika" (the IMF, EC, and ECB) sought repeatedly to impose tax increases on the Greek people as part of the economic adjustment program, it was most unfortunate that they appeared to have an inadequate grasp of the fact that they were up against nearly five hundred years of an entrenched legacy of tax evasion.

CHAPTER 4

BACK ACROSS THE ATLANTIC AND SERVING AS AN ADMIRAL'S AIDE

"'Things are getting better.' Joe Louis, upon reading that Lieutenant Commander Samuel Gravely Jr. had become the first Negro in US Naval history to command a warship."

—Gay Talese, *The Gay Talese Reader*

During 1973, my path diverged from that of Greece for a period of time; actually, for almost five decades. However, during those intervening decades, looking back, I sense that various turns in the road were actually leading me back to Greece, and preparing me for what I would find when I finally arrived there.

The first step in the process was a transfer back to the United States to serve as an Admiral's Aide. I stood on the bridge of the USS *Sampson* one late afternoon, preparing to take some sightings of evening stars, including the moon and the sun, when I was called to come to the Communications Center. This was unusual, and the timing was unwelcome as I only had fifteen or so minutes before the visibility of some of the celestial bodies would disappear. I rushed down to the center and quickly picked up the phone.

"Lieutenant Dallara, here," I said rather brusquely. (I was actually only a Lieutenant Junior Grade [Lt. JG] at that point, but that title was rarely used). A deep voice boomed over the phone. "Admiral Gravely, here." I stood straight up as if he could see me six thousand miles away. "Yes sir," was all I could say.

"I am calling to ask if you would be interested in being my Aide and Flag Lieutenant," he said. No small talk, right to the point.

"I would be honored, Admiral, to have that opportunity." A message a few days earlier from the Chief of Naval Personnel's office had advised me that such a call might be coming, but that was only a possibility. Now it was for real. Admiral Gravely then said, again quite forthrightly, "You know I am an African American, don't you?"

I was very surprised and hesitated before responding. "Yes, sir." I then repeated myself, not knowing what else to say. "I would be honored to serve as your Aide and Flag Lieutenant."

"Good, I look forward to seeing you soon. We will be in Newport, where I have been assigned as Commander of Cruiser Destroyer Group Two."

"I look forward to working for you," I responded, and then he hung up.

Although I had come to consider *Sampson* my "home," I knew it was time to leave and, unfortunately, also time to leave Greece. I was very excited about working for Admiral Gravely. His reputation as an exceptional naval officer preceded him, and I knew it would also be a special experience given his historic role as the US Navy's first Black Flag Officer.

I faced one dilemma, however. How to get back to the States.

In one of the oddities that the US government at times seems to specialize in, there was no money to fly me back to the States. I was asked, therefore, if I would "work" my way back across the Mediterranean Sea and the Atlantic Ocean by supporting the navigator on a cruiser, the USS *Albany* (CA-123), that was returning to its homeport of Mayport, Florida, after a six-month tour of duty in the Mediterranean. It seemed their lead navigator had become quite ill, and they needed someone to support the assistant navigator. I did not mind, as I found it an intriguing challenge to help navigate a larger warship. The *Albany* was 673 feet, one and a half times the length of the *Sampson*, and packed with more firepower, with 8-inch guns instead of 5-inch, and two more missile launchers.

As we returned across the Atlantic in stormy weather, I gradually assumed more and more of the responsibilities for navigating the ship.

During my downtime I discovered the Meditations of Marcus Aurelius and took solace from his wisdom. In particular, I cherished the thought that "you have power over your mind, not outside events. Realize this, and you will find strength." I also spent time during this voyage home to reflect on my experiences in Greece: My visit to Delphi, which I found mesmerizing as I learned about the special power of the oracles of Delphi— the legend goes that the Pythia, or priestess, could utter prophecies, and these prophecies were valued throughout the Greek world; the evenings on the rooftop of my apartment building, gazing at the Parthenon sitting atop the Acropolis like an unchallenged king, surrounded by his court of other buildings from the Periclean period; the Erechtheion, which I found especially captivating, with the Caryatids, the five draped female figures, supporting the "Porch of the Maidens." Although one of the maidens was taken by Lord Elgin, reportedly to decorate his Scottish mansion, the remaining five figures, though partially disfigured by the ravages of time, war, pollution, and looting, are a stunning reminder of the majestic architecture of the ancient Athenians. The Erechtheion also appealed because of its nautical connections, with the marks of the trident of Poseidon, Greece's ancient lord of the sea. As a sailor, I could not help but be drawn to this mythological figure, for it was always tempting when in rough seas to think that you could have someone who could calm the seas on your side, even if it was mythology and even if it often did not work.

During my quiet time on the bridge across the Atlantic, my mind also wondered over the often-competing images of modern Greece. The suffocating pollution of Athens, the unparalleled beauty of Greece's beaches, and the vitality of the Greek people. The Temple of Poseidon at Cape Sounion towering over the Aegean. In every small village, scores of men sat idly in the town square and in front of every café, drinking coffee and smoking cigarettes. The old men, I could understand. They had earned it. But the younger men? Nevertheless, there was an entrepreneurial energy and creativity evident in so many small tavernas and other businesses, contrasting with the sluggish and inefficient presence of the government at every turn. And then there was the seemingly endless decline of the drachma against the dollar. The student unrest toward the government was growing, even as the junta tried to clamp down on Greek citizens. Soldiers were increasingly evident on every street corner, and as I pondered the situation on my US-bound cruiser, I had a sense that the military government would not last too much longer. I also wondered when, or if, I would ever return to Greece. Little did I realize that two seemingly unrelated events in early 1973—the breakdown of the global par value system and the imminent overthrow of Greece's military government—would conspire to help create the circumstances that would eventually bring me back to Greece.

The day after I reported to the cruiser, I went to the ship's barbershop to get a haircut. Another young officer was sitting in the chair next to me. I introduced myself: "Charles Dallara, working my way back across the Atlantic on your ship."

"David Eisenhower, a pleasure to meet you," he responded.

I suddenly realized he was the grandson of President Dwight D. Eisenhower. We began talking, and I discovered he had graduated from Amherst College in 1970 at the same time I had graduated from the University of South Carolina. He was heading back to the *Albany*'s homeport with the expectation of soon being discharged. He was married to Julie Nixon Eisenhower, one of the daughters of President Richard Nixon, who was serving as our thirty-seventh president at the time. I had met Julie's older sister, Patricia, along with President Nixon, at an event for a select number of student leaders at the White House in 1969. This was before the full extent of the Watergate affair was known, and I was at the time a stronger supporter of President Nixon. I also was a great admirer of David's grandfather, Dwight Eisenhower. President Eisenhower had been a magisterial commander of Allied forces in Europe, and he had also shown courage and leadership in advancing civil rights in America during his presidency. David fondly shared stories of time with his grandfather, but understandably was reluctant to openly discuss his father-in-law, President Nixon.

As I got to know David on our sojourn together, he seemed pleasant and highly intelligent. We discussed our respective experiences in the Mediterranean. He seemed particularly interested in my living in Greece, and we chatted about it on numerous occasions during our two-week journey to Mayport.

During my trip I also reflected on my upcoming responsibilities. I was, of course, mentally preparing to work for another exceptional military leader, Rear Admiral Samuel Lee Gravely Jr., not only the Navy's first Black Admiral, but the only one at that time.

Serving as Admiral's Aide/Flag Lieutenant to Admiral Samuel Lee Gravely Jr., the US Navy's first Black Admiral. I am on the far left, with Captain Roger Buck (Chief of Staff), Admiral Gravely, and Lt. Commander Pete Marnane (Flag Secretary) (right). Photo courtesy of the author

Once I reported for duty, I realized that he had two rather distinct roles: first, as the operational head of Cruiser Destroyer Group Two, a modern-day armada of ships—generally twenty-four in number—that could wage a fierce battle at sea if needed against other ships, as well as airborne or submarine enemy targets; second, the titular leader of the Navy's efforts to promote greater integration within its ranks and to promote the role of Black Americans in the Navy. I learned a great deal about leadership, some of which was eventually helpful in Greece and other negotiations, as I supported Admiral Gravely in both of his roles. At sea during a two-month exercise in the Arctic Circle, I witnessed the Admiral demonstrate real-time strategic thinking as we maneuvered one group of ships against another in a joint NATO exercise. We were not in an actual war, but in an exercise that forced us to react quickly to "enemy" maneuvers and deploy our forces to our best advantage, all in a hostile natural environment where glaciers and lack of sunlight challenged both sides at every turn. I had learned how to operate under pressure during my first three years with the Navy, but this exercise took things to another level, and I observed dynamic leadership in an intense combat-like environment. Gravely was cool and collected, as they say, and carried out his duties as if he were made for it.

But nothing had ever come easy for Samuel Lee Gravely Jr. Born in Richmond, he joined the Navy reserve in 1942 and was commissioned as an Ensign in 1944 after graduating from UCLA. He determinedly worked his way up the line, distinguishing himself during the Vietnam War as the first Black commander of a US Navy ship, the USS *Theodore E. Chandler* (DD-717). He broke the racial barriers time and again. He was the first to lead a ship into combat, and at every step of the way, he faced discrimination. But he persisted, with a motto of "Education, Motivation, Perseverance." In 1971, he became the first Black Admiral in the history of the US Navy.

I traveled the country with him in his second set of duties as the spokesman for the Navy's African American community—a community in which he was an icon. I drafted speeches that he gave, often at historically Black colleges and universities. We went into some parts of the country that were hit hard by the recession of 1973–1974, such as Wilberforce University, the nation's oldest predominantly African American private university. It is located near Columbus, Ohio, an area on the eastern edge of the "rust belt," a center of economic decline and rising unemployment in the 1970s.

The experience was an eye-opener for me, working for a man who had faced and overcome discrimination his entire life. At first he was a bit hesitant around me—an Italian-Irish kid from South Carolina who had come of age in a segregated South. I discussed with him the local circumstances of my youth, with which he was quite familiar; while our schools, churches, and buses were segregated for most of my youth, our neighborhood and social life were not. My brother Dale, local friends, and I played many football, baseball, and basketball games with young men from the Black community that abutted my neighborhood. Although these games started as "Black versus white," after a period of time we began to mix the races on each team. During the summer these games often lasted into the evening, and provided a wonderful opportunity for developing friendships across racial boundaries.

I became Admiral Gravely's Flag Lieutenant, looking out for him in every way that I could. He was, after all, the Navy's Jackie Robinson, baseball's first African American in the Major Leagues. He did not want to highlight his status as the Navy's first Black Admiral, since his goal from the start had been to simply become an Admiral in the Navy. But it was inevitable given his unique status and achievements.

I began to learn what it meant to "walk in someone else's shoes" when I was the only white person in an auditorium at Savannah State University that was full of 1,200 people. Sitting high in the balcony in my summer white uniform, I felt a bit lonely and isolated. Was everyone really staring at me? Imagine how so many Black youth must have felt when they were thrust into formerly all-white schools at the onset of integration, often one at a time, as in my own high school.

Listening to Admiral Gravely tell his stories during our trips together, sometimes over a drink after the demanding schedule had subsided, I began to understand the importance of empathy. Few of us would have had the qualities to persist with his motto, "Education, Motivation, Perseverance," with the fortitude and determination he showed. The need to look at issues from the perspective of someone on the other side of the table was a quality that I tried to develop during my career in global finance, and it came in handy more than once during the Greek debt negotiations.

Admiral Gravely reminded me of John Glenn, another American of many firsts: the first American to orbit the earth, in 1962; the first American to fly across the US continent in less than three hours and twenty-five minutes—an astounding achievement in 1957. One was much more of a household name in America than the other, but both were genuine American heroes. I met Glenn at a dinner a few years ago and told him about Admiral Gravely. He said that he had met him and admired him and considered him a fellow pathbreaker.

Sam Gravely's many years of being on the receiving end of discrimination as he nevertheless progressed up the Navy ladder had understandably left some scars and resentment. He told me of the embarrassment he felt when, after having commanded the USS *Falgout* (DE-324) in combat during the Vietnam War in 1967, he returned to duty at the Pentagon only to find that he was "discouraged" from buying a home in a solid, middle-class neighborhood in Arlington, Virginia, due to his race. He did not know how to explain this to his wife, Alma, so he told her he could not find anything "suitable." As he later said to *Ebony* magazine, he was "saving America for democracy, but not allowed to participate in the goddamn thing."[1]

Those years of prejudice took their toll, and at times he was apt to perceive discrimination where perhaps it did not exist. On one occasion, we flew to Roosevelt Roads, a US Navy base in Puerto Rico, to take command of a major naval exercise on board an aircraft carrier. When we arrived, we were scheduled to stay for two nights at the naval station prior to setting sail. He expected to stay at the Visiting Flag Officer's Quarters, a special compound set aside for Admirals and other high-ranking dignitaries. Upon arrival, we were advised that the flag quarters were unavailable due to repairs, and we would have to stay in regular officer's quarters.

The Admiral raised his eyebrows and walked briskly out of the room. I followed him out and we rode together in the backseat of his chauffeur-driven car, replete with his Admiral's flag fluttering in the right rear corner of the car. He was upset. "Charles, I seriously doubt whether there is anything wrong with the flag quarters—they just didn't want me to stay there." I tried to convince him otherwise, that the Navy would not treat an Admiral that way, but he would have none of it. We checked into our comfortable, but by no means luxurious, bachelor officer quarters (BOQ) and I promptly asked the driver to take me to the Visiting Flag Officer's Quarters. As we drove up, it became apparent that the house was torn apart and major construction was under way, with one wall completely torn down due to the need to remove all the asbestos. I returned immediately and pulled the Admiral out of his room. He was already taking off his uniform to relax and did not want to go with me. I insisted, and after a moment, he sighed, put on his khakis again, and walked slowly to the car. Five minutes later, I opened his door in front of the disassembled Flag Officer's Quarters, and he immediately said, "In the future, Dallara, I will trust your judgment in such matters."

CHAPTER 5

POSTWAR GREECE AND THE QUEST FOR STABILITY AND A CAPABLE DEMOCRACY

"Just because you do not take an interest in politics . . .
does not mean that politics won't take an interest in you."

—Pericles, circa 431 BC

The World Economic Forum was a rather chic gathering spot for many of the world's leaders in 2010, especially for the economic and political "elite." Turtlenecks, snow boots, frigid cold, endless security, horrible traffic, conversations over coffee that were interrupted an average of five and a half times, three-minute television interviews, often discussing "Davos Man" rather than the pressing global problems of the day.

It seemed at times that everyone at Davos became temporarily seized by an infectious, globalized version of attention deficit hyperactivity disorder (ADHD). Two thousand ADHD-affected hyperintellectuals in a small conference center, eyes constantly darting away from one's interlocutor to see if someone more important was walking by. "Hi Gordon [Brown, the UK Prime Minister]. How are you today?" "Good morning, George [Soros, hedge fund manager and philanthropist], I'll see you at the coffee area at 3 p.m., correct?" Occasionally, one could encounter an erudite presentation or engage in an unexpected conversation that was exhilarating. A conversation with famed historian Daniel Boorstin in a taxicab as he explained that he thought that *The Discoverers* was his finest work was one of those for me and my wife, Peixin. As the heavy snow slowed our taxi to a crawl, I relished every word, actually regretting our arrival at our dinner destination. A casual chat over dinner with Francis Collins, President of the US National Institutes of Health (NIH) at the time, and one of the world's leaders of the Human Genome Project, was another. I was surprised to learn that his work at the forefront of science had not deterred him from a belief that science and Christianity can be reconciled, as articulated in his book *The Language of God*.[1]

The more pragmatic benefits of Davos for me were the nearly limitless occasions to connect or reconnect with so many financiers—both private sector and official—who were integral to the operation of the IIF. I would seize the opportunity to meet not only with the leading bankers, but with key policy officials, including Jean-Claude Trichet, President of the European Central Bank; Governor Zhou Xiaochuan, the Governor of China's central bank; and Mark Carney, head of the Canadian Central Bank at the time and subsequently Chairman of the Financial Stability Board (FSB), the global body created in September 2009 to guide global financial regulatory reform.[†]

My highly capable executive assistant, Karen Dozier, walked into my office in Washington, DC, one morning in January 2010. "The Greek Prime Minister's office just called and asked if you could meet with him during Davos," she said. I was not expecting the call, but neither was I surprised. I was aware that Greece was in trouble, but with so many other pressing problems on the global financial landscape, I had not yet begun to dig into Greece's problems. I agreed to the meeting and called Jeff Anderson, the Chief Economist for Europe, to discuss Greece's plight. I asked him, "How did Greece get into such a predicament? For three months no one, other than Greek banks who were trapped by the system to continue to roll over short-term debt issued by the Greek government, would touch Greek debt." He reminded me that when I had taken over the reins of the Institute in the mid-1990s, I had to rebuild an economic staff that had been somewhat depleted in the years prior to my arrival. As

† The Financial Stability Board was the successor to the Financial Stability Forum (FSF), originally created in 1999.

we did so, we decided to update our "country coverage"—that is, those economies that we monitored and analyzed on behalf of our member firms: the world's leading banks, investment banks, insurance firms, and private equity houses. Given the growing interest in the emerging markets of Asia, Latin America, Africa, and Central Europe, we expanded our coverage of select countries and dropped coverage of two "Old Europe" countries, Portugal and, you guessed it, Greece. So, for the dozen or so years preceding Greece's crisis, the IIF was not conducting research on the Greek economy. Not my most prescient decision, to be sure. Would it have made a difference if we had alerted our members to the deterioration of Greece's economy during the first decade of the 2000s? Perhaps, but I am doubtful. Many European investors had convinced themselves that the Greek economy was under the umbrella of the Eurozone, especially Germany, its strongest member. This was a classic and powerful case of moral hazard. Money poured into Greece from banks, insurance firms, pension funds, and hedge funds, despite a growing list of warning signs that things were amiss. Just a few examples:

· During 2000–2005, when the average unit labor cost for the Eurozone increased only 1.6% per year, Greece's unit labor cost increased at an annual rate of 4.4% per year, eroding the competitiveness of the Greek economy during its early years in the Eurozone.

· Greece's current account deficit was high throughout the period, averaging 6% of GDP and rising to 7.4% in 2005.

· Greece was seriously unfriendly to business, steadily ranking low in World Bank's rankings. Greece was in the bottom tier of the world in legal rights for both borrowers and lenders and among the top-tier countries in the world for cumbersome procedures for an entrepreneur to register a property transfer, right there alongside Ethiopia and Ecuador. Not the best company for a new member of the Eurozone.

· Greece was tied with Argentina and Ukraine with the most regulations of business startups.

It is tempting here to dive into the decade of 1999–2009 to understand how Greece found itself in such dire straits and elaborate how

Greece got it wrong. But it is necessary to look beyond the key macro-economic and structural variables for the period between 2000 and 2009. It requires looking back at least as far as the end of World War II and Greece's Civil War.

Greece had suffered mightily under German occupation throughout the war. It has been estimated that as many as three hundred thousand Greeks died due to starvation or malnutrition during World War II. Over Christmas in 1944, as it was becoming clear that the Axis powers were losing the war, Winston Churchill made a pivotal trip to Greece. As the Germans evacuated Athens in October of that year, two former anti-Nazi resistance groups were vying for power: the EAM-ELAS group, which was supported by the Communists, and EDES, who were loyalists to the Greek government in exile and had the support of the Greek military. The Greek government, based in Cairo, was led by King George II. George Papandreou became Prime Minister of the government in April of that year (grandfather of the George Papandreou who led the country from October 2009 to November 2011). The elder George Papandreou was only a transitional leader at that time but went on to serve as Prime Minister in 1963 and again from 1964 to 1965. Today, he is held in high regard by Greek citizens as one of the towering political figures of Greece's twentieth century, helping solidify democracy after the war.

A new Greek government of National Unity was organized under Papandreou, along with representatives of the King, EAM-ELAS, and EDES. Archbishop Damaskinos was chosen by Churchill as regent for the King in exile. This was a period of tremendous turmoil in Athens that has historically been referred to as the first phase of Greece's civil war, which tragically lasted until 1949 when the Americans brought enough military strength to enable the Greek government and military to defeat the Communist insurgency.

Churchill's initiative did not achieve its overarching goal of restoring peace in Greece by bringing the different factions together, but it did provide a framework for leadership until the Greek people themselves could decide on their new government and determine whether they would restore the monarchy.

Over sixty thousand people died in the brutal Greek civil war, and hundreds of thousands of Greeks were displaced. The war left long-standing scars in Greek society and in Greece's political system; as Roderick Beaton, one of today's foremost Greek historians, has argued, "The new political and cultural fault lines, between Communism and anti-Communism, between 'East and West' . . . would continue to divide Greece down the middle for two more generations."[2] Some families in Greece today still trace their modern ancestry to whether their parents or grandparents supported the communists or the loyalists.

A compelling account of Greece's civil war can be found in Nicholas Gage's book *Eleni*. It is the story of his mother's assassination at the hands of communists as a result of her successfully arranging for her children to escape the clutches of local communist officials who were deporting young boys and girls to neighboring communist countries as the loyalists closed in on them.

Eleni also has a place in Cold War history. In December 1987, President Ronald Reagan reached an agreement with Soviet President Mikhail Gorbachev limiting the development of long-range nuclear weapons. In his speech announcing the far-reaching accord, he quoted Eleni's last words as she faced the firing squad— "My children"[3]—invoking that powerful statement on behalf of all children.

What is the relevance of all this to Greece's debt problem in 2011? As indicated in Chapter 3, Greece's problem was much more than a debt problem. In 2009, Greece was a structurally weak economy with woeful competitiveness. Yes, the yawning fiscal deficit revealed in the early weeks of the Papandreou administration shocked the markets out of their decade-long somnolence, but what lay beneath was the real shocker. As George Papaconstantinou correctly characterized things in his book *Game Over*, "My own party in its previous stints in government was also to blame for this 'monster' public administration that was incapable of even knowing how much it spent."[4] Monstrous indeed.

During one of my evenings in Athens after an especially wearisome negotiating session, I decided to walk to the northwest corner of Syntagma Square, where I had spotted a bookstore. I wanted to understand more about the modern history of Greece since its creation in the 1820s. I asked the proprietor whether he had an English section with some books on Greek history, and he rather proudly guided me to it.

"I have a number of books on Greek history, and it is a special honor to welcome you here, Mr. Dallara. I have seen you on television and I believe you are trying to help Greece." I thanked him for his sentiments and noticed that he was carrying a broom. He quickly explained with a slight look of embarrassment that he had been forced to dismiss his cleaning staff and was doing it himself.

"I could only pay €10 per hour and the government is still paying well over €20 per hour for cleaning the 2004 Olympic facilities, which are no longer in use. I cannot compete with that. Can you help fix that?" he asked. I didn't quite know what to say. It was not, of course, our job to fix the deep-seated structural problems of the Greek economy, but I fervently hoped that the Troika would make progress in that area.

Take taxes, for example. As Papaconstantinou said, "The tax system was indicative of a broader problem—a broken social contract. Only one in three euros owed as VAT [was] actually collected. Three out of four in liberal professions paid no income tax . . . Tax evasion and tax avoidance permeated the entire economic fabric."[5]

The role of the government in Greece's economy was at the heart of the problem. Successive New Democracy and PASOK governments had decided to forgo important areas of tax collections in order to build support from various segments of society. PASOK appeared to have been particularly adept at building its political base by using the government apparatus. In 1984, PASOK "penetrated the state and gained control of it in an attempt to satisfy its own demands and interests."[6] For example, the position of the General Director of the Ministries was eliminated, and the role of Special Secretaries was introduced, staffed by those who were appointed by ministers. According to Kostas Kostis, this further limited the effectiveness of the administration. As a result of this and many similar policies, the state became bloated with a wave of public employees. From 1974 through 1981, the total increase in civil servants accounted for 13% of total new employment. From 1982 through 1989, that figure rose to an astounding 58%. PASOK was a powerful force in that era, and Andreas Papandreou stated explicitly that PASOK was the political expression of the vision of three generations: the generation of resistance, the generation of the radical movement of the 1960s, and the generation of the Polytechnic uprising.[7]

During the late 1970s and early 1980s, the public sector grew like an amoeba. The state spread its presence into virtually every corner of the economy, creating inefficiencies and distortions and weighing heavily on competitiveness.

Of course, the enormous spread of this state didn't begin with PASOK in 1981 nor the Karamanlis government of 1974—which, as explained earlier, had successfully restored democracy to Greece after the seven-year reign of the junta. Some of the problems go back to the economic model that emerged after the civil war, centered on large-scale industrialization. For the political left, the precursor of PASOK, the state would be at the center of this industrialization, supported by a "backbone of heavy industry."[8] A unique aspect of this approach was that the Greek economy's weakness was due in no insignificant part to Greece's dependence on foreign powers—increasingly on the United States. Despite the huge role played by the Marshall Plan in helping to rebuild Greece after World War II—a process that started even while the civil war still raged—the sentiment grew within the left political circles in the 1950s that Greece's economy should focus on the full vertical integration of production.

In the early 1950s, Greece was a relatively poor country despite the economic rebuilding after World War II and the Greek civil war. Nearly 60% of the workforce was employed in the primary sector, mainly agriculture with some oil and gas. However, this represented only 27.9% of GDP, reflecting very low productivity in agriculture.[9] Greece was the poorest among all the initial sixteen members of the OEEC (the Organisation for European Economic Co-operation; now the Organization for Economic Cooperation and Development [OECD]), which had been established to support implementation of the Marshall Plan. Greece was also beset with a weak currency, reflecting in part the political instability of the country as it emerged from its civil war in 1949. The new government in 1950 had introduced a "new drachma" since the value of the old one had "evaporated." However, "every effort to maintain a stable currency faltered due to the Greek state's inability to restructure its tax system and increase revenue in general."[10] Sound familiar?

Despite the early focus on renewed industrialization, the road ahead was very rocky. The Americans had growing doubts about the economic plan, and the OEEC, which had huge influence on how Marshall Plan funds were spent, began to object to proposals for the creation of businesses in oil refineries, steel, and chemicals, where Greece actually had some potential. Apparently, the objections were based on the concern that investing in these industries would create a surplus of production capacity in Europe.[11]

US aid continued to flow to prop up the economy during the early 1950s, but the economy's structural shortcomings became more pronounced. Monetary instability continued to dog the country. It seemed that very few Greeks wanted to put money in banks to see it inflated away; gold, commodities, and real estate became the preferred form of savings. In 1953, the drachma was devalued 50% against the dollar, and this did help inaugurate a period of growth that lasted for the better part of two decades. The conservative governments of this era were able to reduce poverty as small family businesses began to drive the growth in new areas such as construction, tourism, and shipping. Between 1950 and 1973, growth in Greece was the highest in capitalist countries of Europe.[12]

Serious problems began to emerge, however, in the mid-1970s, when New Democracy took the reins of government after the fall of the junta. As noted earlier, Karamanlis handled a smooth transition back to democracy and led Greece into the European Financial Stability Facility (EFSF), a major achievement toward reinstating Greece into the Western democratic community. The oil price shock of 1973 hit Greece hard, but underlying challenges also started to come to the surface. Greece began to borrow more from foreign sources to support its military. At that time, Greece had the second-highest expenditure on defense, relative to national GDP, of all NATO members after the United States. (As of 2022, Greece now actually exceeds the US and has the largest relative defense budget among all NATO countries.) There were good reasons for that then, and good reasons for that now, but the financing of these expenditures began to place a strain on the budget. Industry also began to face serious challenges as they "struggled to adopt to the new conditions caused by the oil crisis and increased labor costs."[13] Another development would have ominous long-term adverse effects on the Greek economy,[14] as the country's second-largest bank, the Commercial Bank, was nationalized, giving the Greek state control of 60% of the banking system. Through layers of administrative controls, it determined the availability of most of the banking credit to fuel the economy. Such an agreement left little room for the private sector to allocate credit and had inevitable negative effects on the efficient allocation of resources and competitiveness.

The seven-year reign of New Democracy and Constantinos Karamanlis came to an end, ushering in the eight-year period of a PASOK-led government under the leadership of Andreas Papandreou. Both Karamanlis and Papandreou had been in exile during the years of the junta, Karamanlis in France and Papandreou in Canada and Sweden.

During his time in exile, Papandreou wrote a searing personal account of his experience at the time of the coup, when he was held in jail for several months until he was released under pressure from the American government, stimulated in large part by John Kenneth Galbraith, Papandreou's friend and colleague. Despite the intervention on his behalf, Papandreou had developed a deep resentment toward the United States and its influence on Greece during the postwar era. He considered Greece a country without sovereignty: "The first and most important feature [of the political process following the civil war] is the absence of a true national sovereign."[15] He continued with a scathing commentary about the "powerful American factor" in Greece during that period. "As Americans replaced the British in the role of 'protector' or 'sponsor' power, they became increasingly enmeshed in the internal political process. They had come to Greece to protect 'democracy' from the Communist onslaught, then shifted their sights . . . Democracy . . . became secondary and . . . stability became the primary target."[16]

Papandreou brought with him not just an anti-American perspective, but an apparent determination to free Greece from foreign domination by taking over the reins of administration as well as government. As Beaton states quite emphatically, "PASOK also changed the way that government was run. At the highest ranks of the civil service, tenured professionals were replaced by political appointees."[17] It appears that political power and administration became rather merged, as PASOK seized the midlevels of governance from the civil service.

Finding the right balance and forming a government is a never-ending challenge for democracies. If political appointments are not made sufficiently deep enough into the government structure, new governments and their policies can be stifled by bureaucracy. In fact, some civil servants can be quite good at obstructing new initiatives or policy shifts. On the other hand, if political appointments cut too deeply into the staffing structure, they can chip away the institutional knowledge and experience necessary to effectively run a government. Finding the right balance to engage in a dialectic is never easy, but my impression is that Greece clearly did not find the right balance, and they have paid for it.

Beginning under PASOK in 1982, "at the highest ranks of the civil service tenured professionals were replaced by political appointees."[18] It appears that the day-to-day exercise of power became highly political for the first time in the postwar era. This stripped many capable civil servants out of the system. At the same time, two other changes occurred that distorted and weakened the economy. The first was an explosion in hiring by the state. From 1974 to 1981, under the Karamanlis government, civil servant hires accounted for 13% of the increase in total employment in Greece. Even this seems like an uncomfortably high figure to me (currently in the US, the federal workforce accounts for approximately 6% of total employment, including the US military),[19] but between 1982 and 1989, the hiring of civil servants represented over 58% of total job growth in the economy. This is a shocking figure and speaks loudly to the outsized role that the government has played in the Greek economy over the last four decades. But the size of the public sector was not the whole of it. The party "infiltrated the state and gained control of it in an attempt to satisfy its own demands and interests." As indicated earlier, the position of general director of the various ministries was eliminated and the role of "special secretaries" was created, staffed by political appointees.[20]

As the 1980s progressed, Greece's economic performance deteriorated, due in part to the energy crisis that erupted in 1979, but undoubtedly due to the increased economic burden of the government as well. During the 1970s, many Greeks moved from the countryside and joined industry in urban areas, but Greek industry was generally family-owned and focused on the domestic market, leading to low productivity, weak competitiveness, modest exports, and a perpetual trade deficit.[21] New Democracy managed to see relatively strong growth in the mid to late 1970s, but problems of low productivity reflected a lack of investment and rising labor costs.[22] Inflation was 18.9% in 1979, much higher than that of Greece's leading partners. PASOK held power from 1981 through 2004 (except for 1989–1993), and for much of that time tried to make a socialist society based on Papandreou's theories of excess dependency on the West and anti-Western and anticapitalist rhetoric (as Beaton pointed out, the Simitis administration of 1996–2006 did move somewhat away from these policies and toward a more market-based approach). PASOK's economic policies boosted wages but there was, for the most part, no comparable rise in productivity. PASOK formed a group called the Organization for Rehabilitation of Business Firms.[23] Through this the government took control of twenty-one firms. When combined with the nationalizations done under the Karamanlis government, the Greek government at that time controlled, either directly or indirectly, 70% of Greece's domestic industry. This was occurring while much of Europe was beginning to privatize industry, and it left the government with a "bottomless pit" to fill financially, as these OAE companies built up huge operational deficits and debts. By 1985 the budget deficit was an alarming 18% of GDP,[24] while the current account deficit was over 10% of GDP. An IMF mission at the beginning of 1985 was reported to have stated that "Greece was heading for an obvious crisis."[25] In a foreshadowing of what would happen twenty-four years later under his son's government, Andreas Papandreou refused to go to the IMF for a program, and instead applied for help from the EEC. With loans provided both bilaterally from other member states and by commercial banks with the guarantee of the Commission, a 1.75 billion European currency unit (ECU) was approved in November 1985. Just as we at the Treasury were grappling with the Latin American debt crisis, Greece was struggling with its own debt crisis. In September 1985, we launched the Baker Plan, a proposal to reenergize our international debt strategy around a more growth-oriented strategy. As a sign of how much things had changed in the twenty years since the US dominated the political landscape in Greece, we at the Treasury were not even focused on Greece's serious economic problems. Although this was still the height of the Cold War, our national fear of Greece coming under strong communist influence had waned, despite the strong socialist orientation of the Papandreou government. We were vaguely aware of Greece's serious economic problems but assumed that Europe would somehow find a way to solve them. We had a fire burning in our own backyard and were focused on that.

A few steps were taken to stabilize the Greek economy in 1982–83, with some reduction in the deficit (still almost 12%) and a tighter monetary policy. However, these only held temporarily, as the deficit increased again to over 14% in 1984 and investment continued to decline as profits were compressed by a variety of factors, including high wages and increases in interest rates. Meanwhile, external debt had doubled between 1979 and 1982 to $12.8 billion, but only 38.4% of GDP! Still very modest, but a clear sign of things to come. In fact, the companies that had been placed under the umbrella of the new restructuring agency (OAE) were allowed to restructure their debt, with interest payments to private creditors suspended. Although I was the US Executive Director at the IMF at the time, we had not even one visit from a Greek official asking for support. On the other hand, Brazilian, Argentinian, Mexican, and Philippine authorities regularly visited my office, as did the IMF staff who were handling their cases.

The 1985 IMF Article IV consultation report was a carefully worded indictment of Greece's economy and economic policy: "In recent years the Greece economy has suffered from relatively high inflation, declining private investment, and large external imbalances. While some of those problems are rooted in the structural weakness of their economy, they also reflect the insufficient policy responses to the two oil price shocks of the 1970s." It goes on to say, "Wages expanded by nearly 8% *per annum* [emphasis mine] between 1974–78, far exceeding the rise in productivity. Moreover, industrial policy continued to subsidize and protect existing industries . . . weakening the incentive for structural change."[26]

Industry had developed during the decades of the 1950s to 1980s in a highly protected environment. With Greece's entry into the EEC in 1981, the lack of competitiveness of industry in global markets was increasingly exposed. At the same time, the government continued to live under the illusion that a period of tax amnesty for delinquent past returns would contribute to a flood of tax revenue, which of course never happened. The IMF report continues, "the persistence, and indeed, enlargement of the fiscal and external deficits can only heighten the concerns expressed by Director last year."[27]

By early 1986, Greece was forced into an adjustment program to obtain 1.75 billion European currency units, the precursor to the euro. The program actually did strengthen the economy and enabled the Bank of Greece to return to international markets and raise 300 million dollars, led by the ever-hopeful Japanese banks.

But the stabilization program of 1985–1987 did not sit well with many elements of Greek society. Protests erupted, and PASOK lost support in local elections. Papandreou failed to back Costas Simitis, the Minister of National Economy, in matters relating to wage indexation,[28] which eventually led to Simitis's resignation. All of this coupled with the imposition of an extraordinary tax precipitated a 40% decline in the Greek stock market, and the government descended into scandal. Nevertheless, the populist underdog culture that permeated many tenets of society fed by PASOK's dogma of fighting the "metropolis of capitalism" would not disappear.

By 1989 the fiscal deficit had reached 21.5%, fueled by pre-election spending[29] that resulted in a government led by eighty-five-year-old Xenophon Zolotas in 1989. His was a technocratic government with some echoes in the Lucas Papademos government three decades later. Zolotas was also a distinguished economist, but unlike Papademos, he apparently tried to deflect the issue and seek another line of credit from the European Commission without further reforms. However, Jacques Delors, the strong president of the Commission, and Henry Christopherson, the Commissioner for Macroeconomic Affairs, wrote to Zolotas, stating in no uncertain terms that what he wanted wouldn't happen. Ominously, they also argued that "Greek debt bids were growing so rapidly that they posed a threat . . . to the prospect of monetary union as a whole."[30] Little did they know that thirty-two years later Greece would pose a severe threat to a monetary union that was barely a decade old.

The short life of the Zolotas administration was soon replaced by a newly elected New Democracy government under Constantine Mitsotakis, father of Kyriakos Mitsotakis, who was elected Prime Minister in 2019. The elder Mitsotakis brought in new economic ideas and for the first time in postwar Greece tried to implement a market-based neoliberal approach to economic challenges. With the support of the EU, which provided a 2.2 billion ECU loan, he launched a major adjustment and reform program. It involved reductions in the civil service, a sharp reduction in government borrowing, a widening of the tax base, accelerated privatization, and legislation introduced to free up markets in goods, labor, and services. Although implementation fell short in some areas, some stability was restored to the fiscal position, with revenues raised from 25.8% of GDP in 1989 to 30.4% in 1992, and the public sector borrowing requirement (PSBR) was drastically reduced from 21.5% in 1989 to 7.9%. Progress was also made in privatization; a freeze was applied to public sector regulations as the economy went through a much-needed stiff adjustment program. Foreign investors actually came in, a reflection in part of a more pro-business orientation, but the effects of the adjustment policies, when combined with a global slowdown, led to a weakening of political support for New Democracy.[31] This gave political ammunition to PASOK and Papandreou to take the reins of government once again.

Despite the improvements, when the Maastricht Treaty was introduced in 1992 it became clear just how far Greece was from being prepared to join the European Monetary Union (EMU), the precursor to the euro. Greece had not been fully prepared from an economic perspective to join the EU in the late 1970s, but the political value of that decision for the long-term development of Greece and long-term stability of Europe as a collective of Western democracies should never be underestimated. However, prospective euro membership in the early 1990s was another thing entirely. An inflation rate of 20.4% against an EEC (European Economic Commission) average of 6.7%, public debt of 105% of GDP against the treaty benchmark of 60%, and a budget deficit of 14.6% against a target for euro membership of 3%, did not bode well. In a pattern that has been repeated time and again over the last thirty years, Greece would take partial steps to meet euro membership. However, the political system seemed unwilling or unable to take the more radical step that could lead Greece to eventually become economically and financially integrated into the European Union. A system of clientelism and patronage had taken hold of the Greek political system. As Beaton has pointed out, the creation (in the early 1980s) of a genuinely mass party, for the first time in Greek history, also had a transformative effect on the traditional system of patronage. It was no longer individual members of parliament who were expected to distribute privileges to their voters, but the party to its members. Far from abolishing the inherited system of patrons and clients, the effect of PASOK's dominance of the political landscape was to reshape it into a state-run institution.[32]

Soon after PASOK returned to power, Papandreou fell ill and Simitis took over, leading to a somewhat surprisingly conservative approach to economic policies that strengthened government finances. Some of this was real, as the government sought to meet the European Economic Monetary Union convergence targets and signed the Stability and Growth Pact in 1996. At that time the government was posting a primary budget surplus, the economy was responding, and inflation falling. The process of preparing for euro membership, however, was volatile. They had to go through a two-year period as part of the Exchange Rate Mechanism (ERM), during which the drachma was only allowed to move within a narrow range around a fixed parity. Unfortunately, the Asian debt crisis erupted as this process was underway, and the drachma came under pressure, forcing considerable Greek central bank interventions. However, in March 1998 the drachma was admitted to the ERM with a prior depreciation of 12.1%.[33] Paradoxically, even though the underlying fundamentals of the Greek economy had not radically improved, especially with regard to long-term competitiveness, entry into the ERM meant that all of the central banks of the EMU world joined together, defending the Greek currency. This led to immediate capital inflows and a sharp decline in the perceived risk of Greek bonds as the spread over Greek bonds fell within the required range for euro membership. Sadly, this led to a stock market bubble that subsequently burst by the end of 2000, wiping out many businesses and small investors. Despite this, Greece persevered in its efforts to meet the convergence criteria and join the euro. Questions were raised about whether the underlying reform process was being adequately pursued, and government officials continued to sing praises for the role of the state in economic policy. As the momentum to join the Euro Area grew, so did the number of measures taken to fudge the numbers. The government withheld payments to suppliers and engaged in some very dubious accounting.

By December 1999, Greece reportedly brought its economy within the bounds of the convergence criteria, and in March 2000 Greece made a formal application to join the EMU. By January 1, 2001, Greece became the twelfth member of the Euro Area. Prime Minister Simitis spoke of the moment as an opportunity of true transformation, "the beginning of a real economic convergence." This was no doubt a major accomplishment by Greece, but the aspirations for real economic convergence[34] did not come to pass.

CHAPTER 6

THE FLETCHER SCHOOL OF LAW AND DIPLOMACY

"One of the most valuable skills a leader of character can possess, especially in competitive fields like business, politics, or the military, is to . . . chart a course toward a fairly distant desired outcome, and in the process shape what happens."

—Admiral James G. Stavridis, USN (Ret.), *Sailing True North*

As much as I enjoyed and benefited from my time in the Navy, I yearned to gain further education. I resigned my commission from the Navy in July 1974 and knew what I wanted to do: pursue an advanced degree in international economics. Further, I wanted a multidisciplinary environment where I could focus on international economics and finance blended with studies in other areas such as political science, development economics, and diplomacy.

I found the right place for me at The Fletcher School of Law and Diplomacy. Founded in 1933 as a training ground for diplomats, Fletcher had become much more than that. Jointly administered by both Tufts University and Harvard University, Fletcher had such distinguished alumni as US Senator Daniel Patrick Moynihan, Chairman of Citibank Walter Wriston, French Foreign Minister Jean Francois-Poncet, and two Senior Economic Advisors to Henry Kissinger, Fred Bergsten and Bob

Hormats, and I saw a school that could prepare individuals for careers in finance, politics, business, or diplomacy. When I was considering various options for graduate study, it did not hurt that the Dean of Admissions who recruited me was a former Navy Captain, Charles Shane, who persuaded me that a former naval officer could indeed fit into Fletcher. There also was an interesting twist on my decision to attend Fletcher and my subsequent move from Fletcher to the Treasury Department in the summer of 1976. I had interviewed with Fred Bergsten for an opportunity to work as his research assistant at the Brookings Institution, and when he asked what other opportunities I had, I indicated that I had been offered a position at the Treasury. He immediately responded, "Take the position at the Treasury. You won't regret it." I did, and a few months later he was announced as the nominee for the new Assistant Secretary of the Treasury for International Affairs; my new boss after all, three or four layers up.

I became convinced that I had made the correct choice when I was introduced to *Present at the Creation* by Dean Acheson as the first book on Fletcher's summer reading list. I found it an inspiring memoir of the former Secretary of State (also a former senior Treasury official) detailing his experience in helping to shape the postwar world into which my generation was born.

Fletcher had a strong department of International Economics, led by Benjamin J. "Jerry" Cohen. He was an outstanding teacher—one of the best that I ever encountered. Organized, meticulous, coherent, and knowledgeable, Jerry had a precise approach to teaching his students international finance. He was demanding and challenging, but also had a somewhat hidden sense of humor and humanity. Jerry went on to become one of the leading theoreticians and authors in the field of international political economy. Arpad von Lazar was another exceptional member of the Fletcher faculty. A refugee from Hungary, he had escaped under fire from Russian troops in November 1956, and went on to develop a brilliant academic career in political science. Arpad had a unique ability to make this field come alive, and his flamboyance added to the experience of being his student. Whether it was Europe, Latin America, Africa, or the Middle East, he taught with a verve that was at times mesmerizing.

Fletcher also had Deans who were individuals of great distinction. During my time at the school, Edmund Gullion, a distinguished American career diplomat, was the Dean. This tradition of stellar leaders has been carried forward in recent years by Jack Galvin, a four-star army general; Steve Bosworth; and Jim Stavridis. Bosworth served as US Ambassador to the Philippines, South Korea, and Tunisia, while Stavridis served as the Supreme Allied Commander of NATO after an illustrious career in the US Navy.

Complementing the impressive faculty and leadership was a highly diverse group of American and international students. Inquisitive minds from Turkey, Chile, Germany, Ghana, Japan, China, Korea, and a host of other countries enhanced an already fertile environment for learning across a range of fields of study. This multidisciplinary approach proved to be extraordinarily valuable to me, as after I graduated from Fletcher and went on to the US Treasury I quickly discovered that the economic problems of the real world were often woven into a complex nexus of political, institutional, financial, cultural, and historic factors. Effective problem solving at times meant understanding more than one of those dimensions. Never was that more the case than years later in dealing with Greece.

CHAPTER 7

THE UNITED STATES TREASURY AND THE INSTITUTE OF INTERNATIONAL FINANCE

"The truth unquestionably is, that the only path to a subversion of the republican system . . . is, by flattering the prejudices of the people, and exciting their jealousies and apprehensions, to throw affairs into confusion and bring on civil commotion."

—Alexander Hamilton, 1788

The reader may reasonably begin to wonder just how I ended up in the middle of the Greek debt crisis, engaging alongside Lemierre with Merkel and Sarkozy. The Managing Director of the Institute of International Finance? What, pray tell, is the Institute of International Finance, or the IIF as it is colloquially called?

My circuitous route back to Greece wound from my days at The Fletcher School through the US Treasury Department, JP Morgan, and yes, the Institute of International Finance. I joined Treasury straight out of Fletcher in the fall of 1976, when I was immediately posted to support the US Executive Director of the International Monetary Fund (IMF),

Sam Y. Cross. Sam was an exceptional man—knowledgeable of virtually all things in the world of international finance, with almost three decades of experience under his belt at the Treasury. He was a man of integrity and always had a twinkle in his eye. His wife, Nancy Jacklin, called him a raconteur, and he was that in the best sense of the word. He had a remarkable wit and sense of humor, often writing limericks during dull moments of IMF Board meetings. One that appears especially well suited for today's global economy is this:

"If we live to 103,

It may be that we'll live to see

That nice situation

Of zero inflation

That you were describing to me."[‡]

I was also pulled into other issues relating to the international monetary system under the direction of Tom Leddy, another singularly talented and dedicated public servant. Tom served simultaneously as the Alternate US Director of the IMF and Deputy Assistant Secretary of the Treasury for International Monetary Affairs. Tom would typically take two full briefcases home with him at night—large ones at that—to review and comment on multitudes of Treasury and IMF documents, then carry the briefcases back to the office in the morning and put them in his outbox for processing. You knew you were in trouble when a draft document was returned to you marked simply, "See me to discuss!" Tom was a solid man in every sense of the word. He had been a football player in high school and a part-time construction worker during college. In his professional life, he was blunt, frank with everyone, including his superiors (I witnessed him directly challenging more than one Secretary of the Treasury), and had a keen sense of how to reconcile US interests with a stable, effective international monetary system.

With mentors such as Sam and Tom, one could not help but learn a lot about how the international financial system worked. I was then afforded the chance to serve as Special Assistant to Under Secretary of the Treasury Anthony M. Solomon in 1978 and 1979. When Ronald Reagan was elected as US President in November 1980, I was invited by Marc E. Leland, the new Assistant Secretary for International Affairs, to be his Special Assistant. I was reluctant at first because I had been

‡   Sam Y. Cross, circa 1978, courtesy of Ron Myers and Nancy Jacklin

given a year's sabbatical to write my doctoral dissertation and still had four months left and much work remaining. Marc was clear, however: "I want you in the office next Monday." So much for my sabbatical. In both positions I worked for highly talented men and was exposed to economic policymaking at a senior level. When the Latin American debt crisis erupted in 1982, I supported Marc in the initial efforts to cope with the burgeoning crisis.

I subsequently was appointed by President Reagan as the US Alternate and then US Executive Director to the IMF, while continuing to wear hats at the Treasury Department. During those years, I became increasingly involved in the management of debt crises in Mexico, Argentina, Brazil, and a host of other countries. Working under Treasury Secretaries Donald T. Regan and James A. Baker III, I began to help shape the evolution of the international debt strategy. Later in the 1980s, under Secretary Nicholas F. Brady, I was promoted to Assistant Secretary for International Affairs and became an integral part of the team that shaped the Brady Plan (discussed in detail in Chapter 14).

A14   L   THE NEW YORK TIMES, MONDAY, JANUARY 16, 1989

The Economic Team: Ideological Agnostics Who Believe In What Works

Continued From Page A1

At the Top: Economic Policy

ALAN GREENSPAN Chairman, Federal Reserve Board

CARLA A. HILLS U.S. Trade Representative

NICHOLAS F. BRADY Secretary of the Treasury

RICHARD G. DARMAN Budget Director

MICHAEL J. BOSKIN Chief Economic Adviser

CHARLES H. DALLARA Asst. Secy. for Int'l Affairs

Honored to serve in President George H. W. Bush's administration under the leadership of Treasury Secretary Nicholas F. Brady. January 1989. Top, l-r: Alan Greenspan, Carla A. Hills, Secretary Brady. Bottom: Richard G. Darman, Michael J. Boskin, author. From The New York Times ©1989 The New York Times Company. All rights reserved. Used under license.

I also had the good fortune to work under the stewardship of Jacques de Larosiere, the Managing Director of the IMF, and Paul Volcker, Chairman of the Federal Reserve, which gave me a ringside seat to witness not only their stellar leadership qualities, but also to collaborate with them on the formulation and implementation of the international debt strategy in real time.

By the time I left the Treasury in the early 1990s, I had gathered quite a bit of experience in the labyrinthine world of sovereign debt. During two years of working in investment at JP Morgan, I was able to gain sorely needed knowledge in the operation of global capital markets as I helped bring countries to the international debt markets for the first time, including Poland and Turkey.

In 1993, I was offered the opportunity to take the helm of the Institute of International Finance (IIF). The IIF was created in 1983 upon the suggestion of Bill McDonough, the First Vice President of First Chicago at the time. That suggestion was endorsed by de Larosiere at a special meeting at Ditchley Park in England, and the IIF was born within a matter of months. Its original purpose was threefold: 1) to provide the global banking community an independent source of macroeconomic analysis of emerging market economies; 2) to serve as a platform to negotiate sovereign debt restructurings if needed; and 3) to represent the interests of the global banking community on key cross-border regulatory issues. During the 1980s, the first role gained prominence as leading banks across the major industrial countries began increasingly to rely upon the IIF in evaluating the risks and opportunities of lending to emerging market countries. Its economists were highly respected, and their views carried weight as objective analysis.

During the 1990s and 2000s, the IIF expanded its other roles. On issues of sovereign debt, we began to develop policies to help avoid debt crises that were to be followed by the creditors as well as by the debtors. We also formulated best practices to manage such crises when they did erupt. As these efforts gathered momentum, more private financial institutions became involved as members of the IIF, including investment banks, insurance firms, sovereign wealth funds, and private equity houses. The IIF also gained credibility in various official circles, which became important for the eventual unprecedented role played by the IIF in the Greek crisis. Central banks, finance ministers, the Bank for International Settlements (BIS), and the IMF began to recognize the value of our initiatives and, in many cases, participate in them. As explained in more detail in subsequent chapters, the creation of the "Principles for Stable Capital Flows and Fair Debt Restructuring" in 2004 broke new ground by creating for the first time an entity that included key leaders from both the public and the private sectors.

As these systemic endeavors expanded, the IIF's involvement in individual sovereign cases also increased. Debtor countries in some instances sought the IIF's assistance in facilitating engagement with the sources of private capital. Meetings were organized at which the IIF was seen as an honest broker between the creditors and the debtors.

Meanwhile, the IIF's work on global regulatory issues took off, and our role as an intermediary between the private financial community and key national and supranational regulatory agencies gathered force. We mobilized expertise from private firms on any number of key issues, and the regulators found that quite useful even if we had different ideas about how various regulatory issues should best be handled.

During these years, the IIF Board of Directors was gradually transformed from a collection of developing country experts to a group of the world's preeminent financiers. Senior bankers such as John Bond, Chairman of HSBC; Toyoo Gyohten, Chairman of Bank of Tokyo (now BTMU-UFJ); Joe Ackermann, the CEO of Deutsche Bank; and Bill Rhodes, the Vice Chairman of Citibank, became leaders of the IIF, strengthening our credibility in the eyes of finance officials. At the same time, leading insurance executives such as Walter Keilholz, the Chairman of Swiss Re, and Jim Schiro, CEO of Zurich Financial, also assumed leadership roles. In the asset management community, Frank Savage, Chairman of Alliance Capital Management International, and David Fisher, Chairman of the Capital Group, joined the Board and became actively involved in policy activities. On the investment banking front, Sir David Walker, Chairman of Morgan Stanley International, Peter Wuffli, CEO of UBS, and eventually James Gorman, Chairman and CEO of Morgan Stanley, provided leadership. Finally, key emerging market bankers, each a prominent leader in local or regional markets, joined the ranks of IIF principals: Roberto Setubal, CEO (now Co-Chairman) of Banco Itaú (now Itaú Unibanco), one of Latin America's leading banks; KV Kamath of ICICI, India's premier private bank; Ibrahim Dabdoub, CEO of the National Bank of Kuwait, a bank that set the standard for Middle Eastern banks; Cezary Stypułkowski, the CEO of the Bank of Handlowy, Poland's leading bank; Chartsiri Sophonpanich, CEO of Bangkok Bank; and Liu Mingkang, Chairman of the Bank of China. As the bankers came on to the global stage they began to engage through the IIF with global officials, expanding their influence in unprecedented ways.

As the IIF Board and membership was maturing and extending its tentacles, we formed a myriad of committees, working groups, and steering committees to capture the expertise of both senior and midlevel bankers on various specific issues in managing and regulating banks. Matters such as operational risk, crisis prevention, corporate governance, data transparency, liquidity management, and capital requirements all became the focus of intense toil to synthesize the views of the "marketplace" and debate it with the relevant regulatory or central bank authorities. Other senior bankers helped guide these undertakings, including Jorge Londoño, the CEO of Banco Colombia, and Sławomir Sikora of PBK in Poland (later the CEO of Bank Handlowy).

As we built our committee and working group structures, we also invited former officials who could bring additional experience to our products. Jacob Frenkel, former Chief Economist of the IMF and Governor of the Bank of Israel, became a major contributor to our global efforts. John Heimann, former US Comptroller of the Currency, became a valuable Director of the IIF. Tom de Swaan, the former head of the Basel Committee, joined our Board once he joined ABN AMRO. Sir David Walker had been the UK's Chief Securities Regulator before he joined our Board and became a force in our regulatory work. Paul Volcker even became a Trustee of the "Principles" on sovereign debt after he stepped down from his Chairmanship at the Federal Reserve as one of the premier public servants of his generation.

Among the other luminaries who joined the IIF's leadership ranks in the late 1990s and the 2000s was Jacques de Larosiere, formerly the head of the IMF, who had played a central role in steering the global economy through the sovereign debt crisis of the 1980s. After an exceptionally distinguished career in global finance from a public sector perspective, Jacques became a Senior Advisor to the Chairman of Paribas, a highly respected investment bank. When Paribas merged with BNP, Jacques continued to serve as Advisor to the Chairman. He also kindly agreed

Bill Rhodes, Chairman and President, Citibank (left), and Jacques de Larosiere, Advisor to the Chairman of BNP Paribas. Co-Chairs of the IIF's Special Committee on Financial Crisis Prevention. Two giants in global finance for decades. © 2008 Institute of International Finance, Inc.

to actively engage in our work at the Institute. He helped shape the "Principles for Stable Capital Flows and Fair Debt Restructuring" and became a member of the Trustees. Jacques also played a pivotal role in the creation of the IIF in 1982, having endorsed the proposal by Bill McDonough, the Senior Vice President of First Chicago Bank at the time, to create a private sector organization that would provide independent analysis of risks in emerging markets. This exchange led to the creation of the IIF within a year.

Bill Rhodes had worked closely with Jacques during the debt crisis of the 1980s and became very involved in the work of the Institute as an active Board Member in the 1990s, when he partnered once again with Jacques to guide the Institute's activities in dealing with sovereign debt crises. For many years, they co-chaired the IIF Special Committee on Financial Crisis Prevention and Resolution. Bill served as a Vice Chairman, Acting Chairman, and then Vice Chairman of the Board. Both men continued to play a vital role as an informal counsel to me throughout the process, even through the Greek debt restructuring. Together, they were a powerful and sustained positive influence on the functioning of the global financial system for at least four decades.

The net effect of the expansion of the IIF and its dialogue with the public sector was to enhance the overall reputation of the IIF, despite the fact that some observers still considered us little more than a lobbyist organization for the banks. The overall professionalism of the IIF's staff and industry participants, however, generally offset that view. We had, in the eyes of some, successfully blended a profile that represented the interests of the private financial community while also seeking to advance the public good of a safer and more stable financial system.

When the Greek crisis began to simmer and simmer and then boil, no one seemed prepared to step up and pull the trigger to launch negotiations to restructure the debt. The major European creditors were caught between a central bank that was adamantly opposed to restructuring on the one hand, and on the other, market pressures and rising government insistence that the banks "participate in a solution to the Greek debt." The IIF saw not only an opportunity, but a need to break the logjam, and after close consultation with key individual Greek creditors and our Board, we decided to do just that. Somehow, we were prepared to step into the breach, and the negotiations were set in motion.

CHAPTER 8

SARKOZY ON STAGE

"There is something about a live performance
that you just cannot replicate anywhere else."
—Carrie Hope Fletcher, 2018

As we sat down in President van Rompuy's elegant meeting room in the wee hours of October 26, 2011, I noticed there was no table. I had become accustomed to negotiating on various tables, generally dark, long, and imposing, be they in Washington, Paris, Rome, Brussels, or Athens. I kind of missed a table, but I nevertheless eased myself comfortably into my highly cushioned chair. For a moment, I thought that perhaps this would be a civilized exchange during which we would, hopefully, find common ground without too much drama. I was, after all, rather fatigued, as was Jean, and it was then we looked across to Chancellor Merkel as she motioned to President Sarkozy to open the discussions. Suddenly, I found myself sharp and alert—despite the hour, the adrenaline kicked in—and I could see the same look on Lemierre's face as he stared at his president expectantly.

We were ready to listen, but we were not going to be intimidated, no matter how many dignitaries were in the room. We had come too far to be overcome by meekness.

I have met with many political leaders over the years, some more impressive than others. So had Jean, who in his position at the helm of the

EBRD has undoubtedly met every head of state in Europe. Among the most memorable for me was Margaret Thatcher, whose sense of purpose was evident the moment she strode into a room. There was Japanese Prime Minister Noboru Takeshita, whom I met on numerous occasions during lengthy US-Japan negotiations. A small man, but tough and shrewd. I met Cory Aquino on her first day in office as the new president of the Philippines in 1986. A charming person, President Aquino insisted on showing me and US Ambassador Steve Bosworth, Imelda Marcos's vast shoe collection, which filled a huge storage room the size of an airplane hangar. Carlos Menem, the President of Argentina, danced a mean tango in front of Bob Dole during a congressional trip to Latin America on which I accompanied Senator Dole (Dole did not seem impressed with Menem's performance). Carlo Ciampi of Italy, a taciturn former central bank governor who became Italy's tenth president, seemed ill at ease in the role, but who wouldn't be when dealing with Berlusconi? Ernesto Zedillo, President of Mexico from 1994 to 2000, was one of the smartest, most capable, and skilled governmental leaders I have ever encountered.

But this meeting in Brussels with two heads of government, the President of the European Union, and countless other grandees felt different. At stake was not only the future of a sovereign debtor—Jean and I were accustomed to that—but also arguably the future of the Eurozone. Of course, one person commanded the room: German Chancellor Angela Merkel, with French President Nicolas Sarkozy beside her. If Europe had a Royal Court, Merkel would have been its Queen, albeit a reluctant one. Despite her preeminent position, she did not appear to feel the need to radiate authority. Other leaders gain vitality in a crisis; Merkel reacted with caution, thoughtfulness, and a touch of weariness that hinted at wanting to be elsewhere. She had never expected to lead Germany, and now she was being asked to lead all of Europe? And lead it out of the greatest crises in two generations?

I had already come to admire Merkel, for without her pragmatism and innate sense of Europe, Greece may already have been drummed out of the Eurozone, and the Eurozone may well have been in shreds. Time and again, she seemed to rise to her destiny. She may not have always felt she was the person for the role, but she was going to play it all the same. She was always attuned to her political interests in Germany, but now she was being forced to look out for the broader interests of Europe. Of European leaders, she seemed among the most professional to me, and the least inclined to histrionics. I found her to be a terrific listener, and I could tell that she was open in the meeting. At the same time, she seemed reserved.

Sarkozy opened the meeting by standing up and suggesting that before Merkel outlined their positions on substance to Jean and myself, that he would say "what was in their hearts." When I heard that and saw him begin to prance from one corner of the room to the other, it felt like the circus had come to town and we were going to discover what was under the tent.

Sarkozy then launched into an astonishing tirade against the banks. He gesticulated with both arms as he lit into us in elegant but angry French that I couldn't easily follow. I would get a blast of his invective, however, before the translator clued me in to what he was saying. I suspect she deleted a few choice words. In such a sumptuous setting, with the fate of Europe hanging in the balance, he said, with what I'm sure he took to be charm, "We politicians aren't much loved, but Messieurs Lemierre and Dallara, you bankers," and he practically spat the words, "are positively hated. And now look at you. You are making terrible, disgraceful, outrageous demands on Europe and the long-suffering Greek people." That was followed by a litany of "how could you's" as the translator struggled to keep up with his rapid-fire pace. Jean and I sat stoically through this tirade. Marcus Aurelius would have been proud of us.

Sarkozy then launched into a particularly vicious attack on French banks. Speaking directly to Jean, he said "You French bankers are the worst of the lot," with emphasis on the word *French*. "You are putting the European project and France's future at risk by your dishonest conduct and your stubbornness. It is completely unacceptable." Then he turned to both of us and said with solemnity, "If you don't accept our position, in four hours when markets open in Asia,"—and he looked dramatically at his watch—"I will destroy you and the banks you represent and savage you all in the press." With that, the room fell silent. It was, as someone described a subsequent performance by him at the G7 Summit in Cannes, "the full Sarkozy."

I suspect everyone was as floored by this performance as I was; at least I hope so. Then Sarkozy did something that left me even more flabbergasted. He shot us a look that seemed to say, "Don't take this personally, Messieurs Lemierre and Dallara." A twinkle came into his eyes, and the beginnings of a smile, and I believe what followed was a wink. Suddenly, it all became clear to me. He was demonstrating for Merkel and all the others in the audience, letting them know that he could take charge and bash the bankers with great verve and gusto. Startled as I was by all of this, Lemierre must have been even more perturbed, since Sarkozy was his president. But we both maintained our poise. I looked at Juncker, who appeared slightly aghast but successfully subdued his reaction.

Jean responded to Sarkozy calmly but firmly, "We have been working closely with Greece and the Eurozone leadership to resolve Greece's debt problems, Mr. President. We remain fully committed to solving this quandary, but we will need support from Europe to find a workable solution." Sarkozy did not respond but turned to Merkel and asked her to relate what the heads of state had decided regarding Greece. Quite nonplussed, she declared that it was essential that an agreement be reached regarding the Greek debt. She reminded us that the Eurozone had already committed €100 billion, and the IMF €20 billion more, and now it was the banks' turn to sacrifice. "You should reconsider the twenty-one percent haircut of the July agreement and do better." She looked at me intently. "Are you prepared to?"

I looked around the room and saw only Europeans—senior, distinguished Europeans except for me, the sole American. This was their continent, their common currency, their future. I was an interloper. My Italian father and Irish mother meant virtually nothing in that room. My mind flashed back to a book I had read in high school, Mark Twain's *A Connecticut Yankee in King Arthur's Court*. I felt a bit like Hank Morgan, the nineteenth-century engineer who suddenly finds himself in the midst of King Arthur's court in 528 AD. An American in the center of this essentially European drama? I felt similarly transported, not so much back in time, but to a foreign land. Hank at least had the "magic" of a solar eclipse, gunpowder, and a pump to repair a fountain. I had considerable experience in restructuring sovereign debt, but I didn't have any magic bullets in my pockets as Chancellor Merkel stared expectantly at me. Despite all this, I was well prepared to respond to her.

When I was growing up in Spartanburg, South Carolina, you would not have thought it likely that I would end up in the middle of a European debt crisis. Spartanburg is in the Piedmont section of the Carolinas, situated just southeast of the Blue Ridge Mountains. Historically, it had been a center of cotton textiles and peaches. In the 1950s, it was a town of barely 30,000 citizens. Curiously, there was a Greek connection buried in these roots. During the American Revolution, the local militia in this part of South Carolina joined forces with the Revolutionary Army to defeat the British in the Battle of Cowpens in January 1781. This was arguably the turning point of the war in the South. The news of the victory electrified Americans. "Neither before nor after in this war would an American force so completely defeat a British one on the battlefield."[1] The militia fought with such discipline and vigor that they conjured up images of the ancient Spartan soldiers, and the local militia came to be known as the "Spartan Rifles." The nearby town was thus named Spartanburg in their honor.

During World War II, Spartanburg had a more prosaic role, serving as a major training ground for soldiers being inducted into the war. Over two hundred thousand soldiers underwent boot camp at Camp Croft. One of those was my father, who volunteered to serve and was sent there in May 1943 from the Bronx, New York City, where he had grown up during the Depression. He eventually became known in the Spartanburg area as "Mr. Tire" for perfecting the art of selling automotive tires at Sears & Roebuck, and later known as "The Rose Man" at Converse College (now University), when he became a rose gardener. He was renowned on campus for presenting roses to the female students (Converse was a predominantly female school), and for this the 1990 yearbook was dedicated to him. There is now a baseball field in Tryon, North Carolina, named after him, and a foundation in his name dedicated to promoting youth baseball among diverse boys and girls and honoring the unique historical role of Negro League Baseball teams in the South.

Another, more famous personality also came through Camp Croft for boot camp at the same time: Henry Kissinger. When I learned some years ago that the two of them were at Camp Croft simultaneously, I spoke to Henry about this coincidence.

"Henry, I understand you underwent basic training in my hometown in 1943 at the same time as my father. Perhaps you met him in the mess hall." He chuckled and responded, "Most likely in the latrine, Charles!" He went on to say, quite astonishingly to me, that his time in Spartanburg was the most "formative time" of his life. "I had been a Jewish refugee, and when I first arrived in America, I was sent to work in a factory with other Jewish immigrant young men. I was sent to school with other Jewish immigrant boys. When I arrived in Spartanburg, I met men for the first time from South Carolina, Kentucky, Texas, Michigan—from all over the country. I learned their customs, became familiar with their cultures, and their slang. I began the process of assimilating into America. It was the start for me of becoming an American." I didn't know how to respond to him. Most Americans think of him as one of the great minds of the last half century, a recipient of the Nobel Peace Prize, a prolific author, and a highly accomplished global strategist and diplomat. But the transition from his humble beginnings in Germany to a man of greatness on the world stage were apparently greatly facilitated by a few months in Spartanburg, South Carolina. Imagine that.

CHAPTER 9

1999–2009: A DECADE OF DELUSION

"The end of a delusion is invariably sadness or tears."

—Pop Samuel

The prelude to Greece's economic crisis that erupted in 2010 took a surprising turn as Greece settled into its membership in the Eurozone. No more drachmas, only euros. Greece's very entry into the Euro Area had been shrouded in controversy. As outlined earlier, access into this exclusive club was based, inter alia, on the observance by each prospective member country of three criteria (the so-called Maastricht criteria) related to the inflation rate (no more than 1.5 percentage points above the three best-performing EU countries), budget deficit (below 3% of GDP), and public debt (below 60% of GDP, or at least on a declining trend if above this threshold). To meet these criteria in 1999, the base year for her entry into the Euro Area, Greece resorted to several temporary one-off measures, which to some extent had been utilized by some of the other eleven Euro Area countries prior to their entry. These included a reduction in indirect taxes on gasoline and heating oil and the freezing of public utility tariffs, which lowered measured inflation by 1 percentage point in 1999. In addition, Greece changed the timing of current spending and temporarily boosted government revenue by declaring a tax amnesty for tax evaders. Furthermore, the country securitized some future revenue items and EU transfers through the issuance of government securities that were not required, according to methodology used at the time, to be shown as part of public debt, contributing artificially to the reduction in public debt as a ratio to GDP.

Greece also resorted to a now rather infamous currency swap, with the engagement of Goldman Sachs, to reduce the national debt. Greece issued debt denominated in dollars and yen, then exchanged it for euros. The swap used off-market rates, permitted under the rules of the Eurozone at the time, namely historical exchange rates in which the euro was weaker, therefore once again artificially suppressing the national amount of debt, in this case by 2% compared to the actual amount. It should be noted that such swaps were not illegal at the time; they were ruled "out of bounds" in 2008 by Eurostat, the European authority on such matters. (It is also the case that Italy had used swap transactions to reduce its debt at the time of entry into the euro. As early as 1997 Eurostat had approved Italy's creative accounting methods, which would reduce budget deficit figures and improve the country's chance of being admitted to the Eurozone.[1] Additionally, "a 1996 derivative helped bring Italy's budget into line by swapping currency with JP Morgan at a favorable exchange rate, effectively putting more money in the government's hands. In return, Italy committed to future payments that were not booked as liabilities."[2])

The combination of various sleights of hand and manipulation of the data enabled Greece to squeeze by the Maastricht criteria for admission to the Eurozone. In reflecting upon this, I am reminded of a dinner that took place in Rome in 1998 during the IIF's Spring Membership Meeting. Hans Tietmeyer, President of the Bundesbank at the time and a key architect of the euro, had agreed to present a keynote dinner address to the IIF membership meeting in Rome in April of that year. It was only a matter of weeks before Europe's leaders were to make their final decisions on the initial members in the Euro Area, which would occur in May 1998.

Hans was a staunch admirer of the deutsche mark (DM), which had been Germany's national currency since June 20, 1948. It had been the strongman of European currencies since the 1960s, and Hans was duly skeptical of the benefits of trading the DM for a common currency, especially one including a large and disparate number of countries. Over dinner after his speech, we sat at the head table discussing the possible mix of currencies that could be amalgamated to become the euro. Hans and I had been friends and close collaborators for many years, dating back to his time as the German State Secretary at the German Finance Ministry in the 1980s. We had worked intensively together on both the Plaza and Louvre Accords of the mid-1980s, and he had been kind to speak at IIF meetings on a number of occasions during the 1990s.

On this warm spring evening in Rome, he was quite exercised about the prospect of some currencies becoming part of the euro, and turning it, as he saw it, into a weak alloy that would be a pale shadow of the deutsche mark. He was particularly concerned regarding the Italian lira and the Greek drachma. "The lira and the drachma will be part of the euro over my dead body," he protested loudly. Hans was a large and garrulous man, but I had never seen him so animated, his face turning red as his fist hit the table, jostling his beer.

On May 3, 1998, the European Council announced that eleven currencies would form the inaugural group of currencies to become the euro. The Greek drachma was not among them, but the Italian lira was. Two and a half years later, Greece's drachma was folded into the euro.

In the summer of 2013, a year after the Greek debt restructuring was completed, I went to see Hans in his hometown of Königstein, twenty miles outside of Frankfurt. We had a pleasant lunch at a nearby restaurant and reminisced about many issues. Hans had slowed down a bit since our earlier days, but at the age of 81, he still had a ready smile. I reminded him of his statement over dinner in Rome fifteen years earlier, and added, "I am pleased you're still alive and kicking, despite the fact that both the lira and the drachma are now part of the euro." He laughed boisterously, but after a sip of his Riesling, he explained, "Charles, it always was going to be a political project in the end, but it is such a shame. We had stability with the deutsche mark and look what we have now! It was a mistake to proceed with the euro without fiscal discipline in every country." Certainly, events have borne out the validity of his statement, as every Greek citizen knows.

A close friend of mine, Caio Koch-Weser, served as the Secretary of State in the German Finance Ministry at the time of the decision regarding Greece joining the euro. We spent a weekend together with our spouses a few years ago, and as we were wandering the streets of Dresden, I asked Caio about that decision. "Charles, I protested, because I had serious doubts about the sustainability of Greece's membership in the euro. They were just not ready."

Greece's wayward and occasionally misleading policies continued well past its entry into the Euro Area. Greece persisted in recording in the budget what otherwise would have been classified as current spending above the line as financial transactions below the line, thus understating the true budget deficit. Once again, such classification was in theory allowed under the Eurostat rules at the time, and to some extent, once again, was common in other EU countries, but the scale of this practice by Greece was extensive, giving rise to sizable stock/flow discrepancies (the stock of public debt rising much faster than suggested by the recorded budget deficit). In its March 2002 Article IV surveillance report on Greece, the IMF estimated that during the period 1995–2000, these below-the-line stock/flow discrepancies amounted to a cumulative 22 percentage points of GDP, limiting the decline in the public debt-to-GDP ratio to 6 percentage points, despite the cumulative impact of 28 percentage points of GDP from primary budget surpluses and higher nominal GDP growth relative to the average interest rate on public debt. The discrepancy is explained primarily through subsidies to public enterprises disguised as capital transfers for equity contributions, understated military spending, and public debt valuation adjustments.

Eurostat, the European Commission's statistical office, dates back to 1953, when its forerunner was created as part of the Coal and Steel Community. It is the authoritative source of comparative data on European economies. In November 2004, Eurostat issued a report indicting many Greek statistical records and practices and raised fundamental questions about Greece's data reliability. Deficit figures for 1999, a crucial period in meeting the Maastricht criteria, were revised upward from 1.8% of GDP to 3.4%; debt figures from 105.2% to 112.3% of GDP. According to the report, Greece had used various accounting techniques in violation of Eurostat rules, such as failing to report capitalized interest.[3]

Regrettably, just a few months after Greece's glorious staging of the Olympic Games in Athens—which was the site of the original modern games in 1896, and was again in August 2004—Greece's financial problems were resurfacing again. Membership in the euro, however, had given a shot in the arm to Greece's perceived creditworthiness. The government continued to report minimal budget deficits during 2002–2004, and the ratings agencies rewarded Greece for this. The spreads on Greek bonds over the German bonds were declining, but at 54 basis points they were still attractive, the highest in the Eurozone. Thus began what was arguably the second most consequential risk management mistake of this century to date (after the accumulation of highly leveraged securitized subprime mortgages that contributed to the global financial crisis of 2008–2009): mispricing of Greek sovereign debt.

The ratings agencies fueled the creditors' misguided enthusiasm for Greek debt. All three major rating agencies raised their ratings on Greek sovereign debt before and soon after Greece joined the Euro Area. In June 2003, Standard & Poor's rating of Greece's long-term debt was raised from A to A+, right in the middle of investment grades. This was consistent with Moody's A1 rating. Shockingly, none of the major rating agencies downgraded Greece's long-term debt to below A investment grade until April 27, 2010, when S&P moved their rating to BB+. This was seven months after the Papandreou government had announced that the budget deficit for 2009 would be 12.7%, more than double the previous estimate. Seven months!

The ratings agencies were joined by some of the financial media in embracing the idea that Greece had turned a page economically by joining the Eurozone. The *Financial Times*, for example, got caught up in the euphoria: "Greece has passed from economic laggard to disciplined member of the Eurozone."[4]

And what was happening in the Greek economy during this period of euphoria? In late 2004, a restatement of the fiscal accounts for the period 1997–2003 by the New Democracy government (which had won the March 2004 parliamentary elections, replacing PASOK as the ruling party) brought accounting irregularities once again to the fore. This reaffirmed that Greece had in fact manipulated the data to enable its entry into the Eurozone. The restatement entailed a more accurate estimate of military spending and the shifting of most of the below-the-line items to above-the-line regular government spending. As a result, the budget deficit each year during this period was revised upward by an average of 2.2 percentage points of GDP, with the deficit never falling below the 3% of GDP limit in the assessment year of 1999 or any year during this period. Similarly, the ratio of public debt to GDP was revised upward by more than 7 percentage points of GDP. While the restatements of the fiscal accounts were welcomed by the Euro Area institutions and financial markets as a step toward more accurate and transparent fiscal reporting, it nonetheless struck a major blow to Greece's reputation and credibility among its EU peers and led to renewed questioning of the appropriateness of Greece's entry into the Euro Area. Commenting on this, the IMF indicated in its February 2005 report on Greece that "the unreliability of the fiscal data, revealed by the large revisions agreed with Eurostat, has hindered surveillance, policymaking, and [Greece's] credibility." The accuracy of Greece's statistics was further called into question in September 2006, when the authorities announced a 26% upward adjustment of nominal GDP as a result of an update of the base for calculating national accounts statistics. The adjustment was resisted by some analysts as excessive, and was not fully endorsed by the Eurostat, which cut the increase in nominal GDP to only 9%.

George Provopoulos, Governor of the Bank of Greece from 2008 to 2014, captured the overall thrust of Greek economic performance during the 2000s accurately with the following data, which was outlined in a speech in 2014:

- Greece's fiscal deficit increased from 4.4% of GDP in 2001 to 15.6% in 2009;
- The share of government spending in GDP rose from 45% to 54%;
- The ratio of government debt rose from 103.7% in 2001 to 123.7% in 2009;
- The current account deficit rose from 11.5% of GDP in 2001 to 18% in 2009;
- Perhaps most profoundly for the overall deterioration of Greece's economy, its competitiveness, as measured by unit labor costs relative to those of its main trading partners, deteriorated by approximately 30% from 2001 to 2009.

As Governor Provopoulos said rather succinctly, "The Greek crisis was an accident waiting to happen."[5] None of this, however, seemed to matter to the investors—mostly European banks, insurance firms, and pension funds, which poured money into Greece from 2000 to 2009. The following charts indicate noticeably the flows of capital to Greece from the rest of the world, motivated by returns that averaged above the yield on German government debt (the bund), with the misguided perception that the risk was virtually no greater than that of German government debt.

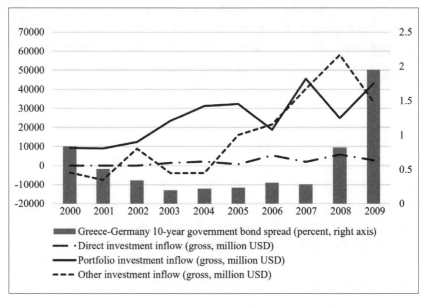

Figure 1 - Sources: ECB Statistics Data Warehouse & IMF Balance of Payments Statistics

Never mind that the Maastricht Treaty had explicitly stated that as of February 7, 1992, neither the European Community nor any EMU member would be liable for the commitments of any other member—the "no bail out" clause. Markets simply did not believe it, and as the endless string of Greek deficiencies and shortcomings began to accumulate, this did not appear to change market sentiment in the least.

During the first physical meeting of the IIF Task Force on Greece, which took place in Paris on June 24, 2011, I asked the representatives of the largest private lenders to Greece how they had missed the country's deteriorating economic and financial conditions during most of the decade leading up to the crisis in 2009. The response was stark—and telling. One after another, they acknowledged that they had, de facto, shut down their sovereign risk analysis over bond purchases from Greece, assuming that the German/Eurozone umbrella would protect them. They let their guard down and would pay the price. They had been "chasing yield," one of the oldest temptations in investing, even though the "spread" over German bonds—the extra return for investors—declined from 84 basis points in 2000, the year before Greece joined the euro, to approximately 30 basis points by 2007.

Of course, this was a time not just of delusions in Europe, but also of delusions globally by investors. Starting with the dot-com bubble of 1997–2000, markets seemed to lose perspective on the underlying value of many assets, and suspension of reality began to run through conduits of the global financial markets. The internet craze of the late 1990s was characterized by the rapid rise in stock prices for a wide range of so-called dot-coms. In what was a classic bubble, prices of many start-ups rose rapidly, despite a lack of profits. In its initial public offering (IPO) in 1998, TheGlobe.com saw its stock price rising from $9 a share to as high as $97 a share before closing at $63.50 on its first trading day.[6] On its IPO, the stock price of eToys.com rose from the opening $20 per share to $85 and closed at $76.56.[7] IPOs proliferated as new ventures attracted large amounts of capital, but, in many cases, with little revenue to sustain their momentum. By 2000, the landscape was littered with debris of companies that had become overnight disasters as quickly as they had become instant successes:

- The Learning Company, worth $3.5 billion in 1999, sold for $27.3 million in 2010.

- The stock of Infospace, whose price reached $1,305 per share in March 2000, one year later crashed to $22 per share.

- Webvan, an online grocery retailer, raised $405 million in its IPO in November 1999. Its stock price reached $34 per share on its first trading day, but plummeted to $.06 a share in 2001.[8]

Of course, investors in the 2000s did not limit their enthusiasm for European sovereign debt to Greece. They lent heavily into the other peripheral economies of Europe as well. As David Marsh notes in his impressive, but discouraging, 2013 book, *Europe's Deadlock: How the Euro Crisis Could Be Solved and Why It Won't Happen*, "At first [in the evolution of the Euro Area] everything went well. Sharply higher balance of payments . . . Deficits were financed more or less automatically. In a form of vendor finance, the countries with export surpluses simply built-up financial claims on the progressively more indebted nations with growing trade deficits . . . Large proportions of the size of the sizably higher liabilities in Greece, Portugal and Spain were financed by short-term cash flows."[9]

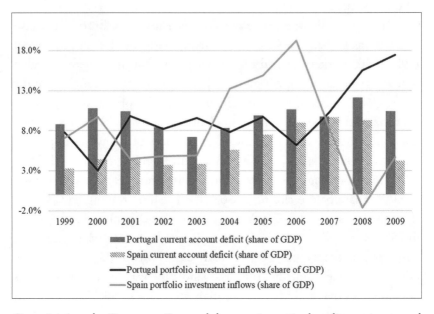

Since joining the Eurozone, Portugal became increasingly reliant on external financing to cover its current accounts deficits. In most of the years during 1999 through 2009, the short-term capital inflows did cover these deficits. The boom and bust of Spanish banks' access to short-term wholesale funding is evident in years 2004–2005.

These short-term flows created, of course, growing vulnerabilities for these economies should the flows cease or reverse. But in these halcyon years of the early to mid-2000s, investors kept piling in, with the "benefit" of implicit encouragement by the rating agencies.

As John Authers points out in his excellent review of the causes of the Eurozone crisis in his 2012 book titled *Europe's Financial Crisis: A Short Guide to How the West Fell into Crisis and the Consequences for the World*, Ireland, Portugal, Spain, and Italy all had, each in their own way, misspent their first decade in the Eurozone.[10] Greece, Ireland, and Spain all benefited from the reduction of risk premiums after joining the euro, leading to lower borrowing costs. But bank regulations and fiscal discipline did not improve to keep up with the credit expansion.

Ireland experienced a boom in housing and private credit expansion in the 2000s after joining the EU, during which period property speculation was rampant. Lower interest rates, imprudent banking regulation, and tax incentives contributed to the boom. While the headline fiscal balance was sound, public revenues relied heavily on the real estate sector, and the structural budget deficit was high. Like Ireland, Spain also experienced a boom in construction and housing that led to excessive credit growth and overreliance on external spending.

Italy, on the other hand, experienced low productivity growth and erosion of competitiveness, leaving it vulnerable thanks to high debt and fiscal deficit due to slack public fiscal management.[11] Unlike Ireland, Portugal did not experience an economic boom following the accession to the Eurozone. But due to weak economic competitiveness, the external deficits deteriorated and were financed by large public and private external borrowing, leaving the high debt susceptible to external shocks.[12]

Greek debt continued to grow throughout the decade, nearly doubling to €151.9 billion. Debt levels had been exacerbated by the cost of measures to complete facilities for the Olympics. While this is common for Olympic countries, Greece could ill afford it. Following the Olympics, the new Karamanlis government had set out to correct many of Greece's economic problems, and expectations were high. As Peter Siani-Davies stated, "During the election campaign Kostas Karamanlis had spoken of reinventing the state, rolling back bureaucracy in promoting meritocracy and more, with a strong popular mandate . . . It was widely assumed that the 48-year-old nephew of the famed Constantinos Karamanlis, with his mixture of easygoing bonhomie and natural self-confidence, would make good on his promises."[13] Unfortunately, he did not. As Beaton described things during Kostas Karamanlis's tenure, "a certain lassitude . . . had been identified as a hallmark of the five-year rule."[14] Nevertheless, in September 2007 he was reelected for a second term, as the economy was growing steadily.

As the chart and table indicate, debt levels of Greece and Italy were, in general, relatively stable for the first seven or so years of the 2000s. Spain's declined, while Portugal's rose steadily, from a low level of 50% of GDP to 69% by 2006. Beginning in 2008, the debt levels for all four countries migrated upward as the global recession began to take its toll. By 2009, Greece's debt level had moved from an already high level of 103% of GDP to 109%.

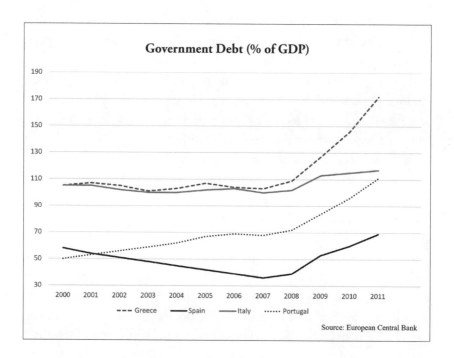

Source: European Central Bank

Government Debt (% of GDP)

	Greece	Spain	Italy	Portugal
2000	105	58	105	50
2001	107	54	105	53
2002	105	51	102	56
2003	101	48	100	59
2004	103	45	100	62
2005	107	42	102	67
2006	104	39	103	69
2007	103	36	100	68
2008	109	39	102	72
2009	127	53	113	84
2010	146	60	115	96
2011	172	69	117	111
2012	160	85	123	126

Source: European Central Bank

Enjoying a moment of levity with Yannis Costopoulos (right), Chairman of Greece's Alpha Bank and the "Dean" of Greece's private banking community. The Greek crisis had yet to envelop us. Louisa Gouliamaki/AFP via Getty Images

Earlier that same year (May 2007), the IIF held its Spring Membership Meeting in Athens, hosted magnificently by the Greek banks, led by Yannis Costopoulos of Alpha Bank. We held a gala dinner under the stars, and Prime Minister Kostas Karamanlis delivered a rousing speech. Another election was approaching, but his popularity seemed to be relatively high, and he appeared confident of the outcome as he talked with him and several Board members over dinner. But not all was well. A number of scandals had undermined confidence in the government, and long-standing underlying economic challenges, such as pension reform, were not being addressed. In early 2007, the IMF had completed its annual review of the 2006 Greek economy. While they noted that growth was continuing to be strong, at 4.1% in 2006, "vulnerabilities had developed in the form of very high credit growth, persistent inflationary measures, eroding competitiveness, and an unsustainably large current account deficit."[15] Other than that, things were fine. Pension reform was desperately needed, fiscal consolidation was on hold, privatization was lagging, and the oft-discussed labor market reform was meager. But the markets still were not focused on the downside risks. Greece was a member of the Eurozone; therefore, the risk was implicitly covered by Germany and other strong members of the Eurozone, so never mind that "indicators suggest a significant erosion of cost and price competitiveness in EMU excessiveness."[16]

Perhaps none of this would have been cataclysmic were it not for a combination of adverse events at home and a gathering storm abroad that would lead to a severe global recession. The overwhelming bulk of the bankers and other financiers gathered for our meetings in Athens appeared rather distant from the growing underlying problems in the Greek economy. Their thoughts were understandably elsewhere. Dark clouds were gathering over the global financial system, and our Board of Directors was concerned. The US housing bubble had begun to crack, and consequently subprime mortgages—of which there were a vast number—started defaulting. As Alan Blinder so aptly described it in his book *After the Music Stopped*, the financial system "has built an intricate financial house of cards—a concoction of great complexity, but also great fragility."[17] In late May, housing prices were only beginning to decline, but as the first card began to fall, the bankers knew other cards could tumble quite quickly. IIF Board Chairman Joe Ackermann led a roundtable discussion of the state of financial markets. It was sobering at first, then frightening. The leaders of many of the world's largest financial institutions saw a tempestuous storm coming. I can still recall many of the ominous comments made by the Board members. Gordon Nixon, the sharp but soft-spoken CEO of Royal Bank of Canada, led off the discussion by stating bluntly that the declining values in US real estate could lead to a chain reaction through the securitization and distribution of mortgage-backed securities (MBS) that had taken place. One senior banker after another elaborated on those risks: Bill Rhodes of Citibank, Doug Flint of HSBC, Baudouin Prot of BNPP, Martin Blessing of Commerzbank; they all spoke to the number of risks that had accumulated in the system, including in many European as well as American banks. Perhaps the most worrisome set of comments were expressed by Ahmass Fakahany, the Executive Vice President responsible for markets at Merrill Lynch, who was especially blunt: "I am quite concerned about the concentration of mortgage-backed risks we see at many institutions, including my own. The embedded leverage has exceeded any reasonable limit." Fakahany, who became a successful restaurateur after he left banking (his restaurant Marea is one of New York's top-rated Italian restaurants, and another of his restaurants, Ai Fiori, is one of my favorites). At times, the discussion had the air of a group confession. The top emerging-market bankers, such as Roberto Setubal of Itaú and Chartsiri Sophonpanich of Bangkok Bank, had steered well clear of the problem. Fortunately, so had the Greek banks (they were obviously not to be so lucky when it came to Greek sovereign debt risk).

When the discussion wrapped up, we took a short break. Everyone in the room had a worried expression on their face. There was one more moment of disquiet before our meetings in Athens concluded. Terry Checki, then the Executive Vice President of the Federal Reserve Bank of New York, gave a speech that turned out to be eerily prescient. I've known Terry for years. He had been mentored, as I had, by one of the United States' finest minds in international finance, Sam Cross. As explained in Chapter 7, Sam had been the US Executive Director at the IMF when I joined the Treasury, and he was a remarkably experienced and wise man. He moved from the US Treasury to the Federal Reserve Bank in New York, where Terry had the good fortune to benefit from his vast knowledge. Terry has always been a very astute observer of the dynamics between market trends and underlying economic fundamentals. Because we had worked together over the years on numerous sovereign debt issues, I knew he had a keen sense of the strengths and vulnerabilities of global markets, and I asked him to speak that day on the outlook for those markets.

He began by giving a somewhat upbeat view of emerging markets, but then segued into a very thoughtful and pointed assessment of risks in global markets. "Low interest rates, low volatility, and the seeming ability to trade out of any risk create obvious incentives to build up leverage, often in ways that are not readily transparent. Leverage contributes to very tight pricing in good times. But it also introduces the scope for large and sudden reversals when the cycle turns. And in this connection, we haven't lived through a full credit cycle with the complex structural products that currently dominate the landscape."[18] As I listened to Terry, I reflected on the discussion I had just heard in the IIF boardroom. All signs pointed in an ominous direction.

Leaving 10 Downing Street after a meeting with UK Prime Minister Gordon Brown and senior bankers during the global financial crisis. I was accompanied by David Mulford (left), Vice Chairman of Credit Suisse at the time and a former close colleague of mine at the US Treasury, 1984–1991. Photo by Chris Ratcliffe/Bloomberg via Getty Images

Two months later, on August 7, 2007, the alarm bells went off. BNP Paribas froze three of its subprime mortgage funds. This triggered a sharp reaction, and the global financial crisis was off and running. Many excellent books have been written about the crisis, and I have no intention of trying to plow this ground once again. In the months leading up to the global financial crisis that erupted in fall 2008, the world economy was in suspended animation. Defaults occurred with increasing frequency in the subprime and Alt A market and in March, Bear Stearns collapsed as a result of its exposure to structure mortgage products. Although that firm was rescued by the Federal Reserve and JP Morgan, the markets were extraordinarily jittery, and underlying growth began to stutter. After a first quarter contraction of -1.6 percent, the US economy picked up growth in the second quarter to 2.3 percent. As the real estate markets continued to collapse, however, real GDP contracted again in the third quarter by an annual rate of 2.1 percent.

In Greece, inflation spiked to 4.2% in 2008 from 2.9% in 2007, and spreads in Greek debt were beginning to widen as the markets finally began to awaken to the underlying vulnerabilities of the Greek economy. Growth was slowing, scandals were spreading around the Karamanlis government, and violence was taking place in the streets. On December 6, 2008, a student involved in the protest was killed by police, inciting weeks of demonstrations in Athens, some of them violent. The demonstrations spread around the country, and a substantial degree of disorder took place in many cities and towns. To give a sense of the mood around the country, one historian described it as "an incoherent explosion of a society trapped by the whirlwind of an institutional, social and moral crisis."[19] That may be a lot to absorb, but you get the point.

The government in Greece was struggling, and by the end of 2008 it was clear that the collapse of Lehman Brothers had catapulted the world economy into a serious recession. Lehman was a lightning strike to the entire global financial system. Greece was drawn into the vortex and by late 2008 was in a recession, along with virtually all of Europe. In 2009, Greece was lucky that its contraction was only 2.5%. But the accumulation of domestic and international pressures led Karamanlis to call for an election in October 2009, two years before the end of his second term. He lost to Papandreou, who gained a slim majority in the parliament.

Of course, no one knows whether the Greek crisis would have been avoided—unlikely, in my view, since it was probably only a matter of time until Greece's economic weaknesses would have revealed themselves in an ugly way. But it is important to recognize that the exogenous negative factors generated by the global financial crisis had at least four transmission mechanisms into the Greek crisis:

1) Throughout 2008 and the first half of 2009, US GDP fell 4.3%, and the Eurozone followed the US into recession quite quickly; by the first quarter of 2008 it was in recession. The contraction of Germany was among the most painful at 6.8%, and the entire Eurozone recession was compounded by contractionary fiscal policies in many Eurozone countries. Although Greece was a relatively closed economy with an export-to-GDP ratio that was the lowest among EU countries, the contraction by the Eurozone economy nevertheless hit Greece, and exports dropped 19% in 2009.[20]

2) More broadly, the suddenness and depth of global recession had undermined investor confidence throughout the world, including in Greece. Investment declined significantly and private consumption also turned negative,[21] and an already woefully weak revenue base was hit further. First quarter 2009 GDP declined by 4.8%, quarter over quarter. Despite all of this, wage growth in Greece proceeded at the alarming pace of 12%, further undermining competitiveness.[22]

3) Greek banks were also hit by the confidence problem that's spread virtually throughout global banking. Cross-border liquidity became scarce and the regulatory pressures on banks began to mount, with increased capital and liquidity requirements among a host of measures put in place. This, in turn, restricted credit to the Greek economy and compounded the domestic economic weakness.

4) Finally, Ireland had preceded Greece into crisis with the collapse of their leading banks in the fall and winter of 2008–2009. Ireland had been among the original members of the Euro Area, and its crisis catalyzed market concerns about a broader problem in the Eurozone. The ECB played a critical role in supporting

Ireland during the first period of Irish crisis, but eventually Ireland had to seek an IMF program in the fall of 2010. Portugal followed Ireland into IMF programs, in May 2011. Thus, three members of the Eurozone—two original ones—became the first Western European countries with IMF programs since Italy and the UK and the 1970s. At the same time, Italy and Spain were facing major economic challenges as well, creating a collective European economic crisis that was characterized by Alan Blinder as "The Big Aftershock."[23]

None of these exogenous factors should deflect us from the core weaknesses of the Greek economy. Nevertheless, they do underscore that the forces contributing to the Greek debt crisis were an extraordinary and toxic combination of national, regional, and global factors. The fact remains that during the first decade of the twenty-first century Greece had the best opportunity since the nation was formed almost two centuries prior to reinvigorate and reform its economy and put it on a path of stability and sustained growth—an opportunity missed that would cost its citizens dearly. The markets and EU funding had done Greece no favor in funding and facilitating this massive lost opportunity. And the stage was set for a crisis of unprecedented proportions.

CHAPTER 10

EUROPE AND THE IMF STEP UP

"It is not what happens to you,
but how you react to it that matters."

—Epictetus, circa 93 BC

Amidst the snowy chaos of Davos in late January 2010, I kept my appointment with Papandreou. I was joined by Bill Rhodes, a banker who was not only a Vice Chairman of the IIF Board but one of the world's most experienced bankers in dealing with sovereign debt issues. I had worked closely with him during my years at the Treasury dealing with the Latin debt crisis. Bill had also chaired many of the advisory committees that represented the commercial banks in restructuring Mexican, Argentinian, Brazilian, and other debt.

Because all of the proper meeting rooms were taken, we met with Papandreou in a café corner of the main conference building, tucked away behind some registration booths by the main common area. He was sitting there sipping an espresso while Davosians hurried past, trying to betray no idea that they knew who he was. The Greek Prime Minister was a tall, slim, bald man with an elegant mustache who spoke American English, having grown up in Minnesota, where his father, former Prime Minister Andreas Papandreou, had gone to teach after his last term in office. Somewhat disconcertingly for a Greek Prime Minister, George Papandreou moved in the loose-limbed style of an American as well. He seemed quite nervous, somewhat plaintive, as though he didn't need advice from us so much as solace.

And for good reason. On October 22, 2009, the rating agency Fitch had downgraded Greece from A to A-. On December 7, Standard & Poor put Greece on negative watch, and a day later Fitch had downgraded Greece again. By January 26, 2010, just two days before our meeting in Davos, the spread on Greek debt over German bonds had risen from mid-October's 130 basis points to over 300 basis points. The Athens stock market was down 25% since early October. The run was on, and Papandreou could feel the pressure.

Once the pleasantries were dispensed with, Papandreou reached into his satchel and handed us each a printout of a few pages, headlined "Program for Sustained Growth." As I thumbed through, it seemed quite impressive at first glance, but could it be implemented? As we talked, he made clear that before he could hope to put through any economic reforms, he'd have to establish Greece's—and his—credibility in the markets. He turned to us. "Do you suppose you could help with that, Bill and Charles?"

If the global creditors represented by the IIF could express some confidence in him and his new program, he reasoned, that would improve the country's standing in the capital markets, which had largely frozen Greece out during the preceding months; drop bond prices back to more affordable levels; and turn the vicious cycle of debt back around in Greece's favor.

We were sympathetic, but told him we couldn't just snap our fingers. I was responsible to the IIF membership and needed to achieve consensus first.

"Your program is ambitious, and will require fortitude to implement," I said.

"Do you intend to seek help from the EC or the IMF?" Bill asked.

"No, I don't believe we need it."

We were skeptical. The Greek economy was already imploding. Industrial production had contracted, and unemployment was rising sharply.[1] Could Greece really stabilize their increasingly dire situation without an IMF program? "We will do our best, George, but it may be very difficult without official support."

He seemed gratified, smiled, and thanked us for our willingness to help. I decided to follow up with a visit to Athens, but by the time I got there a month later, the situation had deteriorated further. As outlined earlier, the IIF had played a constructive role on a number of occasions over the previous twenty years in other cases, facilitating a country's renewed access to global capital markets, often following or during an economic adjustment program. Turkey on several occasions in the late 1990s, Hungary in 1995, the Czech Republic in 1996, even Mexico in 1995 after the tequila crisis. We would often arrange meetings at a time when there seemed to be a substantive basis to rebuild credibility and "road-show" presentations to IIF member firms. It would allow the Finance Minister and Central Bank Governor an opportunity to present their economic plan and attempt to persuade creditors that investing in their sovereign debt would be a good investment. Often, it worked, especially—but not necessarily—if accompanied by an IMF program.

But Greece felt different. It was already part of a regional crisis, as Ireland was in an advanced banking calamity and Spain was also showing growing signs of stress. Furthermore, the role of the Eurozone and the IMF in supporting an adjustment program remained very unclear, as it appeared that Greece could not meet its obligations on its own, and contagion was spreading. Prime Minister Papandreou and Chancellor Merkel were openly disagreeing over the roles of the Eurozone and the IMF in the adjustment program. At the same time, IMF and European leaders were adamant that there would be no debt restructuring. Christine Lagarde, still the French Finance Minister, "rejected the notion."[2] German Finance Minister Wolfgang Schäuble argued that a debt restructuring would spread contagion, and he, along with other European leaders, began to gravitate toward an official support program that would revolve around a contractionary adjustment program. Jean-Claude Trichet, ECB President, was also firmly opposed to any debt restructuring.

When I arrived in Athens, it initially looked as if there would not be much of a role for the IIF. Nevertheless, I had been through enough debt crises to know that events could take unexpected turns. Our member firms held much of Greece's debt, so at a minimum they were anxious for us to analyze and monitor the situation. Perhaps, at some point, we could also be helpful to Greece somewhere along the way. They certainly looked like they needed the help.

Greek Prime Minister George Papandreou and German Chancellor Angela Merkel struggling to get on the same page during a press conference in Berlin, Germany, March 2010. Photo by Alina Novopashina, dpa picture alliance archive/Alamy Stock Photo

My first stop in Athens was to see the Finance Minister, George Papaconstantinou, at his office by the parliament building in Syntagma Square. The Finance Ministry building is old and a bit rusty, somewhat like a used car. It wasn't far from Greece's Central Bank, a building that could hardly be more handsome, with ornate paintings of the heroes of classical Greece on the walls.

I made my way down a long corridor with security guards lolling at desks at irregular intervals, performing no obvious function but nevertheless sending clouds of cigarette smoke into the air.

Papaconstantinou's office wasn't much, just a large wooden desk with a few chairs around it, a conference table off to one side, a spare carpet, and little on the walls. The Minister himself was trim and alert with a thick brush of black hair that seemed to be not only a national birthright but also professorial, which fit a man whose academic background in economics had led to a series of important government jobs. His last post had been Environmental Minister, which included dealing with climate change, another enormous task I took to be good preparation for his new job.

After a business-like greeting, I took a seat in front of Papaconstantinou's desk, and watched to see whether he would remain behind his desk, safe in his fortress. At first, he settled down where he was, seemingly protecting himself behind the trappings of his office. But then he stood up and began stalking about his office, growing angrier by the minute as he railed against the absurdities of the national budget, the padding of governmental payrolls with thousands of useless staff and make-work jobs at ridiculous wages—well above what they'd get elsewhere in the Eurozone—and the fact that privileged sectors like accountants, auditors, and doctors got special treatment from the government to protect their own jobs from open competition. And then he weighed in on the tax system, where thousands of professionals paid virtually no taxes. And all of it, he told me, had contributed to this enormous unsustainable deficit. "Twelve point seven percent!" he cried out, as if one number could sum it all up. "It's inconceivable!"

Unfortunately, it was all too conceivable, as Papaconstantinou well knew. Greece resembled an overextended homeowner, and Papaconstantinou as Finance Minister was the unfortunate homeowner who had bought his house without fully inspecting it and was now horrified to discover that carpenter ants have turned the basement sills to sawdust, and the bathrooms are thick with mold.

Before I left the meeting with Papaconstantinou, he asked me what Papandreou had asked: If Greece could implement its austerity/reform program, could the Institute help put Greece back on a course for renewed market access and reconnect the country with the bankers, investors, and insurance firms that had become estranged because of the financial revelations? I told him that I would do what I could. I emerged with admiration for him for going right at this. However, the waters were rising all around him. I had no idea how high nor how far circumstances would draw me into them.

My colleague Jeff Anderson and I met with a number of our Greek banking colleagues. We started with the dean of Greek bankers, Yannis Costopoulos. Yannis was the epitome of a capable, distinguished, and accomplished banker. With a patrician style befitting his position as the son of the firm's founder, he had guided Alpha Bank for more than forty years, beginning in 1973. He had served as a Director of the IIF, and I had come to rely upon his advice and experience on many matters.

"Charles, this isn't going to work. Even with European and IMF support, I am quite pessimistic. The economy is in deep trouble. Even though this government is trying to turn the situation around, I am afraid it is too much to expect." He shook his head with a sense of resignation.

The other bankers we met shared similar assessments. Then we went to see the Minister of Health, Andreas Loverdos. If the meeting with Papaconstantinou was a stark eye-opener, the meeting with Loverdos was a shocker. He described a ministry that was in revolt against him.

"Charles and Jeff, I have tried but I cannot get control of this ministry. There are at least three to four hundred career employees in the upper ranks of the ministry who refused to follow my instructions. They rebel at the idea of trimming our staff and reducing the cost of medicine to the citizens." If Papaconstantinou was angry and animated, Loverdos seemed frustrated and already defeated. We were amazed at the ability of the bureaucracy to completely stymie the government's efforts to rein in spending and try to clean up the multitude of problems in the health sector.

Our final meeting during this trip to Athens was with the Prime Minister. We were not certain of the timing, so we went to the dining room at the hotel where we were staying. Suddenly Papandreou's executive assistant called, and we were off, leaving our dinner on the table.

Papandreou was at his office in the parliament, and it was getting late. Once again, we walked down long corridors, but this time they were darker and the guards at the security desks were more numerous. We finally made it to his office, and he greeted us cordially.

"Charles, I am facing increased resistance to our program, and the economy continues to contract."

"That is to be expected, George, for your program is focused on contraction in the short term, while the structural reforms will take time. Jobs will be lost before the efficiency gains can take hold."

"I will need support from both the IMF and the Eurozone, and I hope I can count on the IIF as well," he replied.

We knew that our role at that point was rather peripheral, but we assured him that we would do our best. "George, it could be helpful if you came to speak at our Spring Membership Meeting. It will be held in Vienna, Austria, in early June. The key question is whether this program, with IMF or Eurozone support, can rebuild confidence among the private creditors. Many will be in attendance, and they need to be convinced."

"If you think it can help, I will be there," he responded.

In early May, Europe and the IMF stepped up with a €110 billion package of loans, the bulk of which (€80 billion) came from Eurozone countries.

The program provided temporary relief; yields on Greek sovereign bonds declined sharply from 12% to 7.25%. Our Spring Membership Meeting in Vienna in early June featured Papandreou as the keynote speaker. He met privately with the leadership of the IIF and Greece's major creditors, and the meeting went well. He assured the bankers of his commitment to the adjustment program, and then gave an inspiring speech before approximately four hundred senior bankers and investors from around the world. He received a standing ovation as the collective sentiment of the creditors at that time was infused by admiration for his commitment to tackle Greece's deep-seated problems. A degree of hope spread throughout the audience that somehow Greece would avoid restructuring its debt, an event that could cost billions of dollars for the banks represented in the room. Within a year, we were to learn that this was wishful thinking.

Welcoming Prime Minister George Papandreou (second from left) to Vienna for his keynote speech at the IIF Spring Membership Meeting, June 2011. Accompanied by Yannis Costopoulos, Chairman of Alpha Bank (second from right), and Jeff Anderson, Director, European Department, IIF (far right). Papandreou later characterized this occasion as the "high point" of his time as Prime Minister.
© 2011 Institute of International Finance, Inc.

CHAPTER 11

AUSTERITY,
THEN DEAUVILLE

**"I want a man without money
rather than money without a man."**

—Themistocles, circa 480 BC

During the summer of 2010, the pressure on Greece and financial markets eased somewhat, at least initially. The scope of the program had clearly impressed markets, and Greece appeared to be making every effort to implement that program. But the scale of financing was outdone by the scale of fiscal adjustment called for. Greece had agreed to cut the deficit from 13.6% in 2009 to 8.1% in 2010, 7.6% in 2011, and below 3% in 2014. But could it really be compatible with the forecast built into the program of a relatively short-lived recession: negative growth in 2010 of 4%, 2.6% in 2011, and minimal growth in 2012 of 1.1%?

Protests in Greece over the adjustment program grew, with participants willing to cross party lines and ideological divides. Syntagma Square became an almost semi-permanent sight for many of these protests. Thousands turned out on May Day, and unfortunately things turned violent. The protests persisted for many days thereafter as tear gas was used to disperse the crowds.

Credit default swap spreads dropped sharply upon announcement of the Eurozone/IMF support package but moved back up during the summer. The same was the case with spreads on sovereign debt. As the fall of 2010 approached, spreads on sovereign debt of not only Greece but Ireland, Portugal, and Spain all rose further; in the case of Greece, the spread of 900 basis points nearly equaled the peak level in the spring.

Market concerns reflected reality; the contraction in the economy was becoming much more severe than had been forecast. Furthermore, this entire Euro Area was being adversely affected, as growth stalled throughout most of the Eurozone, while economic recovery was under way in the US.

Meanwhile, with no exchange rate to facilitate the adjustment process, the program called for an internal devaluation, focusing on wage compression—almost exclusively from private sector workers—and job elimination. By June, the unemployment rate hit 11.7%, up over two full points since the summer of 2009. By October, that number had been 13.9%, the highest in Europe.

Despite these rather ominous signs, the government, IMF, and European officials tried to shine the best light on the situation. There was talk of Greece having "crossed the Rubicon" and the program having outpaced expectations.[1]

In late summer, Papaconstantinou and I discussed the idea of a road show to meet with investors and creditors and seek to persuade them that Greece was restoring its creditworthiness. At the IIF, we had our doubts, but we also felt that we owed it to Papaconstantinou and Papandreou to try. They were trying to make the best of a very difficult situation, and so we arranged for meetings with investors in Paris, London, Berlin, and Tokyo. IIF staff organized the events, and they were quite well attended. I chaired the one in Paris, hosted by BNP Paribas, and thought it went well. George Papaconstantinou and I, along with our staff and colleagues, met for breakfast before our meeting with investors in Paris.

"George, how are things going at home?" I asked.

"Charles," he responded, "I have to be honest; things are tough. We are implementing reforms, such as opening up the various trading sectors for greater competition, but resistance is strong, and demonstrations persist."

I stressed the importance of the presentation to the creditors and encouraged him to be as positive as possible. He was, and I felt that he made a good presentation. It was endorsed by Poul Thomsen, the head of the IMF's Greek team, who also joined the gathering.

At meetings such as this we aimed to maintain a neutral stance, as our role was not to be an advocate for Greece. Nevertheless, I was pleased that the meeting went well; the bankers asked questions but also expressed support. The meetings in London, Berlin, and Tokyo also were well received, and Greece finally had some wind at its back.

This continued during the IMF World Bank meetings that followed a couple of weeks later. Papaconstantinou impressed his interlocutors in the press and in the official meetings with his steadfast commitment to fiscal discipline and economic reform. He gave an impressive speech at the IFF's Annual Meetings, and received a standing ovation, reminiscent of the one received by his boss in Vienna in June. By the end of September, Greek sovereign debt had once again begun to recede, indicating some degree of renewed confidence in the outlook for the Greek economy.

Then reality appeared in another form: Deauville. Deauville is a small, medieval town that rings a yacht-filled harbor on the Normandy coast of France. In October 2010, a month after we'd completed the road shows with Papaconstantinou, the French hosted a Franco-German summit. Greece was, of course, high on the agenda, but they also were working to stabilize the Eurozone more generally. Ireland was under tremendous pressure to resolve its banking problem, which was becoming more severe by the day. Portugal was also facing growing resistance to its severe fiscal adjustment measures.

The confluence of events on October 18, 2010, was bizarre, to say the least. Fighting fires on a number of fronts, the Eurozone leadership took measures that, at least in the short term, worsened them. In the midst of a crisis that was still spiraling, Finance Ministers, along with Trichet, were meeting to decide whether to impose automatic sanctions on countries that violated their fiscal deficit rules of Maastricht. Fiscal discipline had clearly been a problem for Greece, as well as for many of the Eurozone countries over the years (recall Germany's violation in 2004). But was this really the right time to be debating automatic economic and even political sanctions for budgetary sinners? Europe, after all, was in recession, and another round of budget cuts would hardly help Europe emerge from the recession. Of course, putting in place automatic sanctions would not have necessarily required more immediate fiscal adjustment, but part of the issue was what signal to send both to governments and to markets.

The proposal was not supported, but another important matter needed consideration. The European Financial Stability Facility had been set up earlier in the year as a temporary measure. It needed to be made a more permanent mechanism. But the trade-off for that decision proved to be quite controversial. And to a large extent, it cast the die for a restructuring of Greece's debt, even though that was not immediately recognized.

While the ministers were meeting in Brussels, some 420 kilometers southwest, another meeting was under way that would have a dramatic effect on Greece and its debt. Chancellor Merkel and President Sarkozy had agreed to meet for a Franco-German Summit. (Curiously, they had also invited Russian President Dmitry Medvedev to discuss security issues. Moscow said it was looking to "build a democratic space of equal and indivisible security in the Euro-Atlantic and Eurasia region."[2] What a difference a dozen years make.)

Merkel and Sarkozy went for a stroll on the windswept harbor at Deauville. Deauville had become an upscale holiday destination, famous for, among other things, its casino. I visited there with Peixin and our son Bryan in the summer of 2019 and discovered, unsurprisingly, that it also has outstanding fresh seafood.

Without their Finance Ministers accompanying them, and apparently without any prior consultation with key staff, they made a far-reaching decision. In making the Financial Stability mechanism permanent, they included the following language:

"The establishment of a permanent and robust framework to ensure orderly crises management in the future *providing the necessary arrangements for an adequate participation of private creditors* [emphasis mine] and allowing Member States to take appropriate coordinated measures to safeguard financial stability of the Euroarea as a whole."[3]

From a long-term political and economic perspective, the incorporation of private creditors into a stabilization program makes sense—if it is necessary. But not every stabilization program requires a debt restructuring, and that was part of the problem with the announcement: the implicit assumption that a restructuring of privately held claims would be needed in each and every case. Debt restructurings reflect a profound lack of creditworthiness and can be very disruptive to the overall operation of an economy. Many IMF programs over the years have not had debt restructurings, depending on the overall balance of payments and debt sustainability outlook, of course.

The biggest problem with the announcement was the message it sent to markets. Technically the "bail in" clause would only apply to new bonds issued after 2013. Many creditors, however, saw in this decision another message: that there was a great risk hanging on to or purchasing existing Greek sovereign debt in the months ahead; you may get caught in a "bail in" operation.

There are two different interpretations of subsequent events. Ahsoka Mody argues that Deauville was not a "grave economic error,"[4] and that it had little effect on the market for Greek bonds. George Papaconstantinou, Greece's Finance Minister, had a different view: "European banks immediately took the announcement to imply the prospect of losing money on the Greek bonds."[5] I support Papaconstantinou's analysis. The spread on Greek bonds climbed 150 basis points in the weeks that followed as some of the banks sold down their positions.

Soon after Deauville, I met with Christine Lagarde. She was unhappy about the decision at Deauville, and said that she would not have approved of it had she been there. I talked with numerous Greek creditors, and they were uniformly critical. "We had a gentlemen's agreement to maintain our exposure to Greece and now they have broken it," one said to me. Another told me, "If they want to maintain and have any chance of rebuilding confidence in Greece's economic program, this is not the way to do it."

As 2010 came to an end, the economy back in Greece was flagging. Total deposits in the banking system had shrunk 12% over the course of the year. Credit to the private sector turned negative in December as GDP declined 4.5% for the year. The budget deficit had been reduced a rather sensible 5.75%, but Greece had fallen short of the deficit target due to a rebasing of the deficit by Eurostat. They had found the 2009 deficit to be 15.4% of GDP, not 13.6%. Nevertheless, the IMF staff had refused to adjust the 2010 target, a surprisingly misguided judgment.

When the revised 2009 deficit numbers were announced, Greek spreads jumped another 100 basis points. In retrospect, that may have been the coup de grace.

CHAPTER 12

DEBT RESTRUCTURING LOOMS

"The aim of the wise is not to secure pleasure, but to avoid pain."

—Aristotle, circa 340 BC

The first months of 2011 felt like a train wreck in slow motion. The prospect of a successful adjustment program without a debt restructuring was slipping away. Chancellor Merkel and Prime Minister Papandreou each began to realize this but were uncertain of whether and how to move to a restructuring, especially given the continued firm opposition of the ECB. The endless meetings in Brussels produced no agreed path forward, but instead stasis and bickering.

We will never know whether in the absence of Deauville and the revised 2009 budget data Greece would have been able to make it through without the restructuring. It is, in my view, highly doubtful. It would have required a more graduated path of adjustment, with more financial support from Europe and the IMF. As I will demonstrate subsequently, that would have been feasible had the IMF recognized that this was never a stand-alone Greek crisis; it was a regional crisis that required a regional set of adjustment policies. The IMF could have developed a set of broad adjustment guidelines for all members of the Eurozone and a more specific set of policies for Greece, Portugal, and Ireland, and based its lending to those three countries on the entire Eurozone quota. Feasible according to existing IMF policies? No, but it would have been feasible to amend the policies in those exceptional circumstances. Of course, it would have taken a significant dose of creativity and required burden-sharing of the additional liabilities to the IMF by all Eurozone members. The obvious alternative would have been for Europe to step up more in its regional and bilateral funding arrangements. This would have been the fairest way to distribute the adjustment burden—heavy on Greece, Portugal, and Ireland, but not unmanageably so, and lighter on everyone else, yet significant enough to ease the burden on Greece. It should be remembered that the notion of "burdening the taxpayer" with these additional loans is often exaggerated. The principal of the loans could be repaid, either on schedule or with a stretch-out of maturities. The only direct "costs" to the official creditors would have been the difference between the below-market rates on loans to Greece and the rates at which the Stability Facility could raise money in capital markets. This was a modest spread, generally averaging less than 1.5%.

In spring 2011 things became even more difficult for Greece. The economy continued to contract at an alarming rate, raising further doubts about debt sustainability as the ratio of debt to GDP increased noticeably, even while the nominal level of debt hardly moved. Opposition to the program was growing at home as the "Can't Pay, Won't Pay" movement gathered steam throughout Greece.[1]

In March, Moody's downgraded Greece again, this time from Ba1 to B1, citing, among other factors, "considerable difficulties with revenue collection" and the risk that "conditions attached to continuing support from sources will . . . result in a restructuring of existing debt." For the icing on the cake, they also had a negative outlook. In the parlance of credit ratings, this moved Greece from "speculative" to "highly speculative."[2]

It was hard to argue with the logic of that decision, but Greece found itself in a no-man's-land. Multiple signs were increasingly pointing to a likely debt restructuring, but the program did not allow for it, many voices in Europe continued to resist, and Greece had no choice but to soldier on. Nonetheless, spreads on Greek debt hit 1000 basis points above German bonds in early April 2011.

That month we organized a roundtable at the IIF that discussed, among other things, the Greek debt dilemma. A number of leading

Chancellor Angela Merkel makes a point to Prime Minister George Papandreou during a heated exchange in Brussels, February 2011. French President Nicolas Sarkozy looks on. Photo by John Thys/AFP via Getty Images

voices from the private sector, including Vice Chairman Bill Rhodes of Citibank, took the view that a restructuring may be needed, while Papaconstantinou made a strong case that the program was on track and that restructuring was not necessary. Trichet made an even more emphatic statement that it was unthinkable for a member of the Eurozone to restructure its debt—to undermine the credibility of the country's "signature." I understood fully the principles behind his position, but felt that the principle of "sanctity of the signature" of a Eurozone member was increasingly in conflict with the reality of Greece's position.

I met Papaconstantinou privately around the edges of the meeting, and he confirmed what I had suspected: that Greece was quietly looking at various options for "re-profiling" or rolling over its debt, but until Europe gave a green light, he could say or do nothing publicly.

Later that month, I traveled to Frankfurt to give a speech at Goethe University in Frankfurt, and arranged a visit to Trichet while I was there. We reviewed the situation in Europe, and in particular Greece.

"Jean-Claude, I fear that circumstances are conspiring to make it increasingly difficult for Greece to avoid restructuring. If it becomes necessary, I believe the IIF could possibly play a useful role facilitating a restructuring process. If it comes to that, it is essential that it be done on a voluntary basis. It is at times like this that the Principles that we devised at your inspiration become crucial."

He responded politely but unwaveringly. "Charles, I am certain that the IIF could play a key role if this should transpire, and I agree completely about the Principles. But I have made my position crystal clear: I do not support the restructuring of Greece's debt. Period. We can solve this without such a drastic step that would damage the credibility of the euro." I said I understood but was not at all certain that the program goals would be met without further financial support either from the IMF or the Eurozone governments, or a restructuring.

As always, Jean-Claude was cordial as I walked out of the office, but he looked somewhat perturbed at the thrust of our discussion. It would not be our final words on the matter of Greek debt restructuring.

Upon returning to the US in early May, I began canvassing IIF Board members and key European creditors to gain a sense of their attitude. The tide was turning among most, but not all, key creditors.

"There are serious risks wherever we turn, Charles, but the greater risk is in procrastinating. If we don't lance the boil of Greece, it could bring Spain, Portugal, and even Italy down with it," said the CEO of one of Greece's largest creditors. He continued, "Others share this concern— that the future of the Euro is at stake, and that we have to be willing to accept losses on Greece to protect the integrity of the system."

Yet there was no clear consensus. Joe Ackermann, both the Chairman of the Board of the Institute and the CEO of one of the largest creditors, was uncertain. He understood the case for restructuring, but remained concerned about the strong resistance of Trichet. He reminded me that the IMF also remained opposed to restructuring. Nevertheless, he assented to us exploring further the idea of initiating negotiation on Greece's debt with our Board.

European officials had begun to talk of re-profiling. I had seen that movie before and knew how it ended. Re-profiling was another word for rescheduling, which had been the modus operandi of the 1980s sovereign debt crisis. We had managed to avoid a collapse of the global banking system, but this strategy had also led to many years of weak growth among Latin debtors, and had provided no framework for ultimate resolution of the debt problems.

In mid-May, Dominique Strauss-Kahn had been arrested in New York on sexual assault charges, and he resigned four days later from his position at the IMF. Six weeks later, Christine Lagarde was appointed as his successor. Although a skilled lawyer and highly capable finance minister, she lacked the economic training of Strauss-Kahn.

In late May I touched base with Ackermann again, and then Prot, Lemierre, and other key creditors, and there was a growing willingness to enter into discussions over Greek debt. But the confusion and conflicting signals in the official sector continued to cloud the picture.

I decided to call Trichet one more time to see if his attitude had changed. It had not, but there was a slight shift in tone after he returned my call while I was in an Advisory Board meeting at The Fletcher School. I stepped outside and took the call, standing above and staring at the tennis courts, full of early spring competition. It was a gorgeous day, and Jean-Claude could not have been more courteous. Nevertheless, I could feel the tension on the phone.

"Jean-Claude, the Greek economy continues to deteriorate, and the contagion among the other weak economies is not abating. We believe there is a pressing need to move forward to restructure Greek debt."

There was a pause, and when he responded his tone was cool: "Charles, you need to talk to the governments of Europe, not me. They will ultimately have to decide this vital question."

It proved to be a pivotal phone call. I immediately made two follow-up calls, one to Joe Ackermann, who gave me wise advice: call Juncker and ask him how to proceed. I did, and Juncker was quite clear: "Charles, give Vittorio Grilli a call. He is the head of the Euro Deputies Group, and he can move this forward. It is time." I often found Juncker to be a very astute interpreter of European forces: political, economic, financial, and cosmic. While he himself could often not take independent positions, even as "Europe's Finance Minister," he could guide matters skillfully from the front row.

I called Grilli, who seemed somewhat perplexed by the call, but he nevertheless agreed to organize the Euro Deputies Group for a meeting on June 27 in Rome. "Charles, can the IIF organize Greece's main creditors?" he asked.

"Vittorio, I believe we can," I told him.

"Then I will pull together the Eurogroup Deputies."

"We will be there," I responded. And with that the largest debt restructuring in history was inaugurated.

CHAPTER 13

DESCENT INTO THE MAELSTROM

"I am that quiet place, the centre of the maelstrom.
The dangerous abyss, where few dare to tread."

—Virginia Alison

The IIF found itself at the center of the maelstrom beginning with the first conference call of our Task Force on Greece, which occurred on the morning of June 20, 2011. We at the IIF were determined not to allow the swirl of uncertainties surrounding Greece and the broader turbulence in the Eurozone to distract us from our mission. We knew that the only path forward that could possibly work was for the creditors to agree voluntarily to a restructuring and reduction of the debt. This could involve a so-called "credit event," which could put Greece technically into default, or so we thought at the time. We had only a very preliminary exchange that morning on our conference call. We had circulated a document titled "Greece—Six Guiding Principles for Possible Engagement by the Private Sector." Although it was not formally approved, it served as a useful starting point for our discussions. We also distributed a paper that helped advance our discussions, titled "The Way Forward," prepared by Jeff Anderson, the Director of the European Department of the IIF. Jeff was an outstanding economist and knew the Greek economy quite well, having resumed analysis of Greece in late 2009 when Greece's crisis erupted. His paper, like most analyses at the time, focused on the prospect of the private creditors being asked to "roll over" maturity claims, rather than a larger restructuring. The idea was also beginning to circulate that we could consider an approach to the restructuring that was based on the underlying principle of the "Brady Plan."

Many of us following the Greek crisis did not want Greece to suffer through years of minimal growth, as had most Latin countries, and were increasingly inclined to think that serious debt reduction was necessary to alter the already powerful downward trajectory of Greece's economy as well as to alleviate the pressure that was building on the euro. But the European official sector was at loggerheads on the issue, and a number of my private sector colleagues were also inclined to avoid the harsh pain and losses of a debt-reduction exercise.

Europe did, however, signal the need for some form of restructuring in their statement on June 20, 2011, which included the following:

"The passing of two laws on the fiscal strategy and privatization by the Greek Parliament will pave the way for the next disbursement by mid-July. However, given the difficult financing circumstances, Greece is unlikely to regain private market access by early 2012. Ministers agreed that the required additional funding will be financed through both official and private sources and welcome the pursuit of voluntary private-sector involvement in the form of informal and voluntary roll-overs of existing Greek debt at maturity, or a substantial reduction of the required year-by-year funding within the program, while avoiding a selective default for Greece."[1]

This was, in my view, a step forward in recognizing the reality of Greece's severe debt problems, but only a small step. As Steven Fidler of the *Wall Street Journal* had written somewhat earlier: "For the first time this week a taboo was lifted. European officials can now use the 'R' word 'restructuring' in sentences that don't also have 'not' in them. Restructuring Greece's government debt—changing the conditions attached to its bonds to lessen the burden—is now something that can be talked about in polite company. (With the proviso that it will be the nicest, gentlest, most investor-friendly restructuring possible.)"[2]

Officials in Brussels were using the term re-profiling of debt, meaning to stretch out maturities, and possibly adjust interest rates, but it is not a reduction of debt. This is the course we followed in Latin America for six years, and a number of us at the IIF felt it was essential to sidestep this phase in Greece. However, there remained a major division within the official sector. Although a disbursement of IMF and EC funds had been approved three days earlier, there were two schools of thought. One faction, led by Wolfgang Schäuble, German Finance Minister, took the view that restructuring of privately held debt was necessary—indeed, inevitable. As he had said in Washington two months prior, "We cannot just bail out the private investors with public money. That would reward reckless lending and it would never get through an increasingly impatient German Parliament."[3]

Luxembourg's Jean-Claude Juncker, who led the group of Euro Area Finance Ministers, was also supportive of some move along these lines. He said a "soft restructuring" was possible for Greece after the government in Athens takes additional steps to cut the budget deficit, such as state asset sales. German Deputy Finance Minister Jorg Asmussen stated in Brussels that such a setup would be designed to avert a chain reaction of claims linked to credit default swaps. Christine Lagarde, the French Finance Minister, increasingly looking like she would head to Washington to replace Strauss-Kahn, walked a fine line by telling reporters that any rescheduling that would create a credit event was off the table. "We are not debating that," Ms. Lagarde stated.[4] A credit event leads to a payout of credit default swaps (CDS) and can be triggered by a variety of occurrences resulting from a deterioration in the borrower's creditworthiness. It could be a debt moratorium during which debt servicing is suspended, a switch of currency, or certain types of debt restructuring. (Whether such occurrences count as a credit event is determined by a panel of dealers and buyers from the International Swaps and Derivatives Association, or ISDA. The amount of the insurance payout is derived by the discount from face value established at an auction of the affected bonds that then takes place.). Why were Ms. Lagarde and others so worried about triggering CDS payouts? There was, first of all, a stigma that would attach to Greece and, by extension, to its partners in the Eurozone. Second, there was concern that it would reward speculators against Eurozone bond markets. Most significantly, however, officials were worried that those profits could spur further speculative attacks against other governments in the Eurozone, such as Spain. Avoiding a credit event might also discredit the officially despised CDS market.

So how would you avoid one? The answer was to make restructuring voluntary. David Green, general counsel for ISDA in London, clarified the matter: "Technically speaking, if a restructuring is not in a form that binds all holders [of the debt], it won't be regarded as a credit event. That suggests an offer to bondholders to extend their debt maturities or an offer to repay bondholders with new bonds would not trigger payouts."

But Jean-Claude Trichet and his colleagues at the ECB were still adamantly opposed. He warned against forcing bondholders to put in more money, which would effectively delay repayment. "This is not a good way to go in the monetary union," he said. "Investors would avoid all Euro Area bonds." Trichet, in the twilight of a remarkable thirty-six-year career as a finance official, feared that if Greece didn't honor its bond debts on schedule, the implicit trust that kept credit flowing to many weak Eurozone governments would shatter. More countries and their banks would lose access to capital markets, and a chain reaction with incalculable consequences could occur. Other ECB board members echoed his views.

Meanwhile, things in Greece were, once again, going downhill fast. A report in the *New York Times* captured some of the misery: "Social workers and municipal officials in Athens report that there has been a 25% increase in homelessness. At the main food kitchen in Athens, 3500 people a day come seeking food and clothing, from about a hundred people a day when it first opened 10 years ago. The average age of those who show up is now 47, down from 62 years ago, adding to evidence that those who are suffering now are former professionals. The unemployment rate for men 30 to 60 years old has spiked to 10% from 4% since the crisis began in 2008. Aris Violatzis says that calls to the Klimaka Charities suicide helpline have risen to 30 a day, twice the number two years ago."[5]

According to a June 2011 article in the *Wall Street Journal*, "Greece shook global markets, intensifying fears of a default, as tens of thousands of demonstrators protested a new round of budget-cutting plans, and its prime minister offered to step down to try to preserve them. Protests across the capital sometimes turned violent as Prime Minister George Papandreou sought an agreement with opposition parties on austerity measures demanded as the price of a new bailout by Eurozone nations and the International Monetary Fund. When his offer to step down in favor of a Unity government failed, he instead announced in a late-night televised address that he would reorganize his cabinet Thursday and then call for a vote of confidence in parliament. Mr. Papandreou's Socialist Party has a parliament majority of just four, following two defections in recent days."[6]

Neil Irwin's *The Alchemists* captures the nearly impossible circumstances very well: "The discontent wasn't just on the streets. Tensions between the Troika and Prime Minister George Papandreou's government were growing as the lenders found Greece failing to live up to its commitments, particularly in privatizing state-run concerns such as telecommunications firm OTE and the ports of Piraeus and Thessaloniki. Reforms to the labor market designed to give employers greater flexibility to fire or cut the pay of workers were drawn up by representatives of the IMF and the ECB, translated into Greek legalese by an Athens law firm, and delivered to the government as legislation that was to be passed. By May 2011 . . . Greek unemployment had risen from 12.1% to 16.8%. The yield on 10-year government bonds rate had shot from around 9% to 15%. Public debt had risen from 148% of GDP to more than 171%."[7]

Just a week beforehand, Greece had been downgraded close to default by Standard & Poor's (S&P) rating agency. As my good friend and former IIF Board member John Heimann said, the rating agencies are quite good at arriving at the battlefield after a hard day of battle and shooting the wounded. Quite a crude analogy, but not without some merit on some occasions. On June 13, 2011, S&P cut Greece's rating by three notches to triple C. Greece was then the lowest-rated sovereign in the world, below Ecuador, Pakistan, and Grenada. Greek 10-year bond yields jumped to more than 17%. This drove Portuguese and Irish 10-year bonds to Euro Area highs of 10.66% and 11.34% respectively. Greece seemed increasingly likely to drive the Eurozone into a chaotic breakup.

To add to the sense of disarray, Papandreou fired his Finance Minister, George Papaconstantinou, on June 17, and replaced him with Evangelos Venizelos. Papaconstantinou was a highly capable economist who brought real focus and commitment to the job. Unfortunately, he was no match for the phalanx of Greek political forces that were determined to see the reform efforts falter. He took the blame for failure to get the privatization program going and for shortfalls in the deficit reduction program.

I regretted seeing him go, for I felt a certain kindred spirit with him, but I surmised that if Papandreou was to survive—he had faced a revolt within his own party on the 16th of June—he had to turn it over to someone more politically established in PASOK. And Evangelos Venizelos was certainly that.

Venizelos was a constitutional lawyer from Thessaloniki who had built an impressive career in politics after successfully defending George Papandreou's father, Andreas Papandreou, from corruption charges in 1989. Having established himself as a member of parliament in 1993, Venizelos moved rapidly up the system and had served in a number of ministerial posts, including Minister for Culture, Minister for Justice, Minister of Defense, and Minister for the Press and the Media. But Minister of Finance? It seemed somewhat of a stretch to me, since he had no prior experience in that area, and he was inheriting one of the most tumultuous finance portfolios in modern European history. He was also made Deputy Prime Minister, giving him more authority within the cabinet, and presumably a stronger position from which to push reforms through his recalcitrant party. Taking an optimistic approach, I hoped that Greece was now poised for more progress, and Venizelos had certainly demonstrated his intelligence and talent in a multitude of difficult positions. He was regarded in the press as a pugnacious and former leadership rival of Papandreou. Five months later, Papandreou would learn that bringing a rival into the cabinet carried risks to his own political future.

As indicated earlier, on June 20, 2011, we had our first meeting of the Task Force on Greece via conference call. So much preparation, and yet we still had so much to do to get organized. That call inaugurated an intense month of meetings, discussions, and shuttling among Paris, Rome, Zurich, and Brussels with what seemed like a thousand conference calls along the way.

The first call was fairly orderly, as we began to explore a possible way forward. It was a small group, with only nine creditor institutions represented. I opened the call with brief remarks, followed by Jean Lemierre, who at the time was Senior Advisor to the Chairman of BNP Paribas. Although I was formally the Chairman of the Task Force, I knew that as the representative of Greece's largest private creditor, BNP Paribas, Jean needed to be viewed as de facto Co-Chairman. I could get virtually nothing done without his support.

The June 24 meeting of the Task Force proved to be a much more meaningful moment than was the June 20 teleconference. Participation was much larger, with a growing number of institutions recognizing that we were serious about this process. Representatives from twenty-four financial institutions showed up at BNP Paribas headquarters at 3 Rue d'Antin, a tiny street off the Avenue de l'Opéra—such an obscure street, in fact, that taxi drivers often get lost trying to find it. Many attendees arrived late, a few of them somewhat cross. Not the best way to start a meeting that was already bound to be contentious.

Because BNP Paribas was Greece's largest bank creditor, it was natural that we would hold our first meeting there. It also gave the French some sense of their place of importance in the debate, a factor I thought could prove beneficial in the long run. The building that housed the headquarters of BNP Paribas at the time has a long and illustrious history. Built in the early eighteenth century, more than half a century before the US and French revolutions, it had seen a lot. On March 9, 1796, it hosted a rather prestigious wedding—that of Napoleon Bonaparte and Josephine de Beauharnais. As the legend goes, it hosted their wedding in what at the time was listed as the residence of the Future King. It was her second marriage, and since she was six years older than he was, they falsified his age, increasing it by eighteen months, and reducing hers by several years. This was purportedly done as a sign of gallantry. The house had been confiscated and declared National Property during the French Revolution. It had been turned into the town hall of the Paris second arrondissement, allowing Napoleon to use it for his wedding. The day before the first meeting of the Task Force, Jean Lemierre graciously turned his office over to me and the IIF team to prepare for the meeting. His office happened to be the very room where Napoleon and Josephine had been married. An imposing bust of Josephine was displayed in an antique chest, together with the documents confirming their marriage.

Josephine's eyes seemed to be following us as we hurried in and out of the room. The first Empress of France and a woman whose lineage was sprinkled throughout Europe, she was the grandmother of Napoleon III and great-grandmother of later Swedish and Danish Kings and Queens. The current reigning houses of Belgium, Norway, and Luxembourg also descended from her, which was quite extraordinary and somewhat perplexing to me given that she didn't bear Napoleon any children. She was also the Queen Consort of Italy, and somehow became known as the "patroness of roses," something I found particularly interesting since, as noted earlier, my father was a rose gardener for quite some years.

On the afternoon of June 23, in advance of the first meeting of the Task Force, I also called upon my good friend Jacques de Larosiere. He was, and remains, one of the "eminences grises" of global finance. As noted in Chapter 7, he had been Managing Director of the IMF when I was on the IMF Board and at the Treasury, so we had worked very closely together on debt problems in Latin America. He was a remarkable leader, not only of the IMF but throughout the world of global finance. During the last quarter of the twentieth century, there were two giants who strode across the global economic and financial landscape: Paul Volcker and Jacques de Larosiere. Volcker was literally and figuratively a giant, standing at six feet, seven inches. He had slain rampant inflation in the early 1980s, and likely forever shall be remembered as one of the most independent and effective Chairmen of the Federal Reserve in its history. De Larosiere, while a man of only five feet, seven inches, was just as tall when it came to facing international financial challenges. When the Latin debt crisis erupted in the summer of 1982, he rose to the occasion, working tirelessly and seamlessly with Volcker, my colleagues at the Treasury, debtor country officials, the BIS, key central bankers, commercial bankers, and his own team to forge and implement a coherent international debt strategy that helped to avoid a global calamity and eventually led to economic recovery for the region. More recently, in his late 80s and 90s, he has become a distinguished author, having written a number of books, including his most recent one, *Putting an end to the reign of financial illusion: For real growth.*

De Larosiere and I had become not only close collaborators during this period, but also very good friends. I had learned much from him, and as I walked into his office late on that Thursday afternoon, I had a feeling I would learn once again. I had stayed in touch with him when he left the IMF to become the Governor of the Banque de France, where, in the relatively small world of global finance, he preceded Trichet. He had also served as the second President of the European Bank for Reconstruction and Development (EBRD), which Jean Lemierre subsequently took over. After that, Jacques became Senior Advisor to the Chairman of Paribas, and was still in that role when it merged with BNP in 1999. In that position, Lemierre also succeeded him. I know this all seems a bit odd, but it really isn't.

That afternoon, we sat across from each other in comfortable chairs. The late afternoon summer light angled across the room, as a bust of

Louis XIV, the Sun King, rested behind de Larosiere. He listened quietly as I laid out my thoughts about the prospective Greek restructuring, detailed the obstacles, and conveyed my anxiety about what lay ahead. He responded, "Charles, your destiny has brought you here. Everything you have done in your career has prepared you to lead this historic negotiation."

Perhaps it was true, I thought. I did have the history for the job and was prepared for it. I felt like I was up to the challenge, but I knew that I would have to draw on every bit of my thirty-five years of experience and rely heavily on my staff and colleagues from throughout the banking community as well as Lemierre at BNPP. I pondered the complexity of the task as I left his office.

The next day, everyone gathered around a vast conference table in an ornate room out of France's lavish past. The large number of Task Force members seemed wary. Because of their loan holdings, they had significant reasons for that attitude. But they also had to wonder about my, and the IIF's, role in the negotiations. Would I be there primarily as an analyst, or as an advocate? If an advocate, for whom? The creditors? Greece? The system, whatever that means? In its long history, the IIF's job had always been to support the creditors, and advance their cause, but never to negotiate formally on behalf of the banks. That role had been envisioned in the original concept of the Institute, but had been shunted aside by the Creditor Committees, which had sprung up during the Latin debt crisis and were led, naturally, by the lead creditor bank in each case. But it had become clear to me, and to the main creditors, that in this case the IIF was well positioned to lead the discussions. No other group could hope to match the experience, impartiality, and expertise that the IIF could bring to the matter as an institution. And we were largely seen as an "honest broker" by many in the European official sector and the majority—but not all—of the private creditors.

We were only three days away from our first meeting with the Euro Deputies Group, our counterpart for the negotiations, more or less, so we had a lot of ground to cover. The agenda was very ambitious, largely focused on different options for restructuring. Jean Lemierre and I began with opening statements. All of us knew perfectly well that everyone was here to decide what to do about Greece. I was straight with them: "I want everyone to know that the winds are starting to blow in favor of restructuring. Governments and some key institutions are beginning to go in that direction. Even though the ECB is still opposed, there is simply no other way out for Greece. The question is, are we going to take control of our own destiny here? If we don't, we could be presented with a fait accompli."

As we conducted a "tour de table," many questions were thrown my way, some of which resembled barbs: What authority do you have to negotiate on behalf of the creditors? With whom will they be negotiating? Why not have Greece's largest creditors lead the talks, as is usually done? Are we really certain a debt restructuring is needed for Greece?

I fielded them as effectively as I could, anticipating some pushback. My capable deputy, Hung Tran, parried some of the thrust as well. But still, things got a bit unruly. I had been chairing meetings for the IIF for over fifteen years, and this was shaping up to be one of the most challenging.

Finally, Jean Lemierre stepped in, cutting off one of his own colleagues from BNP Paribas. "None of us want to be here, facing an extremely difficult and challenging, and possibly costly, debt restructuring. But these are the cards we have been dealt, and the longer we wait, the more we will lose control of the process for the official sector. And the IIF and Charles are the right leaders for this unique moment. He has been involved in more debt restructurings than any of us, and he has a strong team to back him up. So let's get on with it."

The grumbling quieted down, and we got down to business, more or less. I could see lingering frustration on the faces of some bankers around the table, but they knew it would be fruitless to continue fighting. And I knew I had a reliable partner in Jean Lemierre.

The focus of the ensuing four-hour meeting revolved around core issues:

- Could, and should, we pursue a simple re-profiling, for which many in the official sector had been arguing;
- Or a new debt reduction operation that would enhance the prospect of clearing away Greece's debt problem, and;
- Would it be possible to avoid costly write-downs?

Hovering in the background were two more basic questions that we knew could not be productively debated by this group but were hanging around like a bad mood when you can't quite identify the source.

· Would we actually be able to negotiate a deal that was, in the end, voluntarily agreed to by both sides? As we subsequently discovered, there were more than two sides in this negotiation. It eventually felt more like a hexagon, but one that wasn't too well put together.

· Would our efforts help the euro—and the Eurozone—survive?

Many sheets of paper and ideas were considered and then crumpled, most of which revolved around the concept of bond exchange, with lower interest rates or longer maturities, but with some form of "credit enhancement" to cushion the blow to the creditors, e.g., a guarantee by the European Financial Stability Facility (EFSF), the temporary mechanism created by Europe in 2010 to help manage the Eurozone crisis.

Allianz, one of Greece's largest creditors from the insurance industry, provided some ideas of an insurance-type solution, based on the creation of a European sovereign insurance mechanism. On the eve of our first meeting in Paris, the French banks had circulated to the press, but not yet to the group assembled around the table, a set of ideas that combined rollover with new collateral provided by zero coupon bonds issued by a "supernational organization," most likely the EFSF. The proposal had ideas that were partially built on the basic structures of the Brady Plan, so I found it intriguing. But I also found it odd that the proposal appeared in the *Financial Times* (FT) as a French proposal, suggesting it had been pre-discussed with the French government, without it having first been discussed in our Task Force. I was not the only one perturbed, and it was certainly not the last time that a group of bankers would try to circumvent the process by working with their government. The Germans, Dutch, and other bank representatives expressed their disgruntlement, but they were not shocked. Although French bankers could be as sharp as any in their criticism of French government policies, including bank regulatory policies, there was also at times a commingling of both people and ideas between the government and the banking community. The French had a way of closing ranks at times like this in the broader threads of French and Gallic tradition. I did not want to be distracted by it, and neither did Lemierre, who said he would look into its origins. The French Banking Federation seemed to have its own sense of direction, as was often the case with national banking associations, and I did not believe Jean was involved with it.

We wrapped up our meeting without a clear strategy, but at least we had not splintered into a hundred different directions. And the IIF's authority to carry on was arguably bolstered, somewhat.

Two days later, the cast had moved to Rome, preparing for our first meeting with the "Grilli Group," the Deputy Finance Ministers' body that had been "designated" as our counterpart in this negotiation.

Our first gathering in Rome was held at the office of Intesa Sanpaolo in Rome early in the morning of Monday, June 27, 2011. It was a gorgeous summer morning in Rome, and fortunately the overbearing heat of a Roman summer had not yet set in. The upper walls of buildings were exhibiting their vibrant ocher hue in the morning sun, mingled with yellow and amber to convey a sense of beauty that never ceases to amaze.

As I walked into Intesa Sanpaolo's ancient Roman architecture amidst modern design, I was focused on the need to gather our forces before this first crucial engagement with European officialdom.

Intesa was Greece's second-largest creditor from Italy, just shy of UniCredit's holdings. Intesa's CEO, Enrico Cucchiani, was an accomplished executive in both banking and insurance. He had just joined the IIF Board and had readily agreed to host our preparatory meeting there. We had decided not to put a formal proposal on the table with the Grilli Group, but we needed to sort through what we thought were the best options. Increasingly, the governments of Europe and the IMF were pressing for some restructuring of Greece's privately held debt, but the ECB remained firmly opposed. In our first preparatory meeting, we got into an esoteric discussion of accounting issues, and I began to realize how important they could be in shaping the way forward. If impairment of the existing bank claims were to be triggered by the declining valuation of Greek government bonds (GGBs) in capital markets, based on the accounting principle of mark-to-market, the quarterly profit-and-loss accounts of the banks would be hit hard. Such a treatment was actually pushed by the independent bank auditors of some European banks for the end of June 2011 financial statements. Thank the Lord we had a number of accounting experts around the table. Tony Clifford, a senior partner at Ernst & Young, and Charlotte Jones, then a regional CFO for Deutsche Bank, were especially valuable. We began to sense that whatever route we took toward restructuring, the creditors would be unable to avoid writing off significant amounts of their Greek debt at the end of the second quarter. And we thought that accepting accounting reality would also help the banks come to grips with the need for meaningful debt reduction.

An accounting impairment would negatively affect bank profits without rendering any benefits to Greece and potentially necessitating further impairments down the line, not only for bank holdings of Greek debt but also for bank holdings of other Eurozone sovereign debt. An early agreement on restructuring would allow banks, with the same losses due to impairment, to also contribute to solving Greece's debt problems.

But things would become even more complicated than that.

The Italian Treasury building in Rome is an imposing postwar edifice whose exterior must have been impressive once. It seemed fitting that we had come here to try to patch up the Eurozone, which like the building, offered contrasting images of grandeur and demise. The elegant stone archways surround a classic Roman courtyard, but the paint and plaster were fading.

To avoid the media that had formed in front of the building, Hung Tran, Mikis Hadjimichael, Jean, and I snuck in a little-used back door of the Treasury, passing along some beautiful marble hallways covered with red carpet, and up a grand staircase. Finally, we reached an ornate, high-ceilinged room where a long table had been arranged for us. There must have been twenty people milling about. We had been asked to keep our numbers down, so I limited it to ten or so on our side, with a similar number across the table. There were officials from many different Eurozone countries, aside from Grilli, including Germany, France, and the Netherlands. They were more junior than I had thought they would be. The most important debt negotiation in the history of the European Union, and they send junior staff? The IMF, the EC, and the ECB were also represented, again at midlevel. Finally, two Greek officials were there waiting, one with a vague look of resignation on his face as if awaiting an unpleasant sentencing from a judge. That was George Zanias, Chief Economic Advisor to the Finance Minister. The other Greek official, Petros Christodoulou, Director of the Greek Debt Management Agency, looked more energized, but also uncertain.

We quickly realized that the junior staff from around the continent had come primarily to listen—essentially stenographers who could report back to superiors who were reluctant to participate at this stage. Inside this knot of low-level dignitaries was the ultimate irony for such a gathering that we, the creditors, had come prepared to propose a restructuring; the "debtor" had not come prepared to ask for one. We were, in an odd fashion, offering to take a fleecing; they were not sure they wanted to give us one. To us, the question wasn't whether there would be a haircut, but how severe it would be. Would it be 20%, 30%, or even 50% or more? All unhappy prospects, certainly, and the creditors were a little edgy on our side of the table. But no one seemed pleased to be there, and no one knew where it might lead. All of this made for a complicated opening round, to say the least. Vittorio Grilli arrived almost a half hour late, looking sharp in his custom double-breasted suit. It would have been difficult for anyone to get the whole production going, but Grilli, who appeared to be a combination of bluster and formality, claimed to speak for Greece, although he actually served other masters—Italy and the Eurozone.

He and I had met the night before, and he hinted that I should run the meeting, but I thought that was absurd. If the creditors took charge, it would look like we were trying to stick Greece with a proposal that ignored their interests. He should run it, but I gave him some thoughts on how it might go. We both knew it would not be the easiest of meetings, and we wanted it to have at least some direction.

I had also had an opportunity the night before to call Christine Lagarde. Although she had not yet been formally elected to the position of Managing Director of the IMF, her selection was widely anticipated. I wanted to make sure she was on board with the concept of a debt restructuring. The IMF senior staff had assured us that was the case, but it was always prudent to ensure that the staff and the Managing Director were speaking with one voice, especially given the ongoing debates about such a fundamental question. She told me that the IMF was behind a restructuring. It would continue to ask for more fiscal adjustment as well, but it had indeed come around to the view that restructuring was necessary. I took some comfort in this.

The meeting began with a rather stiff round of introductions on both sides. Then Grilli began the meeting somewhat haltingly by announcing that this was not to be any sort of negotiation about Greece's debt, stating firmly for all to hear that he had no mandate to negotiate. Little did I realize how much our core team would come to loathe the expression "have no mandate," even though the former government official in me understood why he had to say it. He looked around at "his" side of the table to ensure that his colleagues duly noted his remarks. They had, each writing them on paper or entering them quickly into their computers. Rather, he emphasized, it was to be a discussion among public and private creditors about potential approaches to coordinate actions; to level the playing field (whatever that meant). After that, there were some uncomfortable stirrings on both sides of the table. He clearly did not want to be seen as exceeding his authority. He did go on, however, to state that appropriate "PSI" (the euphemistic term used to refer to debt restructuring) was needed as a precondition for continued official financing. PSI means "private sector involvement," a term coined by the official sector to employ a wide range of options for the private holders of debt to "contribute" to the closing of a financing gap for a debtor country. Of course, such gaps for Greece could be closed through any number of means, including more Greek fiscal adjustment or more lending from the IMF and/or Europe. The focus, however, was on privately held debt, which was understandable given the scale of the private claims on Greece—which stood at approximately €210 billion at the time—and also given that the EU and IMF together had already put in €65.1 billion and another €8 billion was in the works, scheduled for disbursement on completion of the July 2011 quarterly review.[8]

I never liked the term "private sector involvement," because I felt it was a misleading and confusing euphemism. What does "involvement" mean anyway? The private sector was already involved up to its eyeballs, having lent billions of dollars to Greece, some in the most dubious of circumstances. We were already involved due to the creditors' tremendous exposure beyond Greece to the other peripheral countries that were in trouble—Italy, Spain, Portugal, and Ireland. Bank exposure alone—not including insurance firms and pension funds—to these countries amounted to roughly €308 billion, substantially greater than the exposure to Greece.[9] To use one of my all too frequently relied-upon nautical analogies, a hit from Greece would be like taking a shell to the superstructure of a destroyer—damaging, but not necessarily likely to put the combatant out of action or sink the ship. However, a hit for the creditors from other countries as well as from Greece would strike below the waterline—possibly, to continue the analogy, sinking some European banks into the depths of the Mediterranean, near ancient ruins of Greece and Rome that lie buried on the bottom of the sea.

So "involvement"? We had plenty, and we did not need some other official or academic expression to name our engagement. We were determined to decide our fate in a cooperative, transparent negotiation. As time would tell, however, that would be a very ambitious goal.

On more concrete terms, Grilli made mention of an official proposal involving a rolling-over of debt maturing during 2012–2014 with new 5-year bonds at a coupon related to the interest rate on IMF lending. It was odd that he characterized this as an "official proposal," since he readily admitted that the ECB had not gotten on board with the basic idea. He then surprised us by asking that we make our "decisions" and communicate them to the Eurogroup by July 3, nine days away.

He looked across the table at me as he repeated, "It is essential for you to inform the Eurogroup no later than July 3rd so the next round of IMF and European financial support for Greece could be disbursed." He was apparently stipulating, in essence, that a "contribution" from private creditors was a precondition for further official IMF/Eurozone disbursements to Greece.

We resisted the temptation to react angrily, realizing that we were miles apart and that this was likely to be the opening salvo of a long battle. I responded somewhat methodically, "Vittorio, thank you for your opening comments and suggestions. The private sector is willing to cooperate with the official sector to help arrange a voluntary private sector rescheduling based on broad participation, fairness, evenhandedness, and transparency." I then went on to explain, as we had agreed that morning, that the "official proposal" had a number of obstacles, including sizable negative accounting implications for bank balance sheets.

Finally, we added that what the official sector was suggesting was not going to be sufficient and would even worsen Greece's debt sustainability outlook, as the proposed new private sector 5-year bonds would mature at the same time as the 5-year IMF and official financial support being provided to Greece, thus substantially increasing Greece's debt rollover challenge five years ahead. Vittorio was surprised by the fact that private creditors were willing to "contribute" more than he asked. His response was classic. He said he had no authority to accept a higher offer from private creditors and repeated that he had no mandate to negotiate. He needed to consult with the Eurogroup and come back to private creditors with official feedback.

I stressed that this all would take time and added that we should not unsettle financial markets with unrealistic expectations and artificial deadlines. The meeting broke up around 5 p.m., with Grilli concluding with his oft-repeated statement that he "had no mandate to negotiate."

So there we had it. He had no mandate to negotiate, but we were expected to convey "decisions" about debt restructuring to Juncker by July 3. It was all rather surreal, but I think Grilli knew that.

It was at that point that Grilli and I repaired to his office to reflect upon the next steps. I began to realize what an awkward position Grilli was in and just how vulnerable Italy was to market attack.

But Greece was under ever more pressure. Papandreou was working feverishly in Athens to find common ground between a demanding Troika (the IMF, EC, and ECB) and a recalcitrant parliament. He needed to bring an agreed-upon package of measures to Brussels by Sunday, July 3, in order to secure the next tranche of support from the Eurozone and the IMF.

In fact, that very afternoon, he had begun debate in parliament over some €28 billion in cost-cutting measures. Finance Minister Evangelos Venizelos had been in place for only ten days. He was on the front line with Papandreou, looking for the narrow path between parliament and the official creditors. He had already stirred up the ire of Olli Rehn, the Finnish economist who was in the crucial position as European Commissioner for Economic and Monetary Affairs. Olli is a cool, capable man, thoughtful and reserved, true to his Finnish character. Over the many months of our negotiations, I also found him to be a reliable partner. He had a capacity to read the key players of Europe and to understand, if not always fully share, the views of the private sector. I found his taciturn, low-key style somehow reassuring, even when there was actually nothing reassuring about the underlying circumstance. Even the sound of his voice, "Olli Rehn," when he answered his cell phone, was slightly soothing.

On this occasion with Venizelos, he was reportedly far from taciturn, telling him that there would be absolutely no sympathy among official creditors to revisit the scale of the adjustment package that the Greeks had to assemble.[10] It was easy to see why Venizelos had raised the issue; riots were developing on the streets of Athens, and tear gas surrounded the parliament building as they debated into the night on June 27.

Meanwhile, I headed to the airport in Rome for a late flight to Istanbul. Despite the pressure of the Greek negotiations, I had other commitments as the head of the IIF, which I could not ignore. Among them was to continue working with the far-flung membership of banks. We had managed to build quite a contingent of some fifteen or so Turkish banks in the IIF membership, and it was always important to sustain the relationships. Notwithstanding the long history of conflict and tension between Turkey and Greece, banks from both countries had coexisted within the IIF membership with no difficulty. In fact, some years earlier we had organized a joint meeting of leading Greek and Turkish banks that actually led to mergers and acquisitions involving those countries' banks—something unthinkable only twenty-five years earlier. I had a prior commitment to travel to Turkey to give a speech to the Turkish bankers, to see government officials, and to visit with key financial leaders. I had also agreed to join forces with the Dean of my graduate school, Ambassador Steve Bosworth, to explore the participation of Turkish banks in executive training at The Fletcher School. I owed a great deal to Fletcher, and I was always willing in those days to support the school, including their fundraising efforts.

As I boarded the flight, I considered how we might approach the July 3 deadline. There was considerable pressure to deliver something in support of a critical €12 billion combined disbursement from the EU and the IMF. After consulting with Ackermann and Lemierre, we agreed we would try to develop a general statement of support by the private creditors. We were certainly in no position to make a firm restructuring proposal.

A number of ideas were continuing to circulate on our side of the table based on the Task Force discussions on June 24. This included a Brady Bond–like Debt Restructuring. As explained earlier, my experience in helping develop and implement the Brady Bonds of 1989–1991 had left an indelible impression on me. The key ingredients of the Brady Plan had been:

- *That it was voluntary in nature.* While the framework was developed by those of us at the US Treasury under Secretary Brady's leadership, and it took pressure to get the process going, the actual negotiations of the scale of debt reduction for each country was debated and resolved between the debtor and the creditors;

- Upfront stock of debt and debt service reduction;

- · The remaining debt was exchanged with new 30-year bonds with credit enhancements in the form of

  - rolling interest payment guarantees;

  - the collateralization of principal repayment at maturity with zero-coupon 30-year US Treasury bonds.[11]

It was this final element that had been critical to the ultimate success of the Brady Plan. The new restructured debt of Mexico and Brazil, among many others, was essentially no longer Mexican or Brazilian debt; the guarantee of interest payments and, in particular, the collateralization of the principal essentially turned the debt, in effect, into US Treasury debt.

There were, however, difficulties with applying this option to the Greek debt problem. It would require government or market-based funding of the collateral, and with the low, prevailing interest rates in 2011, the cost of purchasing 30-year zero-coupon bonds was much greater than the cost of the US Treasury during the higher interest rate environment of the late 1980s.

In addition, there was resistance in Europe to the idea of an "American-made" solution—the Brady bonds—being used to solve a "European problem." Even Jean Lemierre, who usually approached matters analytically and with considerable reflection, appeared somewhat allergic to an approach based on the Brady Plan. And yet, the proposal released by the French banking association on June 23 in fact included the collateralization of all restructured principal by zero-coupon bonds, one of the key aspects of the Brady Plan.

Sarkozy was in the press the day of our meeting in Rome, reiterating in *Le Figaro* that "French banks were ready to re-lend or rollover 70% of loans they hold."[12] Of course, it was not clear that Sarkozy actually spoke for the French banks assembled in the negotiating room; it was not uncommon for French banks to roll their eyes when advised of one of Sarkozy's pronouncements to the press.

During the flight to Istanbul, I also considered the tense debate still underway within European official circles over whether a restructuring should proceed, and if it did, whether it should be voluntary or forced upon the private creditors. Merkel and Sarkozy had both clearly come around to the view that a restructuring was needed, and on June 17 Merkel had joined Sarkozy to state, "we would like to have a participation of private creditors on a voluntary basis." I was relieved to read this as we prepared for the launch of negotiations, but I also knew full well that this would not be the last word on "voluntary" versus involuntary restructuring. Like a bad penny, the issue kept turning up, despite our determination that any deal, in the end, would have to be negotiated.

I had a 7:15 a.m. meeting with my Fletcher colleagues on Tuesday, June 28, ahead of a day of meetings with Turkish bankers and officials. By the time the meetings were underway, we had quickly scheduled three conference calls for Wednesday, June 29, that I needed to slot in somehow among my Turkish meetings:

- A call of Task Force technicians to work on details of our options;
- A call of the full Task Force to bring all key creditors up to speed as well as get feedback on a draft of a general statement in support of Greece;
- An IIF Board conference call on the same subject.

The need to coordinate our position at three different levels within the rank of the creditors was endless, at times exhausting, but absolutely essential. It had been argued for many years by academics, lawyers, IMF staff, and some sovereign debtors that in the atomistic world of capital markets—where sovereign debt was issued through the bond market and not through syndicated bank loans (as in the 1970s and 1980s)—negotiated sovereign debt restructurings were a thing of the past. Going forward, it would be necessary only for debtors, often with the support of the IMF, to take a few soundings from selected creditors, and then to launch a unilateral take-it-or-leave-it offer.

Of course, this is what Argentina had done, in 2003 and 2004, and many creditors had resented it ever since. Ultimately, Argentina's strategy was seen by all to be fatally flawed, as they were unable to access global capital markets due to the lawsuits and court filings in the United States. In fact, they were unable to issue any sovereign bonds on international markets between January 2002 and April 2016.[13] Not a very successful strategy, I would say, for a country desperate for foreign capital.

It took a new approach of the Macri government in 2016 to restore global market access by pursuing a more cooperative strategy with the creditors. It is, in fact, worth noting that between 2002 and 2010, "Argentina saw a total of 182 lawsuits in the Southern District Court of New York alone, including 11 by NML, 8 by Aurelius, and 7 by Gramercy. The lawsuits against Argentina in terms of value were 'a total of $3.1 billion in face claims by institutional investors (corresponding to about 5% of the 2005 restructurings).'"[14]

But in 2003 and 2004, there was considerable support within official circles, including the IMF and, most surprisingly, the US Treasury, for Argentina's unilateral approach to debt restructuring. Consequently, we at the IIF felt compelled to resist, and the product that emerged was the unique "Principles for Stable Capital Flows and Fair Debt Restructuring." The Principles, and their origins, are described in Chapter 24.

We knew that pursuing a voluntary approach in the case of Greece, against the sentiments of many, would require continuous communication among the various levels of creditor representatives. Thus, the need for three group calls in a day, generally five to ten bilateral calls with IIF Board members and key creditors, sometimes at the CEO level, but often at the CIO or Working Group level, where authority was generally lower but knowledge of the particulars of the deal was greater. I had learned over nearly two decades at the IIF just how crucial it was to sustain dialogue within the IMF's Board membership throughout the member organizations, and Jean and I would often, explicitly or implicitly, divide up the consultation responsibilities, supported always by Hung and Mikis.

We worked our way through the calls on June 29, and it became apparent that with some drafting skill we would likely be able to issue an IIF Board statement of support for Greece, one that would be clear enough to be useful to support a further round of financing from the Eurozone and IMF at their meeting on July 3, but vague enough to allow us considerable room for negotiations with official creditors in the weeks (or months) ahead.

As we tried to get all the creditors on one page, pressure was building in Germany. Wolfgang Schäuble, Germany's Finance Minister throughout this ordeal, announced in Berlin on June 30 that Germany's "leading financial institutions have agreed to roll over €32 billion holdings of Greek debt falling due 2011 through 2014." Ackermann, beyond a doubt Germany's leading banker, played a key role in helping shape this "agreement in principle,"[15] which lent further momentum to the prospect of a meaningful restructuring, although the actual amounts involved in this particular instance were modest.

I struggled to keep my schedule in Turkey while juggling the steady stream of calls and emails needed to keep the process moving. I had planned a luncheon speech at a restaurant on the Bosporus with the Turkish Bankers Association. Just as I approached the podium, my phone rang. It was Prime Minister Papandreou. He wanted to find out how our discussions were going, but also wanted to ask me for assistance in moving forward with his privatization program. I noticed a sense of energy in his voice, buoyed by the parliament's approval two days prior of the latest set of austerity measures. He was, however, concerned about the feasibility of the €50 million goal for privatization over the next four years, a concern I shared. I told him I would take a harder look at this when I had time, and went back to my speech.

Before leaving Turkey, I flew to Ankara to see, among others, Ali Babacan. Ali and I had worked together since he became Turkey's Minister of Economic Affairs in 2002 at the age of thirty-five. When he first spoke to an IIF gathering in the spring of 2003, he was inexperienced and unprepared for the challenges of guiding an economy that had only emerged from a major crisis in 2002. Nevertheless, over almost a decade he had grown steadily into one of Europe's (in my view he was European) leading Economic Ministers—savvy, knowledgeable, an outstanding spokesman for Turkey and, remarkably, able to get along with his Prime Minister, Recep Erdoğan.

On the afternoon of June 30, he was also serving as Deputy Prime Minister. After I walked into his office with Dean Bosworth through a phalanx of security guards and staff, Babacan and I discussed the Greek debt situation, and I explained to him why I thought it was necessary to proceed with a major reduction in Greece's privately held debt if the Eurozone was to survive intact. Somewhat to my surprise, he took a view consistent with that of the ECB: that it was the restructuring itself that posed a grave threat to the Eurozone. He had just recently returned from a meeting where it had been discussed. I tried to persuade him of the necessity to shift gears, but he was reluctant to come around to this perspective.

Indeed, this was the essential question. Everyone was concerned about Greek contagion to the remainder of the Eurozone, especially to Italy, Spain, and Portugal, all of whom were struggling mightily and being buffeted by the markets day in and day out.

But which path forward contained the most risk for Europe: restructuring and fracturing the sanctity of the signature of a Eurozone member country, or avoiding it, and hoping that somehow Greece's problems could be solved without it? The headlines were full of the major step that the Greeks had taken on June 29 in support of a €28 billion package of total increases: "Greece pulls back from the brink."[16] But we all knew that this was just one step on a long road. Presciently, the same *Financial Times* article signaled "Repeat of Greek deadline drama cannot be ruled out." Indeed!

Babacan's views were a foreboding of an eleventh-hour call I received from Ackermann the night of June 30 as I tried to begin a mini-vacation. Peixin and I had planned earlier in the year to have a short Mediterranean break squeezed in among the stream of meetings, calls, and negotiating stops around the continent. The first was to be a few days on a "blue sea cruise" off the southern Turkish coast with our dear friends Gazi and Zeynep Ercel and their daughter Mina. Gazi had been Turkey's Central Bank Governor during 1996–2001, and quite a remarkable governor he had been. He had been selected as European Central Banker of the Year in 1999, as he had strengthened Turkey's position in global capital markets and laid the basis for an eventual reduction in inflation. We had gotten to know each other well on a trip through Turkey together in 1983, when I served as Alternate Director of the IMF, and he served as an Advisor in the Belgian delegation to the IMF led by Jacques de Groote.

At that time, I had challenged a new IMF program for Turkey in the IMF Board. The Deputy Prime Minister of Turkey at the time, Dr. Kaya Erdem, and I met in the spring of 1983 and, aware of my skepticism, he invited me personally to visit Turkey and see firsthand the reforms they were putting into place. I had to travel to Paris later in the year for an IMF meeting, so I accepted his invitation, and Gazi was asked to accompany me on the trip. We met with Dr. Erdem, other senior government officials in Ankara, and bankers and businessman in Istanbul, and drove dusty roads with a trigger-happy security guard en route to Bodrum. When the guard's rifle went off accidentally while we were walking the ancient ruins of Ephesus, I decided that the guard was more dangerous than the troublemakers against whom we were being protected. Gazi and I became fast friends, and we subsequently spent parts of many summers vacationing together with our spouses.

Sadly, he passed away in the summer of 2022, and Yavuz Canevi, one of Turkey's most distinguished bankers, and Gazi's family arranged a special and unprecedented memorial service in his memory. I was the second speaker; the first speaker was Kaya Erdem. It was the first time I had seen Erdem since 1983.

On my visit to Bodrum in 2011, things also got complicated, but in a different way. Joe Ackermann had spent time with Trichet on June 30, and he was having serious reservations about the whole strategy of pursuing the restructuring. It was midnight in Bodrum, and I took the call on the steps of Ercel's summer home. Joe argued that restructuring could trigger contagion through the southern rim of Europe, including Italy. These views were familiar ones, as Trichet and his colleagues of the ECB continued to hold them with force. In fact, if the restructuring produced an event of default—and at least a technical default looked increasingly likely—Trichet threatened to refuse to accept defaulted Greek bonds as collateral for ECB liquidity. This fear was being reflected throughout the region, as the risk of a default in Greece led to bond yields widening dramatically and stocks declining sharply throughout the weaker economies.

I debated this with Ackermann, pointing out that the statement of support had cleared through our Board of Directors, as well as the Task Force, and that the authorities were expecting it prior to the planned July 3 release of funds to Greece. More precisely, an IMF Board meeting was scheduled on that date to consider the IMF's fourth review of Greece's program. The IMF needed assurances that Greece's funding needs could be covered over the next twelve months. Our IIF Board statement on July 1 actually served that purpose. A lot was riding on it—markets could react very negatively if the Eurozone Ministers failed to act because of our pullback.

As our voices grew louder over the phone in the still of a star-drenched summer evening in Bodrum, two dogs started barking, and lights began to come on from homes dotting the hillside. I was certain that my host Gazi was beginning to regret his invitation. Finally, Ackermann relented and agreed to proceed with the announcement the next morning. I dragged my luggage up the hill, apologized to all, and collapsed after a long day that had stretched from Istanbul through Ankara to the Turkish coastline. The following year at his IIF farewell dinner held in Hamlet's castle outside Copenhagen—Kronborg Castle—Joe recalled our rare disagreement that night and, in a magnanimous gesture, indicated that he was wrong, and that we were indeed right to persist down the path of restructuring. I deeply appreciated the mutual respect and friendship that lay behind his comment.

CHAPTER 14

THE BRADY PLAN

"Nick Brady cut through it all with his plan for a new kind of bonds —conceptually brilliant involving manageable long-term commitments by all parties. Suddenly, the financial load was lifted. The market and political mood brightened. Latin America could begin to plan for growth and open economies. An astonishing achievement for a neophyte Treasury Secretary."

—Paul Volcker, 2010

As we began to consider alternative approaches to restructuring Greece's debt, one that arose for consideration on a number of occasions was the Brady Plan. This chapter contains a very brief summary of the Latin American debt crisis, the key elements of the Brady Plan, and an explanation of how the plan was developed and applied.

One of the most remarkable features of the Greek debt negotiation was that, in contrast to every other sovereign debt restructuring exercise in which I had been involved—and there were many of them over three and a half decades—the private sector actually pulled the trigger to open the negotiations rather than being dragged into it by the official sector, which had been typically the case. The public sector had, of course, set the table in a very roundabout way, but it was the private sector that decided to kick-start the talk. Of course, pressure was building for restructuring the debt, both from the marketplace and from official circles, especially

Explaining the potential benefits of a Brady-style approach to Greece's debt problem at a news conference in July 2011. Photo by Daniel Acker/Bloomberg via Getty Images

after the events of Deauville. But no one on the official side had stepped forward to activate the process.

In contrast, from the beginning of the Latin American debt crisis that broke into the global economic scene abruptly in August 1982 through the restructurings of recent years, the general pattern was that private creditors had to be cajoled, persuaded, and in some cases pressured into debt restructuring, especially restructuring that involves forfeiting claims on sovereign debtors. After all, each dollar of debt forgone is not only an immediate loss—with the destruction of bank or creditor capital—but also with any principal written off, the future earnings from the interest payments forgone are lost forever too. This partly explains why private creditors are so loath to write off the principal of a loan. For six and a half long years during the Latin American debt crisis, from 1982 until the Brady Plan was launched in March 1989, the bank creditors—hundreds of them, from around the globe (primarily American, European, and Japanese, with a sprinkling of Canadian, Australian, Middle Eastern, and other banks)—steadfastly resisted writing off the principal of their loans. Time and again, as countries such as Mexico, Brazil, Argentina, and Venezuela implemented challenging economic stabilization and reform programs in the 1980s, the financial support from the banking community would typically involve a rollover of outstanding principal (extending maturities), with slightly lower interest rates and a smidgen of "new money."

On August 20, 1982, the Latin American debt crisis erupted when Mexican Finance Minister Jesús Silva Herzog informed the Treasury that he was unable to meet his debt obligations. He was forced to reach an agreement with 119 banks to roll over the principal of bank loans for ninety days. This "standstill" was essential to avoid default. Subsequently, on November 16, 1982, the bank advisory committee, consisting of Mexico's largest bank creditors, met with the IMF's Managing Director, Jacques de Larosiere. Under the stewardship of Bill Rhodes of Citibank, the committee agreed to roll over the short-term principal by another ninety days. De Larosiere also asked the banks to provide new lending and clear interest arrears that Mexico owed as a precondition for an IMF program. By December 8, 1982, Herzog had reached an agreement with the bank creditors. There would be $5 billion in new money, and $20 billion of debt outstanding due in 1983–1984 would be given a moratorium through the end of 1984 with a repayment period of eight years and four years' grace.[1] And the banks would extend maturities and increase their exposure to Mexico by 7 percent. Thus, the creditors avoided write-off of principal in the hope that with the extension of maturities and implementation of a strong reform program, Mexico would ultimately be able to repay the debt.

This case captures the essence of the international debt strategy that evolved in the early 1980s and remained largely in place, with some changes and reinforcements, from its inception in 1982 until the US Treasury launched the Brady Plan on March 9, 1989. Given the magnitude of such exposure to Latin America in the early 1980s, the original strategy made eminent sense.

Year	US Banks' Exposure to Latin America (year end, million $)	US Banks' Exposure to Latin America (share of banks' capital)
1982	82,873	117%

Source: Country Exposure Lending Survey *in Federal Reserve Archival System for Economic Research (FRASER)*

A serious hit to the outstanding principal could have brought some banks perilously close to collapse. For just the US banks collectively, exposure to Latin America was well over 100 percent of capital. Large European and Japanese banks were in many cases similarly exposed. And in those early years of the Latin debt crisis, most of us believed that Latin America would eventually grow its way out of its debt. Most Latin American debtors did have some growth in the 1980s, but not sufficient to solve the debt problem. For example, Mexico's GDP grew at an average rate between 1983 and 1988 of only 0.1 percent.[2]

I witnessed how Jacques de Larosiere provided brilliant leadership in forging a strategy that, with strong support from Paul Volcker at the Federal Reserve and Don Regan at the US Treasury, managed to avert a global crisis during those stressful years from 1982 to 1985. This period, however, was not without extraordinary challenges, as sustaining the debt strategy through this period was very difficult. For example, in 1983 and 1984 an unprecedented loan was organized from four other debtor countries in the region—Mexico, Brazil, Colombia, and Venezuela—to keep Argentina current in meeting its interest obligations to the banks. This unusual $300 million short-term loan was pulled together with the active involvement of my colleague David Mulford and Mexican Finance Minister Silva Herzog.

With the arrival of Secretary James A. Baker III at the Treasury in early 1985, a new phase of the debt strategy was launched that gave greater emphasis to growth. Called the Baker Plan, with a "program for sustained growth," the strategy helped boost growth in a number of Latin American countries. Supply-side measures such as trade liberalization were strengthened, and sustainable growth for some countries appeared to be achievable. At the same time, we at the Treasury continued to resist fundamental debt reduction. The crisis in Latin America dragged on, however, and by the time Secretary Nicholas F. Brady arrived at the Treasury in the late summer of 1988, there were signs that pressures were boiling over. As pointed out in Richard Frank's excellent book, *The History of the Brady Plan*, the process was seriously fraying. A 50 percent drop in oil prices in 1986 had dramatically reduced resources available to Mexico, Venezuela, and Ecuador to service their debts.[3] In 1987, Brazil declared a moratorium on interest payments. There were growing protests within Latin America, along with rising populism, rampant inflation, and, to top it off, growing resistance among the banks to even implement the "old formula" of rolling over principal with interest rates raised ever so slightly, while throwing in a modest amount of new money.

The process was, in effect, breaking down under the burden of excessive debt and political stress. Secretary Brady, previously a highly successful merchant banker and a US Senator, also had a serious savings and loan crisis to deal with when he arrived at the Treasury in 1988. Nevertheless, when he came on board, he was inclined to take a fresh approach to the debt problem.

We briefed Secretary Brady on the debt strategy as we prepared him for the 1988 IMF/World Bank Annual Meetings in Berlin. David Mulford, Assistant Secretary of the Treasury for International Affairs at the time, and I finished our presentation along with the key Treasury staff one afternoon in mid-September. Secretary Brady did not immediately raise a question about our approach. However, later that evening, he strolled into my office, sat down, and said, "Let me ask you, Charles, do you really believe in this approach?" David and I quickly acknowledged the weaknesses in the existing strategy, and were ready to engage in a fundamental shift in the strategy under Brady's leadership. He directed us to immediately develop a new approach that would leverage recent developments in the marketplace.

This was just the new direction that was needed. As Pedro Aspe, then Mexico's Finance Minister, remarked later, "What do I admire about Secretary Brady? He didn't generate the problem, but the problem was with him, and he took the bull by the horns. That is a combination of wisdom and guts."[4]

We had been debating for some time whether we would have to shift the strategy to something more fundamental. David had, in fact, prepared a paper on the possible shift in the strategy earlier in 1988. This was based in large part on an eye-opening visit that he and I had to New York, during which we visited the trading floors of investment banks. We witnessed traders selling and purchasing Latin American sovereign debt at prices well below par value. This provided compelling evidence that the banks' claims were no longer worth 100 cents to the dollar—no matter what senior bankers or accountants said. This activity was highlighted when in 1982 JP Morgan had sold Mexican debt at an off-market price well below par (the Aztec bonds). We'd been operating for six years on the basis that the Latin American debt problem was primarily a liquidity problem, trying to restore the Latin economies to health by easing the terms of the debt and advancing reforms. But this approach had only limited success. The countries could get out of their hospital beds, but they were never restored to full health. The emerging view in the Treasury by 1988 was that this was indeed a matter of solvency. Countries needed to be able to reduce their debt burden substantially and get out from under the crushing weight of their debt. Secretary Brady aptly captured the problem when he stated, "Our task was clear: decrease the debt burden so the countries could flourish."[5]

The Secretary seized on the importance of the secondary market trading of Latin debt, and gave us the direction to develop a new strategy that leveraged that reality. We began quietly assembling ideas for a fundamentally new approach to the Latin debt problem. Under the strong leadership of Brady and Mulford, and with the support of the highly competent Treasury staff, in particular Mary Chaves and Bruce Juba, we quietly conceived a plan that would provide a framework for a radical shift in the strategy. We would not only endorse write-downs of debt; we also planned to organize funding that could enable the debtor to issue "defeased securities," that is, securities backed up by other assets—in this case, Treasury zero-coupon bonds. The banks and debtors would negotiate a discounted exchange of old loans for new Mexican "defeased" debt (in the case of Mexico, after months of difficult negotiations, the discount was ultimately agreed at 35 percent). There were other options as well—banks could exchange their Mexican loans for securitized debt at par value but would earn only a discounted interest rate of 6.25 percent. Under either approach, the interest payments were guaranteed for eighteen months. Banks could also provide new money.

The "menu" approach was ultimately critical to the plan's success, as banks in different jurisdictions made rather different choices, influenced not only by risk appetite but by regulatory treatment of the options. For example, German banks took 8 percent of their "new exposure" to Mexico in par bonds, while Japanese banks took 81 percent of their new exposures in discount bonds.

Before we got to the implementation phase, however, we had to work our way through layers of resistance. David Mulford was a forceful catalyst of our efforts at Treasury under the overall stewardship of

Secretary Brady. David drafted a paper called the "Truth Serum," which was designed to make the case that there was in fact a strong need for a fundamental shift in this strategy. Secretary Brady described it as "a detailed description . . . of what the irrefutable realities were."[6] We did not circulate it among US government agencies; this was a highly confidential process, and David was never high on interagency coordination in any case. Secretary Brady, accompanied by David, personally took that paper to Brent Scowcroft, President George W. Bush's National Security Advisor, and John Sununu, Bush's Chief of Staff, as well as to Secretary of State James Baker. Following those consultations, Brady then took the paper directly to President Bush, where he received approval to advance the plan. Scowcroft understood that if we did not shift gears, not only would Latin American economies be at risk, but progress that had been made in consolidating democracy in the region could readily be compromised. Secretary Baker also realized that the Baker Plan had served its purpose, but was no longer viable, and he did not oppose the new strategy. Secretary Brady had a long-standing close relationship with President Bush, and he made a compelling case to the president that action was needed. The president agreed. As would be the case with the Greek debt crisis twenty-two years later, the economic and political stability of a major region of the world was at stake. Brady recognized that immediately, and brought a decisiveness to the solution. Of course, others were critical players, and we could not do it without the support of the banks, the IMF, Europe, and Japan. But it was up to Brady and his team at the Treasury to define the way forward. David made a confidential trip to Houston to brief Aspe and his team on our plans, and they were excited.

There were other internal US politics, of course, but they were kept to a minimum because no US expenditures were directly involved in the funding of the Brady Plan. The IMF was initially not supportive, arguing that the financing of Mexico's balance of payments deficits needed to be confirmed "up front" before the program was launched. We countered that this could not be the case, as capital market sources of finance would respond positively, but only spontaneously once they saw the opportunities emerging. In the end, we won the day. The funding to purchase the zero-coupon bonds was provided by the IMF, World Bank, and the Japanese EXIM Bank in the form of loans to Mexico. The Japanese contribution was especially critical, as it covered a large gap that was not provided for by the multilateral institutions. I made a special weekend trip to discuss this with Vice Minister Utsumi, but it took an extraordinary visit by Aspe and his deputy, Angel Gurría, to Japan to secure the loan, as detailed by Aspe in Frank's book.[7] Remarkably, the Brady Plan was implemented without one dollar of US taxpayer funds.

Had the US Congress been directly involved in the Latin debt strategy that evolved throughout the entire 1980s, it's very possible that the process would have broken down. Imagine the US Congress having to approve every program package for Mexico, Argentina, Brazil, and Venezuela. Most likely, it never would have happened. In this regard, despite its defects, the IMF is a well-framed instrument of global financial stability. Even though the IMF Executive Board has to approve every lending program—and the Board Members are either appointed or elected by its member governments—individual country programs are largely sheltered from national legislative politics of member countries.

In contrast, decision-making during the Eurozone crisis was much less coherent. Europe effectively had no one in charge during the euro crisis. At the highest political levels, of course, Chancellor Merkel was the most important voice, and when she took a firm position, it usually prevailed. But beneath her, decision-making on the key issues in the euro crisis most often was, regrettably, shambolic at times. Despite the creation of the stability mechanism, the new package of financial commitments required each Eurozone member to obtain legislative approval for the package. This meant that Greek economic programs on occasion became political footballs, to be kicked around by politicians in some member countries as they so chose. In August 2011, it reached the height of absurdity when Finland insisted that Greek state-owned assets be transferred to a Luxembourg-based holding company and held as security for new loans to Greece. All this for a loan of 1.4 billion euros to a fellow Eurozone member? Other countries jumped on the bandwagon—Austria, the Netherlands, Slovenia, and Slovakia asked for similar treatment. That was quite the show of solidarity for a fellow Eurozone member whose program had already been endorsed by every head of state in the Eurozone.

The lack of legislative complications did not mean that the Brady Plan had smooth sailing. Federal Reserve staff were also initially quite skeptical. Ted Truman, the experienced and well-respected longtime head of the International Department at the Board of Governors, had serious doubts at first, although once the decision was made, he became very helpful in the Plan's implementation. Fortunately, Alan Greenspan, who had succeeded Paul Volcker as Chairman of the Federal Reserve Board, was supportive.

Volcker, however, had not taken such a kind view of the Brady Plan at the outset. When the Plan was announced by Secretary Brady on March 10, 1989, at a luncheon at the US State Department, its reception among the many bankers in attendance was polite but not overly enthusiastic. As I departed the building in an elevator, a very tall man stepped in just before the doors closed. The elevator was packed, but it did not prevent Volcker from spotting me. Peering down from his 6-foot 7-inch perch, he growled, "Well, I hope you're satisfied; you and your colleagues just destroyed the US banking system." I was mortified, and everyone stared at me as if I was a leper. Fortunately, for one of the few times in his career, Paul was wrong. The US banking system had spent much of the 1980s rebuilding capital and was able to absorb the losses that ensued with the implementation of the Brady Plan. As the quote at the beginning of this chapter testifies, Volcker subsequently came around to recognizing the necessity and brilliance of the Brady Plan.

The bankers were another story entirely. The day after the announcement, Secretary Brady, Mulford, and I met with the CEOs of the major US banks involved. The meeting, at which we sat around a long mahogany table in the Secretary's conference room, was far from cordial. The Secretary outlined the plan and made it clear that we expected the banks to cooperate. We were careful not to predetermine the amount of the "haircut" that banks would suffer and the deals to follow. That would be determined by negotiations between the debtor countries and the banks. It would also be influenced by the value of each country's debt in the secondary markets.

Lou Preston of JP Morgan spoke. "Mr. Secretary, your proposal recognizes the reality in the marketplace, and we have to be guided by that. JP Morgan is prepared to work with you to find a way forward." We soon discovered he was a lone voice of support in the room. One by one, the other bankers voiced their concerns, some rather loudly. The Secretary, David, and I answered their questions and tried to reinforce the need to move forward. "The old strategy was wearing thin, and every one of you knows that," David said. "This will enable all of us to turn the page on this long, dark decade for Latin America." Still, they were not mollified. "This will not work" was the theme of their responses. It was a rather disappointing meeting, but Brady persevered.

He knew that this had to be done not only for the future of the Western hemisphere, but for the millions of people who lived in Latin America. As Toyoo Gyohten later said in a tribute to Secretary Brady, "Clearly, you were much more than a simple deal maker. You were the man who knows human beings."[8] Mexico's chief debt negotiator throughout the 1980s, Angel Gurría, described Brady similarly: "Somebody who could understand facts that were contrary to acceptable wisdom . . . But also, somebody who has a generous heart."

The road ahead remained arduous, as Mexico struggled in the midst of a collapse in the oil market to formulate an adequately convincing adjustment program. And the bankers remained obstinate.

Secretary Brady had been invited to present a keynote address at the Annual International Monetary Conference in early June of 1989. It was the gathering of the world's leading bankers—not only American but European, Japanese, and some from emerging markets. He asked me to join him, along with his trusted Chief of Staff, Hollis McLoughlin. When we sat down in his Madrid hotel room to review a draft of his speech, I was surprised to see that after revisiting the key elements of the plan, this speech ventured into American frontier history. After reading it, I feared it might not go over well. "Mr. Secretary, are you sure about this?"

"Yes, Charles," he responded, "They need to understand that all options at this stage involve risks." I wasn't convinced, but he stood his ground and allowed me to make only a few minor edits.

Near the end of his speech, he recounted a story from the diary of John Wesley Powell, who led the first expedition down the Colorado River. Powell was the founder of the Cosmos Club, a Washington-based club of which I am a member. I knew of his legacy as an intrepid explorer, but I was not familiar with the details of this expedition. Brady's speech told of a pivotal moment in the exploration: "At one point in the river, now called Separation Rapids, the party reached a moment of critical decision. Having already faced days of difficult rapids, three members of the crew had doubts about continuing and left the party, preferring, instead, to climb out of the Canyon.

"Major Powell and his remaining crew, including Willie the cook, ran the treacherous rapids successfully and emerged at the other end in calm waters. The other men met a different fate; a plaque that still exists records their end as follows: 'Here on August 28, 1869, Seneca Howland, O.G. Howland and William H. Dunn separated from the original Powell party, climbed to the North Rim, and were killed by the Indians.'"[9]

By recounting this story, Brady wanted to demonstrate that in assessing the risks of following the Brady Plan, bankers should also fully consider the implications of alternative courses of action.

The speech was first met with silence, and then a tepid reaction of halfhearted applause. But it was pure Brady: direct, powerful, and with the message that no one wanted to hear but could not ignore. I was standing at the back of the room during the speech. As it ended and I witnessed the cool reception, I slipped out the door thinking that we had made little progress in bringing the bankers around. I was wrong. Soon after the speech, John Reed, CEO of Citibank, came up to me and asked to have breakfast the next morning to discuss details of implementation. Walter Shipley, CEO of Chemical Bank, spoke to me soon thereafter and said that he wanted to help. Others reached out directly to Secretary Brady. The tide was apparently turning. The bankers had decided to run the rapids after all.

Still, there was the issue of Mexico. They had an outstanding economic team, led by Pedro Aspe, the Secretary of Finance. Three future finance ministers, Angel Gurría, Francisco Gil Díaz, and Guillermo Ortiz, were integral parts of his team. But discussions between the banks and Mexico were proceeding slowly, as were negotiations between Mexico and the IMF. David and I, with support from Federal Reserve staff, were busy cajoling both the bankers and the Mexicans to move toward common ground. He and I had worked together for six years by then, and had become quite an effective duo in handling many issues. We had worked on the Plaza Accord together, when David had played a key negotiating role under the leadership of Secretary James Baker. The Plaza Accord was a successful attempt to realign exchange rates in the context of an overall approach to develop economic policy coordination among the world's major economies. It led to the much needed depreciation of the dollar against key currencies, which helped mitigate the risks of protectionism and a trade war, and stimulated growth. We had also teamed up on numerous US-Japanese negotiations, as well as virtually all of the debt negotiations of the mid to late 1980s. By this point, we were able to work together almost seamlessly. On the Brady Plan, David's long years of operating in global capital markets was a strong advantage for us at the Treasury. My experience in policy formulation and the workings of the US government also came in handy at times.

But by the time of the G7 Summit in Paris on July 14, 1989, progress in the negotiations between Mexico and the banks had stalled. French President François Mitterrand had expanded the Summit to include leaders of key emerging market economies in some associated meetings. (This foreshadowed the creation of today's Group of Twenty, which brings together the major industrial and developing countries.) The French initiative in 1989 meant that President Carlos Salinas was in Paris and his Chief of Staff was there with him. Jose "Pepe" Córdoba was described by the *New York Times* as "discreet to the point of seeming mysterious," and he was considered by some to be the power behind the throne in the Salinas administration.[10]

On Saturday, July 15, Brent Scowcroft told Secretary Brady that the president was meeting with the G7 heads of state Sunday afternoon and needed to demonstrate progress with the new debt strategy. "Nick, you need to get the deal moving, and soon," Scowcroft said to Brady.

On Sunday morning, President Bush was scheduled to join President Mitterrand, Salinas, and many other heads of state at the American church in Paris. Brady and I stopped to talk with Córdoba before entering the church. In front of a relatively new Peugeot, Secretary Brady stressed the importance of concluding the Mexican negotiations.

"Pepe, we have come a long way together, and it's time to close the deal. The banks are willing to agree to an unprecedented discount on Mexican debt. So, let's get on with it." Córdoba hemmed and hawed a bit, and Brady began to lose patience. "Pepe, let me tell you the story of the wheelbarrow." I was puzzled. I had heard Secretary Brady tell many homilies, but not this one. "There was a Russian defense factory where every evening, when a worker left the plant, he would be pushing a wheelbarrow. The guard would let the man pass as there was nothing in the wheelbarrow. They went through this routine night after night. The guard became suspicious that the worker was stealing something and began to look over the wheelbarrow very carefully, even examining the handles and wheels." Córdoba had a look of incredulity on his face as he tried to follow where the story was going. Brady continued, "Finally, the guard bluntly asked, 'I know you're stealing something. What is it?'" Brady paused, looked squarely at Córdoba and recounted the man's response: "Wheelbarrows."

The message was clear: take the wheelbarrows and go home—declare victory. Córdoba paused for a moment, absorbing what he had just heard. He then nodded and responded, "I understand, Mr. Secretary." It took a few more weeks to sort through the details, but the deal was effectively sealed there on the steps of the church. President Bush announced later that day that Mexico had agreed to participate in the new debt strategy. The following day, President Bush held a press conference in the rose garden outside the US Ambassador's residence. When asked whether he would call the new plan the Bush Plan, the president replied, "No, we're going to call it the Brady Plan. If it works, we'll call it the Bush Plan."[11] And so, the Brady Plan—which proved to be enormously successful—was christened. Altogether, it provided the framework for the issuance of over $200 billion in "Brady Bonds," leading to the restructuring and reduction of the sovereign debt of eighteen countries. For additional details, see Appendix 1.

CHAPTER 15

MOVING TOWARD RESTRUCTURING GREECE'S DEBT

"Although only a few may originate a policy, we are all able to judge it."

—Pericles, circa 440 BC

The Greek commitment to new reforms, the release of the IIF Board statement, and the consequent approval by Eurozone Ministers and the IMF Board of the new funding to Greece gave us all a short window in early July 2011 to catch our breath and regroup. I was pleased that we had now publicly committed to a restructuring and, despite the continued opposition from the ECB, it looked increasingly unlikely that the tide would turn back. As reported by the *Financial Times* on July 1, "the world's largest banks signaled on Friday they were willing to take write downs on their stocks of Greek debt to help foster a wider solution to the Eurozone debt crisis."[1]

The morning of July 1, I touched base quickly with Jean Lemierre, Hung Tran, and Mikis Hadjimichael as well as Joe Ackermann and a few other Board members. We set the course for the next round of discussions of the Task Force, aiming toward a July 6 meeting in Paris. I then called Vittorio Grilli, and we agreed to another round of "negotiations" in Rome on July 7.

That afternoon I had a good review of the situation with Jean-Claude Juncker. As Chairman of the Eurozone Ministers Group, he was technically Grilli's superior in the web of Eurogroup structures. He was also an astute student of European power politics and the functioning of Europe's vast bureaucracies. Over the course of the many months of our endeavor, I came to rely upon him as a remarkably accurate barometer of how the Germans and French would react to various proposals and developments. He also gave prescient advice to me time and again on how to proceed in search of a voluntary restructuring. He assured me on that early July call that he would seek formal Eurogroup endorsement of granting authority to the Grilli Group to negotiate with us.

While on the boat during the short "blue sea cruise" with Peixin in late June, I had felt that we needed more public support for debt reduction. I called Martin Wolfe, the esteemed columnist and associate editor of the *Financial Times*. I interrupted him in the middle of writing his excellent book *The Shifts and Shocks: What We've Learned—And Still Have to Learn—from the Financial Crisis*, nestled somewhere in the Tuscan countryside. He seemed a bit perturbed at the interruption at first, but then he listened carefully as I expounded on the fact that the prospects for restructuring remained very much up in the air. He explained he was on an extended leave, but that he would indeed ensure that his colleagues in London gave support for restructuring Greece's debt. He indicated that he thought it was essential. It was so windy on the boat that I had to place the call from the captain's bridge, huddled next to him as the wind buffeted our small boat in the choppy seas. As I had learned years earlier when navigating the USS *Sampson*, the Mediterranean can turn nasty even in the midst of summer heat. The "meltemi winds" often sweep down from the north and create considerable turbulence, even for warships, much less a small leisure boat.

On July 5, I flew to Paris to resume discussions. It was raining heavily as Jean, Mikis, Hung, and I met with Charlotte Jones, an experienced and highly regarded London-based accountant who worked for Deutsche Bank. Ackermann had, in effect, seconded her to the Task Force to provide accounting advice to the entire Task Force, not just to Deutsche Bank. She was smart, industrious, and made herself available around the clock as we increasingly realized how important accounting rules would be in determining the way forward. Somewhat unexpectedly, these rules proved to be an ally to those of us seeking an actual debt reduction, not just a rollover. International Accounting Standards (IAS) 39 laid out the accounting treatment of hold to maturity (HTM) assets on bank balance sheets. As I mentioned earlier, the accounting standards were pointing to the need for most banks' holdings of Greek bonds to be marked to market as of the end of the second-quarter financial statements—due out in late July. Thus, many banks would have to begin absorbing losses as a result of the ongoing negotiations and the unnerving disconnect between the book and market value of Greek debt—which was at that time trading around 49 cents to the euro for bonds maturing in four years (by 2015) while the twenty-year maturities were trading as low as ten cents on the euro.

Given the lateness of the hour, we found a conference room in the basement of the Lotte Hotel to meet over a working dinner. Charlotte was staying at a different hotel, and Mikis, who knew his way around Paris, was dispatched to escort her to the Lotte hotel amidst a major rainstorm. We all entered the lobby somewhat wet, but poor Charlotte, whose train from London was running late, had gotten lost searching for our hotel before Mikis rescued her. She was soaked head to toe. We gave her time to dry her clothes, and then sat down to craft the next phase of our strategy. Jean, however, was perturbed with Charlotte over a note she had prepared on the accounting dilemmas, out of concern that her analysis would, intentionally he thought, put pressure on the French banks to start recognizing losses, something they were still reluctant to do. I did not share his view, and considered that Charlotte was simply providing professional advice, which was complicated as the French in particular had a very specific interpretation of the "so-called International Financial Reporting Standards (IFRS)." Behind his perturbation were reports that German banks had sold part of their exposure into the marketplace contrary to understandings that had been reached between Eurozone finance ministers and their leading banks. We had quite a difficult discussion, but resolved nothing on that issue.

We finally put the accounting issues aside and began discussing strategy. We began drafting a new position paper, seeking to build a list of options. Jean and I asked Hung and Mikis to begin drafting, and they got a start on it as the clock struck 9 p.m. Suddenly, Mikis stopped work on his computer, looked up, and said, "Hungry bears don't dance." He explained that this was an old Cypriot expression, and that he needed food to recharge his batteries. We quickly got our hands on some room service menus and within forty-five minutes had Mikis up and running again.

The next day brought another long day of Task Force discussions. We decided to shift away from short-term rollovers to longer-term solutions that could make a meaningful contribution to putting Greece into a sustainable debt position. We debated options that could be used to meet that goal, but an agreed menu of options seemed far away. Debt buybacks remained one attractive option, but who was going to provide the funds for such an operation? The idea of a "Brady-style" collateralization of some of the Greek debt was also considered, but was it a high priority?

Jean and I led a small group back to Rome that night for a second round with the Grilli Group. We had boiled down our subgroup to eight or so, and Vittorio Grilli had a similar size on his side. We slipped in the back entrance of the Italian Finance Ministry once again, a practice to which we became accustomed. It was one of those Roman summer days that can become unbearable by midafternoon, but in the early morning hours, it sparkled. During the meeting, most of Grilli's "team" again simply took notes on their computers. Both Greek officials, George Zanias and Petros Christodoulou, spoke of the need for major restructuring, but deferred to Grilli. He continued to exhibit ambivalence, repeating his mantra "I have no mandate to negotiate" at the beginning of the meeting. He reminded me of an orchestra conductor, standing in front of a capable but irascible group of musicians, frozen with his baton in the air, waiting for someone to say, "start the music!" I sensed, however, that he was beginning to realize that a major Greek debt restructuring might well occur under his watch.

Our points were fourfold:

- Recent deterioration in market conditions and the possibility of loan impairment made clear the need for a credible, comprehensive solution, not a short-term fix;

- We were committed to a voluntary restructuring as part of a broader reform agenda;

· The July 11 Eurogroup meeting should state clearly and publicly that they welcome such an approach;

· As part of this, the ECB should continue to provide liquidity support for the Greek banking system.

Grilli noted all the points and while he promised to pass them up the line, he asked for a white paper from us to capture the points. We agreed to pull it together, realizing we had precious little time to get it cleared. Although some members of the IIF Task Force were still grumbling about having an American lead the effort, a sense of teamwork was beginning to develop on our side, and I was somewhat optimistic that we could craft a paper. Besides, Jean was functioning as a de facto Co-Chairman, and that helped mitigate the concerns.

The position of the Greek banks was particularly sensitive. They held approximately €56 billion of Greek sovereign debt, representing a massive 45.7%[2] of the total claims by all private creditors participating in our Task Force.[3] On July 6, Evangelos Venizelos had made news when he stated that Greeks were willing to roll over their government bonds as part of a European aid plan. "The Greek banks are ready to participate," Venizelos said in an interview. He added, "We must respect absolutely the voluntary character of this procedure."[4] That was good to see, but did he really mean it? And was Venizelos really in a position to speak for the Greek banks? This became an area of uncertainty for some time. The leading Greek banks with the bulk of exposure had joined forces with our Task Force. The Chairman of Alpha Bank, Yannis Costopoulos, Greece's leading private bank, had been a member of the IIF Board and was committed to working with us while also doing his best to protect Alpha Bank. It was a virtually impossible task. If any institutions were genuine victims of the Greek crisis, they were the Greek banks. They had been essentially forced by the Greek government to buy new government bonds when Greece had lost market access, financed through a scheme of issuing bank bonds guaranteed by the government that could be rediscounted by the ECB. Their holdings of the GGBs thus were not only high, but they also represented a multitude of their equity capital, an existential threat to their viability. It had not been that way at all just a few years earlier. In January 2007, just prior to the onset of the global financial crisis, the IMF had stated, "Financial soundness indicators suggest that the banking system is profitable and well capitalized (Table 10). Solvency remains satisfactory, and profits are robust, driven by rising lending volumes in Greece and southeastern Europe, wide margins, and some cost cutting through the rationalization of branch networks (resulting from mergers), investments in IT, and the implementation of voluntary retirement plans in some banks."[5]

Core Set of Financial Soundness Indicators for Deposit-Taking Institutions
(1998–June 2006, unless otherwise indicated)

	1998	1999	2000	2001	2002	2003	2004	2005	2006
Regulatory capital to risk-weighted assets	10.2	16.2	13.6	12.4	10.5	12.0	12.8	13.2	12.3
Regulatory Tier 1 capital to risk-weighted assets	9.7	15.3	13.5	10.9	8.8	9.8	10.0	10.9	10.3
Nonperforming loans net of provisions to capital	29.3	24.1	23.2	17.4	18.7	16.1	16.3	18.0	19.1
Nonperforming loans to total gross loans	8.7	11.2	7.2	5.6	5.5	5.1	5.4	5.5	5.5
Sectoral distributions of loans to total (enterprises and households, domestic and other Euro Area residents)									
Insurance corporations and pension funds	0.0	0.1	0.1	0.1	0.1	0.1	0.1	0.1	0.1
Other financial intermediaries	0.7	0.4	1.1	2.2	3.2	2.6	2.3	1.6	1.5
Nonfinancial corporations	75.0	72.2	70.5	65.7	60.4	57.5	54.4	50.4	49.5
Consumer credit	7.3	8.4	9.3	10.6	11.3	12.3	14.3	15.2	15.7
Lending for house purchase	17.0	18.8	18.8	21.0	24.3	26.1	27.6	31.4	32.0
Other lending to households and nonprofit institutions serving households	0.1	0.2	0.3	0.4	0.6	1.2	1.2	1.2	1.2
Return on assets (after taxes; on a nonconsolidated basis)	0.7	2.4	1.4	1.0	0.5	0.6	0.3	0.9	1.2
Return on equity (after taxes; on a nonconsolidated basis)	13.7	28.6	15.4	12.4	6.8	8.9	5.6	16.2	21.7
Interest margin to gross income	55.1	44.5	54.5	62.8	72.5	73.9	76.3	75.3	71.1
Noninterest expenses to gross income	62	48	53	59	69	63	62	55	48
Liquid assets to total assets	55.2	50.3	46.4	41.1	39.5	37.0	33.4	34.0	34.2
Liquid assets to short-term liabilities	62.6	64.6	60.7	53.0	48.7	46.5	43.2	47.0	46.8
Net open position in foreign exchange to capital	---	---	---	3.5	7.2	5.8	3.5	2.9	0.6

Source: Bank of Greece

- *2007 Article IV Consultation*: "The Greek banking **system remains healthy, adequately capitalized, and highly profitable**, but some developments will need to be monitored closely. Continued rapid credit growth has increased banks' exposure to credit risk and their vulnerability to swings in the economic cycle. The increasing exposure in Southeastern Europe (SEE), while entailing significant benefits, carries foreign exchange, credit, and country risks. Spillover effects from the turmoil in mature financial markets have been limited thus far."[6]

- *2008 Article IV Consultation*: "The banking sector **appears to be sound** and has thus far remained largely unaffected by the global financial market turmoil. However, continued rapid credit growth and increasing presence in southeastern Europe, financed partly by wholesale funding, have increased banks' exposure to credit, country, and liquidity risks."[7]

The following tables outline the exposures of Greek banks and other European banks to Greek sovereign debt at different points in the crisis. It should be noted that the data on the table "European Banks' Exposure" are net of provisions and impairments as required by accounting rules. Thus, the gross holdings were higher, especially after June 2011.

Exposure of Greek Banks and of Other European Banks to Greek Sovereign Debt

Country Banking Exposure to Sovereign Debt of Greece (as of August 2010)

EUR Millions	Exposures to Greece	Exposure/Tier 1 Capital
Greece	56,148	226%
Germany	18,718	12%
France	11,624	6%
Cyprus	4,837	109%
Belgium	4,656	14%
United Kingdom	4,131	1%
Netherlands	3,160	4%
Italy	1,778	2%
Portugal	1,739	9%
Spain	1,016	1%

Greek Bank Exposures to their Own Sovereign Debt (as of August 2010)

	Exposures to Greek Sovereign Debt			Exposure/ Tier 1
	Euro million	o/w Banking Book (%)	o/w Trading Book (%)	%
National Bank of Greece	19,756	91.8%	8.2%	260%
Agricultural Bank of Greece	10,187	93.5%	6.5%	807%
Piraeus Bank Group	8,306	87.1%	12.9%	244%
Eurobank EGF	7,458	98.7%	1.3%	139%
TT Hellenic Postbank	5,371	97.2%	2,8%	418%
Alpha Bank	5,070	96.9%	3.1%	86%
Greek Banks	56,148	93.3%	6.7%	226%

Source: Adrian Blundell-Wignall and Patrick Slovik, "The EU Stress Test and Sovereign Debt Exposures." OECD Working Papers on Finance, Insurance and Private Pensions, no. 4, August 1, 2010.

Greek banks' holding of Greek government securities—quarterly data

Values in parentheses refer to total exposure that include bonds
that were subject to restructuring

	2010 Q4	2011 Q1	2011 Q2	2011 Q3	2011 Q4	2012 Q1	2012 Q2	2012 Q3	2012 Q4
Alpha	5,475	907 (4,600)	3,072 (6,139.6)	-	-	-	-	-	-
Eurobank	8,740	-	5,483 (9,839)	-	4,115	4,224 (14,378)	4,887 (14,664)	5,722 (16,329)	5,339

European Banks' Exposure

Other European banks' holding of Greek government securities (million €)

	2010 Q4	2011 Q1	2011 Q2	2011 Q3	2011 Q4	2012 Q1	2012 Q2	2012 Q3	2012 Q4
BNP Paribas (France)	5200	-	3500*	1600	1041	200	0	0	0
Dexia (Franco-Belgian)	3500	-	3785	1292	747	-	-	-	0
Marfin (Cyprus Popular Bank)	3400	-	2953.85	2848.83	817.41	-	364	-	-
Commerzbank (Germany)	3100	2900	2200	1400	800	0	0	0	0
Société Générale (France)	2800	2500	1800	800	400	200	0	0	0
Bank of Cyprus	2400	2025.87	2221.28	1699.08	1133.2	971.6	1387.01	1202.12	595.82
Deutsche Bank (Germany)	1800	-	1154	881	448	-	35	67	39
HSBC (UK)	1300	-	1000	500	400	100	100	0	100
Royal Bank of Scotland	1200	-	981	705	400	0	0	-	-
Credit Agricole (France)	700	631	326	177	7	18	31	0	0
Intesa Sanpaolo (Italy)	600	-	559	446	219	-	10	12	1
KBC (Belgium)	440	600	500	300	200	0	0	0	0
Erste Group Bank (Austria)	350	-	4	-61.6	4	4	1	0	0
Banco BPI (Portugal)	330	-	530.4	-	-	-	23	0	0
Natixis (France)	230	-	181	146	170	-	-	-	5
Barclays (UK)	190	-	69	22	13	4	9	7	0
Banco Santander (Spain)	180	-	-	-	84	-	-	-	-
Grupo BBVA (Spain)	130	-	101	-	109	-	-	-	0

Source: Bloomberg
Note: 2010 Q4 data are from EBA's July 2011 stress test
These banks are selected as they were the top holders of Greek bonds as of 2010 Q4
*Estimation based on Financial Times *report (http://www.ft.com/intl/cms/s/0/9dfd3a52-060d-11e1-ad0e-00144feabdc0.html)*

On July 10, as we were finalizing the white paper, we received a balanced letter from the CEOs of the National Bank of Greece (NBG), Alpha Bank, Eurobank, and Piraeus. While endorsing the broad thrust of our proposals, they stressed the need to "ensure that any measures are introduced in a prudent way that takes account of the current state of the Greek banking system."[8] The letter was a model of statesmanship that was rarely replicated by any party during the following nine months of negotiations.

After another flurry of conference calls over July 8 and 9, and some exceptionally skillful compromise drafting by Hung and Mikis, we had a white paper by July 10 (see Appendix 2). We had held a number of calls with Moody's and Standard & Poor's, two of the key ratings agencies, and they informed us that a "selective default" for Greece was fairly likely with a restructuring, even with a voluntary deal. This made our task all the more difficult, for Trichet and many other officials, including Lagarde, had expressed opposition to any restructuring that triggered an event of default, arguing that it would require the ECB to cut off funding to the Greek banking system. The more we studied the problem, however, the more we understood that there was a world of difference between a "technical" default, which would likely only last for a few weeks, and a "pure" or "complete" default, which could indeed be devastating to Greece and the Eurozone. We became confident that a technical default, reached in the context of a cooperative, voluntary agreement for reducing Greece's debt, would be viewed very differently by the market than would a default that resulted from Greece's utter unwillingness or inability to pay. We knew, however, that the issue of ECB collateral policies with regard to Greek bonds could still lead the restructuring to "come a cropper." I called Trichet to discuss this. He advised me that while I should continue my discussions with the "government institutions," he had not changed his mind: "A restructuring of Greek debt would be a big mistake." I hung up the phone wondering whether we were doing the right thing by persisting. If he held firm, would this turn out to be a disaster? His conviction that a restructuring was unwise was understandable, built on his vision that the sovereign debt of Eurozone member countries was inviolable, unalterable. His view was that a debt restructuring for Greece would lead to an unraveling of the euro, a very real risk given the tenuous nature of Italy, Ireland, Portugal, and Spain. On the other hand, stabilizing Greece without debt reduction was proving increasingly out of reach. We were all truly on the cusp of a dilemma.

Our white paper covered a lot of ground, including the growing prospect that many of the banks' loans to Greece would be wholly or partially impaired beginning the third week of July, requiring them to recognize losses in their income statements. This would adversely impact regulatory capital positions in some cases. While I was concerned that this could lead to contagion, I could also sense that the resistance to a restructuring among some financial institutions was eroding: the reality that Greek debt was worth nothing even close to 100 cents on the euro was seeping into every corner of these discussions, like a bad odor pervading a room. At first, polite people would try to ignore it. Then people would begin to look around and eyes would meet, often above upturned noses and crinkled faces. So it was with Greek debt: the odor was becoming too strong to ignore.

Our white paper asked for clarity from the ECB, reaffirmed our commitment to a voluntary, broadly based deal, stressed the need to avoid triggering credit default swaps (our advisors had given us some comfort on that point), and emphasized the importance of Greek reforms (what else was new?). We also made a strong case for credit enhancements, à la the Brady Plan. In addition, we proposed a debt buyback program, which could take advantage of the huge discount in the market value of Greek debt. To be funded by whom? That was the question.

CHAPTER 16

THE DEAL IS DONE
(OR IS IT?)

**"Money makers are tiresome company,
as they have no standard but cash value."**

—Plato, *The Republic*, circa 375 BC

As we waited for the Eurogroup reaction to our white paper, we began to sense that the markets were closing in on Greece and the Eurozone. The back and forth between our Task Force and the various European authorities was not keeping pace with the anxiety of the markets. On the day that the Eurogroup met in Brussels to consider our white paper, the spreads on Italian and Spanish sovereign debt soared by record amounts—10-year Italian paper rose 0.44 percentage points to 5.72%, while Spanish yields jumped 0.41 points to 6.09%—which in turn drove down bank shares and stock markets around the world. As I opened my iPad and surveyed the day's damage in the markets, I realized we had to find some way to accelerate the negotiations, despite the lack of a full consensus on our side of the table and the bureaucratic hydra on the other.

Moody's had downgraded both Irish and Portuguese bonds, which according to some reports was due to a perception that the EU had changed "the rules of the game"—that is, requiring private creditors to write down debt in order to obtain Eurozone support.

Against this tumultuous background, shares in Italian banks—the largest holders of Italy's sovereign debt—came under sharp pressure. Intesa Sanpaolo was down 8% on that single day of trading, with UniCredit off 6%. Over the previous eight days, the losses were more painful: 20% and 25%, respectively.

The markets were full of reports that our white paper would vastly expand the scope of the Greek bailout and could see billions in taxpayer money used to buy up swaths of Greek bonds at discounted levels. That aspect of our proposal (a possible debt buyback facility) appeared to have stoked contagion further. We were on a knife's edge: if we did not move forward to try to reduce Greece's debt, the crisis could mushroom into an even more severe European or global crisis. If we did move forward, every step, every idea was subject to instant analysis and risked adding to the sense of instability circling in global markets.

We also were acutely conscious that beyond market gyrations, the real economy of Europe was stagnating, while the US economy was beginning to recover from the global recession of 2008 and 2009, growing 1.8% over the course of 2011 as Europe hit a wall. Even Germany grew at only 0.1%, while the French economy was completely stalled at zero growth.

In Greece, the picture was becoming bleaker by the day. The economy shrank 6% from July 2010 to July 2011, an alarming collapse. In the second quarter of 2011 the decline gathered even more speed, with a 7% annualized contraction. Domestic demand contracted sharply as private consumption pulled back. Unsurprisingly, the austerity measures imposed by the Troika program were biting hard, further undermining confidence regarding Greece's future in the Eurozone. Total employment was on track to fall 6% in 2011, with the unemployment rate rising to 16%.

Sitting at the desk of my small hotel room in Rome on the evening of July 11, I decided to reach out to Juncker to see how the meetings of the Eurozone Ministers went. It was closing in on 10:30 p.m., but I knew their meetings often ran into the wee hours of the morning. He took my call, and I waited as he stepped out of the room where their dinner seemed to be in full swing. After a minute or so, he came back on the line.

"Charles, how are you my dear friend, how wonderful to hear from you! Please, what I can do for you?" A real gentleman—and a rare one in those days, even in diplomatic circles.

I asked him how his colleagues had reacted, and he reported, "We are making some progress, but there are still many complex issues to resolve." He reported that some of the group was coming around to the idea of accepting technical default in order to gain the benefits of reducing Greece's debt. "But many are not supportive of official funding for a buyback."

I then briefed him on the avalanche of negative news from the markets and asked what could be done to move things forward at a faster pace. "The markets are not moving at the glacial pace of our negotiations," I said.

"I understand," he responded, "but this is how Europe functions." Or doesn't, I thought. "Nonetheless, I share your sense of urgency. I will seek clearer instructions for Grilli. If you make some progress with him, then we can meet to strategize and possibly reset the stage for a decision at the next Heads of State meeting."

Early the next day, Jean Lemierre, Hung Tran, Mikis Hadjimichael, and I turned our attention back to Grilli. I informed him of my discussion with Juncker and asked for another urgent session between our two sides. He too was shaken by the market gyrations and agreed to another meeting in Rome. Jean and I decided to have yet another conference call of our Task Force ahead of the next Grilli gathering. We still had too many options on the table, and some were not clearly articulated. We needed to narrow our focus if we were to make progress in Rome. We had formed working groups of the private sector firms to flush out some of the proposals and worked overnight at the old premises of Banco Nazionale del Lavoro in Rome. At the same time, we arranged a technical meeting in Rome between Task Force representatives and a small official delegation, led by Maarten Verwey of the Dutch Finance Ministry, who was also serving as Grilli's Deputy.

The Eurozone Finance Ministers meeting was aptly described in the press: "European Finance Chiefs cast about for a strategy to halt Greece's debt spiral . . . as the rot spread to Italy."[1] They reopened the debate on the possibility of a debt buyback, an option we had mentioned in our white paper. This option had the considerable advantage of enabling Greece and Europe to take advantage of the heavy discount in the price of Greek debt (approximately 45% of the face value at the time).

Our Task Force felt this could be an attractive element on a menu of options, possibly reducing Greece's debt by 10% just from a buyback alone. That had been previously stymied by both Germany and the Dutch, but it appeared that they were rethinking this as Europe searched for anything that could anchor the Eurozone amidst the rising market turbulence. Of course, the key question with a buyback was, who would finance it? European resistance was cracking, but it remained very unclear that the Eurozone would spend the €10–20 billion needed to finance a meaningful buyback.

The Eurogroup statement officially opened the door to a voluntary restructuring by welcoming the "proposal from the private sector to voluntarily contribute to the financing of a second program." But the vagueness of the language left confusion in the market about the exact intentions of the Eurozone. And what was meant by the fact that only the ECB confirmed its position "that a credit event or selective default should be avoided"? Did this mean that the government would accept a credit event? And for the first time Greek Finance Minister Venizelos mentioned the possibility of a selective default. "Selective default is not an actual event; it's an assessment by ratings agencies," he stated. At the same time, Trichet "maintained his fierce opposition to roping bondholders into a bailout," according to one report.[2]

Thus, the authorities of Europe remained rather disorganized, and some still seemed oblivious to the rising tide that could swallow up the Eurozone if not properly managed. Nevertheless, I felt mildly encouraged. Through the fog, Jean and I could begin to see the prospects of a meaningful restructuring growing. But the key question remained: whether we could bring it to closure before contagion spread throughout the entirety of the Eurozone.

The next few days were riddled with endless conference calls as we prepared our white paper. Sprinkled among those calls were frequent consultations with key IIF Board members Ackermann, Prot, Oudéa, Wallenberg, Blessing, and others such as Cucchiani of Intesa Sanpaolo and Achleitner of Allianz. It was essential to seek their advice as we barreled ahead in this unprecedented process. The members of the Task Force were in some cases seasoned veterans of debt negotiations in Latin America, but they could not realistically provide a CEO perspective on what was at stake, especially the broader risks if Greece failed and Italy was also pulled into a restructuring. Thus, Jean and I found it essential to maintain the dialogue at several levels as well.

I also talked with Hans Humes, the CEO of Greylock Capital. Hans was a savvy hedge fund executive, but he was also the rare hedge fund veteran who had a strong sense of how the financial system should work to find an orderly path to debt restructuring. I called him often in the following months and found his perspective increasingly of value.

On July 12, my first day back in my Washington, DC, office, Hung and Mikis chaired a private creditors group conference call on debt buyback options as Jean and I initiated another round of consultation calls, including to Olli Rehn, who had become quite a constructive force in this process. There were so many competing power centers in Europe, and negotiations sometimes felt like trying to navigate a maze with no exit. Rehn was widely respected and knew how to operate in Brussels. Furthermore, he firmly supported a voluntary restructuring of Greece's debt.

I briefed Rehn on our plans to meet with Grilli again on July 14, and he gave me further perspective on the Ministerial meetings on the 11th. Together we explored how to move the Grilli group forward on the 14th. As usual, our discussion focused on how to deal with Germany. Perplexingly, although they were moving toward supporting a debt restructuring (voluntary or otherwise), they seemed to lack a sense of urgency. In fact, on the 13th "Berlin made it clear that it sees no pressing reason to hold an emergency Eurozone Summit at the end of the week." One trillion dollars in stock market value had been destroyed by the market anxieties on July 11 and 12 alone, and yet the German authorities saw no pressing reason?

Rehn stressed that he would do all he could to push both Germany and Grilli, but at the same time he said resignedly, "Charles, I cannot assure you of anything at this point." I hung up the phone, somewhat dejected that some of the most important political and economic leaders of Europe, who should be at the forefront of understanding the systemic risks to the Eurozone, seemed somewhat out of touch with market realities and at times apparently resentful of the force that markets brought to the political structures and processes of Europe. Of course, markets can behave erratically, and their movements are generally correlated with fundamentals only over the medium and long term. But ignoring market signals comes with great peril. Markets can be regulated, influenced, cajoled, berated, jawboned, or framed with supportive policies, but not ignored.

The next morning, I had breakfast with Howard Davies at the Sofitel Hotel close to my office. I had gotten to know him well during his time as the UK's first consolidated financial regulator, the Financial Services Authority (FSA), created in 1997 by Gordon Brown and the UK government. Davies led the FSA from 1997 to 2003 with energy, balance, integrity, and not a small amount of wit. He was widely known for a unique capacity to combine sharp analysis, erudition, biting critique, and the capacity to greatly enliven an evening with a sense of humor that often contained a zinger or two. He had spoken at a number of IIF gatherings over the years, and never failed to both inform and entertain.

We sat down at 7:15 a.m. for an early bite. I unloaded my Greek woes and anxieties, and he was momentarily taken aback. While a Europeanist at heart, he was nevertheless a strong critic of the Eurozone. He shared my view of the urgency of the problem but was concerned that we might not be able to mobilize sufficient support for a restructuring in time to avoid a rupture of the Eurozone. I found his judgment sound, but a good night's sleep and the challenges ahead that day convinced me not to slip back into pessimism.

After breakfast, as I walked into my office two blocks away, I found the usual swirl of confusing and conflicting views emerging from the official sector. The IMF issued a report that was perceived as supporting Germany's push for debt restructuring. The fact that the IMF and other officials were steadily moving toward support for a restructuring was helpful at that stage. It was one of those rare moments during the negotiations when it appeared that, on at least some core issues, the interests of the IMF, the German government, and the IIF were aligned. But when you looked more closely, you could see that the alignment broke down. Germany was, in fact, resisting attempts by other Eurozone partners to accelerate negotiations in their effort to limit contagion in Italy and Spain. French officials were pushing back on Germany, and I remained hopeful that the Heads of State meeting tentatively scheduled for July 21 would take place despite apparent German intransigence.

We had a Task Force conference call—private creditors only—at 9 a.m. Washington time that presented an important opportunity to refine and narrow our options before a meeting with the Grilli group the next afternoon. As with the official creditors, positions were far from united. We had a diverse group of creditors, ranging from large banks such as BNP Paribas and Société Générale in France, Deutsche Bank and Commerzbank in Germany, and Intesa Sanpaolo in Italy, to large insurers such as AXA and Allianz, and of course, the Greek banks, with their own unique challenges.

Interest in a debt buyback option remained high, but we had not solved the essential question: Who would finance it? We also prepared a note summarizing the experience under the Brady Plan and considered possible sources of financing for a "Brady Plan" for Greece. There was a big difference, however: the official creditors were moving away from the idea of using any available funding to collateralize Greek debt, as was done in the Brady Plan.

I boarded a plane that evening heading back to Rome for another meeting with the Grilli group, not knowing what to expect. Would our discussion make a difference in their willingness to deal, or would the European officials continue to do a good imitation of Nero? But the great fire of Rome, during which Nero supposedly fiddled or sang the "Sack of Ilium" (which actually derived from ancient Greek literature) only lasted one week. Not to blame Brussels for all of this, but destabilization of European financial markets had been going on for many weeks, with no end in sight.

I got off the plane in Rome on a sunny summer day, longing for some rest. However, a shower would be all that I would get, as I had a meeting with Grilli scheduled for noon at the Italian Treasury. I had asked for a private meeting ahead of our group "negotiations" in order to gauge the situation and see how the messages were filtering down from Brussels, if at all. Jean joined me for the meeting, despite it being Bastille Day. Although this was a distant bit of European history for me, not so for Jean—it is a significant national holiday. As we slowly climbed the steps to Grilli's office, I expressed regret for events pulling Jean to Rome on that day. He shrugged and smiled slightly, then replied, "Ah, yes. The revolution—people revolt when the elite do not take care of them." I briefly wondered whether the modern Greeks, and even the Italians, would someday revolt against their ruling classes—if so, hopefully in a less violent way than the French did in 1789. In fact, that is what Greece did in 2015. More on that to come.

Our minds were drawn back to current realities as Grilli greeted us warmly, but with a worried expression on his face. I asked him if it was due to Greece or Italy.

"Both," he responded. "We need to auction nearly €5 billion of Italian paper today, and it is driving rates up further. As for Greece, the message coming from Brussels, Berlin, and Frankfurt remains muddled, while Greece has been downgraded once again."

I responded that I was aware that Fitch had downgraded Greece four notches further to "deep junk territory," despite the recent release of EU and IMF funds. This came on the heels of Moody's downgrading Ireland to junk status the previous day, underscoring that contagion was continuing to spread.

"I do not believe we should be preoccupied with what the ratings agencies are doing," I said. "A technical default is highly likely, but it will be short-lived if we do our jobs right."

It turned out that Grilli had heard from both Juncker and Rehn following the Eurogroup Ministerial meeting of July 11. Grilli confirmed what we already knew: that both were pushing Europe toward a Greek restructuring, but that the way forward remained very cluttered. The Eurogroup statement on July 11 had mentioned the possible use of collateral arrangements, alluding to the possibility of debt buybacks or a Brady-type deal, and noted the exploration of modalities to improve sustainability of Greek public debt. And yet the statement also indicated that the ECB confirmed its position that a credit event or selective default should be avoided.

Grilli said, "I still do not have clear guidance." How we had come to loathe that phrase. Jean and I knew that, once again, this did not bode well for meeting between our two teams. Nevertheless, we pushed ahead, gathering the "core team" of our Task Force at Intesa Sanpaolo's Rome office to finalize our preparations.

We had a superb luncheon of insalata caprese and spaghetti con pomodoro e basilico that temporarily lifted the mood. Then we had a fruitful exchange despite the market pressure breathing down our necks. Everyone in the room realized that while we were technically negotiating to salvage some of our claims against Greece, there was much more at stake. The shakiness of both Ireland and Italy added to the stress, and most of us clearly perceived the need to get something done on our side, even at the risk of wiping out a substantial part of our claims.

We proceeded back to the Italian Treasury in the heavy heat of the afternoon and met a rather truncated group of a half dozen European and

IMF officials. After courtesies, we presented a draft proposal, which outlined three options for debt reduction: a "Committed Financing Facility" with credit enhancements, a debt exchange (which would require official collaboration along the lines of Brady bonds), and a cash debt buyback, which also would have required additional official financing. The reaction was muted, with many questions, and we felt like we were pushing on a marshmallow. When Grilli repeated his already exceptionally tiresome phrase, "I have no mandate to negotiate," I tried to exercise restraint, as we all did on the private side, but we asked impatiently that he convey our proposal to his Ministers in the Eurogroup before the Heads of State Summit, which appeared to be taking shape over the next week or so. Jean underscored the need to bring our ideas forward, using a measured and effective tone. The meeting broke up at 5 p.m. in a rather desultory fashion. Many jumped on planes back to their home bases.

Jean, Hung, Mikis, and I went to dinner to assess the situation, and decided that we needed to reach out to Ackermann and then connect to Juncker. Somehow, we had to break out of the cycle of roundabout discussions while the markets continued to swirl. I called Ackermann immediately after dinner and we agreed that I would try to reach Juncker to arrange the small meeting with him that he had offered. I immediately reached out to Juncker, and although it was nearly 10 p.m., he answered promptly and cordially, despite the once again obvious interruption of his dinner. I described the meeting in Rome and our concerns.

He listened and responded, "Charles, you are right. We need to meet so we can consider a way forward before the Ministerial next week, which still is not pinned down. We cannot schedule a summit unless we have a solution in sight, and we simply do not have a consensus." I agreed on the last part and explained to him that it would be four of us: myself, Joe Ackermann, BNP Chairman Baudouin Prot, and his colleague, Jean Lemierre, my informal but vital Co-Chair.

He then surprised me. "For this informal meeting, I only want you and Joe from your side. I know both of you well, but don't know the French bankers." I pushed back, saying that we would need the French banks, which were the largest creditors, but Juncker was firm.

"Charles, I understand, but not at this tête-à-tête, please."

I asked for time to consider this, while we agreed to meet in five days, on Tuesday, July 19. I called Ackermann back.

"The good news is that Juncker agreed to meet, but we have a problem. He only wants you and me, not our French colleagues." We discussed the dilemma, and Ackermann agreed to call Juncker to raise the issue with him again. He did, but it did not change the outcome. Juncker wanted to meet with only the two of us. It would be a decision that would backfire.

The next morning, July 15, we quickly shifted our attention to having a round of discussions with our full Task Force. We scheduled a conference call for that afternoon, to prepare a document that we could use as a basis for the next round of discussions in Brussels. Before the conference call, I touched base directly with Henri de Castries the CEO of AXA and with Paul Achleitner, who was then CIO of Allianz, to ensure that we had our largest insurers on board. Also, I called Frédéric Oudéa, CEO of Société Générale, and Rich Waugh of Scotia Bank. Oudéa was a major creditor to Greece, while Scotia had no exposure whatsoever. But he was a very experienced banker and had dealt with many sovereign debt problems in Latin America. I often found his independent views quite useful.

Hung and Mikis, somewhat detached, worked feverishly to shape proposals that we felt would be acceptable to our private creditors and yet also workable for the EU, the IMF, and Greece. It was an exacting challenge, but we felt like we were inching forward. The creditors had agreed to accept options that would involve a 15% haircut—a loss of 15% of their claims in net present value (NPV) terms. It had been difficult in the past to push a 10% loss, but both the technicians and the leadership of the private creditors knew that 15% was the minimum needed (or at least that is what we thought at the time). Even then, we had to demonstrate that a 15% loss would sufficiently reduce Greece's debt and that it would, along with official support and adjustment measures, lead to a sustainable debt outlook for Greece.

Ahead of the meeting with Juncker, Joe Ackermann wisely suggested that we have a quiet strategy session in a small group. He invited Hung, Mikis, and me to his home in Zurich. We flew there, and his wife, Pirkko, fixed a wonderful lunch for the four of us. Pirkko is a lovely, vivacious Finnish lady whom I had gotten to know well during the many years Joe and I worked together at the IIF—fifteen at that point. But I never knew that Pirkko was such a good cook.

We debated ways to nudge the process toward restructuring without compromising too much on the scale of debt reduction, now that we had the bankers largely on board. To bring the governments around, Ackermann thought we should cut to the basics, and he asked Mikis to draw an isosceles triangle indicating at each corner the costs and benefits of restructuring to the three major interested parties—private creditors, Greece, and the Euro Area official creditors. We worked to devise a strategy that boosted benefits and minimized costs for each of the three sets of interested parties. That would not only demonstrate the need for restructuring but also could provide a system for gauging how much.

For the Greeks, restructuring meant they had to be willing to ride the rapids of a temporary technical default and the risks this could bring to ECB support, as well as undergo the contained painful costs of the adjustment process. However, if the debt reduction were sufficient to put them on a sustainable debt course, they not only could mobilize further support from Europe, but more important, they could begin the vital process of restoring market confidence.

The private creditors would have to endure the financial costs of a major write-off on their Greek holdings, but if it helped stabilize the Greek situation, and if a Greek exit from the euro were avoided, they could steer clear of an even more catastrophic event such as Italy being forced out of the euro on the heels of Greece, the potential result of the powerful contagion that was sweeping Europe at this time. The banks, insurance firms, and pension funds of Europe had roughly four times the exposure to Italy than they did to Greece. As for the official creditors—they would have to accept the fact that sovereign debt in the Eurozone was no longer sacrosanct and take the risk that a restriction of Greece could trigger further contagion. They would also have to make their own financial contributions to the solution. But if it worked, Greece would be stabilized, the private creditors would have provided a major contribution to addressing Greece's financing needs, and the Eurozone would be saved.

As Ackermann and I walked into our meeting with Juncker on the afternoon of July 19, we knew it was going to take more than a 15% reduction in NPV to get the job done. The meeting with Juncker provided remarkable insights into the perspectives of Berlin, Paris, Brussels, and other key Eurozone capitals. As he sat in the Luxembourg Ambassador's conference room, smoking one cigarette after another, Ackermann and I listened intently as he explained the complex dynamics in each capital.

Juncker then paused, looked us in the eye, and asked, "How much debt relief to Greece can you offer?" Ackermann explained that we had agreement among the creditors for a voluntary set of options that would likely lead to a 15% loss in net present value. Juncker responded by saying that it was unlikely to be enough. Ackermann sighed, looking first at me and then at Juncker, and said, "We will see what we can do."

Next, we exchanged views on the problem of Italy, Ireland, and Portugal, and agreed that if we continued to procrastinate with Greece, the entire structure of the Eurozone could be rent asunder.

Juncker said, "I will talk to Merkel, and also ask Grilli to come prepared to negotiate, but you will need to move the banks along." Ackermann responded succinctly: "We will aim for a 20 percent NPV loss, but it will take some work."

Ackermann and I went back to our hotel to review the bidding with Hung and Mikis, and were greeted by three irate calls. The first came from Jean Lemierre, quite upset that we had met with Juncker without inviting him and Baudouin Prot, his CEO. I explained the circumstances, but he was not impressed. Realizing that we were already in a bad moment, I decided to go ahead and broach the subject of the discount embedded in the options.

"Jean, while I have you on the phone, let's discuss the NPV loss. I don't believe we can get away with 15 percent and credibly argue that we will sufficiently reduce Greece's debt. We need to move to 20 percent." Despite his ire, Jean paused, and said simply, "Let's think about it," and hung up abruptly.

Within minutes, irate call number two came in, this one to Ackermann from Prot, whose anger boiled over and was expressed in language that was much more colorful than Lemierre's had been. Not only was he furious over being excluded from the meeting, but he fiercely resisted the idea of a move from a 15% loss to 20%. "I do not agree to that!" he screamed, rather emphatically. Shortly thereafter, call number three, this one from Prot to me. He was as incensed with me as he had been with Ackermann, and he threatened to resign from the Board of the Institute. "I am personally very disappointed in you, Charles, for not reaching out to me."

Ackermann and I felt strongly that we had to move to 20% if we were to secure an agreement, and I asked Hung and Mikis to prepare options along those lines.

I called Ray McDaniel, the head of Moody's, in New York, to ensure that I fully understood the implications of a technical default. He had been briefed and confirmed that while there would be no avoiding it, Greece could emerge within a matter of weeks to an improved position with the ratings agencies if the exchange were successful. We touched base with our core creditors to see if they would agree to a 20% NPV loss. Gradually, but reluctantly, they were coming around. Ackermann and I worked the phones. A 9 a.m. meeting was scheduled the next day that would not only involve Grilli and his band of "warriors," but the Finance Deputies of Germany and France as well as Chancellor Angela Merkel's Chief Economic Advisor.

I called Jacques de Larosiere to ask him for some assistance with Prot. He was, after all, a highly distinguished alumnus of BNPP, even though he had relinquished the title of Senior Advisor to the Chairman to Lemierre. He called back as Joe Ackermann and I were getting a quick bite at a nearby French restaurant. Stepping away from the table, I took the call and explained the need to persuade BNPP to move from 15% to 20% NPV loss. He listened carefully, as always, and then responded.

"I certainly agree with you and Joe that 15 percent is too little of a restructuring. However, I seriously doubt that 20 percent will get the job done. In fact, although I have not recently studied the numbers, I would not be surprised if it took a 50 percent haircut to put Greece on a sustainable course." I was stunned.

"Did I hear you right, Jacques—50 percent?" I asked incredulously.

"Yes," he responded with a sigh. "I am afraid so."

I had great respect for de Larosiere. He had been my mentor on sovereign debt issues for many years, but I felt that he was woefully out of touch. I told him that 50% was neither practical nor necessary to put Greece on a more sustainable debt track and risked too deep a cut into the banks' capital.

I hung up, returned to the table, and summarized my conversation with de Larosiere. Ackermann agreed that he was not being realistic, and we returned to strategizing about the next day. Little did we suspect on that hot Brussels afternoon that ultimately, we would agree not only to a 50% loss, but even more.

We prepared a set of documents designed to persuade the officialdom of the EU and IMF that a 20% debt reduction would be sufficient. We argued in the documentation that a very large discount would impair a very large share of the value of GGB bank holdings—a 20% reduction was estimated to impair €44 billion, while a 50% haircut would lead to impairment of €77 billion as of June 30, increasing to €110 billion in subsequent quarters. If contagion led to impairment being triggered on bank holdings of bonds of other vulnerable Eurozone members such as Italy and Ireland, the losses on banks could surge to as much as a total of €310 billion (including Greece), which would have severely damaged the capital base of some of Europe's largest banks. It would also have done severe damage to the Greek banks, which held approximately €56 billion of their own sovereign debt. Such damage would directly boomerang on the EU, as they would have to mobilize funds to recapitalize the Greek banks.

We also put forward the case that our menu of options would stabilize the markets and contain contagion. We cited previous experience, in which a country entered into "selective default"—the term for a technical default used by the ratings agencies—and was upgraded within a matter of months, with restored market access within a year or two (the cases were Indonesia, Uruguay, and Jamaica). We also reminded the officials of the dramatic decline in spreads that occurred following the Brady bond restructurings of the early 1990s, when a spread as high as 1200 basis points for Mexico declined to 750 basis points within six months.

Beyond the basic reluctance of the ECB and others to engage in a debt restructuring of a Eurozone economy, our proposals presented one other major challenge: it would require additional funds from the Eurozone and/or the IMF. Such funds would be used for collateralization of the principal of the newly issued bonds, for an insurance scheme, or for the purchase of some bonds at face value. We estimated that €20 billion in funds would be needed for collateralization, and another €10–20 billion for debt buyback.

We outlined four options that would be presented to the private holders of Greek debt, with a heavy emphasis on Brady-style techniques of collateralization that would embrace the underlying value of the newly issued claims after restructuring:

- An exchange for "Par Bonds," with a new maturity of 30 years, and a coupon structure equivalent to 4.5% fixed coupon rate, the entire principal of the new bond collateralized by 30-year zero-coupon AAA bonds.

· An exchange for discount bonds, also with a maturity of 30 years, offered at a 20% discount to the face value of existing debt, also 100% collateralized.

· A "Par Bond" offer involving rolling over maturing Greek government bonds into 30-year installments, again with full collateralization of the new principal.

· A discount bond exchange offered at 80% of par value for a 15-year investment, with principal only partly collateralized.

We estimated that with adequate participation (90%) by the banks, insurers, and pension funds holding Greek debt, these options would reduce the stock of debt by €21.9 billion, and with stronger growth by Greece—1% more per annum—Greece's debt-to-GDP ratio would be brought down to below 100% by 2020. The private sector would contribute €51.9 billion during 2011–2014, and another €83.1 billion during 2014–2020, leaving a total of €135 billion for the financing of Greece from mid-2011 to the end of 2020. At the same time, the total official funds to be used would be €78.9 billion.

We felt confident that this was a credible package, but nevertheless expected the next day's negotiations to be difficult. Would the EU and the IMF commit such a magnitude of funds to solve the Greek problem, while taking the heat out of the markets for other Eurozone sovereign debt?

Joe Ackermann, Hung, Mikis, Charlotte Jones, and I discussed last-minute strategy over dinner that night at the hotel bar. We ate in a private room at the hotel, and it turned out to be one of the strangest dinners of the entire negotiations. We discussed how to approach the next day's negotiation, and we all agreed that we had to hold the line at 20%. Suddenly Joe received a text on his cell from Berlin. It was Chancellor Angela Merkel. She and Nicolas Sarkozy had sat down for a private dinner to iron out the Greek situation, and both wanted to proceed with the restructuring. They represented the two most important economies in the Eurozone, and while Merkel and Sarkozy made for vivid contrasts in personalities, when they were aligned on a specific issue, they almost inevitably ruled the day. On this issue of Greek debt, however, Jean-Claude Trichet was a difficult hurdle. He had steadfastly refused all of our efforts to persuade him to support the restructuring, and likewise had resisted pressure from Paris, Berlin, and the IMF. He had been invited to join Merkel and Sarkozy for coffee following their dinner. This was Merkel's last-ditch attempt to win Trichet over, for she knew that the success of the Euro Summit the next day hinged on a successful resolution of Greece. A failure could mean an even fiercer round of market pressures on the Eurozone.

The message to Joe came directly from Merkel, not one of her aides. As Joe stepped aside to study the text, I could not help but be somewhat amused by the fact that Angela Merkel would reach out directly to Joe on his direct cell number. With reflection, however, I should not have been surprised. In February 2008, Merkel hosted a party for Joe's sixtieth birthday. It was sensible and pragmatic that as Germany's leading politician and Germany's leading banker, she would work with Joe at crucial times. As described earlier, in fact, Joe had played an instrumental role in the 2008 bailout of Hypo Real Estate, one of Germany's largest banks.

Merkel had undoubtedly not forgotten that, and she frequently relied on Joe's banking expertise at times of market stress. She wanted to be assured that there would only be a temporary judgment of "selective default" by the rating agencies, and no credit event in the credit default swap (CDS) market. Joe gave her that assurance in a return text.

He sat down, briefed us on the message, and we resumed our strategy session. A few moments later, he got another text from Merkel. "Joe, if we restructure Greece's debt, what will this do to Italy?" she asked. In his response, he tried to assure her that this was the right move. At that point, I got a call from Jean Lemierre in Paris. He had just received a call from Xavier Musca, Sarkozy's Chief of Staff, asking for some details on our proposal. Musca was apparently not in the room with Merkel, Sarkozy, and Trichet, but just outside. Sarkozy had asked for clarification on how much our proposal would reduce Greece's debt, and Lemierre wanted to keep us informed.

Back to our dinner. The exchanges were mildly encouraging, but we had been through too many hurdles, and engaged in too many circuitous discussions, to allow our hopes to rise too much. As we were about to wrap up and get some rest, two more messages came in, in rapid succession, as the clock approached 11 p.m. The first was from Merkel to Joe, asking if the banks would all come on board if she and Sarkozy authorized the collateralization package. Joe responded affirmatively without hesitation, stating that we could get 90% of the creditors. I thought to myself, that will be tough, but we have no choice. Five minutes later, Musca called Lemierre again: it appeared that the deal was struck. Trichet had reluctantly agreed to a restructuring of Greek debt, despite his enormous misgivings about the "sanctity of the signature" for Eurozone currencies.

To his credit, Trichet had extracted two commitments from Merkel and Sarkozy that made the restructuring more palatable to him. First, Eurozone governments would have to insure Greek bonds against default so that the ECB could continue to accept them as collateral. He also received a commitment that no other euro country except Greece would have its debt restructured. So the logjam was apparently broken, but we knew it was still premature to celebrate. How would the actual negotiation go the next day?

The word was given to the press in Berlin almost immediately. Steffen Seibert, Merkel's spokesman, stated that "a common German-French position" had been agreed upon, and that this had been "discussed" with Trichet and Herman van Rompuy, President of the EU. Sarkozy was described as a savior, having "rushed to Berlin to hammer out a Greek rescue plan." He must have been delighted with that.

We arrived early for an 8 a.m. breakfast and pre-meeting with only German and French officials. Brussels being very much part of the French tradition of continental breakfasts, they only served coffee, juice, and croissants. Not my idea of breakfast, but after all, we were in the heart of Europe.

When Ackermann checked in for the meeting at security, he was somehow given Jean Lemierre's badge. Strange, but it was Brussels, and it was the European Commission. When Lemierre arrived, there was no badge for him. He called me and I looked at Joe's badge. Sure enough, it said 'Jean Lemierre.' Jean could be very persuasive at times, and he then managed to somehow convince the guard to give him Ackermann's badge. After the tension of the last few days, it provided a moment of levity when they exchanged badges in front of their German and French colleagues. Prot also surprisingly showed up and joined us, but relations with him were still frosty.

The breakfast meeting was mildly useful, as the participants mainly asked technical questions. At the same time, it was downright surreal. No Greeks anywhere in sight. No IMF, European Commission, or European Central Bank. Did Berlin and Paris really have this much control? Maybe so. We would find out as we took a break and proceeded to a slightly larger, but still cramped room with representatives from all the groups that were missing in the first round. Indeed, the breakfast meeting had been the warm-up act before the main event.

As we settled in, Ackermann took over. He made a compelling argument that a 20% NPV loss was as far as we could move the creditors voluntarily, and none of us wanted to see a breakdown ahead of the Summit, which was scheduled to start that afternoon. The Greeks were the first to push back, with Petros Christodoulou arguing that the debt reduction was insufficient, and that the Greek banks would need special treatment. I disagreed with the former but shared his concern on the latter. I told him that we would see what could be done, but I knew our scope was limited in that all banks had to be treated equally.

We were asked many times whether we could really deliver the creditors, and as with Merkel the night before, Ackermann assured all that we could. The French Deputy, Ramon Fernandez, then took the lead on the official side—not Grilli, nor the IMF, nor the Germans. He argued that our proposal was not acceptable, and he could not recommend it to President Sarkozy. We believed we had Sarkozy and his Chef de Cabinet Musca on our side, but neither Lemierre nor Prot wanted to test Fernandez at that point. Neither did I.

Ackermann and I asked for a short break. Our team, consisting just of Ackermann, Prot, Lemierre, and myself, returned to the breakfast room. We discussed further options and decided to agree to a 21% NPV loss, without further consultation with our creditors. I did not think it would be accepted by the official side, believing that it would take something near 30% to secure an agreement. I was wrong.

Ackermann was masterful, and Lemierre and I were astonished. The IMF staff member hardly said a word. Where was Lagarde? Where was her Deputy, John Lipsky? Nowhere in sight. When the French deputy nodded his concession, we stood, shook hands all around and walked to the door.

As we entered the hallway, I hesitated and pulled Lemierre aside. "Jean, there are many questions unresolved. Will this agreement be woven into the statement of the heads of state tonight, or will it simply be referenced? How will the officials mobilize the finances for the collateralization, and in what structure?"

He looked at me, touched my arm, and responded quietly in my ear, "Charles, let's go before they change their minds. We can sort out the details later."

I knew immediately that he was right, and we proceeded swiftly down the corridor to the elevator, out of the building, and into a car waiting for us. We were a bit cramped, the four of us, and we said nothing until we arrived at our hotel. We then jumped out of the car and congratulated one another on a "job well done," or so it seemed at the moment.

We briefed Hung and Mikis, and then engaged in a flurry of phone calls, dictation, and memo writing. We had little time to call each major creditor again individually, but we crafted two quick, similar memos— one to the Task Force, and one to the IIF Board seeking their immediate concurrence. Simultaneously, we called the CEOs of key creditors and Board members, including Henri de Castries of AXA; Enrico Cucchiani, the CEO of Intesa Sanpaolo; Paul Achleitner of Allianz; Frédéric Oudéa of Société Générale; Marcus Wallenberg of SEB (not a large creditor but a key Board member); Paco Gonzalez, Chairman of BBVA; and of course, the Greek and Cypriot banks. Based on feedback from the creditors, we decided to break one of the options into two different maturities, so there were five options in total, including the buyback:

1. A Par Bond exchange into a 30-year instrument,

2. A Par Bond offer involving the rolling over of maturing Greek government bonds into new 30-year instruments,

3. A Discount Bond exchange into a 30-year instrument,

4. A Discount Bond exchange into a 15-year instrument, and

5. A buyback program (the new option).

Each of the exchange options would be collateralized by 30-year zero-coupon AAA bonds, with the fourth option being only partly collateralized.

We maintained continuous liaison with Grilli throughout the afternoon and evening as the heads of state met, along with the leaders of the EU, the EC, the IMF, and the ECB. We had moved into the early morning hours of July 21, 2011. Resistance was emerging. Reportedly, when advised that the deal would only immediately cut Greece's debt by €19 billion, Dutch Prime Minister Mark Rutte balked. Finland also balked. There was inevitable confusion over the exact terms of the restructuring, and Lemierre and I volunteered to return to the building and brief the heads of state directly. Grilli contemplated this offer, but declined it, despite the lack of clarity in the room.

We had done an enormous amount of preparation and analysis and had marked up the total value of the private sector's "contribution" far from €51.9 billion to €54 billion as a result of the concession that morning. We had touched base repeatedly with all the ratings agencies and understood the actions that each would take. At the same time, creditor firm after creditor firm was agreeing to the deal as we worked the phones incessantly. We updated our offer with the latest data and list of supporting firms and submitted it to Grilli in the early evening. We had lined up all the key creditors, including BNP, Allianz, Deutsche Bank, ING, Intesa, and the key Greek Banks: Alpha, NBG, as well as the Bank of Cyprus.

Nevertheless, Grilli kept calling with more and more questions, each one of which we answered. We began to fear that "Merkozy" had lost their touch and would be unable to get it through, notwithstanding Trichet's support.

Despite the resistance, Merkel and Sarkozy—mostly Merkel—bulldozed it through. I was quite surprised that there was no strong resistance from the IMF, who fully understood that the debt reduction from the package would be modest. We nevertheless were all thrilled when Grilli signaled just before midnight that the heads of state had agreed to the package.

The banks, insurers, and pension funds would suffer losses, but they would be manageable. The EU and IMF would have to step up with additional funds, but that was inevitable with or without a restructuring of the privately held claims.

More important, we believed it would help halt the hemorrhage of both the Greek economy and the wider Eurozone. Italy had been on the precipice, and this should, in our view, remove the risk of default by Italy, at least temporarily. We had laid out a credible medium-term vision for Greece and showed that with some growth, the debt-to-GDP ratio would decrease from 170% to just under 100% of GDP. At the same time, we knew there were risks that markets could interpret this as a prelude to additional restructuring in the Eurozone, and put ever more pressure on other countries, especially Italy, but also Ireland and Portugal.

We sent out a press release outlining the "IIF Financing Offer for Greece" once it had been agreed (see Appendix 3). Concurrently, the heads of state issued a statement that announced a package of €109 billion, which "welcomed the measures undertaken by the Greek government to stabilize public finances and reform the economy, as well as the new package of measures, including privatization."

They lengthened the maturity of their own loans, and noted that "the financial sector has indicated its willingness to support Greece on a voluntary basis through a menu of options." The net contribution of the private sector was estimated at €37 billion, while in a footnote it was mentioned that the net contribution of the private sector for the full period 2011–2020 was estimated at €106 billion (Appendix 3).

We had insisted upon the reference to "a voluntary basis," considering that to be a crucial element of the entire exercise. The agreement also included improvements to the EU lending terms to Portugal and Ireland, comparable to those provided to Greece. And finally, a strengthening of the "firefighting" instruments of the EU was agreed by increasing the powers of the EFSF and the EMU.

I collapsed in my room around 3 a.m., a flood of thoughts running through my head. Was it possible that after months of frustration, of inconclusive discussions that could hardly be dignified by the word "negotiations," that it would all come together so quickly, with approval all the way through the heads of state? Would it really lead to the renewed growth and expansion for Greece that we had baked into our calculations? And how would the markets react? Would contagion to Ireland, Portugal, and especially Italy be stymied? And the most meddlesome question—had we reduced the debt sufficiently? While I welcomed the virtually unanimous comments by the private creditors that it was a job well done by the IIF, I could not completely put to rest the nagging sense that the events of that July 21 had been too easy.

CHAPTER 17

THE GREEK ECONOMY IMPLODES

**"Hope is an expensive commodity.
It makes better sense to be prepared."**

—Thucydides, circa 440 BC

We had arranged a press conference the next morning, but neither Joe Ackermann nor Jean Lemierre stuck around for it. Joe had to catch an early flight back to Frankfurt, and Jean an early train to Paris. Hung and Mikis joined me for a quick press briefing at the hotel, which had already been preceded by comments in the wee hours of the morning by various officials. Frank and Emily Vogl, a couple who were also a public relations team, had somehow managed to organize the conference from their base in Washington, coordinating with our team on the ground in Brussels. We were prepared for some skeptical questions, but it was manageable. It appeared that the press was as fatigued as we were.

I jumped in a car and dashed for the airport, hoping to make the late-morning plane for Washington. There were numerous requests that morning for TV interviews, but no time. I did, however, agree to be interviewed by Larry Kudlow on CNBC upon arrival in the US, as long as they sent a truck to my home. Larry and I had developed a good working relationship, and I thought it would be useful to give the deal a boost in the US media given the importance of the US market for the overall tone of global markets. As is often the case, Larry was quite energized over the agreement, but asked some probing questions over its ultimate success.

"Charles, can this historic move really help Europe turn the corner, or will it simply be another false start?"

I assured him confidently that this would turn the page on the Greek crisis and the broader problems of Europe, citing all the numbers that had been embedded in my brain about the deal. He kept pushing, but then I signed off, seeing Peixin behind the cameraman in my living room with a frown on her face—and understandably so. Our schedule that summer had been incessantly disrupted by the endless sounds of conference calls, sudden trips to Rome or Paris or Brussels, and frequent delays of meals as I had one more word with someone, often Jean or Joe. Finally, I was home, but sitting in front of a TV camera instead of reconnecting with her and the rest of the family.

We went for a long walk at a nearby park as I relayed the gist of the last few days, and she listened patiently. Finally, I realized it was time for me to stop and listen to her for a while. She had her own private equity advisory business, having spent almost twenty years in the field, and she was also exceptionally skilled at managing our household, which included virtually everything: finances, taxes, and the cat—a strange full-bred Bengal that was constantly violating the normal rules of cat behavior, if there is such a thing. The cat was a gift to our youngest son, Bryan, on his eighth birthday, for which Peixin has forever blamed me. She brought me up to date on things at home, and I tried to disconnect from Greece for a few hours.

The initial media, market, and policy reaction was positive. The *New York Times* noted that "after years of resistance, European leaders agreed on Thursday to reduce Greece's debt burden in a last-ditch effort to preserve the euro and stem a broader panic." That part of the article hit the nail on the head in my view—this was not just about Greece; it was "to preserve the euro." Unfortunately, the article got one item wrong when it said, "It will force many investors in Greek debt to accept some losses on their bonds."[1] If there was any beauty in this otherwise rather ugly and ungainly agreement, it was that the investors were not "forced" into anything. They chose to make the investment in the first place, and they chose to write part of it off under market and political pressure, to be sure, but nevertheless it was a choice. In the "Principles for Stable Capital Flows and Fair Debt Restructuring," the remarkable document put together in 2004 by a unique combination of creditors and debtors under the sponsorship of the IIF, the voluntary nature of any debt restructuring was considered essential. For many years, a debate had raged among economists, lawyers, and policymakers as to whether it was feasible in the capital markets of the twenty-first century to have a voluntary restructuring of sovereign debt. This demonstrated that it was indeed.

The article also noted that "financial markets in Europe and the United States rallied Thursday [the day of the deal] on news that a broad agreement was imminent." Papandreou also welcomed the deal, stating, "We now have a program and a package of decisions which create a sustainable debt management by Greece." CNN repeated that US stocks "surged on Thursday following news that European leaders reached an agreement to contain Greece's debt."[2] The Dow was up 153 points (1.2%), and the S&P added 1.4%.

The European markets were up the next day, July 22, but the Dow was down 43 points (.34%), and US markets began to refocus, as they often do, on another issue: the attempt by President Obama to reach agreement on a deficit reduction package and avoid a default by the US, shifting the markets' attention from one technical default to another. Which was the most important? It was hard to say. The tendency of the US Executive and Congressional branches to play chicken with the debt ceiling has sadly become a bipartisan tradition, despite the absurdity of it. S&P had announced a negative outlook on the US AAA rating in April 2011. On August 5, the S&P downgraded the US to AA+. This was no modest event, and in an ordinary world a downgrade of the US would have a much more serious long-term impact than that of Greece, as the US economy was about one hundred times the size of the Greek economy. In fact, global stock markets had reacted sharply on the US downgrade, declining between 5% and 7%, although Treasury bond yields actually declined. Meanwhile, we put forward a positive thrust on the July 21 deal. "This is a move toward reality for the markets, for investors, for Greece and for Europe," I was quoted as saying at the press conference on the morning of July 22. "This acceptance of reality is the first step toward moving to a brighter future."[3] What I did not realize was that this brighter future would take many years to emerge.

For a brief period after the deal was struck, the next steps unfolded in a surprisingly constructive fashion. Late on Friday, July 22, I talked to

Finance Minister Evangelos Venizelos, and we finalized plans for him to visit Washington the next week and mobilize support for the deal. Following his arrival, he met with a small group of senior bankers at IIF headquarters and did an excellent job of presenting the need for support of the agreement. Venizelos was an articulate speaker and had developed a dramatic style. During his speech that afternoon at the Peterson Institute for International Economics, a Washington-based think tank formed three decades earlier by my friend Fred Bergsten, Venizelos stated, "I'm finding myself in a battlefield of debt, deficit, and economic growth." He went on to state, rather convincingly, I thought, "All of us together—the IMF, the IIF, the American government, the European Union, the European Central Bank—need to send a strong and clear message: we have a program, we trust in its implementation and its prospects, and we will collectively achieve our goals."[4]

Messages of congratulations and support continued to cascade in from around the world. The Institute's Board of Directors was uniformly supportive of the deal, including Baudouin Prot, who had been so adamant just a few days prior that we should not go beyond a 15% haircut. Our Task Force was pleased also, taking their CEO or Chairman's support as a declaration that they had done a solid job.

I especially appreciated the statement issued by Zhou Xiaochuan, the Governor of the People's Bank of China (PBOC). As discussed earlier, Governor Zhou was one of the world's most capable central bank governors—and one of China's most effective economic policymakers. He had already been in the post for a number of years by the time of the crisis and had built a global reputation as a savvy central banker. He was consistently reform-minded, and he also knew how to position himself within Chinese political circles to preserve his credibility. He had been supportive of the IIF since he came to the bank in 2002. I had always interpreted his support as partly a recognition that our work with Chinese banks could facilitate their internationalization and progress—albeit gradual—toward global standards in crucial areas such as a risk management, governance, and transparency. We had worked closely with many Chinese banks over the years, bringing the largest ones into IIF's membership and involving them in our committees on risk management and many other activities.

On July 23, Zhou issued a statement of support: "This will help solve the Eurozone debt problem and maintain financial stability across the Eurozone and its member countries. It will also protect market confidence, boost a recovery and a strong, sustainable, and balanced growth in the European Union and the world economies." He added, "As a responsible investor in the international financial markets, China has always [maintained] its confidence in the Eurozone and the euro."[5] I smiled as I read the statement, but I also silently hoped we would not let him down.

Other respected financial analysts also issued constructive feedback. *Financial Times* journalist Wolfgang Munchau noted, "The best news relates to the decision on private sector participation. It is good that the Eurozone has come to closure in this tedious debate. The terms of the various debt exchange offers are still bank friendly, but not nearly as cynical as some of the earlier proposals." He continued, "Contrary to what the European Council said, the private sector participation will be a blueprint for things that are yet to come. Second Irish and Portuguese programs are likely. The northern Europeans will once again demand private sector participation . . . Thursday's argument succeeded in staving off collapse of the Eurozone. This is undoubtedly its greatest achievement."[6]

The reaction was also positive, even playful at times, in Greece. On July 28, a cartoon appeared in Greece's most popular daily, *Kathimerini*, showing Papandreou admonishing Venizelos for delivering to him George Dalaras rather than me. As virtually every Greek knows, Dalaras is one of the country's most accomplished and popular musicians, with over eighteen million copies of his albums sold. On this one occasion, however, Papandreou wanted the "other Dallara" to participate in his bond buyback!

It did not take long, however, for questions to be raised about the sustainability of the agreement. The *Financial Times*' "Lex" column concluded that "the haircut of only 21 percent would only lead to a reduction of Greece's total debt to GDP from 170% to 130%. A future, larger haircut looks unavoidable."[7] When I read this, I became quite uncomfortable, fearing its accuracy.

There were also questions about whether sufficient investors would participate. It did not help that we accidentally posted a list of participating banks on our website that dropped five names from the list. We corrected it shortly thereafter, but other analysts pointed out that "some less risk-averse bondholders with shorter investment horizons have reorganized potentially lucrative secondary market trading opportunities while they wait for more details to emerge."[8]

These were all fair points, but I had also dealt with widespread skepticism regarding the Brady Plan for months after it was launched. I knew

I Kathimerini, *Greece's popular daily newspaper, ran this cartoon in July 2011, featuring George Dalaras, the well-known Greek singer whose name is similar to my own. George Papandreou and Evangelos Venizelos had asked for me to be brought in for negotiations, and are frustrated to find singer George Dalaras at the office door instead. "There must be some mistake!" Papandreou exclaims. Sketch ©Andreas Petroulakis, published in I* Kathimerini, *July 28, 2011.*

the value of maintaining confidence in a plan of attack even in the face of criticism. And I knew there would be difficult points along the way. One press article stated, "'If you thought the French Plan was complicated,' says one banker involved in the talks, 'then wait till you have a look at this.'" The article went on to say "Another banker involved in the IIF talks with Greece argues that strong participation from bondholders is likely in part because the alternative could be worse."[9]

At the same time, the International Swaps and Derivatives Association (ISDA) issued a helpful statement providing support: "Credit default swaps on Greece plunged 500 basis points to 1500 . . . the biggest decline on record, down from an all-time high of 2568 basis points on July 18."[10]

It did not take long, however, for serious analysis to emerge from Wall Street that cast more doubts on the prospect of this agreement solving Greece's debt problem. JP Morgan published a note on July 25 that somehow suggested that we had underestimated the element of the haircut, disputing our choice of a 9% discount rate. We knew of course that any discount rate would be subject to challenge. Market rates for the 30-year Greek bond were near 12%, and JP Morgan used that as the discount rate, stating that the average haircut for investors would be 34%, not 21%.[11] On the other hand, Barclay's published a research note finding that the "effective haircut range" was 6% to 19%.[12] Both expressed serious skepticism regarding the ultimate success of the agreements, with JP Morgan forecasting a "forced" (involuntary) exchange on long-dated bonds, while Barclays called for more realistic privatization targets.

Another sign of uncertainty—and potential trouble—related to the IMF's financing role. Although Christine Lagarde had supported the package in Brussels, she was notably silent on the issue of the IMF commitment. They had already committed thirty-two times Greece's quota, the highest multiple of quota ever for the Fund. (Korea had been the second-largest at twenty times quota in 1997.)

During the remainder of July and August, we worked to build support for the restructuring within the investor community while the Greek government and its advisors prepared material for the debt exchange.

S&P cut Greece's rating to CC from CCC on July 27, 2011, considering Greece was in "selective default." We had fully anticipated this and were not particularly concerned. In addition, Moody's had warned on July 26 that Greece would be considered technically in default. At the same time, Moody's also said that the plan would benefit Europe "by containing the contagion risk that would likely have followed a disorderly default on existing Greek debt payment."

I was pleased to see this statement from Moody's. In fact, European bank shares had rallied on Tuesday, July 26, "as investors appeared to agree that institutions emerged stronger from the Brussels talks."[13]

Meanwhile, back on the home front, the Greek economy was not doing well at all. In June, Greece had missed a key Troika program target: the general government primary cash balance was -4.9% of GDP compared to the target of -4.3%. In order to respond to this negative fiscal development, on June 29 the Greek parliament approved "Medium Term Fiscal Strategy 2012–15 (MTFS)," which was already the fourth austerity package Greece had implemented. Among the key measures were aggressive commitments on privatization, pension cuts, and increased taxation.

Earlier in 2011, domestic demand and the labor market had been deteriorating, with consumption, savings, and investments all shrinking.[14]

It was not as if fiscal adjustment was not taking place. Since May 2010, the government deficit had been reduced by a remarkable 5% of GDP. But with unemployment rising and tremendous uncertainty surrounding the economy, both domestic demand and investment shrank. Greece's Public Investment Program experienced a significant cut as part of the effort to rein in expenditures.

The economy plummeted over the course of the summer. After a contraction in GDP of 10.4% on an annual basis in the first quarter, the second quarter showed a contraction of 8.5%, and the third quarter 6.7%.[15] The intensity of the recession was lessening, but it nevertheless was having a severe impact on employment. The unemployment rate, which had been 15.5% in March, rose to 17.8% in July, and 18.6% in August. Retail trade turnover collapsed. Withdrawals from the banking register were, unfortunately, accelerating from 8.6% in July, already a very large number, to 10.6% in August. See the following table for more detail on these crushing days in Greece.

State of the Greek Economy (July through Sept 2011)				
	Q1 2011	Q2 2011	Q3 2011	Q4 2011
GDP Growth Rate	-10.4	-8.5	-6.7	-10.0
Final consumption expenditure of households (% change)	-15.4	-7.9	-5.9	-10.7
Gross fixed capital formation (% change)	-18.1	-15.8	-9.3	-23.7
Unemployment rate	15.5	16.8	18.5	20.7
Government deficit (% of GDP)	-8.6	-13.7	-10.2	-8.1
Government gross debt-GDP ratio	154.9	157.8	163.6	171.3
Manufacturing production (% change)	-5.8	-5.6	4.2	-8.2
Retail trade turnover (% change)	1.0	-4.7	-0.3	-3.9

	Jul	Aug	Sept	Oct	Nov
Unemployment rate	17.8	18.6	19.1	20.2	20.6
Manufacturing production (% change)	6.6	-4.3	4.5	-10.0	2.4
Retail trade turnover (% change)	2.0	-0.8	-2.0	-0.3	-.08
Inflation rate (2009=100)	2.4	1.7	3.1	3.0	2.9
Bank deposits (% change)	-8.6	-10.6	-16.3	-18.2	-17.7

Sources: Eurostat; Bank of Greece

The bad economic news began to flow back both to us at the IIF and via global markets as we pushed ahead on our path of restructuring. On August 15, we sent out letters to more banks seeking additional support for the July 21 deal. At that time, we had lined up thirty-six financial institutions and other holders representing a total of approximately €68 billion to support the deal. This was meaningful progress since July 21, but still represented only approximately 50% of all Greek bonds eligible for the exchange, and we knew we had a lot of work to do. Jean Lemierre and I, with the ever-present support of Hung Tran and Mikis Hadjimichael, spoke regularly during this period and divided up the various duties of outreach to firms not yet in the fold.

Some smaller investors were simply waiting to decide whether to opt out in order to seek full payment from the Greeks, while some banks were still studying the options and trying to understand them fully. For example, on August 15, we received a letter from Deke Bank asking for more details on the four options and for the concrete legal documentation. We knew that Greece's attorneys were working on it, but we had also become concerned at reports that some of the lawyers, as well as Lagarde, were seeking to persuade Greece not to proceed, but to launch a unilateral restructuring with a much larger discount.

A day later, on August 16, we put forward an innovative debt buyback proposal in a letter to Jean-Claude Juncker, Olli Rehn, and Venizelos. We proposed to double the resources available for the debt buyback from €20 billion to €40 billion through borrowing from non-EU surplus countries, such as China, Japan, Saudi Arabia, United Arab Emirates, and Qatar, with co-financing from the IMF.

We had informally tested the waters on this idea with their sovereign wealth funds, and there was openness, but our contacts revealed a great deal of concern—understandable concern—that the quality of Greek sovereign credit was far from the level that could generate support among these investors. There was still way too much uncertainty, and despite our efforts to mobilize European support for this—which would leverage the EU resources—there wasn't much willingness in Brussels or Berlin to join our effort.

There were other financial developments that were disconcerting as well. Finland had resisted putting the July 21 deal forward to parliamentary support without obtaining collateral from Greece. Olli Rehn, who was Finland's Commissioner in the EU and a strong supporter of the deal, was firmly opposed to this request by his fellow countrymen, but he was unable to dissuade them from this demand. These were signs of the growing sense of disintegration and the "every man for himself" attitude that one could observe in Europe in the aftermath of the global financial crisis. I was not altogether surprised that Finland would seek some backup for joining the new Greek support package, since they had been one of Greece's most vocal critics. Nevertheless, they had been asked to provide only €2.2 billion as part of the new Eurozone three-year funding for Greece.

There had been substantial resistance in Finland over the idea of continuing to participate in Greece's support program. The government had reportedly suggested at one point that Greece offer the Parthenon, the Acropolis, and its islands as a guarantee for the return of the loans.[16] When I heard this during the course of the early summer, I had told Hung that I was not too concerned; that this was just political posturing. I was dead wrong. Finland was not the only country having an allergic reaction to more support for Greece—the Netherlands, Austria, and others also exhibited strong antagonism. I felt that if they opened the door to one country for collateral, the system would break down, as others could be shamed into also seeking collateral. I was, therefore, rather astonished when the rest of the EU allowed this to happen. Greece became isolated, as was so often the case that summer, and my call to Venizelos in mid-August to caution him against the collateral arrangement fell on deaf ears.

"Charles, I have no choice. Without it, the July 21st deal will not go forward," he lamented.

The collateral for Finland ultimately came in the form of cash and AAA-rated securities, amounting to €880 million, along with its commitment of €2.2 billion over 40 years. No Parthenon, no islands, but nevertheless, a set of collateral assets that added to the fractures within Europe.

Most years, I attended a mid- to late-August gathering in Aspen, Colorado, called "Aspen Institute Program on the World Economy." I had been doing so since the early 1990s and generally found it to be a useful forum for exchanging views on the latest trends in the global economy. The format is a roundtable, with about forty participants gathered for a closed-door, off-the-record discussion. Over the years many distinguished economists, financiers, and officials had participated, including Paul Volcker, Nicholas Brady, Martin Feldstein, Alan Blinder, Gordon Brown, Stan Fischer, Agustín Carstens, Bill Rhodes, Francisco Gil Díaz, and Axel Weber. Often the sidebar conversations were as informative as the formal discussions.

At the August 2011 program in Aspen I sat down with Mark Walker, an accomplished attorney who was very experienced in sovereign debt restructuring. I first ran across Mark during the Latin debt crisis of the 1980s, when he represented many of the debtor countries, including Mexico. He was now part of Lazard's team, serving as Financial Advisor for Greece. Our talk revealed a decided distaste on his part for the July 21 deal, with Mark suggesting that Greece was not really intent on following through. I knew there was disquiet in the ranks, which was understandable given that Greece's representatives were given little voice during the actual July 21 negotiations. Nevertheless, I believed that Greece would proceed with the exchange. I called Venizelos the next Monday, and he assured me that they had every intention of following through. I was somewhat reassured, but nevertheless was left with a nagging feeling that trouble was brewing.

I was further comforted a few days later when I sat down with Jean-Claude Trichet in Jackson Hole, Wyoming, the gathering place of central bankers every late August. We grabbed a table outside in the crystal-clear late afternoon sun with the Teton Range of the Rocky Mountains in the background. This was our first face-to-face meeting since the drama of July 20 and 21, and I wasn't certain what to expect: the old friend whom I had known for decades, or the rather stiff central banker I had encountered in recent months. He was courteous, cordial, and as professional as ever, and I quickly realized that we had passed through these difficult months into a new phase.

"Charles, I still have reservations about the Greek restructuring, but with the protections which the ECB has received I am prepared to work with you and the governments of Europe to make this a success. I believe it is critical that we continue to affirm that this is an isolated case, and I appreciate the effort you have made in this regard."

We discussed the impact of selective default, and I brought him up to date on the process of preparing for the exchange. We discussed his pending departure from the ECB, only a little more than two months away, when Mario Draghi would take the helm of that organization. It had been an exceptionally challenging eight years for Trichet as the ECB's leader. The first few years were largely those of convergence among Eurozone inflation rates and relatively strong growth. 2008–2011 were, however, full of stress. He implemented extraordinary measures in early 2009 to support Europe during the period when market pressure was building on the entire Eurozone, with a special focus on Ireland.

Trichet had been a dedicated supporter of the euro from his early days at the Trésor. At the end of his term, however, he had seen how the Euro Area had struggled during the crisis despite his extraordinary efforts to stabilize the region. His work to support Ireland in fact had been remarkable—and ultimately successful. He had also raised interest rates twice during 2011, the first in April and second on July 7 while the crisis around Greece raged. Jacques Cailloux, Chief European Economist at RBS, described his view of this move to *Bloomberg News*: "Trichet has drawn a line in the sand on Greece and he's now focusing on the day job. The ECB has done more than governments have to prop up the Euro Area and it really is losing patience with political leaders. It's up to them to fix the problem."[17]

Trichet's move had been criticized by some European officials, coming as it did the week after Portugal had been downgraded to junk status by Moody's, Italy was struggling mightily, and we were desperately striving to stabilize Greece. Trichet had consistently emphasized, correctly, his responsibility for price stability. "There is no contradiction but full complementarity in doing what is our prime mandate, which is to deliver price stability."[18] It should also be noted that at that time, inflation was pushing up to 2.6%, well above the target rate of 2%.

At the same time, this left the ECB well ahead of the Federal Reserve, the Bank of England, and the Bank of Japan, and in risk of compounding the growing economic problems of the periphery.

However, Trichet had at the time affirmed the willingness of the ECB to continue to accept Greek, Irish, and Portuguese government bonds as collateral for ECB loans, which was in all three cases essential to their survival. This certainly helped mitigate the adverse effects of the interest rate increases.

As we sat on the deck at Jackson Hole enjoying a late cup of coffee, I asked Trichet if he had any regrets about the interest rate increases. He hesitated and then responded, "No, Charles, we were simply doing our job. Now it is time for governments to do theirs, and I will do what I can to support you if the governments step forward." I could not disagree, and thanked him as we concluded our discussion with a warm embrace.

The next day I left the invigorating air of Jackson Hole for the heavy, humid heat of Washington. Things were also heating up on the restructuring. The Greek Ministry of Finance, under the direction of Petros Christodoulou, issued a document titled "Letter to All Regulated Holders of Greek Government Bonds," also known as a letter of inquiry (LOI). The purpose was twofold: 1) to request bondholders to report to their national regulators their holdings of GGBs as of June 30, 2011; and 2) to gauge the interest of investors in participating in each of the four options, on a nonbinding basis. This was sent out via national finance ministers as the EU had requested, although we had doubts regarding the effectiveness of this approach. Would the various ministries mobilize to obtain and aggregate the data?

We reviewed the LOI and had a number of concerns. We decided to convey them immediately to Venizelos in a letter, emphasizing the following:

- Incorrect wording on the participation threshold of 90%, implying that Greece intended to pursue a less cooperative approach in the event of a shortfall;

- Lack of an explicit reference to the IIF financing offer;

- The LOI falling short of the firm official commitment of July 21 to provide financial support for debt buyback operations; and

- New restrictions imposed on Option 4 (the discount bond exchange into a 15-year investment)

Venizelos called me and we reviewed each concern. He expressed regret for the mistakes and omissions and said he would look into correcting them. When I hung up the phone, however, I thought that he was not in control of the process, and that the legal and advisory team, along with Petros, were not following through with unwavering support for the voluntary exchange.

CHAPTER 18

THE ACCOUNTING CONUNDRUM

"I am no weakling. I deal with Accounting."

—Unknown

On August 30, 2011, the International Accounting Standards Board (IASB) sent a letter to the European Securities and Market Authority criticizing the inconsistent way in which banks and insurers were writing down the value of their Greek sovereign debt. "This is a matter of great concern to us," said Hans Hoogervorst, IASB Chairman. Apparently, the IASB took a dim view of the efforts by some creditors to minimize their write-down of claims on Greece: "People familiar with the IASB's thinking said the intervention was unprecedented and reflected its belief that some European companies had not been making enough provisions for Greek sovereign debt losses.[1] The truth is that accounting issues had been a major source of contention in the events leading up to July 21. As much as all the European banks were reporting on International Financial Reporting Standards (IFRS) as endorsed by the EU, they are still open to interpretation in their application and, at that time, different countries' practice and application were quite varied. As financial experts are aware, accounting issues exact tremendous influence over the performance of a financial institution, especially so when they have consequences on the regulatory capital and the key ratios that are used for assessing balance sheet resilience. In fact, they are often more important than they should be, but that is simply the way it is. They can play a major role in how a debt crisis plays out.

A question that continues to hang in the now distant shadows of the Latin debt crisis of the 1980s is whether an accounting system aligned around mark-to-market values of Latin debt would have precipitated an earlier resolution of the crisis. While it is the height of counterfactual supposition, there are reasons to believe it could have. I recall with clarity the collective efforts that my colleagues and I at the Treasury Department, along with key staff at the Federal Reserve and the Office of the Comptroller of the Currency, made to preserve the fiction that the claims on Latin sovereigns could continue to be valued at book value. This avoided the pain of write-downs and artificially preserved capital as banks worldwide were seeking to avoid the reality that Mexico, Argentina, Brazil, Venezuela, and other countries outside the region (e.g., Cote d'Ivoire and the Philippines) were simply unable to repay their debt in full, notwithstanding the brilliant system designed by Jacques de Larosiere, Paul Volcker, and my colleagues at the Treasury in the early 1980s to keep the world economy going while the debt problem was being addressed. Perhaps the reality is that Jacques, Paul, and others fully realized that the debt was actually worth much less than book value but took the view that the banks were simply not adequately capitalized to deal with the reality of the Latins' lack of debt sustainability.

As explained in the chapter on the Brady Plan (Chapter 14), it was only when a secondary market for Latin debt developed in the late 1980s that there was a reliable benchmark for the "actual" market price of Latin debt. This was finally captured in a landmark transaction between JP Morgan and Mexico in 1988, in the so-called Aztec or Mexican bonds, which involved Mexico's issue of $2.6 billion of bonds in exchange at a discount. This transaction helped, a year later, to lay the basis for the Brady Plan. However, at the time, the accounting standards for US, European, and Japanese banks still allowed banks to maintain the value of their holdings at book value. This partly explains the anger and hostility of many banks in March 1989 when we at the Treasury announced the Brady Plan. They knew the game was up—they would be forced to recognize the losses between the actual value and a more realistic market value.

Of course, by 2011, the accounting world was a much more demanding world for bankers, and hiding behind book value was no longer so easy. Nevertheless, there was room for "interpretation," which meant that some holders of claims in Greece could, in effect, "fudge" the issue. The differences were further confused because, often, the accounting and regulatory classifications were conflated.

Contrary to popular misconception, private firms (banks, insurance, and pension firms) held the majority of claims—67.9%—on the Greek sovereign as we entered the first round of negotiations. The bulk of those, in turn, were classified as either "available for sale" (AFS) or "trading." However, many of the Greek banks, some of the smaller regional German banks, and the ECB itself classified the bonds as "hold to maturity" to avoid losses. The following table outlines the holders of the claims on Greek debt as of December 2010.

Table 1—Greek General Government Debt (As of Dec 2010) *

	Billion €
Total debt	328.6
Short Term (ST)	8.9
Long Term (MLT)	319.7
Debt to Official Creditors	31.5
Euro Area	21.1
IMF	10.4
Debt Held by the ECB	65.0
MLT debt held by the private sector **	223.2
of which:	
Greek banks	54.0
Greek non-bank sector	30.0
Non-Greek banks	44.5
Insurance companies	15.0
Investment advisors	9.0
Unidentified	777
Memorandum items:	
Privately held Greek bonds maturing (mid 2011–mid 2014) ***	57.7
Privately held Greek bonds maturing (mid 2014–end 2020)	92.3

* IIF negotiation documents (July 19, 2011)
** If both ST and MLT debt were considered, the total Greek debt held by the private sector was €230 billion, according to "Greece —An Approach to Private Investor Involvement"
*** For bonds maturing up to July 2014, estimated notional held by private sector was €68 billion (based on a separate IIF document titled "Project Phoenix 30 Jun 11 summary DRAFT updated post EU WG")

Sources: IMF Staff Report on Greece, July 2011; European Banking Authority; and IIF estimates

As described earlier, Charlotte Jones, our highly capable British accountant working for Deutsche Bank at the time, became the reliable "expert" on accounting issues for the Task Force. She quickly gained the confidence of the team, and even some of our French collaborators came to rely upon her, perhaps grudgingly. Charlotte conducted an analysis of the accounting classifications based on three scenarios.

Within each scenario, all bonds were held in only one classification. In all the scenarios, a voluntary debt exchange would occur in 2011 to restructure bonds maturing between 2012 and 2014, including 5-year extension at 4% coupon, with no credit protection:

- If *all* debt were classified as loans: **€6 billion loss**
- If *all* classified as trading: **€15 billion loss**
- If *all* bonds were classified as **AFS: €119 billion loss**
  - A loss of €45 billion for the 2012–2014 bonds
  - As the 2012–2014 bonds would be treated as impaired, all other Greek government bonds would also be impaired. This would lead to
    - Loss of €6 billion for bonds maturing in 2011
    - Loss of €1.6 billion for bonds maturing in 2015
    - Loss of €33 billion on €74 billion of bonds maturing 2016–2019
    - Loss of €11.4 billion on €24 billion of bonds maturing 2020–2024
    - Loss of €22 billion on additional bonds of €42 billion maturing 2025 and beyond
  - In aggregate therefore the loss under an AFS approach was estimated as €119 billion.
- IIF's impairment assessment had been shared with the official EU Summit on July 21, 2011:
  - If impairment was triggered on the €220 billion of Greek debt held in the private sector, the loss could be up to €77 billion for June 30 (second quarter)—based on 65% of average market price of bonds on June 30.

- In many jurisdictions (e.g., France, Netherlands, UK) the impairment would directly drive a regulatory capital impact of the same magnitude adjusted for tax. At an effective tax rate of 30%, this would be €54 billion and would have significant negative impacts on the Regulatory Capital ratios of the sector.

- If the restructuring led to a 20% reduction in NPV, an argument could be made to scale the impairment back to this level—thereby reducing the impairment to €44 billion.

- If the debt were restructured at 50% NPV reduction, then the losses for those participating would be 50%. Full impairment loss of €77 billion as of June 30 would then likely increase in subsequent quarters to €110 billion.

- Greek banks held 67% of the Greece sovereign holdings. Under a 50% NPV reduction, the loss for Greek banks would be almost €26 billion.

Accounting classifications determine whether the restructured assets are de-recognized and/or impaired, which ultimately shape repurchase prices and profit and loss (P&L) impact.

- **De-recognition**: According to International Financial Reporting Standards (IFRS), de-recognition occurs when the restructuring involves a change of substance of the assets, rather than extension or rollover. In other words, after restructuring, a bond may become a new instrument for accounting purposes or simply modifications of the original instrument.

- **Impairment**: It is possible to avoid impairment if there is increase in coupon or credit enhancement.

Complexity was also enhanced by differing accounting classifications:

- Depending on the accounting method, the restructuring of an asset may be reflected differently in the financial statement.

- Consequently, it was difficult to directly compare the accounting effects of different debt restructuring options.

- During our early July negotiations, the IIF proposed establishing several concurrent Working Groups (WGs), one of which would be on accounting issues.

The Working Group found the following accounting classifications of GGBs:

- A high portion were in the banking book—meaning they were in the available for sale (AFS) classification, although some talked about them being held to maturity (HTM).
- The rest were in the trading book—carried at fair value.
- As of July 2011, many Greek bonds seemed to fall under AFS.

P&L impact of the following sample scenario:

- Restructure bonds maturing between 2012 and 2014: 5-year extension at 4% coupon.
- Accounting assumptions: impairment occurs, but no de-recognition.
- Impact—AFS bonds likely to exert the biggest loss:
  - If *all* bonds were classified as **AFS: €119 billion loss**
  - If *all* debt were classified as loans: **€6 billion loss**
  - If *all* classified as trading: **€15 billion loss**

The fundamental point that could be derived from these various scenarios is that whatever classification a bank applied for their holdings of Greek debt—and there were many variations across jurisdictions, with many different tax treatments as well—the reality was that many banks would be substantially affected. The end quarter results for June 30 were bound to show a loss based on the market's continued downward pressure on the value of Greek debt. Thus, firms increasingly realized that there was nowhere to run, nowhere to hide.

Despite numerous efforts by individual banks and bankers to minimize the write-down, banks' second-quarter earnings, through their varied and bespoke interpretations of the "so-called" International Financial Reporting Standards (IFRS), were inevitably going to capture some, if not all, of the losses that were affected in the ongoing negotiations. Thus, in contrast to the debt negotiations of the 1980s, the accounting system provided wind at the backs of those who (myself included) wanted to move forward with a negotiated debt reduction for Greece. At times, it was painful to watch the contortions the banks put themselves through, often to no avail in the end. The collapse of Greek creditworthiness was unavoidable, and the sooner they recognized it, the better.

CHAPTER 19

ADJUSTING THE SAILS

"The pessimist complains about the wind; the optimist
expects it to change; the realist adjusts the sails."

—William Arthur Ward

As September arrived, we continued to hold out hope that the debt reduction operation could be successfully concluded in the fall and we would be done with it. I had occasion to discuss the situation with Paul Volcker on the night of September 3. Paul and I had birthdays near one another—of course separated by a couple of decades. His was September 5, mine August 25. Some years before we had begun having a joint celebration when schedules allowed. That year we had dinner at Daniel, the elegant Upper East Side French restaurant owned by Daniel Boulod. Paul was a man of great modesty when it came to personal financial matters, so he was hesitant to have dinner there, but we persuaded him that it was an important celebration—eighty-four years for him—and he rather grumpily assented. Joined by our spouses, Anka and Peixin, we had a wonderful evening.

Over dinner I brought him up to date on the situation in Greece. He listened carefully, and offered only a brief comment. "Dallara, I doubt you will get it done on the terms you agreed in July—things sound pretty grim to me. The economy has not stabilized." I pushed back, arguing that we still had momentum, but the seeds of doubt in my mind grew a bit.

Paul and Anka Volcker enjoying a birthday dinner together with Peixin and Charles Dallara.
Photo courtesy of the author

We sent our trusted Deputy, Mikis Hadjimichael, on a road show in early September to London, Paris, Frankfurt, Amsterdam, Madrid, Tokyo, Hong Kong, and Singapore, along with representatives from the three investment banks supporting Greece for the debt exchange (HSBC, BNP Paribas, and Deutsche Bank). On the whole, things went well, as holders of Greek claims were receptive to the exchange. Many were beginning to realize that a 21% haircut of their claims was a bargain under the circumstances. They asked many legal and technical questions, as was to be expected, but there was nothing to indicate fundamental problems with the deal.

Huge difficulties, however, emerged elsewhere. Key European leaders remained skeptical of the deal, and this bled into market sentiment. On September 11, in an interview published by *Die Welt*, German Economy Minister Philipp Rösler stated that default should be an option to solve Greece's debt problem.[1] This was preceded by ill-advised comments by Mark Rutte, the Dutch Prime Minister at the time, and his colleague Jan Kees de Jager, the Finance Minister. In an op-ed published on September 7 in the *Financial Times*, they wrote that "countries that systemically infringe the rules must gradually face tougher sanctions and be allowed less freedom in their budgetary policy. . . . Countries that do not want to submit to this regime can choose to leave the Eurozone."[2] However sensible this may have sounded to the Dutch citizens for whom it was likely intended, there were two problems with it: 1) There were no provisions whatsoever for a country to exit the Eurozone, nor for a country to be expelled from the Eurozone. 2) This statement by the Dutch lenders added further to the bearish sentiment regarding the Greek debt restructuring, which had been agreed to by all Eurozone governments, including the Dutch, only six days prior.

Other officials continued to pile on. Hans-Peter Friedrich, Germany's Interior Minister, stated that "Greece should withdraw from the Eurozone if the country does not fulfill bailout conditions." Volker Bouffier, Governor of Hesse and Deputy Chairman of the Christian Democratic Union (CDU), Merkel's party added, "If the Greek government's austerity and reform efforts are not successful, we will also have to ask ourselves whether we need new rules to enable a Eurozone country to withdraw from the monetary area."[3]

We understood the frustration felt by northern European leaders. The Germans, the Dutch, and others were making increasing amounts of loans to Greece with little convincing evidence that Greek reforms were taking hold. Whatever the merits of their frustrations, it was obviously also part and parcel of the populism and nationalism that was spreading like kudzu through the world's democracies at that time. Their doubts further weakened market confidence in the July deal.

It was not the spreading negative commentary about Greece by European authorities that posed the most serious threat to the July deal— it was the alarming shrinkage of the Greek economy and the concomitant widening of the financing gap. The IMF seriously underestimated the negative effect of the austerity measures they had insisted upon. This mistake, however, did not just pose a problem for the durability of the July 21 agreement; it went to the heart of why the Troika program rendered a near-disastrous effect on the Greek economy, the Greek people, and Greek society. To understand the impact of this, one has to go back to the design of the original Troika program, and perhaps even to the IMF's basic approach to the euro crisis.

Let us start by focusing on the summer and fall of 2011, then look back before tracing the implications of these difficulties to the debt negotiations.

In June, as we were engaged in the first round of negotiations on Greece's debt, the Troika—comprising the International Monetary Fund, the European Commission, and the European Central Bank—was reviewing the overall state of the Greek economy and economic program. After more than a year under the initial Troika program, which started in May 2010, the Greek economy was in serious decline. In fact, after a slight uptick in the first quarter of 2011, when GDP actually increased by 2%, the economy shrank at an alarming rate of 7% in the period of April–June. But this was not adequately perceived by the IMF staff at the time, as actual data on key macroeconomic variables for that period were not fully available at the time of the review in June. In fact, the review appeared oddly optimistic on a number of fronts, and out of touch with the underlying damage being done through successive rounds of austerity. The Executive Summary began with the rather bold statement that "the programme of economic policies has shown to be appropriate to help Greece in reducing its macroeconomic and fiscal imbalances."[4] Certainly the fiscal imbalance was declining, but key macroeconomic imbalances were growing as the economy contracted. Total employment was falling by almost 6%, with the unemployment rate pushing upward to 16%. Private consumption also declined sharply, by 6% in the first half of the year, although the data available in June only suggested a 4% decline.

There were many factors that lay behind the sharp deterioration as the year unfolded. The political environment was highly unstable, and there was turbulence across the EU, with Ireland, Portugal, and Italy all simultaneously experiencing severe difficulties. Social unrest in Greece was clearly also a factor, and the tremendous uncertainty surrounding the handling of Greece's debt added yet another heavy layer of doubt that undermined investor and consumer confidence. Further, there were understandable doubts in many quarters about Greece's ability and determination to persevere in the face of such difficult conditions.

At that point, Greece had already applied a significant dose of fiscal restraint. Beginning in January 2010, initially under its own "Hellenic Stability and Growth Program," Greece had implemented, at least partially, four different adjustment programs.

Greece unquestionably had needed to rein in its unsustainable fiscal deficit, which, as indicated earlier, had swelled dramatically to 15.4% of GDP toward the end of the Karamanlis administration in 2008 and 2009. Major structural reforms were also long overdue. But the key question was the pace, balance, and sustainability of the adjustment effort, especially fiscal adjustment, in the context of a very unstable European economic and financial environment. Unfortunately, the adjustment path set forth by the Troika was neither sound economics nor sustainable politics.

By the time of the first Troika program review in August 2010, the first round of adjustment had clearly been implemented. This included successive increases in a range of taxes, in particular VAT. In the Hellenic Stability and Growth Program, the immediate tax increases were mainly one-off measures, such as a special levy on profitable firms, a special levy on property of high value, and higher taxes on mobile phones and gasoline. There were, of course, longer-term tax reforms outlined, as well as measures to mitigate tax evasion and tax avoidance. Their eventual success, however, was deeply questionable given the historical Greek aversion to paying taxes and the extremely weak Greek public administration. The program had a bold and dubious goal of increasing revenues as a percentage of GDP from 39.3% in 2009 to 45.7% in 2013. When Prime Minister Papandreou mentioned this goal to me and Bill Rhodes in Davos in late January 2010, soon after the publication of the program, we were taken aback by the idea that this was a practical path to restoring growth and stability, but we did not respond. Perhaps we should have.

Subsequent programs ratcheted taxes up further. The second program included a further hike in fuel prices and a number of VAT increases, including a further increase on food and medicine from 9% to 10%. The May 2010 package of measures, the first under the IMF-led official creditor community, involved another round of tax increases, such as yet a further increase in the VAT on food and medicine to 11%, and common goods from 21% to 23%. A host of other tax assessments were also put into play, including increases on real estate and, once again, on "profitable enterprises."

As these tax measures, along with expenditure cuts, were being implemented, more or less, the economy was already struggling. Quantitative performance criteria were met as of June, as the program had a strong start. By November, the program was broadly on track.

Nevertheless, problems had emerged surrounding the state of the economy. In November 2010, the IMF warned that "the GDP contraction has been slightly deeper than initially expected. . . . Fiscal revenue shortfalls thus far have been met through continued under-execution of budgeted spending. GDP declined by 4.5% year over year, 0.5% larger than expected. According to the IMF, the retrenchment was led by lower private consumption and investment."[5]

By early 2011, at the time of the third program review, the fiscal performance was remarkably perceived as "on track," despite multiple headwinds. As the IMF explained, once again it was "because the government under-executed the investment budget in order to offset revenue shortfalls and overspending at local levels."[6] Structured reforms, however, continued to lag, and the economy continued to struggle. It sank 4.5% for 2010, while Greece nevertheless managed to reduce the fiscal deficit by 5.25% of GDP in that same year. This was a massive adjustment and was much greater than the fiscal adjustments called for in Ireland and Portugal.

As our debt negotiations began in earnest in June 2011, fiscal adjustment stalled, and although structural reform was legislated, it was generally not implemented.

· In June, Greece missed a key Troika program target: the general government primary cash balance was -4.9% of GDP when the target was -4.3%.

In response to the negative fiscal developments, on June 29 the Greek parliament approved Medium-Term Fiscal Strategy 2012–15 (MTFS), or the fourth adjustment package. Its key measures included privatization of state assets, pension cuts, and another round of tax increases. Among them were an increase in property tax rates, a decrease in the tax benefits for heating oil and for investment, and another increase in VAT rates on non-essential goods.

During July and August, the cumulative effects of the repetitive rounds of fiscal adjustments were weighing heavily on the economy. Unemployment was continuing to grow, investment was shrinking, and all of this was exacting downward pressure on demand and gross domestic product. In the third quarter, the economy shrank at an annual rate of 6.7%, and in September, the unemployment rate shot up to 19%. The recurrent rounds of measures to raise taxes and reduce spending were having less and less effect on the fiscal deficit as the downward momentum of the economy—reinforced by the austerity measures—was overtaking the effort at fiscal consolidation.

The IMF, and the entire Troika, appeared either unable or unwilling to see that some of its policies were becoming counterproductive. Part of this was a continued underestimation of the depth of the recession that Greece was experiencing. In July they had estimated that real GDP would decline for 2011 by 3.8%. The actual contraction turned out to be 10.1%, an enormous undershoot.[7]

Despite additional efforts by Greece, fiscal consolidation inevitably slowed as the shrinkage in the economy outpaced efforts at fiscal adjustment. In September, before Greece was allowed to receive the €8 billion tranche from the first IMF-led support package, the Troika demanded yet another round of measures: €1.7 billion of new measures to meet the fiscal target of 2011, as well as a €4 billion tax increase and spending cuts for 2012.[8]

After some debate, and resistance in Greece, the Greek government conceded. On September 12, they announced a new "prosperity" tax to help cover the €2 billion fiscal shortfall of 2011.[9] The government also expedited the parliamentary vote on the 2012 budget. Despite these measures, Lagarde threatened on September 15 that the IMF would not disburse the next tranche if Greece did not deliver more implementation.[10]

By the time negotiations resumed in September over the €8 billion disbursements, the patience of the Greek people was wearing thin. On September 12, there was more unrest in the streets, and on September 20, an unruly protest by government workers.[11]

The new measures were extremely demanding of Greece, as they involved further adjustment equivalent to a total 3% of GDP. They included:

- A further reduction of 20% in public sector salaries (in addition to the 15% already implemented for the civil service and the 25% cut in the public enterprises). These wage cuts were combined with a structural change in the public sector wage grid that ensured long-term savings and public sector productivity improvements.

- A further 4%, on average, cut in pensions (in addition to the 10% already implemented).

- The creation of a labor reserve to which thirty thousand public sector employees would move by the end of 2011.

- The application of the rule of one recruitment for every ten retirements for the duration of the Medium-Term Fiscal Strategy.

- Significant tax expenditure cuts of 0.6% of GDP implemented retroactively from January 2011.

- The introduction of a property tax to be collected via the electricity bills mechanism with an annual yield of 1.1% of GDP for the duration of the Medium-Term Fiscal Strategy.

As we watched the downward spiral of the Greek economy, we knew that this would further weaken the chances of closing the debt restructuring on the July 21 terms. In early September, IIF staff colleagues discussed our concerns with the IMF staff, but to little avail. They refused to acknowledge that the IMF-induced measures were adding to the recession, and of course they had never been fans of the July 21 deal, so they were not at all concerned about the risk of undermining it. Furthermore, we all knew that slower growth meant a larger financing gap and that they would ask for a larger haircut from the banks in order to cover a significant portion of that gap.

Jean Lemierre and I talked in early September and agreed that the ground was beginning to shift but felt that it was premature to reopen talks. I called Venizelos on September 11, confirmed that he would be presenting a keynote address at our Annual Meeting in late September in Washington, and discussed the overall economic and financial situation with him. He reassured me that despite the difficulties at home, things "were on track." He stated that they were working out the details in the exchange offers with their attorneys and investment bank advisors.

Nevertheless, when I got off the phone, I felt uneasy once again. Were things really "on track"? Venizelos had sounded under pressure, which was completely understandable. But the tone of his voice conveyed less confidence than his words. I concluded that there was little to do, but I nonetheless called Hung and Mikis into my office, briefed them on the conversation, and asked them to start doing some quiet thinking about new debt restructuring options. They were not surprised at all and were quickly off to contemplate the matter and develop options.

Our concerns proved to be well-founded. On September 23, just two days before Venizelos was scheduled to speak at our IIF Annual Meeting in Washington, a report leaked that Greece was considering alternative scenarios to "resolve the issue." A fresh round of labor strikes was unfolding in Greece, and popular resistance to another set of budgeting cutbacks grew. Venizelos was reported as having told Socialist deputies that he saw "three scenarios . . . including one involving a 50% haircut for bondholders."[12] A government spokesman promptly issued a denial, stating that "All other discussions, rumors, comments and scenarios, which are diverting attention from this central target and Greece's political obligation . . . do not help our common European task."[13]

Two days later, before Venizelos's speech, Joe Ackermann, Jean, Hung, and I met with him privately to have a frank conversation. Venizelos

German Finance Minister Wolfgang Schäuble delivering a stern message to the assembled bankers at the IIF Annual Meeting, September 24, 2011. © 2011 Institute of International Finance, Inc.

could be eloquent, but often he laced his eloquence with drama. This was the case that day. He described the pressure building on him from all sides: protests on the streets, the IMF breathing down his neck for more policy measures, parliament resisting, and the markets showing little confidence in either the debt agreement or the Greek economy itself. Greek debt was being priced at near-default levels. Nevertheless, he assured us that the agreement would be ready to come to the market for creditors to choose their option soon.

We were at least momentarily somewhat reassured, and he gave a strong speech to the three hundred or so assembled bankers gathered to hear him. I remained hopeful, but at the same time I could feel the deal slipping away from us. The crowd over lunch gave him polite applause, but it was far from the rousing response Papandreou had received at our Membership Meeting in Vienna, Austria, in June 2010, only fifteen months prior. Of course, Venizelos's speech was not the only important moment at the 2011 IIF Annual Membership Meeting. The day before Venizelos spoke, German Finance Minister Schäuble had presented his own views and they were, predictably, quite stern. As Landon Thomas Jr. of the *New York Times* put it, Schäuble argued that "because banks had made bad lending decisions, they shared the blame for Greece's predicament and should also share in the cost of resolving it."[14] It was hard to argue the point, but it contributed to growing doubts about the sustainability of the July agreement. Juxtaposed against these two speeches was a wonderful tribute to Trichet. Senior officials and bankers from far and wide joined us on Saturday the 29th to honor Trichet as he stepped down from the ECB after a remarkable career of over three decades in global finance. Despite the differences of views and tense moments of the past year, there were few people who had contributed more to the stability of the global system in the preceding years than Trichet, and the crowd gave him a standing ovation, putting aside for the moment the perils of Greek debt.

As we moved into the fourth quarter, the situation became dire. The contraction of Greek GDP intensified as the program significantly constrained disposable income and domestic demand.[15] On October 2, the Greek government announced that the economy would shrink by 5.5% in 2011, while the budget deficit would be 8.5%, much higher than the target agreed with the Troika, as the exceptionally weak economy outpaced government revenues.

(Left to right) Paul Volcker with Toyoo Gyohten, former Vice Minister of Finance for International Affairs in the Japanese Ministry of Finance and former Chairman of the Board of the IIF, congratulating Jean-Claude Trichet, President of the European Central Bank, on his many years of distinguished service. September 2011. © 2011 Institute of International Finance, Inc.

Paying tribute to Jean-Claude Trichet (right) at the IIF ceremony in his honor. © 2011 Institute of International Finance, Inc.

The IMF, EC, and the ECB refused to disburse funds in light of the shortfalls, adding further to the already swirling doubts that Greece could avoid an outright default. Greece's supply of available liquidity was down to less than one month.

Against the background of these debilitating developments in the Greek economy and throughout much of the periphery of the Eurozone, the bureaucratic machinery of Europe was grinding away. A critical part of the July 21 deal was the amendment of the European Financial Stability Facility (EFSF) to increase the financial scale of the EFSF and to provide it with the scope for new long-term financing. The EFSF would be increased in size from €440 billion to €780 billion. There were other amendments needed as well, including authorizing the granting of loans for the purpose of recapitalizing financial institutions. Understandably, these amendments needed approval in national parliaments. The pace of such approval was, however, agonizingly slow. As the *Economist* pointed out in an October 1, 2011, article, "All 17 members have a vote on key decisions, which must be then ratified by unruly parliaments. Now the Eurozone is trying to redesign itself even as it sinks—and every country is wondering whether to help others or save itself."[16]

Pressure was growing on Trichet to buy unlimited amounts of sovereign bonds in the secondary market if a solvent country was under pressure.[17] However, there were a number of problems with that idea. In particular, he wisely understood that it would take pressure off creditor and debtor governments to bear their responsibilities to solve the crisis. Furthermore, Germany would never have supported the ECB taking such a drastic step, even if it brought some degree of stability. I felt that there were times when Merkel understood the need for more dramatic decisive action, and perhaps this was one such time. But she was held back by her proclivity for small steps even in the face of large problems. As the *Economist* put it, for her "Europe is a cost-benefit calculation rather than historical destiny."[18]

I consulted once again with Hung and Mikis. They confirmed that with the collapse of the Greek economy and the widening of the financing gap, the July 21 deal no longer looked credible or sufficient. More would be needed by both Greece and the creditors to stabilize the economy and market sentiment. Of course, the "more" that had been asked of Greece over the last six months was actually *increasing* the gap by draining the economy of further growth and revenue. I knew where the extra adjustment would come from—the private creditors—so I asked Hung and Mikis to advance their development of options for our consideration, and immediately called Lemierre. He agreed that it was time to reopen talks, but we were concerned that we would be dragged toward an unacceptably large haircut.

On October 3, I called Ackermann to discuss the increasingly grim outlook for Greece, and indeed for all of the Eurozone. We both realized that the ground was shifting and that we had little choice but to move with it. He authorized me to make some calls to explore how other members of our Task Force felt about the situation.

This was not just a European crisis. The Dow Jones Industrial Average and S&P 500 both were falling to their lowest closes to date in 2011, while NASDAQ hit its lowest end-of-day figure since September 2010. On September 30, the Dow was off 2.36%, with the S&P down 2.85%. The prospect of turbulent times ahead in Europe—after Greece admitted that it would not hit its deficit target—significantly upset the global markets.

It was not only Greece that was weighing on market sentiments. Italian Prime Minister Silvio Berlusconi announced his intention to propose a stimulus package. This was not received well by either his Minister of Economy and Finance, Giulio Tremonti, or the markets, which feared that Italy would end up with an even greater fiscal deficit—one that Italy could ill afford.

It was becoming obvious to most analysts and observers of the Greek economy that the fiscal aspects of the adjustment package were becoming counterproductive. In fact, many distinguished economists had warned of the risks of excessive fiscal tightening amid a recession. In his sharp critique of this period, Ashoka Mody, a former Deputy Director of the IMF's research and European Department, framed the challenge facing Europe: "Policymakers face a dilemma. Addressing the debt problem required governments to undertake austerity measures—to raise taxes and reduce spending—but austerity would lower the demand for goods and services, which would cause income to fall and further setback growth prospects."[19] The quandary for Greece was, arguably, even greater. And yet, fiscal austerity had become a mantra throughout the Eurozone. As Mody put it succinctly, "austerity had become a part of the Eurozone's identity."[20]

During the Latin debt crisis of the 1980s, in virtually every case, fiscal discipline was needed as a crucial pillar of economic adjustment powers to reduce both the balance of payment financing gap and the fiscal deficit, and to rebuild confidence among creditors. This key element of the debt strategy had not really changed. But in the Latin debt cases, exchange rate adjustment and basic monetary policy were also key elements of the adjustment process.

In the cases of Greece, Italy, Spain, and Portugal, they had forsworn the option of having their own currency in the interest of price stability, putting much of the pressure for adjustment on internal productivity gains and relative prices. For a country such as Greece, with an overblown public sector and few sectors of the economy that were competitive in global markets, the process of adjustment was exceptionally painful.

Another difference was that the pace of fiscal adjustment during the 1980s in Latin America was moderate compared to what Greece was experiencing. Much has been written about the pace of Greece's fiscal adjustment being too severe. In fact, the IMF has even acknowledged it. A rather remarkable report issued in July 2016 by the IMF's Office of Independent Evaluations concluded that "the IMF-supported programs in Greece incorporated overly optimistic growth projections. More realistic projections would have made clear the likely impact of fiscal consolidation on growth and debt dynamics."[21]

The report went on to say, among many other criticisms, "that perhaps the most conspicuous weakness of the IMF-supported programs in the Euro Area was their lack of sufficient flexibility. As a result, an increasingly unworkable strategy was maintained for too long. In Portugal as well as in Greece, where GDP contracted more than anticipated, the nominal deficit ceiling was routinely tightened in order to achieve the original targets."

Additionally, the report said that the overly optimistic assumptions regarding privatization revenues as well as the "deeper than expected contraction of output caused the underlying debt dynamics to start overshooting program targets by a large margin. . . . The original growth projections were marked down substantially early in December 2011."[22]

In other words, the IMF program was driving the economy deeper into a hole. At one point, as Lemierre and I mused over the problem in Paris over a late-evening glass of wine, I described this phenomenon as follows: "It is like trying to chase a rabbit down a hole. Rather than catching the rabbit, it simply goes deeper into the hole." Looking back, I am not certain of the relevance of this analogy. But it sure made sense at the time.

What the IMF did has been explained in technical terms as underestimating the "fiscal multiplier"—the extent to which cuts in government spending have a negative impact on the economy, or the ratio of a change in national revenue to the change in government spending that causes it. The IMF staff used a .5 multiplier. The report concluded, however, that "this assumption was inappropriate for the Euro Area program, given the country's inability to ease monetary policy let alone devalue the currency."

In October 2012, only a year after the sharp contraction of the fourth quarter of 2011, IMF Chief Economist Olivier Blanchard and a colleague had published a paper that squarely stated that the IMF forecasts "significantly underestimated the increase in unemployment and decline in domestic demand associated with fiscal consolidation."[23] As Mody summarizes, Blanchard estimated that if the economy was already weak and the government cut spending (or raised taxes) by a euro, GDP would fall by nearly two euros; thus the fiscal multiplier during a period of contraction was close to 2.0, and not 0.5 as the IMF had previously assumed. Aggressive austerity was causing GDP and hence tax revenues to fall far too rapidly, and so, paradoxically, austerity was increasing the burden of repaying debt.

The media drew considerable attention to this paper. A January 3, 2013, article by Howard Schneider of the *Washington Post* wrote that "The IMF's top economist today acknowledged that the Fund blew its forecasts for Greece . . . because it did not fully understand how government austerity efforts would undermine economic growth."[24] Binoy Kampmark of the *International Policy Digest* headlined his article "The Errors of Austerity: The Blanchard Prescription."[25]

The publication of the report of the IMF's Office of Independent Evaluations three and a half years later created something of a firestorm. "IMF admits disastrous love affair with euro and apologizes for the immolation of Greece," wrote Ambrose Evans-Pritchard in the *Telegraph* (July 23, 2016).

Christine Lagarde, the IMF's Managing Director, acknowledged that 2011 was a "lost year" for Greece, partly because of miscalculation by the

EC and the IMF. Later, in November 2016, Lagarde stated "We have acknowledged one mistake, which had to do with the fiscal multiplier."[26]

One other reason that the IMF and the Troika's adjustment strategy for Greece did not work was the fact that despite the very large financing package provided, the balance between adjustment and financing was not appropriate and was unduly tilted toward adjustment. To make things worse, given the Eurozone political constraints in providing additional financing, any shortfalls in fiscal performance were not addressed, even in part, with more financing but with more adjustment, causing an even more severe recession—driving the rabbit deeper into the hole, to use our analogy.

A close reading of the report by the Office of Independent Evaluations reveals many other mistakes made by the IMF and its sister organizations in the Greek drama, the EC and the ECB. Most of those "mistakes" appear to relate to the work of the IMF. This is especially unfortunate since the Fund was indisputably in the lead on most, if not all, macroeconomic issues, especially program design.

Among the other shortcomings noted were the following:

- The decision to provide exceptional financing to Greece—well above the existing guidelines—without transparency.

- The lack of a serious IMF Board discussion about how the IMF could or would engage with a Euro Area country with an adjustment program.

- The lack of balanced, insightful surveillance of the Greek and other crisis countries in the years leading up to the crisis, as I have already described in detail.

- The lack of a balanced critical assessment by the IMF of the euro and the vulnerabilities of the Euro Area.[27]

From the announcement of Greece's fiscal deficit explosion in the fall of 2009, the IMF clearly should have been on the alert. At least markets started to wake up, as spreads widened steadily in the first half of 2010. But not the IMF. For the IMF to acknowledge in 2016 that "no Executive Board meeting ever took place to discuss, let alone articulate, how the IMF would engage with a Euro Area country in a program relationship" was stunning.

As mentioned earlier, I served on the IMF Board during virtually the entirety of the Latin debt crisis, first from August 1982 to September 1983 as the Alternate Executive Director, and then as the Executive Director from April 1984 to January 1989. At the outset, there was also a great deal of uncertainty about how the IMF should approach these countries. How much should the IMF contribute financially? How to ensure that the bank creditors—who had in many cases lent rather irresponsibly to the sovereigns—would "pay" their fair share of the burden of avoiding default and catastrophe? What would be the role of the US, the IMF's largest member and the country most geopolitically aligned with Latin America? What would be the right balance between economic adjustment by the Latin debtors, the multilateral institutions and others in the official sector, and the private banking community? What should be the appropriate pace of fiscal adjustment, since fiscal imbalances lay behind most of the debt challenges facing these countries? How could stopgap financing be mobilized while a program of adjustment measures supported by an IMF standby arrangement could be negotiated?

These were among the many issues swirling in the fall of 1982 as the debt crisis erupted.

At the onset of the crisis, there were very few guideposts. Jacques de Larosiere took charge, and as indicated earlier, he did so in a very consultative way. He became, in effect, an orchestra conductor, knowing when to bring each instrument into the concert. For example, in the early years, it became necessary to develop bridge finance arrangements that would cover anywhere from three weeks to two months of urgent financing needs in order to help ensure that a country did not go into default while an IMF program and a restructuring of the debt were being negotiated.

He therefore launched a process of urgent consultation with key central bankers, especially Paul Volcker, Karl Otto Pöhl of the Bundesbank, Fritz Leutwiler, who ran the Swiss National Bank, and Gordon Richardson of the Bank of England. Through the process, the Bank for International Settlements (BIS) was mobilized to provide bridge financing. Simultaneously, de Larosiere engaged in close discussions with the US Treasury, the US Executive Director of the IMF (at the time, Richard Erb), and the IMF Board.

Numerous meetings were called in the fall of 1982 as well as continuing in 1983, in a conference room just outside de Larosiere's office. Organizing the meetings there meant that they could not be considered formal board meetings—at least not at that stage—but rather took the form of informal briefings and consultations. At times, he would invite key bankers into the meetings, bringing them into the picture at an early stage in order that they would feel they too had partial ownership of the process and eventual outcome.

As the Latin debt strategy took shape under the leadership of de Larosiere, every group involved was asked to share part of the burden but was also made to feel consulted at every step along the way.

In the fall of 2011, that was certainly not the atmosphere. As we moved into October, we laid plans for another round of negotiations, but there was not a sense of teamwork among the major groups—the private creditors, the IMF, the regional institutions, and Greece. During our first conference call of the Task Force, which took place on October 5, we tried to move forward with a few ideas on how to bring down Greece's debt ratio without generating substantially higher losses for the creditors. Hung and Mikis had prepared some options for consideration, and there was a rather unenthusiastic exchange over them.

There were two key questions: Could we hold the course on a "voluntary" negotiation, according to the "Principles for Stable Capital Flows and Fair Debt Restructuring" that we had devised in 2004, or would the pressure build on Greece to declare a unilateral debt restructuring? And, secondly, what size of a haircut would be needed to satisfy the IMF and the Germans?

On the first point, we knew there were views in both the IMF staff and within Greece's legal counsel, the law firm Sherman and Sterling, that Greece should not go to all the trouble to negotiate an agreement with their creditors, but unilaterally announce a restructuring, backed by the IMF and possibly the ECB and the European Commission, that would radically reduce the debt.

That method had been used by Argentina in 2003 and 2004, surprisingly, and disappointingly, with the support of the US Treasury. It was viewed by some as a "victory" for the debtors, and even a blueprint for future negotiations. But Argentina was, as explained earlier, frozen out of the international capital markets for more than a decade following their actions due to lawsuits, so this approach was hardly an appealing precedent for Greece or other debtor countries. Nevertheless, it had some appeal, partly romantic and naïve, to some of the advisors of debtor countries.

The second issue, that of the extent of the haircut, was the center of our concerns. We all knew that we would have to move, but there was great reluctance to move substantially for fear of getting dragged to an extremely large "haircut." At that first call, therefore, we focused more on broad strategy.

We lined up meetings in Europe over the next week, ready to look for a way forward. Hung, Mikis, and I first headed to Paris to meet with Lemierre, key bankers, and officials there. On Monday, October 10, we met with senior bankers at Credit Agricole, one of France's largest banks, albeit heavily domestic in its activities and orientation. They were reluctant to give more ground. I then stopped by to talk with de Larosiere again.

I found his advice useful and timely: "Greece clearly needs more debt relief, and it is becoming increasingly urgent as the Greek economy is contracting and the markets are increasingly anxious about a hard Greek default, possibly followed by a default of Italy. Time is of the essence, my dear friend," he said, in his courteous but forceful fashion. He added, "It is essential, however, that you fully negotiate a new debt restructuring, and not allow Greece or the IMF to take a unilateral approach. We put too much work into the Principles to allow them to be ignored in this crucial case."

I assured him that we would not allow that to happen and thanked him for his advice. At the age of eighty-two Jacques was as sharp as ever, still possessing one of the keenest intellects in global finance. But as I walked out of his office, I felt that the road ahead would be very bumpy.

I then moved quickly to the Banque de France, where the Governor, Christian Noyer, awaited me. I had visited the Banque many times over the years and had never failed to be impressed by its ornate Renaissance architecture. Established by Napoleon Bonaparte in 1800, the Banque de France was housed in a complex mix of buildings dating back to the late seventeenth century. It is filled with beautiful paintings, such as three hunting scenes by Francesco Giuseppe Casanova, "brother to the famous libertine," as the Banque de France's website refers to Giacomo

Girolamo Casanova, the eighteenth-century Venetian known for his many liaisons.

Christian Noyer is a seasoned man of finance, having joined the French Treasury in 1976, the same year that I joined the US Treasury. He had risen through the ranks to become Chief of Staff to Finance Minister Jean Arthuis in 1995, and in 2003 was appointed Governor of the Banque de France by French President Jacques Chirac.

Christian was one of the most experienced central bankers in Europe. He was well aware of what was at stake for Europe as well as French banks. He greeted me warmly, and we sat down for a lengthy discussion. I briefed him on our thinking in the private creditor community, on our concerns about the IMF pushing too hard for an unacceptably deep haircut, and about the risks of a move toward unilateral debt reduction. He said, "Charles, I fully support you on the crucial importance of a voluntary debt reduction. This is vital for the system, and for the stability of Europe."

We exchanged thoughts on the stakes overall and the European economic landscape. He confirmed that the French economy was growing again after a sharp recession and negative growth of 2.3% in 2010. He was quite concerned, however, that it would slip back into recession if the Greek and Italian debt crises were not resolved cooperatively and in a timely fashion.

I asked him to use his influence in both Frankfurt at the ECB and with the IMF. "I will certainly do what I can, Charles," he said firmly as we wrapped up.

I scurried back to BNPP at 3 Rue d'Antin, where I had a 2 p.m. meeting with Baudouin Prot and Lemierre for a thorough review of the situation. Prot had put behind the tensions that had developed between us in July and greeted me with enthusiasm. A bright and intense man, he was constantly pushing us to take a firm stand on the many difficult issues we faced, and this occasion was no different: "We cannot give much more ground, Charles—we have already given a lot."

The next day, on Tuesday, October 11, we were off to Rome to resume the quest for a more meaningful dialogue with Grilli. We met him that afternoon at his office at 97 Via Venti Settembre, where the security staff were beginning to be familiar with us, mercifully simplifying our life somewhat by ushering us quickly into the building. It appeared that Grilli had been encouraged to find a way forward (by Rehn and Juncker?), but in reality, he had little to offer. We had a rather desultory discussion that led nowhere. Even our willingness to move forward toward a net present value loss of 30% seemed to produce little response on his part.

"I am still searching for guidance, Charles and Jean—please understand that this remains very difficult for me. Our situation in Rome is quite fragile, and I have to concentrate on stabilizing matters here."

We responded, with exasperation, that we understood, but that time was seriously running out. We left his office and repaired to our hotel. Jean and I knew at that point that we would have to reach out, once again, to more senior officials in Brussels and in capitals if we were to get anything accomplished. The situation had the uneasy feeling of a ship adrift, floating randomly with the winds toward the shoreline, heading for a grounding that could sink the ship. We learned that there was an EU/euro heads of state meeting slotted for October 25–26 and decided to aim for that. Jean and I made calls to various European officials as well as to our banking network. I scheduled an IIF Board conference call for October 14 after consulting with Ackermann, then headed off to Paris once again.

The next day Jean and I had lunch, just the two of us, to talk through our strategy. Our perspectives were quite similar, although I found him, perhaps predictably, more understanding of the mysterious ways of Europe working—or not working. I was frustrated with the inability of Europe to have anything approaching a coherent decision-making process on the critical matter of Greece. Jean assured me that "things would begin to come together," but I saw scant evidence of this.

What we did see were statements emerging from Brussels and other European capitals. "Losses for private investors on Greek debt . . . are likely to be between 30 and 50 percent, rather than the earlier agreed 21 percent, Eurozone officials said."[28] We were not pleased at the public speculation by officials that the range could go up to 50%. It was, however, somewhat comforting that the statements by unknown officials added that "The haircut will be set at a level compatible with the voluntary nature of the private sector involvement."

The speculation about a much larger haircut began to increase on October 14. Bloomberg reported that "European officials are considering a write down of as much as 50% on Greek bonds . . . as the key plank in a revamped strategy to combat the debt crisis. Political, technical, and legal constraints cloud the crisis' resolution strategy."[29]

Indeed, many uncertainties obscured the outlook, in particular the lack of a sense of direction within Europe. The French economy was now being put under scrutiny by the markets as French government bond yields widened by 17 base points to 3.13%, their highest yield since the formation of the euro in 1999.

Lemierre and I became quite concerned about the expectations that were building for a much larger discount, and we realized we would have to push back if we were not to be dragged into unacceptable levels of NPV loss. Of course, we both knew that another round of real negotiations lay ahead at some point, and that there would be tremendous pressure to concede more losses to the banks. At the same time, we realized there was much on the line. What exactly was our job? To negotiate the lowest possible loss for the banks? We had already done that, and it didn't work. So, what now? Surely it was, in part, to continue to protect the interests of our banks, insurance firms, and pension funds who had invested so heavily in Greek bonds, notwithstanding the apparent blindness with which some of the lending took place. But as former government officials we also realized that our obligations went beyond that. We both had a deep respect for the rules, defined and undefined, through which the global financial systems operated. Some were spelled out in the Articles of Agreement of the IMF (first set forth in 1945), others in the framework of global banking regulation that had evolved since the first Basel Accord in 1988.

Still others did not need to be articulated formally. They were just understood, not only by Jean and me, but also by Hung, Mikis, and many of our fellow bankers who were aware that there was much more at stake than just bank earnings. Was the future of the Eurozone at risk? It certainly felt that way. Was it our responsibility to help save it? Perhaps so, but shouldn't officials take the lead on such a profound issue? We scheduled a Board conference call for the next day, October 14, in order to brief the other members on the state of play and take their temperature on the question of further restructuring. Ackermann began the call by focusing on the challenges that banks were facing with the new definition of capital based on stress tests, and the increase in core tier-one capital requirements to 9% in Europe. There was a discussion on whether, given the amount of market losses already taking place against exposure to Greece, Italy, Portugal, and Ireland, it would be feasible to raise the needed capital from the marketplace, or whether injections of capital from governments would be needed, as during the global financial crisis in 2008 and 2009. After an exchange around the board, there was no consensus, but I detected a growing level of concern. At this point, banks were facing a cascade of difficulties, particularly European banks. The 9% core capital increase was faster than that required by the Basel Committee on US, Japanese, and other banks. The tightening of regulatory requirements on banks globally was necessary after the crisis of 2008–2009, but I had serious doubts about the pace of it, especially in Europe. Not only were banks under stress due to the sovereign debt crisis in Europe, but the entire Eurozone remained in recession. The interest rate increases of July, along with the tightening of capital requirements and the recession, made it more difficult than ever to find creditworthy borrowers—or the capital to extend credits where they could be found.

"We will have to play hardball in these negotiations if we are not to be trampled upon," said one director. "The July restructuring has opened Pandora's box," he muttered. Of all the references to Greek mythology that I heard during these long negotiations, I disliked this one more than most. I believed that Pandora's box had actually, if inadvertently, been opened in a series of steps beginning with the entry of Greece into the Eurozone in 2001, continuing with the large amount of lending that took place from 2002 to 2008 under the notional umbrella of Germany, and then the third "evil," which was let out of the box with the exorbitant increase in Greece's fiscal deficit in 2007–2009. I actually thought we were, through these negotiations, trying to put the "evils," as the myth goes, back in the box. Whether we could, of course, remained to be seen. I bit my tongue during most of the Board discussion, realizing that at times it was best to let the discussion run its course.

Jan Hommen, the CEO of ING Bank, said he was surprised by the accelerated mandatory capital increase, and wondered whether the EFSF could help mitigate the losses from a deeper discount of Greek debt. Douglas Flint, Chairman of HSBC at the time, spoke to the issues of governments recapitalizing the banks as had been done in the US. He was concerned about government control. "I am also quite troubled by the risk of contagion from Greece spreading further to Italy and Spain," he stated.

Paco Gonzalez, the Chairman of BBVA, weighed in on the conversation to stress the importance of Merkel and Sarkozy stepping in to "ringfence" Greece by affirming the uniqueness of the Greek case and clarifying that there was no intention for either Italy's or Spain's debt to be similarly restructured. "We need a comprehensive plan that would deal with sovereign debt, recapitalize the banks, and involve more substantial use of the EFSF," he stated firmly. Paco did not speak frequently at Board meetings, but BBVA and the other leading Spanish banks were now also feeling the heat. Frédéric Oudéa, CEO of Société Générale and someone that I frequently consulted, spoke to the discussions within the French government about recapitalizing the banks, and stressed that we must follow through to resolve the Greece debt issue to regain the confidence of the markets. Nevertheless, he stated, "there remains a large gap between what the governments are seeking and our position."

Baudouin Prot stated that he felt we should move slightly higher to accept a large haircut by the creditors, but it "should be part of a broader solution that involves a major contribution by the EFSF and adjustments to the mandatory recapitalization requirements for banks."

I had considerable sympathy for his points, and certainly we were in fact expecting a major financial contribution from the EFSF—I believed that without it, a deal would not come together. I also fully understood that the increased capital requirements could not have come at a worse time, as the European economy was struggling mightily, and this would make it even more difficult to extend credit to worthy borrowers. At the same time, we sensed that the European regulators were not thinking in a holistic fashion, and they were not to be persuaded.

At that stage in the conversation, Ackermann asked me to summarize the call. I had tried my best, capturing the marginal additional flexibility that had emerged during the call, while also emphasizing the need for burden-sharing with the official community. Like many such calls during that era, it allowed the Board to express its views while venting its frustration, at the same time providing us scope to advance with Grilli— or whomever else we could find as a negotiator on the other side of the table. Such exchanges also strengthened Lemierre's and my hand, as we could authoritatively use the guidance from the Board to give little new ground during the negotiations.

The next day Lemierre and I met with Grilli at BNPP. I was somewhat disgruntled, as I was supposed to be on my way to Dubai. One of the initiatives I had taken soon after assuming the helm of the IIF was to reach out to the leading banks in emerging markets. When I took over, the IIF touted itself as a global association of financial institutions. The problem was that it was not truly global; 80 percent of its members were headquartered in countries of advanced economies—so-called "G10 countries."[§]

I was supposed to be in Dubai at our Mid-East CEO meeting, involving approximately fifty senior executives from across the region, and it was with great reluctance that I decided to withdraw from the gathering. Such events had been vital to the success of the Institute, but I also knew that the Greek negotiations had to take precedence. There was simply too much at stake for me to put the organizational priorities of the IIF above the future of Greece and the stability of the Eurozone. In addition, I also knew I had a superb Chair of Mid-East Department at the IIF—George Abed. George had a background, having served as the head of the Middle East Department at the IMF and subsequently as Governor of the Palestine Monetary Authority. He had come to the IIF in 2007 as part of a trio of high-quality talent acquisitions by the Institute; the other two were Phil Suttle, a highly seasoned senior economist from Barclay's, and Hung Tran, the Deputy Director of the Capital Markets Department at the IMF.

As Lemierre and I prepared to meet Grilli, we decided to push him harder to mobilize a response from the Eurozone. We knew that time was running out, and we also knew that Brussels was feeling the pressure from the marketplace. That morning there had been an article in *Bloomberg* stating that unnamed European officials were considering "write-downs of as much as 50% on Greek bonds, a backstop for banks and continued central bank bond purchases as key planks in a revamped strategy to combat the debt crisis."[30] There was also mention of a "five point plan foreseeing a solution for Greece." The article further said that "political, technical and legal constraints cloud the crisis solution strategy."

Lemierre and I could not resist a chuckle over this when we met in his office and he mentioned the article. As he sipped his espresso, I looked at him and said, "Do you think they realize just how disorderly this process has become?" He smiled and replied, "It is bad, Charles, very

§   The G10 actually comprises eleven of the West's leading industrial countries: Belgium, Canada, France, Germany, Italy, Japan, the Netherlands, Sweden, Switzerland, the United Kingdom, and the United States.

bad, but maybe it is not as bad as you think. Let us try our best to pull it together, as I believe they will work with us." I was not convinced by what I considered at times Lemierre's overconfidence in the messy process of decision-making in Europe. At the same time, I respected the fact that he knew the process inside out, and had insights that I could not possibly have.

With that, we got down to business and discussed our upcoming meeting with Grilli and next steps. As we did so, one of Lemierre's assistants knocked at the door and handed him a note. He looked at it, grimaced, and handed it to me. Even with my limited French skills, the message was clear: French government bonds had come under further pressure. The 10-year yield was up another 17 base points to 3.13%. The previous day's rise of 38 base points was the highest for French government bonds since the euro was introduced in 1997. This was increasingly not just a Greek debt crisis, not just a crisis of the periphery, but a full-fledged Eurozone crisis. Lemierre and I both knew that we either had to find a way to calm the markets in the days ahead, or the Eurozone could well fragment before our very eyes. It sounds overly dramatic as I write this now, but it was reality in October 2011. How could we convince Grilli and his cohorts in Brussels, Berlin, and elsewhere that we could not continue the pattern of waltzing around the mulberry bush? We decided we would not only push Grilli, but would also take it up the line as needed. I knew that US Treasury Secretary Tim Geithner was in Paris for the G7 meetings. I decided to call him after our meeting with Grilli and ask for his direct involvement.

At 6 p.m. we greeted Grilli cordially for a meeting among just the three of us. I had met Grilli bilaterally a number of times, but as we were in Paris, Jean and I hoped we could double up on him.

As Lemierre sat down in his elegant office, he jumped right in, delivering a stark message to Grilli. Either we finalize a new debt restructuring in Brussels at the upcoming Euro-Area Summit on October 25, or we risked that not only Greece, but Italy as well, would be swept away by the tides of contagion that were sweeping through Europe. I added that it had to be done on a voluntary basis if we were to avoid destroying the potential to return Greece to the capital markets after the restructuring.

Grilli agreed, stating, "Jean, Charles, I know you are right on both counts. But firewalls are needed. We need to protect my own country, as well as Spain and Portugal, from being infected by a Greek default. I was supportive of the July 21 agreement, and with a deeper Greek recession than we had anticipated, I know we will need a larger restructuring and that this will require more support from the official sector. However, we do not have a commitment to support a larger private sector restructuring. Furthermore, I do not believe the firewall is sufficient to protect my country and other vulnerable economies from the inevitable pressure for restructuring our debts. Jean, Charles, we cannot let that happen."

We could not seem to advance this play into the final scene of the second act. Despite the growing market tumult, Grilli seemed paralyzed. While his anxiety over Italy was, as always, understandable, it was becoming very counterproductive. "We are open to having a dialogue," he said plaintively, as if a "dialogue" would be sufficient. Throughout my career, I had often encountered the word "dialogue" as a meager substitute for action. It certainly was in this case.

Jean reacted more calmly than I would have. "Vittorio, we need your leadership to mobilize European support if we are to avoid a collapse of the entire Eurozone. The heads of state meeting is only days away, and we must succeed there." Grilli nodded his assent, but it was a nod without conviction. We walked him to the top of the stairs on the second floor of BNPP's headquarters and walked back to Jean's office in a rather discouraged mood. Nevertheless, we planned the next steps in his office before calling it a day. I agreed to call Geithner and Juncker, and Jean would arrange a meeting with Xavier Musca, Sarkozy's Chief of Staff. We would also both touch base with our friends in Brussels in an effort to engage in crucial meetings days ahead of the summit.

I called Geithner immediately following the meeting. He took the call as he was moving to a G7 dinner, so the timing seemed propitious. Tim and I had overlapped at the Treasury, with him joining in the 1980s as a young civil servant, as I had in the 1970s. He had risen through the ranks during Democratic administrations, while I had progressed during Republican. However, I always thought our approaches were broadly similar at a technocratic level, were they not at a more political one. I briefed him on the status of the Greek discussion, and I asked him to reach out to his G7 counterparts, especially German Finance Minister Schäuble, to encourage support for a conclusive negotiation in the days ahead. I acknowledged our willingness to move higher than the 21% NPV loss agreed in July but stressed the need for solid financial support from the EFSF if a deal was to come together. I also described the drift and disorder that continued to characterize the Eurozone's approach, and underscored the need to avoid "cram-down" on the banks, emphasizing that it was essential that any agreement be voluntary.

"Charles, I share your concerns about the need for a deal to come together and I am glad you are prepared to be flexible. I also support a voluntary approach. And I will discuss this tonight. But you must understand, Europe doesn't really want to hear from the US when it comes to resolving the Greek debt crisis." He reminded me that during a G7 Finance Ministers meeting in Marseille, France, in mid-September, he had tried to inject some urgency into the matter, but without much success. "They believe this is their problem, and that they should solve it without American involvement."

"Tim, you and I both realize that Greece has gone global, and a forced exit from the Eurozone could throw the world economy back into another global recession." We were not even three years removed from the outbreak of the global financial crisis and the extraordinary global recession. "I am fully aware of the risks and will do my best," he replied.

The next morning, Jean and I went to meet Musca. Xavier had served as Director du Trésor prior to being brought into Sarkozy's inner circle. He was, like virtually all his predecessors whom I had known, a highly skilled, competent, and globally minded public servant. Throughout my career I have been impressed with the competence and dedication of public servants in the Finance or Treasury Departments of several countries. France, the United Kingdom, Canada, and Japan stood out on this regard—each well trained, highly professional, with a keen sense of long-term national interests.

On this Saturday morning during our meeting at the Elysée Palace, Jean and I asked Xavier for his support in breaking the logjam.

"Xavier, we need you to ask for Sarkozy's help to close a deal at the summit scheduled for October 26 in Brussels," Jean said. "The markets cannot afford another failure, or for that matter, further doses of uncertainty."

"Are you flexible on the size of the haircut?" Xavier asked.

"Yes, within reason," Jean responded, "as long as the deal is reached cooperatively with the banks and does not impose an unmanageable financial loss on the creditors."

"Xavier, we are making virtually no progress with Vittorio Grilli and his team, despite good intentions on his part. We need him to have the authority to deal," I emphasized, "or we need to meet with someone who has the authority."

Musca looked tired and under pressure. President Sarkozy had asked to see him later that morning, and he was busy preparing material for the meeting. We discussed the need to ameliorate the German and IMF instincts to push the creditors too far. After thirty or so minutes, Musca thanked us for coming, and politely but firmly escorted us toward the door. As we departed, he said, "Jean and Charles, I see your problem, and I will do what I can." There was an air of determination in his voice, even though it was combined with a forced smile.

He departed, and Jean and I walked down the Escalier Murat—the Murat Staircase—which links the ground floor and first floor. It is majestic, with its regal red carpet and gold filigree banners running up and down its length. Like many buildings in Paris, the Elysée Palace had seen more than its fair share of history. I had visited there several times over the years, but it never failed to impress. Although the French Revolution had put an end to the monarchy in France, the Palace, built originally in 1722 and serving as the office and residence of France's President since the formation of the Second Republic in 1848, still has a regal air to it. The main study is called the Salon Doré, or Golden Room, after gold-colored trim that adorns the walls, doors, and chairs (it should be noted that neither Valéry Giscard d'Estaing nor Emmanuel Macron used this as their main study).

Passing through the courtyard entrance gates with its four iconic columns, I recalled faintly that the Palace had its name rooted in Greek mythology, although on that cold October morning I could not precisely recall its derivation. Once I returned to my hotel, a little research reminded me that the Palace was named after the Elysian Fields, the paradise where Greek gods and nobles spent eternity in the afterlife and "where life glides on in immortal ease for mortal man."[31] Inhabitants are believed to live in perfect happiness, making music, singing, and playing sport. Although I'd left the Palace somewhat optimistic, I could not help but wonder whether these negotiations might leave the Greek economy in some part of the afterlife much less desirable than that of the Elysian Fields. The Greek mythological counterpart was, of course, Hades, named after the ancient Greek god of the underworld. I had an uneasy feeling that night that even if we were able to reach a new agreement on a voluntary negotiated basis, the Greek economy might continue to suffer mightily until confidence was restored, akin to a modern-day version of Hades. It was not a good feeling.

CHAPTER 20

THE ADVENTURES OF TINTIN IN EUROPE

"Le Scoutisme—boys together, word of honor,
survival skills, good deeds."

—Simon Kuper, 2011

Sunday afternoon, October 16, was a cool, overcast day. Hung, Mikis, and I caught the 3:35 p.m. train from Paris Nord station for the short trip to Brussels. We began discussing the potential for a breakthrough, but the attention of two likely executives sitting across the aisle discouraged us from further conversation. We arrived at 4:45 and jumped in a taxi for our hotel.

We were staying for the first time in the Rocco Forte Amigo Hotel, which proved to be an inspired choice. As we were checking in, we noticed a film crew in the lobby, replete with numerous cameras, video equipment, and screens. I asked what movie they were making. A young man explained that Steven Spielberg was just releasing a new movie on Tintin, the famous Belgian comic strip character created by Georges Remi, who used the pen name Hergé, and they were making arrangements for a major release in Brussels the next week. Suddenly, we saw the signs going up advertising the film, which was titled *The Adventures of Tintin*, and we realized that an economic summit was not the only big event planned in Brussels for that week.

That night we had dinner with Jean and learned more about the history of Tintin. Jean recalled that among many Europeans of his generation, Tintin was very popular. His parents read the books to him from the time he was very young, and then he began to devour the stories himself. Although Hung, Mikis, and I had already been aware of Tintin, we all become rather intrigued by and wanted to learn more about the character that evening. Immediately after dinner we found a bookstore still open and purchased copies of some of "the adventures of Tintin." With advance marketing of the movie already underway, we were able to find copies not only in French, but also in English. The film to be released was based on three different Tintin books published between 1941 and 1944: *The Crab with the Golden Claws*, *The Secret of the Unicorn*, and *Red Rackham's Treasure*. Tintin himself was based on the author's fascination with scouts and the ideology of scouting—"boys together, word of honor, survival skills, good deeds." His comic strips were a huge hit in the 1930s, with "many of the villains fascist."[1]

I purchased several Tintin books, later giving one each to my grandchildren, Oumar, Vanessa, and Alya. Oumar and Alya's father is from Senegal, and I thought the French roots would intrigue them. Some time afterward, we went to see the movie, which they found very entertaining.

The next day, Jean decided I should have a new nickname—"Tintin." He thought that my role had certain Tintin characteristics, and Hung and Mikis quickly endorsed the idea. So Tintin was integrated into our negotiations, and each day as we saw the advertisements spreading throughout Brussels, we laughed about our own private story of Tintin. I actually thought Tintin was a good metaphor for the four of us—a strong team, bound together by duty, aiming to achieve good deeds.

On Monday morning, Joe Ackermann flew in from Frankfurt and joined us. We had managed to organize a meeting involving the President of the European Council, Herman van Rompuy, along with Jean-Claude Juncker, Grilli, Olli Rehn, and one staff person. On our side we had Ackermann, Lemierre, Hung, and me. Although we had worked with van Rompuy's staff—Hung had held a number of meetings with them—it was our first meeting with van Rompuy himself. He had been quite a successful politician in Belgium for many years, including a stint as Minister of Budget during which he had brought down the Belgian debt from 135 percent of GDP to less than 100 percent He also had a master's degree in applied economics, so we were hopeful that he would see the importance of finding a cooperative solution to Greece's debt problem, and one that did not further crush the economy. We had also arranged the meeting with a hope of putting pressure on Grilli to find a solution—to "authorize" him to get something done!

The meeting started promptly at 3 p.m. in van Rompuy's office. He greeted us cordially, and then invited us to sit down. He immediately turned the meeting over to Grilli, who began to explain the difficulties he had in advancing the negotiations. My impatience was just about to get the best of me when Joe interrupted, addressing van Rompuy and Juncker. "President van Rompuy, Jean-Claude, the situation in the markets is dire. It is essential that next week we have an agreement if we are to avoid a market meltdown." Joe Ackermann had credibility with both of them. Van Rompuy turned to Juncker, who responded, "Joe, we understand the urgency, but the decision-making process is very complicated. Germany is insisting on a very large haircut and is unwilling to provide a backstop for the banks. The political mood is terrible when it comes to providing any assistance to the banks."

Lemierre explained that pushing the banks too hard could lead to bank failures and a collapse of the European financial system: "We understand the need for compromise on our part, but the markets will not give us much more time." Rehn intervened to support the need for decisive negotiations but emphasized that "you will need to accept a greater loss if there is to be an agreement." I turned to Juncker and asked if he could speak to Chancellor Merkel and obtain authorization for Grilli to begin serious negotiations ahead of the summit. He said he would try. "I will do my best, Charles." How many times had we heard that?? Before we left, Joe reiterated the need for Berlin to lend their full support for conclusive negotiations.

Publicly, we were trying to keep options open. Joe stated that "the question is whether banks will be able to ensure the financing [of European business] in the future, or whether they will be practically forced to implement restrictions [on lending] due to possible debt haircuts in the Eurozone."[2] Joe's dual position as the CEO of Deutsche Bank, at the time not only Germany's largest bank but also one of its strongest, and as Chair of the IIF gave his views added weight in the marketplace and with media.

The issue of a larger reduction in Greek debt was now also hotly debated in the media and by analysts. Emiel van den Heiligenberg, CIO of BNB Investment Partners in London, captured one view when he said "Everyone is coming to the conclusion that a much deeper restructuring is needed to make Greece in any way sustainable. If the stock of debt doesn't diminish, the problems are going to be bigger and bigger, and Greece will require rescue package after rescue package."[3]

Others, however, were concerned that larger haircuts could increase contagion risk in other indebted European countries. "One risk to changing the agreement [of July 21] is that forcing bigger write-downs could be viewed as a default, triggering insurance bought against a credit event, known as credit default swaps, and risking contagion to larger countries such as Italy and Spain."[4]

As Richard McGuire, a senior fixed-income strategist at Rabobank International in London, put it, "A managed default in Greece may increase speculation of restructuring elsewhere, which would certainly put Portugal under pressure, also Ireland and we would see Italy and Spain under greater speculative pressure. It is a very difficult balancing act."[5]

Difficult indeed. My view was increasingly that we had to "run the rapids." As I went to my room after dinner on the night of the 20th, I remembered Secretary Brady's homily about Colonel Powell running the rapids on the Colorado River.

On October 18, Jean and I had one of the most unusual meetings of the Greek debt negotiations. It was strange in large part because it was not directly about Greece, but it certainly was closely related. It was a meeting with a person who seemed to know that what he was doing would be counterproductive, but he did it anyway. At 5:30 on the evening of the 18th, we met with Andrea Enria, the first Secretary General of the recently established Committee of European Banking Supervision. The Committee had only been created on January 1, 2011, in the aftermath of the global financial crisis. During the crisis, banks everywhere, in virtually every corner of the world, had come under some form of pressure in the markets. Following the collapse of Lehman and the near collapse of AIG, Goldman Sachs, and Morgan Stanley, the American banks were forced to take government capital in order to both shore up their capital base and to boost confidence in the system more generally. Europe, on the other hand, decided against a systematic requirement that the large banks had to take government capital. Some were forced to do so by market conditions, such as RBS and ABN-AMRO. Others resisted, and in some cases, the market was quite skeptical of their capital strength. The results of a stress test on European banks were published on July 15, 2011, and the markets reacted with even greater doubts. The results were controversial in a number of respects, including the fact that one German bank did not pass the test, but authorities refused to publish the results. The test was also criticized for not having included exposure to sovereigns, which was arguably the most important concern at the time. *Bloomberg* reported that "as many as 24 European banks will be under pressure to show they can raise capital after failing, or barely passing, a second round of stress testing regulators."[6]

Two key issues facing the European banks and Enria that October night were whether to accelerate a requirement for European banks to increase their capital holdings to 9%, and how to cope with a new stress test that was being imposed, this one to include bank claims on sovereigns.

We argued that it was the wrong time to accelerate the requirement to increase capital and to impose a test that would clearly result in large capital shortfalls for many banks—potentially undermining confidence in the banking systems of Italy, Greece, Spain, and Portugal in light of the low market valuation of those countries' sovereign debt. Credit supply was very weak in much of Europe, markets were fragile, and we feared that increasing capital requirements would only further intensify the recession in Europe. Enria acknowledged that the "buffer" of 9% was asking a lot, and he himself was concerned that it would lead to deleveraging and further weakness in the European economy.

We discussed the particular problem of Greece, and he seemingly understood the precarious nature of the entire Eurozone. Nevertheless, he argued that sovereign risk was not risk-free, a point on which we fully agreed. We also agreed that no other country in the Eurozone should engage in such a debt reduction exercise.

We wrapped up after nearly three hours of discussion. Enria said that he had little choice but to proceed with the acceleration of the capital requirements and the stress test as planned. "Our credibility is at stake as regulators, and even if we have to pay the price of weakening the European economy, we have no choice."

"The price may actually be the Eurozone," Jean said, as we broke up the meeting.

Early the next morning, October 19, I got a call from Paul Achleiter, the CFO of Allianz and subsequently the Chairman of the Supervisory Board of Deutsche Bank. He was very concerned that we needed to erect a firewall that would prevent Greece from taking down Italy and Spain. We discussed various options to try to achieve this, but I hung up the phone without much confidence that we had a clear plan to do just that. The longer Greece dragged on, the greater the risk that it would indeed undermine the rather thin veneer of confidence in Italy and Spain as well.

Later that afternoon I met in our hotel with Mikis to review our options for debt reduction. How much grace period would we give Greece on repayments of the new debt? What would be the repayment period? And what would be the assumed participation rate among the creditors? Eighty percent, we concluded. We made various assumptions, Mikis made the calculations, and we tried to determine what would work not only for the banks, but for Greece. We knew that the IMF had recalculated the "residual financing gap" and would seek to have the private creditors largely fill that gap.

The IMF had been very evasive about how the gap was calculated, and despite repeated requests, they had refused to share the underlying assumptions of the model with us. This was a far cry from the IMF that I had come to know during the 1980s, when the IMF was virtually completely transparent in outlining to the banks both the detailed elements of the adjustment program as well as the methodology for calculating the financing requirements.

By 2011 the inclusiveness of the 1980s had disappeared. Nevertheless, Mikis had his ways. He had been a member of the IMF staff for twenty-eight years after graduating from a university in Athens and earning a PhD in economics from the London School of Economics. He was deeply schooled in the ways of thinking of the IMF. He could explain virtually any aspect of IMF methodology. At times, this came across as defending the policies and practices of the Fund. However, I learned, after some exchanges, that what may have initially come across as a defense of the IMF policies was more often than not simply demonstrating the depth of his expertise. Hung Tran, Mikis's boss at the IIF and previously the Deputy Director of the IMF's Monetary and Capital Markets Department, had a keen sense of both policy and markets, but also could not match Mikis for his years of IMF staff experience, nor his remarkable ability to provide chapter and verse of particular IMF policies.

In this particular case, Mikis was able to overcome the IMF's reluctance to share their debt sustainability analysis (DSA) assumptions by convincing them to share their DSA summary for his perusal for one hour before a scheduled meeting of all of us with the EC officials, the IMF, and the Greek representatives. The IMF insisted on Mikis staying in the room with them while he studied the one-page DSA summary document, so they could receive his comments and address his questions.

Mikis was very familiar with reading and deciphering summary DSA tables. He quickly discovered that the IMF had indeed increased the financing gap substantially and built in assumptions that the bulk of that would be financed externally, by either private or official creditors. Since we knew the official creditors would be highly unlikely to step up with more funding at that time.

Mikis's debriefing steeled our determination not to be pushed into "excessive" haircuts, even while we were at the same time anxious to move the process forward and face whatever music may be out there.

The meeting that followed with Grilli and his team was a contentious one, the most contentious to date. Jean and I did not feel comfortable with the legal advisers in the room; we wanted a discussion only among principals. We insisted that the advisers leave the room. They were not happy, but we nevertheless stood our ground, and they packed their computers, their phones, their papers, and grumbled their way out the door.

During the meeting, Jean and I stressed that we would not be dragged into unreasonable and unrealistic debt/GDP targets based on the IMF's "black box" methodology. We knew that this would put even more pressure on the amount of debt reduction. Grilli and his small team listened, then stated that the IMF approach was something that they could not challenge, could not "open up." We agreed to disagree, and the meeting ended.

We went for a late dinner at a nearby Belgian restaurant, and we joked about Tintin, but I don't think any of us felt much like Tintin that evening. We felt uneasy about the direction of negotiations, fearing that we could get pushed into an unacceptably large discount on the debt. Not even a good glass of French wine could cheer me up.

On the morning of October 21, the news brought two rather conflicting, and even confusing, pieces of news.

The preceding day had witnessed over seventy thousand people protesting in Syntagma Square in Athens, Greece, with over seventy-four individuals injured and one death occurring in the melee that broke out. They were protesting the tax hikes and other austerity measures embedded in the latest version of the adjustment program. A parliamentary vote had been scheduled that day, provoking demonstrations. Throughout the country, a general strike had paralyzed the nation, and tensions boiled over at the Square. As we have seen elsewhere in recent years, hardliners appeared intent on fighting the authorities, and both the demonstrators and the police were attacked by "hundreds of masked protestors in motorcycle helmets who threw gasoline bombs and chunks of marble into the crowd."[7]

As I read the news that morning, I realized that from both market and political perspectives, time was indeed running out. The stress in global markets was palpable, and the tensions on the streets of Athens were obviously at the boiling point. "There's no precedent for this," said Anastasia Dotsi, a retired seventy-year-old bank worker, who said anger had driven her out to protest, adding that after two years, "we have been crushed as a people."[8] She said that her son and daughter, both of whom worked in the private sector, had not been paid in months and were struggling to pay their mortgage and support their families. "I have never been a leftist; I voted for PASOK, the Socialist Party of PM Papandreou, but they've pushed us to become extremists."

In reading this in my hotel room in Brussels that Friday morning, I was simultaneously perplexed and concerned; perplexed because I had viewed PASOK as a "leftist" party of sorts. I surmised, however, that in the parlance of Greek politics, 2011-style, "leftist" meant "radical left." After all, according to Reuters and many other media outlets, "Communists were among the ringleaders of the protest."

Despite the protests, parliament approved the package of measures, which included cuts in wages and pensions as well as thousands of layoffs in the public sector. Could the Papandreou government hold together in the face of the protests, the demonstrations, and the general strikes? After all, PASOK's majority in parliament was razor-thin, with 154 seats out of 300. As one paper reposted, "Europe continues to debate the country's fate, Greece's government has lost its popular consensus."[9] It was

Thursday morning, and the summit meeting scheduled for Wednesday, October 26, seemed like a long way off. The Ministers of Finance were scheduled to meet on Tuesday, the 25th, but with the heads of state scheduled for the following day, it was unlikely that any final decisions would be made on Tuesday.

On Friday evening we met with Venizelos, who was freshly returned from Athens, where he had overseen the passage of the painfully achieved legislation. Mikis and I met him at his hotel and asked him to support us in not being pulled into an excessive debt reduction that we could not sell to the banks. I stressed that if the deal was not voluntarily agreed to, we would never put it to the creditors for a vote. He asked what we could accept, and I indicated that we could possibly consider a 40–50% haircut, but nothing more. He pleaded impotence, stating in his elegant but defeatist tone, that "I cannot go against my partners. Brussels and Washington control us, and there is nothing we can do about it." He looked at me plaintively, with his hands up, sitting forward in his chair. I was disappointed that the Greek authorities, even such a capable one as Venizelos, seemed to have so little sense of ownership of their program or control of their destiny. I had dealt with multitudes of sovereign debtors over the years, as had Lemierre, many in exceptionally weak financial and economic circumstances. I think of Mexico in 1982, when Finance Minister "Choo" Silva Herzog stated to Treasury Secretary Regan, "Mr. Secretary, we are broke." Or Brazil in 1983, when Finance Minister Ernane Galveas said (also to Secretary Regan), "Mr. Secretary, like Mexico, we cannot pay our debts. We need help." Or Brazil again in 1998, when George Soros stated that Brazil needed "a wall of money" to survive. There were endless other cases where debtors were in weak, vulnerable, dependent positions, but I cannot recall any situation in which the debtor seemed so incapable or reluctant to represent its own interest. Of course, they were bound by various strictures: membership in the Eurozone, which deprived them of a national currency and monetary policy; dependence on the ECB to keep their banking system afloat during this crisis; requiring new funding from the EU and the IMF to meet and pay their unmanageable debts. Nevertheless, their virtually utter impotence was rather shocking.

Mikis and I reiterated that there were limits on our ability or willingness to commit the creditors to excessive haircuts, and that an involuntary restructuring would backfire and be vehemently opposed by the IIF and its members. As we walked back to our hotel, we reflected on the modern history of Greece, which involved numerous similar circumstances in which Greece's fate was in the hands of others.

Sunday was a cool autumn day. We had agreed to meet Grilli and a small team of cohorts. Jean, Hung, Mikis, and I made our way to the place where the meeting was being held. We were all increasingly aware of the dire situation surrounding the Greek economy. The *Financial Times* had just published a "leaked" report late on Friday, October 21, that was apparently a Commission document confirming the swift demise of the Greek economy in recent months and concluding that both the scale of needed EU/MF financing as well as the size of the required haircut by the private creditors had grown considerably. The headline, "EU looks at 60% haircuts for Greek debt,"[10] came as no surprise to us. Just as the political circumstances in Greece were at a breaking point, so were Greece's finances.

Grilli basically used the meeting to summarize the results of this new study. "We have run new scenarios, gentlemen, and they call for much larger debt reduction, on the order of 50 percent plus." I thanked him for this new information and asked for a copy of the debt sustainability analysis. He first refused to share anything, but we insisted. After an hour of debating the fundamental issue of debt sustainability, we took a short break to discuss matters.

It was a timely break. The 2011 Rugby World Cup Final was being played at that time in Auckland, New Zealand, pitting New Zealand's All Blacks against the French. As all rugby fans know, and many non-serious rugby fans such as I have learned, the All Blacks are legendary. Their traditional haka, a Māori ceremonial dance that would intimidate Godzilla, was performed to start the game. The French, however, were not frightened, and played the All Blacks a match of "grim physical attrition."[11] Given the respect that the All Blacks have earned over the years, I had expected that New Zealand would win quite handily. I also went into the game with a slight inclination to pull for the All Blacks given that their Deputy Prime Minister and Finance Minister at the time, Bill English (who subsequently became Prime Minister) had become a good friend during the global financial crisis.

However, since we were in the French mission to the EU and given that my colleague Jean Lemierre had a strong interest in the game, I gradually began to root for France. That wasn't too hard. Even though America's relations with France in recent years has been choppy at times, I was educated at an early age about the immense contributions the French had made to the American Revolution, and I had never forgotten that historical reality.

Jean is a serious rugby fan, and one of his sons played rugby in his youth. We checked on the game during our break, and as France remained competitive late into the game, we were hopeful of a major upset. As we took another break to consider how to deal with the debt sustainability analysis, we saw the All Blacks win this very tough contest through a penalty kick. It was momentarily depressing, as we had all become invested in a French victory, and we needed something to cheer us up.

When we resumed the meeting, Jorg Asmussen, Germany's State Secretary in the Ministry of Finance, indicated that the "leaders believe that the funding requirements for Greece are much higher, and that default must not be excluded." Jean responded swiftly, almost defiantly, that a unilateral default by Greece would be a mistake, not only for Greece, but for Europe as a whole. The meeting concluded just before dinner, and we retreated to our hotel, where we once again encountered the crew filming the new Tintin movie. It seemed like we could not get away from Tintin.

Monday morning, October 24, was a rainy and windy day. We resumed our negotiations at midday after a round of consultation with Board members and key bankers. Our "gang of four" had concluded that we were going to have to move considerably if there was to be a deal, and we needed to prepare the banks for this. We divided up the calls. I touched base with Ackermann, Wallenberg, Oudéa, Cucchiani of Intesa, and Jan Hommen of ING. Overall, they understood the pressure, and were prepared to move, but most expressed a desire to cap the haircut around 40%. I cautioned on the difficulty of that and stressed that we would "do our best." Sound familiar?

Our discussions with Grilli and his team that day focused once again on the issue of debt sustainability. Grilli began by emphasizing the need for Greece to achieve a debt/GDP ratio of 120% by 2020. He argued that the IMF debt sustainability analysis had concluded that this was the level necessary in order for Greece to have a sustainable level of debt. Jean and I refused to accept this as some biblical requirement. We all knew that this number was somewhat arbitrary; there was no single debt-to-GDP ratio that could be asserted for Greece or any other country to be a magical place of debt nirvana. As discussed in detail in Chapter 21 and Appendix 7, debt sustainability depends on so many other factors. We made it absolutely clear that we did not accept the legitimacy of that "magical number."

We also knew that their goal was to press us for additional haircuts, since we all knew there was a limit to how much pain the Greek economy could endure, and there was also a limit to how much funding Europe could continue pouring into the Greek economy. The banks were, for better or worse, the swing variable.

As we were debating this issue, a question arose from the Greek delegation that we had not faced before. Petros Christodoulou argued that we did not represent the Greek banks, and that the Greek government "controlled their voice in these negotiations." This was not, however, the case.

We had recognized this to be a very important matter from the start, and as stated earlier, Yannis Costopoulos of Alpha Bank had firmly cast his lot with us, as had the other Greek banks. These were Eurobank, Ageas, Emporiki Bank, Piraeus Bank, and the largest state-owned bank, the National Bank of Greece. In addition, we had two Cypriot Banks in the Committee, the Bank of Cyprus and Marfin Popular Bank.

We realized that the Greek government, the IMF, and the EU institutions were trying to weaken our influence over the banks, while at the same time positioning the Greek banks to take a smaller haircut. We also knew this would never work—the leading global creditors would never accept this. Petros was trying to create a wedge among the banks, sow dissent, and create weakness in our negotiation potential. Jean and I called their bluff and stated that, if needed, we could get signed statements from each of the banks. Petros backed off, but we knew this would not be the last of that question.

Our meeting with Grilli on October 24 eventually led to some specifics: How long of a grace period would we propose? What would be the cash payment that the banks would expect at the time of any debt exchange? What would be the appropriate discount rate to be applied in calculating the net present value loss to the banks? If Europe were to put up some funds to support the operation, how would it be used by Greece and the creditors?

We were somewhat encouraged that Grilli and his team were willing to begin to talk details, but as we began to reveal our thinking, we realized once again that we were dealing with the same vacuum of authority by the officials that we had faced all along. The grace period? Perhaps ten years. The cash down payment? Fifteen percent if we could mobilize enough funds from Greece, via European government coffers, for them to make such a large down payment. It was, once again, problematic to say the least not to have clear feedback on these specific issues, which were at the heart of the negotiations.

DEBT SUSTAINABILITY, IMF STYLE

"Walk the plank—a nautical metaphor for having to submit to consequences beyond one's control."

—Cynthia Barnett, *Three Sheets to the Wind*

Grilli's comments about the importance of achieving a debt-to-GDP ratio of 120% began to hang heavy over our discussions. The issue of debt sustainability is one of the most complex in macroeconomics. It is also one of the most hotly disputed. This chapter does not attempt to provide a detailed underpinning of the analytical basis for determining debt sustainability. Nor does it seek to develop a broader perspective on debt sustainability as argued by various academic experts. This chapter does, however, introduce the concept in order to provide a frame of reference for following this difficult debate, which shaped much of the latter phase of negotiations between Greece and its private creditors.

The IMF's debt sustainability analysis (DSA) was becoming a frequently analyzed issue in the context of sovereign debt restructurings at that time, and yet it remained a rather obscure, esoteric, and often misunderstood and controversial subject, even among experts. The IMF plays a critical role in the sovereign debt crisis prevention and resolution process, and its views and leverage through the provision of the financial assistance to sovereign debtors in distress are of fundamental importance to all stakeholders involved, including, naturally, private creditors and investors.

In the case of Greece, the IMF played a particularly influential role in framing the ultimate targets for Greece's public debt as a ratio to GDP over the medium term, and by implication the required debt relief from private creditors. This may sound rather natural and appropriate on face value, given the IMF's expertise and mandate. However, the sometimes dogmatic, non-transparent and arbitrary way the IMF imposed its views on both its Euro Area official partners and the Greek authorities on the one hand, and the private creditors on the other, left a bad taste and created unnecessary antagonism and controversy. Furthermore, it undermined trust in the IMF, a precious commodity among parties in any negotiation. Analytically, the IMF's DSA methodology and determination of the targeted debt-to-GDP ratio was challenged and criticized by private creditors, as will be highlighted in this chapter and the Appendices. Ironically, while the IMF staff was unyielding in justifying and defending their DSA methodology during the negotiations, they did come around to recognizing and adopting the thrust of the private creditors' views in the revised DSA framework for market access countries endorsed by the IMF Board in May 2013, and in the proposed IMF new lending policy framework and sovereign debt in June 2014.

By way of background: Traditionally, the IMF serves as a lender of last resort to its member countries in financial distress, a function that is particularly valuable when all sources of financing have dried up, as was the case in Greece. More specifically, the Fund provides financial assistance to its member countries facing balance of payments (financing) difficulties under a number of lending programs and facilities designed to address the nature and scale of the member's funding requirements. This assistance is based on uniform, pre-agreed rules and cost of funding and is invariably associated with detailed economic policy undertakings—financial and structural policy conditionality—designed to enable the country to lay the foundations for reversing its economic and financial imbalances and thus to restore its financial health over time. The IMF financial assistance is intended to support the country authorities' economic adjustment program, which normally covers a one- to three-year period. Inherent to these programs are detailed multi-year macroeconomic projections (financial program) that aim to capture the likely impact from the corrective policy measures envisaged by the authorities. These projections take into account specific understandings or assumptions about the likely financing committed by or expected from other financial institutions, bilateral official creditors, and intended government borrowings from the international capital markets. As an integral part of this financial program, the IMF staff prepares projections about the country's public and external debt outlook. IMF-supported programs are designed to achieve public debt sustainability over the medium term through appropriate reform policies, and, where this is deemed unavoidable, debt relief from its official and private creditors.

Debt sustainability prospects are routinely covered and assessed in all IMF staff reports to its Board of Directors on member countries' policies (Article IV surveillance reports) as well as in financial assistance requests or program reviews. These assessments are presented in a special appendix prepared by the IMF staff titled "Debt Sustainability Analysis," which was made available for public or external audiences. The baseline of this DSA for countries in an IMF lending program reflects the baseline of the macroeconomic projections underlying the adjustment program supported by IMF financial assistance. But the DSA appendix also includes a range of sensitivity tests and alternative scenarios designed to demonstrate or evaluate the robustness of the underlying public debt outlook relative to possible changes in inherent assumptions. The IMF staff had somehow come to consider its independence and exclusivity in the preparation of the DSA as a manifestation of the IMF's role and mandate and had tended to guard this responsibility with religious fervor. Accordingly, it became secretive about the contents of its DSA assessment until the publication of its report and zealously fended off real or perceived attempts by the authorities of the country involved, official and private creditors, or even members of the IMF's Board to probe into this process, notwithstanding their legitimate interests in having insight into it.

This defensiveness and bureaucratic rigidity in sharing information about the projected public debt outlook, or in discussing the rationale for the DSA conclusions, was clearly present in the case of Greece and was one of the factors that complicated the negotiations.

The IMF staff's assessment of Greece's public debt sustainability and its related strategy with regard to the desired private creditor involvement, changed substantially during the period from the Greek program inception in May 2010 through the eventual conclusion of the negotiations in February 2012, and has continued to evolve since that time. The initial position was that, based on the adopted corrective policies and the envisaged reform program, the Greek public debt was sustainable.

No restructuring was needed. John Lipsky, the IMF Acting Managing Director, made that very clear in May 2010 when he stated categorically, "There is no Plan B. There is only Plan A [to support Greece without debt restructuring]. And that is it." This position was maintained until July 2011. The IMF staff took a somewhat detached position on the need for the restructuring of the private debt during the negotiations for the first private debt restructuring during June–July 2011, leaving it primarily up to the Eurogroup to secure a financial "contribution" from private creditors. The new IMF Managing Director, Christine Lagarde, however, gradually came around to the view that debt reduction was needed. During August 2011, and into the fall, in the face of repeated major slippages in policy implementation by Greece, and as the output contraction became deeper than initially projected, the financing requirements for Greece grew, and the IMF shifted its position. It then took the lead in arguing that Greece's public debt was clearly unsustainable, especially on the basis of scaled-down, more realistic policy commitments by the Greek authorities, and that a far-reaching debt restructuring by private creditors was needed.

Beneath the surface, major differences of view existed between the IMF and its Euro Area partners (the Euro Area Finance Ministers, the European Commission, and the ECB). The IMF was brought in to support Greece for two reasons: to contribute to the financing, and to provide its expertise in designing a complex adjustment program and monitor its implementation. The amount of financing needed at the time was exceptionally large according to traditional IMF yardsticks, totaling €110 billion for the three-year period of 2010–2012, or some 50% of Greece's GDP. At that time, the Euro Area did not have any policy mechanisms or frameworks to provide financial assistance to any of its members on such a large scale. It only had a modest short-term facility for balance of payments support that could not in any way handle the needs of Greece. Bringing in the IMF and its policy conditionality had become somewhat of an ugly "game of tag" in early 2010 between

Chancellor Merkel and Prime Minister Papandreou, each threatening to resort to the IMF as a way of pushing the other side to go along with its position. At that time, Greece was resisting the adoption of a more demanding stabilization program designed to both reassure markets and address over time the deep adjustment needs of the Greek economy. Chancellor Merkel, the Eurogroup, and the ECB, on the other hand, felt initially that it would be humiliating for the advanced and wealthy economies of the Euro Area to turn to IMF financing and its associated policy conditionality, an activity that had been pursued solely by emerging market or developing countries for the prior four decades. In fact, the UK and Italy, which were the last western European countries to obtain IMF support in 1976 and 1977, both viewed their experiences as ignominious. It was widely viewed as "beneath" an advanced economy to be forced to accept "subjugation" to the IMF. In addition, the idea that a member of the Eurozone would have to seek IMF financial support was unfathomable until the Greek crisis erupted in the fall of 2009. But Prime Minister Papandreou, sensing the extreme discomfort of the Euro Area governments with a potential IMF involvement, suggested in early 2010, as a tactical move, that Greece would in fact be willing to ask for IMF assistance if the EC did not moderate its demands—despite the fact that he had publicly ruled out such an option in earlier months. Finally, Chancellor Merkel accepted his offer, and the Troika was born!

But the required IMF financial contribution was exceptionally large and unprecedented—at least as measured against Greece's quota in the IMF. It amounted to €30 billion, roughly thirty-two times Greece's quota. No other IMF member country had enjoyed such access until then or has ever since. The highest previous accesses to IMF resources were for Korea in 1997, at less than twenty times its quota, and for Turkey in the early 2000s, at fifteen times its quota. In theory, under the prevailing IMF lending policies, the IMF could go along with such a request under its exceptional access policy, provided four key criteria were met. One of these criteria required the IMF staff and Board to agree that a rigorous and systematic analysis indicated that a member's public debt was sustainable over the medium term with "a high probability." To overcome this constraint in the case of Greece, the IMF changed the rules. In a very unorthodox move and without publicity, this criterion was modified during the May 2010 IMF Board meeting to provide an exception to the normal expectation of debt sustainability with "high probability" in cases such as Greece where "there is a high risk of international spillovers." In assessing the observance of this criterion, the IMF staff report stated that "On balance, staff considers debt to be sustainable over the medium term, but the significant uncertainty around this make it difficult to state categorically that this is the case with a high probability. Even so, Fund support at the proposed level is justified given the high risk of international systemic spillover effects. Going forward, such an approach to this aspect of the exceptional access policy would also be available in similar cases where systemic spillover risks are pronounced."[1]

The ex-post assessment report prepared by IMF staff also criticized several other positions taken by the IMF at the beginning of the program for Greece. It argued that a) Greece did not meet essentially three of the four eligibility criteria for exceptional access; b) the initial program growth projections, fiscal retrenchment targets, and tax collection targets were too optimistic; and c) Greece's commitment to reform and administrative capacity to effectively implement the program were grossly exaggerated.

The latter assessments, with the benefit of hindsight, are in fact widely shared by most analysts today. Nonetheless, it is not clear whether the team of the Troika that negotiated the initial Greek program were indeed overly concerned about public debt sustainability. The policy measures anticipated under the program were projected, too optimistically, to lead to primary budget surpluses of 6% of GDP during 2014–2020 and to facilitate a regaining of market access by Greece by early 2012. Based on this misplaced optimism, the maximum maturity of the €110 billion financial assistance by both individual Euro Area governments and the IMF was five years, which would have created a huge bunching of maturities in the mid-2010s. Even as late as June 2011, the Euro Area official sector requested private creditors to contribute €30 billion to the covering of Greece's widening funding requirements during the program period through a rollover of maturing Greek government bonds and their replacement with new bonds of five-year maturities, which would have aggravated the future debt rollover risk even further.

Another indication that the IMF team was not fully convinced at the time that Greece's public debt was unsustainable, and that a debt restructuring was needed, were comments made by the IMF Mission Chief for Greece, Poul Thomsen. He and other Troika officials participated in the "no-deal road shows" organized by the IIF in September 2010 in London, Paris, and Frankfurt to highlight Greece's strong performance under the program up until then and facilitate a successful return to market financing. Addressing private investors and other market participants in the road show hosted by HSBC in London, Poul was not only upbeat about the prospects for Greece, but was rather forceful in responding to questioning from private sector road-show participants about the suggestions of some analysts that a debt restructuring was inevitable. Poul declared emphatically that such views were unreasonable, and investors who believed them and reduced their holdings of Greek government bonds would not be serving their best financial interests. He stressed that, if Greece continued its strong performance under its ambitious reform program, it would be unlikely that the Euro Area authorities would "abandon Greece" and seek a debt restructuring.

The question remains open, however, as to whether an upfront debt restructuring by Greece would have been possible, as had been claimed in the ex-post assessment and other IMF reports in mid-2013. Were such a restructuring to have taken place, it would likely have resulted in only a small contribution by private creditors given the Greek program design at the time. The budget primary surplus and other macro targets in the initial program were similar to the framework used for the first restructuring concluded in July 2011. The financial contributions by both the Euro Area authorities and the IMF were of a very short maturity (five years). With the early major successes in implementing the program, the spreads on Greek debt actually declined by 600 basis points during July–October 2010. But with the deteriorating performance in subsequent months, had a debt restructuring taken place in 2010, a new debt restructuring may well have been needed down the line.

As indicated earlier, the IMF's strategy on seeking a restructuring of the Greek debt held by private creditors changed over time. In the first phase, covering the period from May 2010 to May 2011, the IMF was taking a backseat to the Eurogroup and avoided taking a strong public position. In its staff reports for the quarterly reviews in 2010 and even early 2011, the IMF staff reiterated its position that Greece's public debt remained sustainable, but not with a high probability.

The IMF position moved toward calling for a restructuring over time, driven by a number of considerations and developments on the ground. In late 2010 and the first half of 2011, there were significant slippages in tax collections, the control of spending by non-central government agencies deteriorated, and the implementation of key structural reforms that were facing increasing political resistance, including within the ruling PASOK party, began to lag. The deeper-than-expected contraction in output and employment, combined with upward revisions of the 2009 budget deficit and public debt and increasing resistance to further fiscal adjustment and to privatization of public enterprises, led to steep increases in the yields on Greek government bonds in the secondary markets.

Moreover, efforts within the Euro Area to establish a new policy framework to deal with potential new bailout programs for other stressed peripheral Euro Area member countries—namely the replacement of the European Financial Stability Facility (EFSF) established in June 2010 for a three-year period with a new permanent mechanism, the European Stability Mechanism (ESM)—included policy initiatives that called for private sector involvement. Within the Euro Area, confidence in the Greek authorities' resolve to implement the agreed program waned during the course of 2011, and strong opposition emerged to extending additional financing to Greece to cover the emerging financing gaps, leading to a very public discussion about options for so-called "private sector involvement." Not surprisingly, these developments induced a worsening in market sentiment toward Greece, and heightened expectations among financial market participants that a debt restructuring was more likely.

The IMF staff report for the fourth review, issued in early July 2011 as we were engaged in a first round of negotiations and discussed by the Board in mid-July, marked a turning point. The report noted that major prior actions—including the adoption by the Greek Parliament of a medium-term fiscal adjustment strategy and privatization targets—were needed to correct for major delays in program implementation and allow for the completion of the review. The stepped-up fiscal adjustment called for the realization of much higher primary budget surpluses for the period 2014–2020 than did earlier programs (7.7% of GDP instead of 6% in 2015 and 6.4% of GDP instead of 6% in 2014 and 2016–2020), in addition to the realization of the targeted €50 billion of privatization proceeds during 2011–2015. Both objectives were very ambitious, much higher than the average of 4% of GDP primary surpluses that Greece achieved in the second half of the 1990s and at the high end of any international experience with sustained surpluses. The tougher fiscal adjustment requested from Greece, against the backdrop of evident implementation difficulties and the social and other adjustment costs for the Greek population, was clearly unrealistic.

The July 2011 IMF staff report included several comments that distanced the IMF staff from the Euro Area authorities, and implied strong skepticism that the efforts to "pile up" additional adjustment on Greece would be successful. Yet the IMF staff stopped short of calling for a more ambitious debt reduction than envisioned by the Euro Area official sector (private sector financing of about €30 billion at five-year maturities). The IMF report noted that "open discussions of Greece's financing challenge and euro-zone countries' insistence on 'private sector involvement' to resolve this have convinced markets *that Greece will restructure its debt*" (emphasis added). The IMF staff also distanced itself from the push for a voluntary debt restructuring. The report stated that "a purely voluntary roll-over scheme may yield very little." It pointed out that "the challenge posed by Greece's heavy debt burden has, from the time of program inception, been enormous" and that "it was unlikely that Greece would regain private market access by early 2012, as initially envisaged under the program."[2]

Against this background, it was not entirely surprising that the outcome of the restructuring deal agreed with the European Council on July 21, 2011, was not adequate to cover Greece's funding needs and pave the way toward debt sustainability. The underlying macroeconomic program on which the deal was based—which had been agreed between the Troika and the Greek authorities without any involvement of private creditors—was unrealistic. This became obvious to the IMF and the Euro Area official sector by October 2011, and ushered in the second, more activist, phase of the IMF strategy toward debt restructuring.

The key emphasis of the new IMF approach, with support from the German government, was to focus on supposedly more realistic (but still ambitious) policy commitments by Greece and targets for the primary budget surplus in outer years, as well as some very conservative projections for output growth, privatization proceeds, and the prospects for regaining market access. Unfortunately, they continued to seek more and more fiscal adjustment when their approach was counterproductive. The consequence was a large funding gap for Greece that needed to be covered by both additional financial support by the Euro Area official sector and a more substantial contribution by private creditors under a new debt restructuring deal.

This new strategy underpinned the IMF position during the prolonged negotiations of a successor, second three-year program with Greece. As outlined earlier, these program negotiations and the related negotiations of a new debt restructuring took place under an exceptionally difficult economic climate in the Euro Area and were fairly protracted. The weak Euro Area growth outlook and the well-publicized emphasis on a private sector "contribution" in the new sovereign debt crisis management policy framework underpinning the ESM contributed to the spread of the sovereign debt crisis to Spain and Italy, going beyond Ireland and Portugal, which had already been under Troika-supported programs since December 2010 and early 2011, respectively. More broadly, the declining market sentiment and mounting pressures on sovereign debt markets contributed to steep increases in the bond yields of all Euro Area problem countries. This in turn weakened the balance sheets of all regional banks exposed to sovereign bonds, and lowered bank share prices to very low levels as well as unprecedentedly low price-to-book value ratios for all European banks (below 0.5). This amplified a negative feedback loop between sovereigns and national banking systems, disrupting bank credit expansion throughout the Euro Area and blockading the monetary transmission mechanism. The market pressures on the euro mounted amid increasing market concern about a possible exit from the Euro Area and a disorderly sovereign debt default by Greece.

Increasing adjustment fatigue by Greece and escalating political resistance to the reform program within the ruling PASOK party magnified these concerns. The negotiations of the new Greek adjustment program became very testy and were temporarily suspended during September and October 2011, when the new Finance Minister, Evangelos Venizelos, made very little progress in implementing agreed structural reforms and advancing fiscal adjustment.

Throughout this, the IMF staff became increasingly fixated on the notion that a debt ratio of 120% to GDP was the necessary target for debt sustainability. No matter the interest rate on the debt, no matter the maturity structure of the debt, no matter the access to private capital markets, the number of 120 took on biblical proportions as we prepared for our negotiations in Brussels in late October.

A question about the overall approach to the euro crisis arises. It may appear to the reader to be a rather technical one, but it is far from it. Should the IMF have stepped back and taken a fundamentally different approach to the Euro Area crisis? Should they not at one point have recognized that the crisis merited a broader strategy that encompassed all of the struggling economies of the Eurozone as well as the stronger members? Why was the central bank of the country under duress not part of the negotiation for the "debtor" side, rather than appearing on the "creditor" side of the table? Was the ECB not Greece's central bank? Why should it not be expected to contribute to the adjustment program of Greece? Was it ever approached by the IMF and the European Commission with that in mind? Toward the end of the negotiations, the IMF did press both European governments and the ECB to shoulder part of the adjustment burden, as discussed in Chapter 30, and in fact they finally did.

But arguably was there a huge opportunity missed in 2010 and 2011 to develop an adjustment program that involved not just Greece, but Germany, other surplus countries, and perhaps even Italy, Portugal, and Spain? Of course, it would have been unprecedented to develop such a wide-ranging adjustment program for a currency union. It would also have been politically very difficult, to say the least. But this would have had two substantial advantages. First, it would have enabled the IMF "quota" of all countries involved to be the basis for the IMF lending, including the "surplus" countries such as Germany and the Netherlands. For cooperative purposes, Greece's IMF "quota"—the basis on which the amount of lending to Greece could take place—was approximately €900 million in 2011. The quota of the entire Eurozone was approximately €53 billion. It was evident from the start that this was not a typical individual country's sovereign debt problem, but a regional crisis. As the crisis unfurled, it became even clearer that it was the integrity of the Eurozone that was at stake, not just the viability of Greece's membership in the euro. So why should not the full membership of the Eurozone bear some of the costs of supporting the program for Greece as part of its IMF membership, in addition to or in place of the financing being provided through the new European Financial Stability Facility?

The EFSF was nascent and hardly sufficient to meet the financing needs of Greece and the other Eurozone countries under stress. To supplement the EFSF with IMF funding geared only to the quotas of the countries in distress (Greece, Ireland, and Portugal all obtained funding from the IMF, while Italy and Spain did not) seemed somehow to miss the heart of the matter—that it was the very existence of the Eurozone that was under duress. Using the quotas of all Eurozone members would, of course, require that the liabilities be shared jointly and several by all Eurozone members. This would undoubtedly have been hugely controversial politically, but it would have shared the burden of adjustment much more equally throughout the Eurozone and avoided such a cataclysmic effect on the Greek economy and Greek society.

CHAPTER 22

SARKOZY SITS
AND MERKEL SPEAKS

"Do not say a little with many words but a great deal in few."

— Pythagoras, circa 520 BC

As we resumed our meeting with Grilli and his team in Brussels, it became difficult again to maintain any traction on specific issues. Despite the pressure that was building around us—pressure from the markets, pressure from senior political leaders in Europe (who were meeting in two days!), pressure from the Greek people, and pressure from our own banking constituency to find a solution that could stabilize the region—it remained seemingly impossible to negotiate a deal. No one on the official side wanted to take the responsibility for giving Grilli negotiating authority. The dysfunctionality of the Eurozone decision-making arrangements regarding Greece was, regrettably, on full display. And the more they procrastinated, the worse the situation became in the markets and on the streets. It's not that we were opposed to their position; they had no position. We were used to negotiating at different levels: technocrat, head of state, Finance Minister, IMF, or EU official; that was not the problem. But searching through the backstreets of Europe for someone with whom to negotiate, to try to cut a deal—this was entirely new to all of us.

The summit loomed and things were languishing. On the morning of October 25, we decided to put a concrete proposal on the table to see if it would win the day before the summit. It basically revolved around a 40% haircut, premised on a €30 billion payment by the Eurozone to Greece that would be used to pay down roughly 15% of the outstanding debt to private claimants.

We met with Grilli to give advance indication of what was coming. He said that he was not in a position to entertain the proposal and was still without a mandate to negotiate with us. We agreed to meet again that night to see if he could obtain authority in the interim. It was increasingly difficult for all of us not to explode at this continued remarkable display of institutional rigidity. They were frozen, despite the storms that were gathering over Europe.

Jean and I had scheduled a conference call that afternoon with our full Committee to advise them of our plans and to get any feedback. There was some hesitation among our constituents, but many were feeling the pressure to get something done. They were especially mindful of Italy's fragile situation, and increasingly felt that if Greece was not solved soon, Italy would indeed fall, and some banks would be devastated. We discussed various scenarios of net present value losses, since that is what ultimately mattered to the banks, not the nominal haircut.

Following the call, Lemierre and I decided we could make another round of calls to our key Board members. We knew something could happen that night, with market expectations very high, and we did not want our leaders caught off guard. Joe Ackermann was supportive, as were the others we were able to reach. Despite the sword of Damocles hanging over his head, we received a strong word of support from Spyros Filaretos of Alpha Bank, and Prot also confirmed with Jean his support to seek a deal.

The early part of the evening of October 26 was described in Chapters 1 and 8. We had somehow transitioned from a dark room in the basement of the Berlaymont building in Brussels to the glorious upper reaches of the European Commission headquarters. French President Sarkozy had just put on quite a performance, during which he lambasted the banks and threatened to destroy them if agreement wasn't reached. It was in the wee hours of the morning on October 27 that Sarkozy returned to his seat, obviously pleased by his brilliant display. Jean had responded calmly, but firmly. Chancellor Merkel, seated to Sarkozy's left, then took the stage. We knew it had already been a long night for Merkel. There had been reports of intense debates at the heads of state meeting earlier that evening, including disagreements between Papandreou and Merkel. Tempers were getting short, and yet Merkel spoke with aplomb. "Mr. Dallara, M. Lemierre. It is critical that we reach a new agreement on Greek debt tonight. Europe has already provided Greece €100 billion, and the IMF €20 billion more. It will be necessary for the banks to go beyond the 21% haircut of this past July."

Her fluent English impressed us both. But Jean explained that we were prepared to do so and that we were even willing to consider a more than 40% haircut. He added that we would need a reaffirmation of the €30 billion that had been agreed as part of the July pact.

Merkel balked and said she did not think that would be possible. "Chancellor Merkel," I implored, "this was part of the original agreement, and the banks cannot accept that they would increase substantially the haircut while losing the original support indicated." She then changed tack.

"Gentleman, I know that you understand the gravity of the situation. Europe has been under tremendous economic pressure over the past two years, first from the global financial crisis, then from our own difficulties. Greece is now the center of the crisis, and we need to stop it here, with your help." Her tone was plaintive, not threatening. After the violent storm of Sarkozy, she was like a calming breeze.

"Madame Chancellor," I responded, "we are fully aware of the gravity of the moment. The private sector, in fact, initiated discussions with your governments this spring and has been trying to find common ground with Mr. Grilli and his colleagues since negotiations resumed. It has been difficult in part due to his lack of negotiating authority."

"Thank you, gentlemen, for your efforts," Merkel responded. She then went to the heart of the matter. "Mr. Dallara, M. Lemierre, can you increase the debt reduction to 50%? We believe this would be sufficient, along with European and IMF support, to put Greece on a path to debt sustainability."

Jean and I looked at each other. We knew this point was approaching and we also knew that the markets would soon open in Japan. Jean responded, "We cannot firmly commit at this moment, but we will consult with our superiors and let you know as soon as possible, hopefully within the hour." I nodded my assent.

Then she surprised us by raising a technical issue. "I understand that you are reluctant to agree to bring Greece's debt down to 120% of GDP by 2020." She looked over at Christine Lagarde, but Lagarde said nothing.

I explained that I had been working on sovereign debt issues for most of my career, and that there was nothing magical about a particular figure, such as 120%, or any other figure. "The ultimate test of sustainability is market confidence. If confidence in Greece's economic future is restored, then debt above 120% can be quite sustainable. Much revolves around the quality of economic management and expectation of future policy implementation." I added, "In my view, it is not feasible to be so precise—in fact, it creates a false sense of precision."

Lagarde obviously did not welcome my comments, since the IMF had been the leading proponent of the view that "120%" was "the target"; Germany's Finance Minister Schäuble, who was not physically present at this meeting but still making his influence felt, was also strongly of that view.

Chancellor Merkel responded by drawing on her own experience. "I understand, gentlemen. I have a doctorate in quantum chemistry, which is supposed to be a very precise science. But even in my field, precision can be elusive." The room fell silent. Merkel stood up, walked across the room, and handed me a sheet of paper. "Here, Mr. Dallara. This is our draft press release to be issued if we can all reach agreement. Please mark up the section of debt sustainability to your comfort. Please return it to us as soon as possible, preferably with your commitment."

We were shocked. It was a brilliant negotiating move. I thanked her, and both Jean and I got up to leave. We shook hands all around, and Jean and I walked out of the door. We found our way back down to the basement, met up with Hung and Mikis, and debriefed them. It was nearly three in the morning, and we knew we could not alert the full Board at that hour. Jean and I nevertheless felt that we had to try to reach a few key leaders. I tracked down Ackermann on a business trip to Moscow. Once he was awake, I quickly briefed him. He just as quickly responded, "I am fine with it, Charles, let's get it done." Jean got the same answer from Prot. Mikis called two of the Greek banks, and I was also able to reach Oudéa of SocGen, Enrico Cucchiani of Intesa, and Wallenberg of SEB, all of whom agreed. We were off and running.

We sat down to review the draft document handed to us by Merkel, concentrating on the language around debt sustainability. We had the complete draft of the "Euro Summit Statement," but we knew better than to edit the language on "Sustainable public finances and structured reforms for growth," the paragraph on Italy, etc.

In paragraph twelve, we modified the language on debt sustainability from "the PSI should *ensure* [emphasis mine] the decline of the Greek debt to GDP ratio to 120% by 2020" to "the PSI should secure the decline of the Greek debt to GDP ratio *with an objective of reaching* 120% by 2020 [underlining mine]." The change may seem modest, but we considered it crucial by placing the goal of 120% of GDP as an objective, not as a firm commitment. With this edit, we had achieved more flexibility with regard to the debt-to-GDP ratio. We knew this could mitigate the risk that if the debt-to-GDP ratio was off track, the private creditors could be forced into yet another restructuring.

The rest of the language was already there, including the 50% nominal discount on Greek debt and, critically from our point of view, the €30 billion contribution from the EU.

After we agreed on the changes among the four of us, we encountered an unanticipated and serious logistical problem: we had laptops, but no way to print an updated version of the draft statement to return to Chancellor Merkel. The building was completely shut down. We wandered into a few offices to see if we could wake up a computer or a printer, but of course we had no such luck given that we had no passwords. We walked back to our conference holding room, momentarily dejected. We really did not want to send a copy that had been marked up by hand back to Merkel—how embarrassing!

Suddenly we stopped. Mikis spotted a security guard sitting in front of a desk. He was staring at a bank of video screens, monitoring the entrance and corridors, an especially important task with so many heads of state in the building. But sitting in front of him was a computer. Mikis brusquely walked in and explained our situation, in French.

The guard was at first incredulous, and Mikis explained again who we were and what we were trying to do, referring to our meeting with Merkel. I joined Mikis to add my presence and a touch of additional authority, but I don't believe it made any difference. The guard pondered matters for a moment, then promptly swiveled in his chair, faced the computer, and fired it up. Within seconds it was humming. Standing up, he motioned Mikis to the computer. Mikis eagerly jumped into the seat and started retyping paragraph twelve, the one on Greece. Within minutes, he was done. Now our challenge was to connect to a printer. A dusty one sat idle in the corner of the guard's post, probably rarely used, and both Mikis and the guard went over to look at it. Soon, they got it going as well and printed off two copies.

I called Grilli and asked him to meet us at the entrance to the elevators. I handed him a copy to give to Chancellor Merkel and asked him to confirm to her that we agreed to the 50% haircut. He nodded, turned, and jumped back on the elevator, and we walked back to our disheveled office, beginning to feel the fatigue set in. We huddled one more time and decided to hold a short press briefing in the morning to share our perspective on the agreement. At the same time, Hung and Mikis were busy drafting a private communication to our creditor group, so they did not receive the news first from the media.

As we returned to the hotel in a taxi, I had a strong urge to go home that day. I had not seen Peixin or our family for weeks, and I yearned to sleep in my own bed. I know that each of us in the quartet felt the same way. I sent a note to my trusted executive assistant Karen Dozier and asked her to book the first flight out of Brussels for Dulles. Then I collapsed back at the hotel for two hours as 6 a.m. approached.

As I got on the plane a few hours later, after our short briefing, it was obvious that the agreement had been initially well received by markets. Of course, as noted in a *New York Times* article, "failure here would have been a disaster." Sarkozy stated, accurately, but this time without his remonstrations, "The results will be a source of huge relief to the world at large, which was waiting for a decision." Merkel added, "I believe we were able to live up to expectations that we did the right thing for the Eurozone, and this brings us one step farther along the road to a good sensible solution."[1]

We issued our own statement welcoming the deal. We referred to the agreement as "a comprehensive package of measures to stabilize Europe, to strengthen the European banking system, and to support Greece's reform efforts."

Importantly, the measures agreed that night also included a plan to recapitalize European banks, requiring banks to raise substantial additional capital to increase their capital base. European leaders also agreed to increase the size of the European "bailout" fund that would be used to support Greece and other struggling European countries.

As I settled into my seat on the flight back to Washington, I felt that we had finally turned the corner in our effort to stabilize the euro. I was also hopeful that this could eventually lay the basis for a turn-around in the Greek economy, but I remained very concerned about its continuing contraction, as I know did Jean, Hung, and Mikis. In addition, we knew that the deal we had struck the night before left many questions unanswered. Particularly, we realized that without pre-cisely defined instruments for a debt exchange, the "nominal discount of 50% on national Greek debt held by private investors" quoted in the press release could mean many different things. The net present value loss that the creditors would suffer could vary widely, depending on the interest coupons attached to the new bonds as well as other terms. At least I felt comfort that we had secured Europe's commitment for a package of support "up to €30 billion," in addition to new support to Greece for balance of payments, financing, and that recapitalization of Greek banks. In total, Europe and the IMF were providing new financ-ing of up to €100 billion between the end of 2011 through 2014. This was a massive amount in total, but the IMF's portion of this was quite modest, reflecting the fact, as exhibited earlier, that a large commit-ment relative to Greece's quota had already been made by the IMF. This was a function of Greece's relatively small quota. I was still troubled by the notion that given that this entire exercise was clearly not just about stabilizing the Greek economy but also about defending the credibility and durability of the euro, using Greece's quota was a misguided basis for determining the appropriate amount of IMF support. A more real-istic approach would have been to measure support against the entire quota of the Eurozone.

After taking a good rest during the first part of my flight home, I began ruminating on other issues. As already noted, six days before our agreement in Brussels, over seventy thousand people had demonstrated in Syntagma Square in the heart of Athens over the austerity measures that had been built into the IMF program. I always paused when I read about very sizable demonstrations in Syntagma Square. It had been at the center of Greek political and social life since the middle of the nineteenth century, when Greece's first king, Otto, formerly a Bavarian prince, had issued a constitution in 1843—the word "syntagma" meaning "constitu-tion" in Greek. During my time living in Greece in 1972–1973, I became

Demonstrations in front of the parliament building in Athens, as the pressure builds on Prime Minister George Papandreou. June 2011. Orestis Panagiotu/EPA/Shutterstock

very familiar with the square, as it was a transportation hub, especially for those of us moving around the city by bus. My recollections are of a hot, noisy center of commerce, with innumerable buses belching noxious fumes all around it. On many afternoons, however, the square served a dual purpose, as it also became the center of protests.

That had certainly been the case throughout 2010 and 2011, as protests frequently erupted in Syntagma Square. Such protests had died down somewhat in the early part of the fall of 2011, but the protests of October 20 had once again led to sharp confrontations with the police, contributing to over seventy people being injured.

It seemed that the passage of a new round of support by Europe capped by the major concession by the banks for a large write-down was doing nothing to quell the ire of the Greek people. The reality on the ground was, in fact, getting worse: unemployment was still rising, and the economy was still shrinking. Inevitably, it would take considerable time for the benefits of additional financial support to work their way through the Greek economy. Did the government have enough time?

I thought so, especially with the benefit of a positive market reaction to the measures announced in Brussels. The Dow Jones Industrial average soared over 400 points after we announced the deal. One news source characterized the markets as "giddy with excitement." Some observers declared the end of the European debt crisis. "The crisis in Europe is basically over," said Gennaro Pucci, the CIO of PVE Capital, a London-based hedge fund.[2] It was, of course, a premature call, but yields on all manner of European debt fell. The yields on Greek debt fell almost 8%, and as prices spiked, Spain and Portugal's debt yields also dropped, although not as sharply (both were down about 2.1%). The euro also gained ground against the dollar, moving up 2% to a remarkably high 1.41.

I was pleased to see the markets' reaction when I landed in Washington, although I knew not to make too much of it. Too many times I had seen markets reverse course after such a sharp move.

CHAPTER 23

GREECE FRACTURES

"We must free ourselves of the hope that the sea will ever rest.
We must learn to sail in high winds."

—Aristotle Onassis

I returned to the office in Washington hoping to spend a few days on other matters, since I had missed a number of IIF activities during the negotiations, including two regional CEO meetings. However, on the morning of Friday, October 28, when Hung, Mikis, and I met to strategize, events in Greece once again captured our attention. President Karolos Papoulias, a largely symbolic figure who handled ceremonial duties, had been in Thessaloniki to commemorate "Oxi Day," the anniversary of Greece's rejection of Italy's ultimatum to surrender in 1940. The day marked a courageous stand by the Greek people against the Italians as well as against the gathering storm of the Axis powers; Greek Prime Minister Ioannis Metaxas reportedly responded to the demand with a simple "no." Although considerably outnumbered and outgunned by the Italians, the Greek army subsequently pushed back the invasion, which came through Albania, and fought the Italians to a stalemate that held for five months until the government fell to the more powerful German forces in April 1941. That moment of resistance on October 28 remains a day of national remembrance of heroism.

It was somewhat shocking then to read that the President was called a traitor by protestors, who also blocked the commemorative parade. In Athens, the rhetoric was equally harsh, with a banner unfurled that read, "No to the 4th Reich."[1] Hung, Mikis, and I exchanged our concerns, but thought that the anger would die down as it became clear that the additional support provided by both the banks and the EU was substantial and would ease the plight of the Greek people. We were wrong. Very wrong. The important lesson for all of us to learn: don't expect economic logic to always prevail on the streets of a country under strife.

As Jean, Hung, Mikis, and I were busy looking at various scenarios to meet the parameters of the October 26 agreement in principle, energized by having achieved this important milestone, riots erupted once again in Athens. On top of that, George Papandreou faced a revolt on the Brussels deal from both the opposition party and his own PASOK colleagues.[2] There appeared to be little genuine understanding of what the deal really meant, and the Greek people simply saw more hardship.

Papandreou decided to put the latest Brussels agreement to a referendum. The announcement was made on Monday, October 31, and came like a bolt out of the blue—not only to me and the creditor community, but apparently to Merkel, Sarkozy, and the rest of the EU leadership. It was a roll of the dice, and he did not come up with a seven or an eleven. Rather, it was, for Papandreou—but fortunately not for Greece—snake eyes. Papandreou called me in Washington that morning, presumably after he had called Merkel and others. I was dumbfounded and hardly knew what to say. In fact, I had trouble absorbing what he had done. Why? For what purpose? He explained that this was necessary to consolidate support for the program, as his majority in parliament was paper thin and he seemed quite convinced that he would win the referendum.

"Don't worry, Charles," he said in a calm voice, "this will strengthen our hand to implement the program." I was too stunned to say much at all in response and mumbled something like, "Thank you for the call, and good luck." I was not so sure Papandreou would succeed, and immediately called Venizelos to ask his view of this sudden development. To my surprise, he answered the phone from a hospital bed. He explained that he had severe abdominal pains and was undergoing tests. I apologized for the intrusion but explained I had called regarding the proposal for the referendum, which had come as a complete surprise. "It was just as much a surprise to me, Charles.

I will explain later." Against background noise of doctors and nurses speaking loudly in Greek, the phone disconnected. I then called Ackermann and Lemierre to alert them. Both had already heard the news.

Ackermann was, like me, perplexed. "Why now? What if it does not pass?"

Lemierre was displeased, and prophetic: "This will backfire."

Jean was also acutely aware that the French were hosting a G20 Summit in Cannes in just a few days. He knew that Papandreou had suddenly cast a large cloud over the gathering. He voiced his dismay in no uncertain terms. "This is a huge mistake and will not likely stand!"

On that point, he was also correct. Papandreou was summoned to Cannes to meet with the EU leadership in a side meeting of the Summit. The side meeting, as it turned out, became the main event.[3] The markets quickly soured as soon as news of the referendum broke. Yields on Greek bonds soared again, rising over 16% in a single day.

Against this background of both political and financial turmoil, Papandreou was forced to change the nature of the proposed referendum profoundly. Sarkozy gave him an ultimatum: the referendum would not be on the October 26 agreement; it would now be on the issue of membership in the euro. Reports indicate that Sarkozy had delivered another tirade, his second in less than a week.[4] This time, Papandreou and Venizelos were the targets instead of Lemierre and me. We will never know which one was more orotund, but apparently this one was quite withering.

Sarkozy's ire was understandable, if not diplomatic. It was one thing to rant at a couple of bankers; it was another to do it to a Prime Minister, in front of his peers. As Peter Spiegel meticulously reported in a special *Financial Times* series written two and a half years later, Sarkozy's view was "we've done everything to help you, we've done everything to keep you in the Eurozone, we've taken financial, political risk. We have agreed to the biggest debt restructuring in the world, ever, and now what you do is betray us."[5]

As this phase of the Greek crisis was unfolding in Cannes, the Italian crisis was right alongside, almost as if Italy was trying to compete with Greece in destabilizing. For those of us dealing with Greece, there was this never-ending awareness that Italy was just around the corner, hovering there, larger than Greece. The scale of Italy's bank debt, at four times the size of Greece's, meant that Greece had to be defused, one way or another, before it blew up Italy and potentially destroyed the integrity of the Eurozone.

Italy sometimes felt like a ball and chain to those of us focusing on Greece. Everywhere we went, we dragged Italy along, always looking for a way to break the chains. Like the scene from the movie *Cool Hand Luke* in which actor Paul Newman is chained to a number of other prisoners as they work in the sun digging ditches, Greece, Ireland, Portugal, Spain, and the biggest of all, Italy, were seemingly all bound together under the searing sun of the markets in 2010 and 2011. In one sense, the entire membership of the Eurogroup was chained together. In 1999, the group had started with eleven countries; in addition to those "troubled five," it also included the initial core members of Germany, France, Austria, the Netherlands, Luxembourg, Belgium, and Finland, eventually adding Slovenia, Malta, Cyprus, and Slovakia. Estonia joined the group in January 2011 to become the seventeenth member, all united through their common currency arrangement.

At many times during 2011 it felt as if Greece or Italy, or both together, would drag the entire Eurozone down. They were clearly the two weakest links, and either one seemed capable of sinking the fleet. The first week of November certainly was one of those times. Greece was falling apart at the seams politically, and Italy was fragmenting.

At the end of the extraordinary meetings on Greece, Papandreou conceded in a press conference that the referendum would be "a question of whether we want to remain in the Eurozone," and retreated to Athens to ponder his next move. The markets not only reacted negatively to the referendum announcement by pummeling the value of Greek assets, but also predictably turned pessimistic on Italian prospects. The Athens Stock Exchange declined by 6.9%, and the Italian FTSE MIB by 6.8%. Spreads on Italian debt widened to a new euro era high,[6] and Italy had €2 trillion in sovereign debt—the fourth largest in the world.[7] Italy had been trying to cope with its problems on its own without the direct support of either the IMF or the EU. But there was a growing sense in some quarters that the time had come to bolster Italy with a program of IMF support as well. IMF Managing Director Lagarde reportedly arrived in Cannes with a plan to put Italy into an €80 billion precautionary program. This line of credit could backstop a monitoring program to reinforce economic reform and fiscal tightening. According to a reported statement by Lagarde, "Italy has no credibility."[8]

Italy's Prime Minister, Silvio Berlusconi, despite his weak standing among the G7 and EU leaders, was able to resist Lagarde's idea. US President Obama apparently threw his lot in with Berlusconi, and that was that. Berlusconi had survived with less scar tissue than Papandreou. For the moment.

But neither would endure for very long. Before the Greek delegation left Cannes, Venizelos and Barroso reportedly exchanged words about the need to "kill the referendum." When the plane landed in Athens, Venizelos issued a statement indicating that leaving the Eurozone was out of the question. "Greece's position within the Euro Area is a historic conquest of the country that cannot be put in doubt."[9]

This was a direct challenge to Papandreou's plan and reflected a government in disarray. A vote of confidence was held, which Papandreou barely survived, but the handwriting was on the wall. Amidst the cacophony and international uproar, Papandreou gave a speech in which he foreshadowed his resignation. Efforts were made to form a new "unity government," but decades-long animosities between PASOK and New Democracy made that difficult, to say the least. On November 9, Papandreou resigned with no successor announced. Three days later, Berlusconi resigned and was replaced by technocrat Mario Monti. Within a matter of a few days, the governments of the two most troubled Euro Area countries had been toppled. Although poor economic management, market pressure, and strategic political blundering had clearly played pivotal roles in the demise of both Papandreou and Berlusconi, it could be argued that the ham-fisted handling of their cases in Cannes also helped push them over the brink. Looking back, it was extraordinary that the other leaders of Europe were, whether intentionally or not, instrumental in bringing about these changes in government. Is that how the Eurozone should function? When a member gets into serious economic difficulty, the other members weigh in on the suitability of leadership of that country? Of course, Greece has a long history of foreign influence and interference in its political leadership; Italy less so. Nonetheless, this is the twenty-first century, and the question warrants reflection.

It is, however, hard to argue with the result from one perspective: both Italy and Greece brought in technocratic governments that helped settle their respective political landscapes, calm the markets, and pave the way toward economic stability and eventual recovery.

Greek Prime Minister George Papandreou waving goodbye. A smile of resignation precedes his formal resignation on November 9, 2011. REUTERS/Yannis Behrakis

Meanwhile, back at the ranch, we felt helpless. As this stunning display of political chaos unfolded, we sought to reassure our creditors—and the markets—that the deal from October 26 was still valid, and we intended to pursue finalization of the details as soon as a new government was formed. Privately, we had our doubts, but we could not allow them to be seen for fear of injecting even more instability into the markets. I had committed to give a speech at a conference in Beijing hosted by the International Finance Forum, a quasi-government group in China led, at the time, by economics professor and politician Cheng Siwei. A fascinating man, Cheng was a prolific author, having written numerous books on economic development and reform. He was also a noted political figure, having served as Vice Chairman of the Standing Committee of China's National People's Congress. Although he always seemed to pack too much into his programs to allow ample time for debate, he attracted top-quality participants and speakers.

Among the speakers in this program were former Korean Prime Minister Han Seung-Soo, IMF Managing Director Christine Lagarde, Governor Zhou Xiaochuan of China's Central Bank, and Andrew Sheng, former head of Hong Kong's Securities Commission. During our visit, I had a wide-ranging lunch with Governor Zhou. He was one of China's most capable economic officials, having served at the helm of the Central Bank (People's Bank of China) since 2002. One of China's most internationally respected and well-known officials, Zhou had become the face of China's international financial relations. He had also become a personal friend as well as a staunch supporter of the IIF. It certainly did not hurt that I was married to a native of Beijing. My wife Peixin was born, raised, and educated in Beijing. She was a graduate of Beijing University, arguably China's most prestigious institution of higher learning, colloquially referred to as "Beida." Immediately following her graduation, she had served as a foreign service officer in China's Foreign Ministry for three years. She left China for the United States in 1987 and never looked back. She had long since become a US citizen, deeply embedded in American society. After acquiring both her MBA and a master's degree in diplomatic history from the University of Washington, she established herself as an investment professional in the private equity world. Furthermore, she was a leading member of the team that brought pension-fund investors into China under the auspices of the Frank Russell Company, which invested more than $1 billion in China's infrastructure, financing some of the first major highways in that country.

Lunch at the People's Bank of China (PBOC) with Governor Zhou Xiaochuan (center) and Steffen Meister, CEO of Partners Group (right). Photo courtesy of the author.

Governor Zhou was trained as an industrial engineer, with a doctor-ate from Tsinghua University. He ascended in the system to become Vice President of the Bank of China, which is China's leading state-owned bank. He then took the helm of SAFE, the subsidiary of China's Central Bank that is responsible for managing foreign exchange. He moved back to the banking industry in 1998 to become the President of China Construction Bank, another large state-owned bank. In 2002, he was appointed to the governorship of the PBOC (China's Central Bank).

An urbane person, Governor Zhou has a civilized manner about him, with a warm, personal smile at virtually every encounter. Even though he had not been educated in the West, he has an innate sense of how to connect with Western leaders and build trust while fulfilling his duties to China with great effectiveness. He often invited me and Peixin to lunch when I visited Beijing, and this occasion was no exception. Alas, Peixin was not with me, so it was a small private lunch, just the two of us.

Zhou was always curious about US policy, and we inevitably spent the first thirty minutes discussing US economic and monetary policy. He was perplexed that the US had not used more capital to write off bad loans during the global financial crisis. Our discussion then turned to the crisis in Europe, and in particular, Greece. I outlined my frustration that after having reached an agreement with Merkel and Sarkozy, political developments in Greece had potentially upset the implementation of this agreement. He assured me that I was on the right path, and that persever-ance would pay off. However, he was alarmed about the instability of the Eurozone as a whole. Chinese exports to Europe had soared during the previous decade, and accounted for one-fifth of Chinese exports, totaling $356 billion in 2011. The EU had, in fact, become China's largest export destination. China was also a major outlet for German exports, totaling approximately €90 billion in 2011. The strength of the Chinese economy in 2010 and 2011 was one major reason why German unemploy-ment remained low during the euro crisis, at only 5.5% in October 2011. Governor Zhou therefore probed about the depth of the Euro Area crisis. I wished that I could give him more assurances than I actually could.

"Governor Zhou, I am afraid the entire situation is quite precarious," I said.

Our conversation then turned to China and the efforts under way to promote economic reform and allow market forces to gain more influence in the Chinese economy. The focus in 2010 had been to sustain growth in the Chinese and world economy while the US and European economies struggled to emerge from the sharp recession of late 2008 and early 2009. The US economy had shrunk 0.3% in 2008 and 3.5% in 2009; Europe ground to a halt in 2011, with Germany growing at a rate of only 0.1% in the second quarter as the euro crisis gripped the region. The US had by then re-established some degree of economic momentum, growing 1.5% for the year, but that was still quite tepid.

On the other hand, China had charged ahead. With the benefit of strong stimulus from both the government and the central bank, the Chinese economy expanded rapidly in both 2010 (10.4%) and 2011 (9.2%). This provided much-needed ballast to the global economy, and China was "feeling its oats." As the fragility of the international finance system became evident in 2008 and 2009, many in China, as well as other parts of the world, began to question the validity of the free-market system that had spawned such volatility and severe recession. The argument was made that China's more "controlled" statist economy was more desirable in the long run.

Governor Zhou had no interest in plowing that field on that afternoon. Although he was well aware of the weaknesses of the Western global financial system—and would subsequently give a speech arguing that the SDR should be enhanced as a global currency—Governor Zhou was focused in the long run on how to support an orderly transition for China into a more market-based economy. The PBOC had injected considerable monetary stimulus into the system in 2009 and 2010, but one of the consequences was a rapid buildup of debt to state-owned enterprises as well as local governments.[10]

"I am quite concerned about the sharp rise in debt levels over the past two years, Charles, and this has been accompanied by a worrisome rise in inflation," he said with a furrowed brow.

Our conversation took place on November 9, as we dined together at a luncheon that he hosted in his private dining room at the PBOC. We were joined by two of his senior staff, including Madame Jin Qi, the Director of the International Department at the PBOC. She was a highly competent career official at the Central Bank who clearly had the trust of Governor Zhou. When she spoke, we knew she was speaking for Zhou. Needless to say, my conversations with Governor Zhou were always conducted in English. But he was extremely busy, and given the time zone issues I often found it convenient and timely to call Madame Jin to discuss particular matters when I was outside China. She was always reliable, and if my call required a reaction from the Governor, she would ensure I received it.

In December 2008, Madame Jin had been quoted as stating that China could sustain economic growth during the crisis, but that there was a need for "timely, effective and pre-emptive measures to tackle the deepening financial and economic crisis,"[11] conveying excerpts from a speech Governor Zhou had given at the opening session of a Sino-American Strategic Economic Dialogue.

China did just that. They managed their economy well during the crisis. But in the fall of 2011, it was clearly time to shift gears and curtail the excess debt that had accumulated in some quarters. Zhou played a pivotal role in that effort.

"It has been necessary to rein in the banks, Charles, in order to successfully dampen the real estate market. We began raising interest rates late last year, and we also stiffened lending standards while increasing reserve requirements," he said. Indeed, the PBOC had shown a remarkable degree of steadfastness in raising interest rates over the preceding twelve months. They had moved rates upward five times, and the banks' reserve requirements a stunning nine times, to fight inflation and steady the real estate markets. At the same time, Governor Zhou continued to pursue a course of reform involving liberalizing the interest rate market and expanding a yuan trade settlement scheme allowing market forces to play a greater role in determining the value of the yuan. It was a remarkable balancing act, which I believed no one other than Governor Zhou could have pulled off.

"I'm impressed that you've persisted in raising interest rates while at the same time persevering with continued reforms," I told him.

He smiled and said simply, "This is my job, Charles." He was a policymaker who could manage to earn the admiration of his professional colleagues at the Bank and central bankers abroad while also maintaining the respect and support of China's political leadership. Even though China was at the time—and remains—far from a market economy, he and his team were quite skillful at reading market signals.

For years, I'd known that Governor Zhou was a pragmatic reformer. I had seen firsthand evidence of this early on during his tenure as the

Governor of the PBOC. In the spring of 2003, the IIF organized a Spring Membership Meeting in Shanghai. It was the first time we held a global membership gathering in China, and we were anxious for it to go well. We managed to line up a Vice Premier as a keynote speaker, as well as the Mayor of Shanghai. We knew, however, that their speeches would be far more diplomatic than economic, and that we needed a senior economic spokesperson from China as well. Zhou had only taken the helm of the People's Bank of China in late 2002, and we were uncertain whether he would agree to give a major address before a gathering of international bankers. We were very pleased, therefore, when his office confirmed his acceptance. Attendance for the meeting was building, as many leading private bankers from the US and Europe were interested in visiting Shanghai and seeing firsthand the near miraculous development that had taken place there during the previous fifteen years, the futuristic shape of the skyline arising almost overnight. There was also growing interest in the Chinese economy, as it was poised to become more integrated into the world economy following its ascension into membership of the World Trade Organization (WTO) in late 2003.

Then came the bad news. I received a call from Madame Jin inform-ing me that Zhou had been injured, having fallen and fractured his leg. As I expressed my regrets and best wishes for a speedy recovery, my mind began racing to consider alternative speakers. Could we reach out to the Finance Minister? What about the Chief Banking Regulator? But before I could lock on any one idea, she interrupted my thoughts by informing me that Governor Zhou still wished to give the speech, but might need a stool. I was quite surprised, and quickly assured them that we would make any arrangements necessary.

I was certainly relieved, but at the same time wondered whether he could pull it off. I did not know the seriousness of the fracture, but I could hardly imagine him standing there and presenting an entire speech in front of three hundred international bankers with a broken leg, even with a stool on which to lean.

But he did! That night, he hobbled up to the stage with a cane, accompanied by his devoted staff carrying his notes, and settled gingerly onto his stool. He then took his notes as one of the IIF staff moved the microphone closer to him. He proceeded to deliver, in a steady and strong voice, one of the most memorable speeches I have ever heard.

The essence of his message was that China would reform their financial system, with the banks at the forefront. They had tried to do this through internal measures: raising auditing standards, strengthening governance, developing more rigorous risk management systems, and limiting banks' lending to state-owned enterprises. Progress has been made, but he continued, it appeared that internal reforms alone were not sufficient to place China's banks on a strong, competitive footing globally. The government decided to augment domestic reforms with the benefit of influence from global markets, and would allow foreign banks to make substantial investments in state-owned banks, bringing their expertise and technology into their banking system. They would also allow their banks to raise capital in international markets, thereby subjecting them to global auditing and accounting standards. China would invite foreign banking experts onto the Boards of their banks, bringing their vast knowledge and experience. And finally, they'd allow private banks to expand their activities, providing stronger competition for the state-owned banks.

It was a bold vision of how to reform the Chinese financial system, and the crowd rose to give him a standing ovation as he slowly walked off the stage with his cane.

During my entire trip to China in November 2011, I was also naturally preoccupied with Greece. Searching on my phone for news on the selection of a new Prime Minister, I had also been in touch with friends in Greece. Rumors were rife that Lucas Papademos would be the next Prime Minister. I had known Lucas for many years, dating back to his days as the Chief Economist at the Bank of Greece. He had been appointed to that position after teaching economics at Columbia University for eight years. We first met during my years at the Treasury when I was in charge of international affairs, and we stayed in touch when I transitioned to JP Morgan and then the IIF. Lucas became Governor of the Bank of Greece in 1994, and we often interacted in Greece at a conference held each summer organized by a mutual friend, Minos Zombanakis. Minos pulled together a fascinating group of Greek, European, British, American, and Middle Eastern leaders for what was called the Athens Seminar. It was a mixture of public officials (including the Saudi Finance Minister and Central Bank Governor), top journalists and writers, European leaders such as former German Finance Minister Manfred Lahnstein, academic leaders such as Graham Allison of Harvard, energy experts such as Ed Morse, and several officials from international organizations such as Bob Zoellick, the former President of the World Bank. It always included, of course, several Greek bankers and officials, Papademos often among them. The gathering was usually held in Athens, and it became a tradition that when the meeting was held there, the Governor of the Bank of Greece would host a dinner on the rooftop of the Bank's headquarters. An impressive stone structure dating back to 1938, it had a lovely view of Athens, and by late evening the temperature often dropped sufficiently, even in the middle of summer, to allow for a pleasant reception and dinner on the rooftop.

From 1994 to 2002, Papademos was the Governor, and always hosted these dinners with grace and dignity. During the program, he and I would often find an opportunity to skip off and have a cup of coffee while discussing the Greek, American, or global economies. I came to admire both his intelligence and his open-mindedness to debate and exchange views. He not only had a doctorate in economics from MIT, but also degrees in physics and electrical engineering. It struck me in those early years of our interactions that this eclectic educational background gave him a certain advantage in seeing the different dimensions of a problem, whether economic, political, financial, or institutional.

During the late 1990s, his focus was preparing the Central Bank for the transition from the Greek drachma to the euro. Soon after Greece joined the Eurozone, Papademos succeeded Christian Noyer as the Vice President of the ECB. Given the questions that surrounded the state of the Greek economy at the time of its acceptance to the EU, it was clearly a statement of respect for Papademos—and not a vote of confidence in the Greek economy—that he became Noyer's successor in 2002.

When I arrived in China on Tuesday evening, November 8, I was focusing on whether Papademos would succeed Papandreou. There was still no word, so I called Papademos directly to ask where things stood. He and I had been in touch after the head of our European Department at the IIF, Jeff Anderson, had pointed out an article Lucas had written in which he expressed concern over potential undesirable side effects of a restructuring of Greece's debt, especially if it did not provide sufficient debt relief or if it turned out to be a "hard, involuntary restructuring." Lucas and I had discussed the matter and I brought him up to date on the current state of play, indicating that we had already "crossed the Rubicon" on the debt restructuring issue, and that there was no way back. He listened carefully, and explained that he had been addressing several issues pertaining to the ongoing discussions, not making a general statement against debt restructuring. Two points he made were especially relevant to the way forward. He had argued that the restructuring would have adverse effects on Greek banks, pension funds, and insurance companies. Second, he had emphasized the consequences of a "hard" restructuring, with potential spillover in the Eurozone. I recalled that although the Rubicon was only a small river in today's northern Italy, Julius Caesar had actually made his famous statement about "crossing the Rubicon" in Greek, referring to a play by the Greek playwright Menander. Lucas responded by saying, "I am impressed by your knowledge of classical Greek and Roman history. Indeed, the Rubicon has been crossed, and the reference has acquired particular meaning given the problems that Greece and Italy are facing. I consider it very positive that your agreement on October 26th refers specifically to a voluntary debt restructuring."

I was assured by his explanations and wholeheartedly agreed with him and continued to stay in touch. I called him the night of my arrival in Beijing to see where things stood. He did not answer, so I left a message.

Early on the morning of November 9, as I was in the middle of breakfast at my hotel in Beijing, I received a return call from Lucas informing me that things looked poor for his selection as Prime Minister.

"Other candidates are being considered, and the discussions are ongoing. There are also certain factors which have not been clarified," he said. "It is essential, Charles, that the political leaders reaffirm their support for the October 26th agreement and that they agree on appropriate framework and timeframe for the attainment of the objective set at the October summit. In addition, it is virtually impossible to complete the debt negotiation by mid-February, so the new government should extend beyond that period. Finally, New Democracy should participate sufficiently in a new government to ensure effective commitment.

I knew it was after midnight in Athens, and Lucas sounded, understandably, very fatigued. I asked whether there was a chance that things could still move in his direction.

"I seriously doubt it, Charles," was his response.

I had only the vaguest idea of what machinations were under way in Athens, but one thing was clear: both PASOK and New Democracy were trying to distance themselves from the Brussels agreement. Wisely, Papademos was trying to use whatever leverage he had to secure their commitment.

"I'm sure you're doing the right thing, Lucas," I told him, "But I am frankly quite disappointed that we will not be working together. I had already begun to look forward to it. Get some rest." I hung up the phone with absolutely no idea of what would happen next. Once again, it seemed, the political class of Athens was unable, even in this moment of national desperation, to find a way forward. I had seen in the past how a technocratic government could step in to stabilize a country—and its economy—in a moment of crisis. In 1997, a close friend of mine, Josef Tosovsky, had been asked by then President of the Czech Republic Václav Havel to take over as Prime Minister in the wake of a scandal regarding the previous government. Josef had served with distinction first as the head of the Czechoslovakian National Bank and then as Governor of the Czech National Bank following the split of Czechoslovakia into the Czech Republic and Slovakia. Like Papademos, he had established a reputation as a highly competent and apolitical central banker. He was selected as Central Banker of the Year in 1993 by *Euromoney Magazine* for having steered the bank through the complicated process of separating into two banks without a hitch. He served as Prime Minister from December 1997 until July 1998, having succeeded in stabilizing the banking system and allowing a new government to be elected. It was quite a successful seven months, and I could envision something similar evolving in Greece.

The next day, both Christine Lagarde and I presented keynote addresses at the conference in Beijing. Both speeches seemed to go well, although all the keynote speakers were rushed and there was no time for questions and answers. Both Christine and I were both visibly frustrated by that, but the program was clearly too jam-packed to allow for good exchange.

Later that afternoon, she and I had a brief meeting about Greece. I expressed my concerns about the IMF staff's handling of the negotiations. In particular, I stressed that it appears that the constant downward revisions to Greece's growth outlook—resulting in part from the continued increases in taxes—was building greater pressure on more and more private debt reduction, potentially more than could be voluntarily agreed among the creditors. She noted my concerns and said she would look into them, but it was clear she wasn't there for an in-depth discussion of Greece. The only IMF staff with her was the China desk officer, so I didn't pursue the matter further. Nevertheless, it was useful to establish rapport with Lagarde in her new role. In any case, we were both expected soon at another meeting, this one with Chinese Vice Premier Wang Qishan.

I'd known Wang since his days as Beijing's Mayor, from 2004 to 2007. The IIF was building its membership in Asia in those days by conducting our Annual Meetings of our Asian CEOs at various Asian capitals. In 2004, the meetings were held in Beijing. Through the intercession of our former Chinese Board Member, Liu Mingkang, Wang agreed to present the keynote address at our formal dinner in the spring of 2004. He had been called to become Mayor on short notice following the rapid spread of SARS in the city during the spring of 2003, having already established himself as a highly capable leader, with considerable experience in the financial sector. Previously, he served as the Chairman of the China Construction Bank.

Wang is a slight man with a ready smile and a confident nature. At our dinner that night, he spoke authoritatively about financial reform in China, and over the meal we conversed quite informally—through a translator—about the United States and the world. Over the years I had called upon him regularly during my visits to Beijing, and during the financial crisis he and I often exchanged views. In 2008, he was promoted to Vice Premier in Charge of Finance and Commerce, and in that capacity chaired the Economic and Trade Components of the US-China Strategic and Economic Dialogue.

As the European crisis unfolded, our contacts became more frequent. China's Vice Minister of Finance for International Affairs, Zhu Guangyao, was a friend of mine from his days as China's Executive Director at the World Bank. Like my wife, he hails from Beijing, and the three of us got to know one another in Washington. Zhu is an animated man who speaks his mind frankly.

During the global financial crisis of 2008–2009, in addition to the European crisis that followed, Zhu became a frequent interlocutor, by phone and in person. As the Greek crisis intensified during 2011, Vice Premier Wang would occasionally ask Zhu to call me regarding specific issues of concern. In particular, was Greece going to be forced out of the Eurozone? How vulnerable were global markets? Most often, Zhu and I would talk directly, and he would relay the essence of my points to Wang. On one occasion, however, Wang got on the phone directly and Zhu served as the translator. It concerned the substantial amount of Greek debt held by the PBOC. The ECB policy of protecting the value of such holdings by the member central banks of the ECB was apparently not being extended to the PBOC, and they were exposed to a potential haircut equal to what the private sector would experience. China was understandably concerned, since their purchase of Greek debt had been an act of solidarity to support Greece and the ECB, and now they were being thrown into the sea alongside private creditors. Although my job was to represent the interests of the private creditors, it was not difficult to see the validity of China's concerns regarding the treatment of their holdings of Greek debt. I committed to do what I could for the Vice Premier, but stressed that my influence on this was limited. After consulting with Lemierre and our team of Hung Tran and Mikis Hadjimichael, I called Mario Draghi and discussed the situation with him. He said he would look into it, but I was not terribly hopeful.

On the afternoon of our conference in Beijing, Lagarde and I joined approximately a half dozen other participants in the IIF program for a meeting with Wang. He was, as always, cordial, but this afternoon he dove right into the Greek crisis by peppering us with questions. What happened to the agreement in Brussels? Why did Papandreou resign? Would Greece now be forced out of the euro? And why so much disagreement among the Europeans? As Lagarde and I tried to explain the complex relationships between the northern and southern members of the Eurozone, Wang made a rather fascinating observation.

"I hope that they have real 'sense and sensibility.' If so, perhaps they will quarrel less." I was rather surprised by his comments, although it was not the first nor the last time he would make literary reference during our meetings. I could only reply, "I hope so."

In accordance with custom, numerous other Chinese officials sat in rows to the left of Wang. This included various party officials and note-takers, but only Yi Gang, then the Deputy Governor of the PBOC (now the Governor), sat in the front row. As we walked out at the end of the meeting, Wang asked me how I relaxed during my long days and nights in Athens.

"Vice Premier Wang," I responded, "there really is little time to relax." I often take a short break at the end of the night before I go to bed to look at the lights shining on the Acropolis with the Parthenon and the smaller but equally gorgeous Erechtheion. I explained that I had been struck by the beauty of the Caryatids on my first visit to the Acropolis in 1970. Even though the Erechtheion was barely visible from the balcony of my room in the Grande Bretagne, I nevertheless could take inspiration from the sight, thinking that the civilization capable of creating those marvelous statues and buildings to their gods could somehow find its way out of its twentieth-century economic quagmire.

When I recounted this to Wang, he chuckled. "I understand your sentiments, but I would suggest instead that you watch American TV shows. Old Westerns can be very relaxing and entertaining." I thanked him for his advice and the meeting as we walked out.

The day following the meeting with Vice Premier Wang, I talked once again with Lucas Papademos, who told me:

"Charles, I wanted to let you know that there is an agreement on the formation of a coalition government and it is likely that I will be the Prime Minister." He added that he believed that "appropriate conditions would be in place that should effectively support the restructuring of public debt and the negotiations of the economic adjustment program in line with the decisions of October 26th."

I was elated; this could possibly provide a path toward finalizing the agreement. Of course, I knew that many obstacles remained, but I also knew that Lucas was a person of honesty and sensibility, with a deep understanding of the economics of Greece, and I could trust him. Had the Greek gods intervened? If so, which one? Most likely Athena herself, goddess of wisdom.

I sent a quick note to both Joe and Jean, informing them of the encouraging news.

CHAPTER 24

STRUGGLING TO CLOSE THE DEAL

"Wrong must not win by technicalities."

—Aeschylus, circa 480 BC

From Beijing it was off to Frankfurt. I had agreed to speak at the Annual Frankfurt European Banking Congress, a prestigious gathering of European and global leaders who came together each November under the traditional banner of Germany's three largest banks: Deutsche Bank, Commerzbank, and Dresdner Bank. Dresdner was acquired by Commerzbank in 2009, so now there were only two host banks. On this occasion, it was hosted by Joe Ackermann, as CEO of Deutsche Bank, and Martin Blessing, CEO of Commerzbank.

They had invited me to speak on the topic of "Shifting Financial Markets," which could be defined in many different ways in the fall of 2011. Commercial and retail banking was under pressure throughout the world thanks to the global financial crisis as well as the subsequent wave of regulation that swept over the global banking system. In the run-up to the crisis, investment banking and capital market operations had become heavily involved in the subprime crisis and had lost a considerable amount of credibility.

I chose to focus on two themes: the need to revitalize bank lending to support the recovery, especially in Europe, and, of course, the necessity to complete the restructuring of Greece's sovereign debt.

Having attended the European Banking Congress for some years, I found it to be a useful place to meet European-based IIF members as well as stay in touch with European officials. But this year I had more on my mind. As we prepared to engage in a further round of negotiations, numerous questions were being raised about our position representing creditors' interests. We knew that the attorneys representing Greece would prefer to have someone else on the other side of the table. Our insistence that any restructuring terms be fully and voluntarily negotiated between creditors and debtors ran against the grain of the sentiment in some quarters: staff of the IMF, members of the academic community, and voices in the official sector.

Insisting that everyone in the Greek negotiations adhere to the IIF's "Principles for Stable Capital Flows and Fair Debt Restructuring" was not popular in many quarters of the official community. Debtors had gradually acquired more leverage and influence in the official sector, especially after the Argentinian restructuring of 2003–2004. A practice had emerged in this murky world of sovereign debt restructuring whereby the debtor would present a "proposal" to a loosely formed, rather small group of creditors, often including those who were most inclined to accept terms favorable to the debtor. This was often much more appealing to the debtor—and to the debtor's advisers—than having to negotiate every time with a different, larger group of creditors.

A report emerged that even the Chancellor's office in Germany was looking for "other groups" to represent the "creditors." We had, to be frank, acquired our authority in a very unusual way. We assembled the first group of "creditors" in Paris in the spring of 2011 with the support of a few key creditors and the Board of the IIF. We did not, in contrast to past practice, organize a formal creditors committee at that time.

The lack of one had not noticeably hindered our effectiveness, especially as Lemierre and I had worked very closely together. However, at one point during the summer of 2011, especially when the need for a restructuring was still very unclear, my old friend Bill Rhodes and I had a lengthy discussion about the pros and cons of organizing a more formal "Advisory Committee," as such committees had been called. Bill had enormous experience in dealing with sovereign debt rescheduling in the 1980s and early 1990s from his senior position at Citibank. I had also worked closely with him in his position as Vice Chairman and then First Vice Chairman of the IIF. As I waited to catch a plane back to the States in early July, he made a strong argument that we should formally organize into a Steering or Advisory Committee to strengthen our position. I listened carefully, and subsequently discussed it with Jean Lemierre, Hung, and Mikis, but we all thought that we might be only weeks away from wrapping up the negotiations and saw no pressing need to move in that direction.

By mid-November, things felt different. We knew we'd be under pressure to agree to an even larger discount on the debt, and if we were to withstand at least some of that pressure, our credibility representing the creditors needed to be rock solid. We were also aware that there were now numerous hedge funds holding some of the debt, purchased at a considerable discount. It was very possible that they would agree to terms that would not appeal at all to some of the original bank and insurance holders.

Reflecting on this, we decided to organize a meeting in Frankfurt on November 17, hosted by Deutsche Bank, to decide how to move forward organizationally. Most of the leading creditors saw the need to consolidate and reinforce our position. After nearly a full day of discussion, the group agreed to form a "Private Creditor-Investor Committee for Greece." The Committee would represent any creditor with at least €100 million in Greek sovereign bonds.

Private Creditor-Investor Committee for Greece

The overall Committee consisted of thirty-three financial institutions, six from Greece, two from Cyprus, and the rest from Europe and the US, with a Steering Committee consisting of twelve creditors. Below is a list of the Committee members, effective December 21, 2011, with the names of the Sterring Committee Banks marked by an asterisk.

Ageas	Credit Agricole	Intesa Sanpaolo*
Allianz*	DekaBank	Landesbank Baden-Württemberg*
Alpha Bank*	Deutsche Bank*	MACSF
AXA*	Dexia	Marathon Asset Management
Bank of Cyprus	Emporiki Bank of Greece	Marfin Popular Bank
BayernLB	Eurobank	MetLife
BBVA	Generali	National Bank of Greece*
BNP Paribas*	Greylock Capital Management*	Piraeus Bank
BPCE	Groupama	Royal Bank of Scotland
CNP Assurances*	HBC	Société Générale
Commerzbank*	ING*	UniCredit

As mentioned earlier, the years preceding the Eurozone debt crisis, the nature of sovereign debt restructurings had undergone considerable evolution—in the wrong direction, as far as many creditors were concerned. During the 1980s and for most of the 1990s, sovereign debt restructurings were negotiated through Creditor Committees, formed by the creditors themselves. Usually, the main creditors were banks, and the largest bank creditor often took the lead. Bill Rhodes's book, *Banker to the World*, describes this process in great detail. Every restructuring had a "negotiated solution."[1] Although many times the US Treasury, the Federal Reserve, or the IMF would put some pressure on either the banks or the debtor nation when they felt that one side was becoming unreasonable or too obstinate (I was involved in that more times than I can recall), the process had a negotiated and largely "voluntary" feel to it. Neither side was able to present a fait accompli to the other side. Sometimes it was voluntary with a capital "V," sometimes with a lowercase "v," but it was voluntary.

But during the 1990s and 2000s, the process changed in favor of the debtors. The IMF gradually, almost imperceptibly at times, began to put more pressure on the creditors for large debt reductions. This was partly the unintended consequences of the crucial bridge that had been crossed with the Brady Plan in 1989 and 1990 (as discussed in Chapter 14). Until that time, privately held debt was rescheduled with new maturities and interest rates, but not reduced in nominal value. Once the Brady Plan broke the mold, sovereign debtors often looked to not only reschedule but to reduce significantly the nominal and real value of the debt.

Another factor was the evolution of creditors from a bank-dominated group to a more diversified group of capital market creditors, hedge funds, asset managers, private wealth investors, investment banks, etc. This more atomistic world also shifted power to the debtor, making it more difficult for the creditors to organize themselves effectively.

In hindsight, it is rather remarkable that we were able to initiate negotiations earlier in the year of 2011 without a formal structure—a negotiation that actually led to an agreement, albeit one that would not hold. The move in November to formalize our structure into the Private Creditor-Investor Committee for Greece was, as explained, a move to consolidate our position as the legitimate and sole "voice" of the private creditors. It worked, despite the fact that the thirty-three members of the Committee held only approximately 40% of the total outstanding Greek government bonds (GGBs) held by the private sector. Notwithstanding the rumblings among some officials, including IMF staff and Greece's legal advisers, there were no other credible representatives for the creditors, so they had little choice but to deal with us.

Jean and I were officially appointed as co-chairs of the Steering Committee and, importantly, the IIF staff (primarily Hung and Mikis) were confirmed as the Secretariat. Nothing really changed, de facto, in terms of leadership. We did, however, hire Blackstone as Advisor to the Steering Committee on financial issues, and hired Allen & Overy and White & Case as legal advisers. The mandate was clear: we were to negotiate a voluntary agreement within the framework of the October 26 agreement. The various agreements among the parties necessarily injected fees for the advisers into the discussion, which were not fully resolved for quite some time after the negotiations ended. With this formal structure in place, we set about to develop our own negotiating position for the next engagement.

Before our Task Force meeting in Frankfurt, during which we consolidated the formation of our new Steering Committee, Jean and I decided to go to Athens for a meeting with Papademos in his new position as Prime Minister. We arrived on November 16, and first went to see key Greek bankers. We had lunch with Yannis Costopoulos and his Deputy, Spyros Filaretos. They were encouraged by the appointment of Papademos but highly uncertain that this would lead to progress in the negotiations. The banking system was virtually frozen, and the economy continued to shrink at a frightening pace. We went to see Evangelos Venizelos. He was in a formal mood and stressed the need for him to work with his "European and international partners." Perhaps unfairly, we took this to mean that he might need to succumb to the prospective pressures of IMF and Germany for an even larger haircut. It was the first meeting between us since his brief hospitalization during the referendum episode of early November, and we inquired about his health. He had recovered, both medically and politically, as he had survived the turmoil of those two weeks, maintaining his position as Deputy Prime Minister and Finance Minister. He stressed the weakness of the economy, which was certainly the case, and asked for our assistance.

"Evangelos, we will make every effort to reach an agreement fully consistent with the understandings reached in Brussels in late October," we told him. Jean reinforced the message by stating unequivocally that now it was time to come together on the details around the 50% haircut, not to seek further advantage. We left Evangelos's office and went to our first meeting with Papademos as Greece's Prime Minister.

As I walked into his new office, my spirits were lifted. He greeted us with a warm smile and showed us in. I said, "Lucas, I bet you never expected to be working in this office."

"You are absolutely correct. I did not expect it until last week," he said as he gently laughed. "I am still learning my way around, but I'm learning fast." He then went on to explain that he had already been spending considerable time on the phone with the leaders of the political parties forming the coalition government, speaking on the phone with European leaders and presidents of institutions, as well as with leading parliamentarians, seeking support for the technocratic government, especially in view of the next round of adjustment measures that would be needed.

We brought Papademos up to date on the debt negotiation from our perspective and assured him of our willingness to work with him to find a mutually agreeable solution. As Jean and I left his office, we better appreciated the pressures he faced on many fronts, but we nevertheless had hopes that his professionalism, patriotism, economic skills, and unassailable credentials would prevail over dysfunctional local and regional politics, economic collapse (unemployment had jumped to 20.4%), and strife on the streets. In the end, he did prevail, but not before overcoming multiple challenges along the way during his seven-month tenure as Prime Minister.

In the weeks that followed, we set about developing with our fellow creditors a detailed proposal to share with the Eurogroup Working Group chaired by Grilli and key European officials. On November 30, we submitted a proposal to the Grilli group. At the outset of the proposal, we stressed that the Greek banks should be recapitalized with preferred shares financed by official financial assistance. We also underscored the importance of Greek banks having "adequate liquidity support by the ECB." We approached the restructuring of the €206 billion in privately held GGBs as follows:

1) 50% upfront nominal haircut on the total, eliminating approximately €103 billion in debt.

2) The remainder of this debt to be exchanged for new GGBs with the following features:

a. English law (a very critical feature to the creditors)

b. 30-year maturity

c. Use of collateral in the form of AAA-rated zero-coupon bonds issued by a sovereign or supranational to defease in full the principal of new GGBs. The collateral would amount to €30 billion, the amount committed by Merkel and the Eurogroup leadership on October 26.

d. An average coupon of 5% on the new GGBs.

e. The net present value (NPV) of the new instruments would be calculated based on market prices at the time of the exchange.

f. Comparable treatment of all privately held GGBs.

g. GDP warrants would be an integral part of the exchange based on higher-than-expected GDP growth (this was an important component to the creditors, providing a potential means to recoup some of their losses as the Greek economy recovered).

h. Goal of December 16 for full agreement.

i. The proposal left open the door to alternative approaches without credit enhancements whereby the €30 billion would be used to pay down a portion of the debt.

The inclusion of the section on collateral was based in large part on the experience of the Brady Plan. I had seen firsthand the powerful effects of zero-coupon collateral. It had provided a major boost to the underlying creditworthiness of Mexican, Brazilian, and other Brady Plan sovereign debt, fueling a strong demand for the new assets, and providing substantial returns to those who purchased the new paper.

However, times and attitudes were different in 2011. In 1989, long-term (30-year) US Treasury rates were 10.32%, providing zeros with considerable earning power over the life of the bond and thus reducing the amount required for the initial purchase of zeros. In 2011, however, interest rates were very low, reflecting the weakness of the European economy and the preceding global recession, with 10-year German bond rates at 1.82%. Thus, €50 billion of new Greek debt would require many more zero-coupon bonds to defease than was the case in 1989.

There were other problems with the use of EU money to purchase zeros. The private creditors had little confidence in the future of Greece at that time. Many of them preferred to use the €30 billion pool of EU funds to receive direct partial payment on their Greek exposure, even if it was only fifteen cents on the euro.

In early December, I attended a Group of 30 meeting in New York. The Group of 30 is a group of financial leaders who meet regularly to exchange views on global finance issues as well as develop ideas for addressing those issues. It consists of a distinguished group of central bankers, commercial bankers, and academic economists. Although I was not a formal member, I was invited regularly to participate, which I found quite useful for my role at the IIF. In early December, I discussed the Greek crisis with a number of attendees, especially Lael Brainard, then the Under Secretary of the US Treasury for International Affairs. I implored her to step into the Greek crisis and pull the IMF away from its strategy of excess austerity. She said she would look into it, but I was not able to discern any meaningful engagement by the Treasury.

The proposal was presented to the official sector just ahead of a meeting with them on December 12 in Greece, hosted by EFG Eurobank, now simply known as Eurobank. The current CEO of the bank, Fokion Karavias, a highly capable banker, was then serving as the Eurobank's representative on the Creditor Committee. He hosted the meeting and did an excellent job. His strength of character and realism, mixed with a touch of resignation, was impressive to observe. Despite being caught in the vise of this crisis—between the Greek government's collapsing creditworthiness on the one hand and the need to support the economy as best they could on the other—the Greek bankers behaved with a remarkable degree of professionalism.

This meeting on December 12 was largely uneventful and mostly involved the presentation of our proposal to the Eurogroup. Jean and I, with strong support from Hung, Mikis, and our legal and financial advisers, walked them through each element. There were many questions, but few reactions. They actually seemed somewhat relaxed. Perhaps if we had all taken a walk through Syntagma Square and the streets of Athens to see firsthand how weak the economy was and how volatile the situation was in the city, they would have been more concerned.

They assured us they would contemplate our proposal, and we agreed to meet again, in short order, in Paris. Even with the benefit of the agreement in Brussels in late October, they did not appear to have a mandate to take the negotiation further. Admittedly, there were reasons to be distracted. Grilli was still chairing the Group, but the Berlusconi government had fallen within a week of the collapse of the Papandreou government. The markets were on fire. Grilli remained the Under Secretary at the Italian Ministry of Economy, and Mario Monti had become Prime Minister and had also taken over the portfolio of Economy and Finance. Perhaps expecting Grilli to focus on Greece at that moment was just too much to ask.

The Creditor team left Greece to reposition in Paris, and we saw the meetings there as potentially definitive. We were wrong—very wrong.

Prior to the next round of negotiation, Jean and I were once again scheduled to see Xavier Musca at the Elysée.

He looked distracted, but he listened. Jean made only two points: 1) this has to be done, and quickly; otherwise, the markets could tear the

Attending a Group of 30 Meeting with Peixin. Joining us is Sir David Walker (to my left) and Joseph Ciechanover. Photo by Dan Porges/Getty Images.

Eurozone apart, country by country, piece by piece, and even France could come into the crosshairs; and 2) there was no room for further concessions from the banks. We were prepared to take the previous losses as agreed, but anything more would likely cross the line from voluntary to involuntary.

Xavier understood and said he would speak to both Sarkozy and Lagarde. As we walked down the red carpet of the Elysée once again, we cautioned him that the IMF would likely push for a greater haircut as the Greek economy continued to sink into the Mediterranean. He thanked us for our visit, and we then went to see one of his successors, Ramon Fernandez, as the Director General du Trésor at the French Treasury. Ramon had been the central person who had agreed to the 21% haircut in July, on behalf of the debtors. He was somewhat surprised that we had given ground to a 50% haircut; he therefore found it quite reasonable that we did not wish to be pushed further. He also had a sense of the market pressure and assured us we had his support.

It was at times like this that I was very thankful that I had Lemierre by my side. He had a sense of European intricacies that often eluded me, and many officials, including but not limited to Musca and Fernandez, looked up to him.

The meeting the next day, held at BNPP's headquarters in Paris, was a disaster. Jean and I held a pre-meeting in his office with one of the key representatives of the "debtor" side of the table, Gerassimos Thomas, a senior and well-respected European Commission official. He is a thoughtful, highly professional economist who brought a balanced view to many issues. We wanted to see what his thinking was about some of our proposals, especially on interest rates and warrants. We also wanted to express our concern about the perceived lack of urgency on the part of the official sector. He shared our concerns on the latter point, but had little definitive insight to offer on the other questions. As we walked out of the room, one of the other delegates from the Greek side of the table saw us, and apparently became concerned.

We then began our formal discussions in the larger conference room and began to make some progress in discussing the critical variables. There was a willingness to engage in further work on a co-financing scheme, possibly an A/B loan structure linking the €30 billion to the new bonds. Furthermore, there were indications that English law would be accepted as the new governing law. The Greek delegates, Petros Christodoulou and

Georgios Zanias, began to engage on the issue of the maturity and coupon of the new debt. We were moving forward in dealing with key issues, and it was shaping up to be a productive meeting. At that point, however, the IMF delegate returned to the room, having apparently conferred with IMF leadership in Washington, and with the support of Greece's legal advisers, the IMF intervened to say that the Greek representative had no authority to express a position on those issues.

We were appalled. Our side of the table looked around at each other in disbelief. Was this real? It was embarrassing to see the Greek officials undermined by their own counsel, as well as the IMF. Isn't it remarkable how suddenly circumstances can change? On a dime, the air went out of the room. It appeared that the IMF, and perhaps some of Greece's advisors, felt that the Greek officials were moving too rapidly or were too flexible.

We asked for a break, and Jean, Hung, Mikis, and I went back into Jean's office. Exasperation. Fatigue. Concern. We decided that we could not negotiate with the European Finance Working Group any longer. We asked for a private meeting with the Creditor Committee to inform them and seek their support. They were unanimously in support. We agreed to let Jean-Claude Juncker and other key officials know that the current engagement was broken.

We returned to the meeting room and advised the Eurogroup that we were not prepared to continue negotiating in this fashion.

"The meeting is over, and we will be in touch," Jean Lemierre stated succinctly. There was a look of surprise among the officials, some of whom most likely thought we were bluffing. We packed our bags, shook hands with the officials, and walked out of the room. Little did we realize at that time that this was the last occasion when the Private Creditor-Investor Committee would meet with the Eurogroup. Negotiations went in another direction, which were ultimately more productive than anything that had been realized in the "Grilli" format.

Less than two months after the breakthrough with Merkel, Sarkozy, et al., the process had gone seriously off track. We pinned our hopes on working with Papademos and Venizelos in Greece, and Juncker, Olli Rehn, and other key officials in Brussels.

However, Papademos had his own challenges. He was settling into the job and realizing the enormity of the challenges he faced. Surrounded

Prime Minister Lucas Papademos (right) and Finance Minister Evangelos Venizelos addressing the press at a low point in the debt negotiations. December 9, 2011, in Brussels. Photo by Thierry Charlier/AFP via Getty Images.

by pressure from the markets, recalcitrant politicians in Athens, our team representing the creditors, and in particular, the Troika, he was feeling the heat. He had, nonetheless, developed a solid working relationship with Venizelos, and the widespread respect with which he was held in many quarters gave him some room to maneuver. However, as he moved through December and in light of the breakdown in our talks in Paris, he must have felt that the room for maneuvering was steadily declining.

CHAPTER 25

ROUNDING
SECOND BASE

"If you are rounding second base, you are only halfway home."

—Charles Dallara, 2012

The lack of willingness, or preparedness (we were not certain which), to engage on the coupon and financing structure perplexed us, although it was not altogether a surprise. On the one hand, while the Greek economy continued to deteriorate, and market pressure continued to build, there was at last a broad framework in place, and there were clear issues on which both sides could focus: interest rates on the new debt, maturity structure, co-financing schemes, etc. On the other hand, calls made by Jean Lemierre and me to senior officials in the days following our failed meeting in Paris revealed that the European authorities remained quite divided on key issues, including the coupon (interest rate) of the new debt, as well as on other terms. But more disconcertedly, we learned from conversations with Juncker, Rehn, and others that a non-voluntary approach to the restructuring of Greek debt was being considered. This could take the form of a proposal being sent directly to the creditors without prior discussion and negotiation with the Steering Committee. The October 26 statement by the Euro Summit had clearly invited Greece, the private sector, and all parties concerned to develop a *voluntary* [emphasis mine] bond exchange. Nevertheless, some of the lawyers for Greece as well as others, possibly including some IMF staff, were agitating for a "unilateral" approach. We had stymied these efforts somewhat with the formation of the formal Creditor Committee, but voices were being raised again in support of this idea. After all, in the eyes of some in the sovereign debt arena, this had become the norm, as demonstrated by Argentina. Despite the G20 endorsement of the IIF's "Principles for Stable Capital Flows and Fair Debt Restructuring," which had solidified the crucial importance of voluntary debt negotiations, some officials still wanted to flirt with the idea of involuntary approaches. Many leading emerging-market officials—such as Agustín Carstens, then Governor of the Bank of Mexico, and now the head of the BIS; Arminio Fraga, then Governor of the Central Bank of Brazil; and Zhou Xiaochuan, then Governor of Central Bank of China—had become Trustees of the Principles, demonstrating their support for the basic tenets of a market-based fair debt restructuring, including the core principle that any restructuring should be voluntary. The Trustees always had, in fact, become somewhat of a Who's Who in global finance in the years leading up to the Greek crisis.

Despite such broad support in the official sector, and virtually total support for the Principles in the private sector, the risk of an involuntary approach wherein Greece developed its own proposal and presented it to the entire world of private sector GGB holders, without prior consultation, generated considerable anxiety in the marketplace, further weakening the secondary market value of these bonds. We knew that Papademos would not find this approach attractive, as he had previously argued that a disorderly default could have severe consequences for Greece and the Eurozone, but other forces were pulling Greece in their direction.

We engaged in intense consultation among the key creditors, at the Committee level as well as with many CEOs, and decided to present four options to the European and Greek authorities for consideration. On December 20, on the eve of the holidays, we offered these possibilities:

1) Do nothing—make no formal offer but engage in informal discussions with Greek and Euro Area officials.

2) Send a letter to Merkel and Sarkozy with a revised offer involving 30-year maturity, 10 years' grace, with a weighted average coupon of 6.2%, producing a debt-to-GDP ratio of 123.8% in 2020.

3) Send a letter to Merkel and Sarkozy with the same new maturity structure but with a weighted average coupon of 5.25%, bringing the 2020 debt-to-GDP ratio down to 121.5%.

4) Send a letter to Merkel and Sarkozy with no formal new offer but highlighting our willingness to engage in further discussions.

Importantly, each of the new specific options (2 and 3) acknowledged that the net percent value loss to the creditors would be well above 50%, depending upon the discount rate used to make the calculations. At a 9% discount rate, the net percent value loss would be 56.8%.

These options were vigorously discussed among the creditors in a series of conference calls over the holidays. They were also tested out informally with key EU officials including Juncker, Rehn, Musca, and Papademos. By then we had developed a steady line of communication with these officials. Jean often concentrated on the French and European officials in key capitals while I focused on deepening the dialogue with Papademos and Juncker. As the leadership of Italy and Greece had changed in the fall of 2011, two other important changes had taken effect. Thomas Wieser had replaced Grilli as the Chair of the Eurogroup, and Mario Draghi had become the President of the ECB. I didn't know Wieser, but Jean did, and he immediately struck up a dialogue with him. This proved to be very useful in the ensuing months. Wieser was an experienced hand in European economic policy circles, having served as Vice President and then President of the Economic and Financial Committee of the EU. As Director General in the Austrian Finance Ministry, he was well placed to step in to chair the Working Group. While Grilli had certainly done his best in a very difficult set of circumstances, Wieser assuming this role, eliminated the tension between Italian and Greek fortunes that had bedeviled Grilli's role.

Joe Ackermann, Jean, and I all had worked with Draghi during the course of his career as a senior official in the Italian Treasury and then as Governor of the Italian Central Bank. Draghi had built a reputation as an excellent economist, but also possessing savvy political skills, both of which were amply demonstrated throughout his tenure at the helm of the ECB and then subsequently as the Prime Minister of Italy.

Jean-Claude Trichet had been, and remains, a close friend and outstanding collaborator for many years, and I hold him in the highest regard. But his strong resistance to a restructuring of Greek debt, while certainly based on a principled view of the fundamental nature of the Eurozone, had certainly complicated the process. Draghi had not been vocal about his position on this in 2011, and therefore did not have to deal with that baggage. Ackermann and I met with him over drinks in the fall of 2011 in Washington, and we knew that while his first priority would be protecting the ECB's stability and strength in dealing with Greece, he was also inclined to work with us to find pragmatic solutions to the debt restructuring.

After intense debate among our Steering Committee members, we settled on option three. We sent a letter on the 5th of January to Merkel and Sarkozy under the signatures of Ackermann, Lemierre, and me. We copied Papademos, Juncker, van Rompuy, Barroso, Rehn, and Lagarde—not to leave out any of the seniors! In the letter, we recalled their personal involvement in forging the agreement of October 26–27 and asked them to step in again to avoid a disorderly default. We also reminded them that in the October deal they had set an end goal of 2011 for the new arrangements to be agreed, and cautioned about reopening the basic parameters of the October agreement.

Based on our extensive discussions with Papademos, we concluded our letter with the following, "We understand that Prime Minister Papademos shares our view that a voluntary agreement needs to be included as soon as possible, with agreement in principle no later than mid-January. Any further delay is likely to present insurmountable operational challenges to concluding the voluntary debt exchange in time to avoid default by Greece." We were all aware that a large repayment of principal by Greece was due in mid-March 2012. The heat was on.

We had been made aware that IMF staff, seeing that the economy's contraction was increasing the financing gap substantially, were re-basing the debt sustainability analysis. Accordingly, they sought to increase the haircut of the private creditors by a sizable amount, as well as to obtain greater fiscal adjustment. We'd received assurances from both Juncker and Rehn that they would not support such a move, but we were nevertheless quite concerned. We felt that we were very close to the point at which we would have to reject any further haircuts.

CHAPTER 26

PAPADEMOS STEPS
FRONT AND CENTER

"A leader is a dealer in hope."

—Napoleon Bonaparte, 1805

With the breakdown of the talks at the Working Group level, and the direct re-engagement with Merkel and Sarkozy, as well as Juncker, Papademos, Venizelos, Rehn, and others, this finally had the feeling of a real sovereign debt negotiation—perhaps for the first time. With the brief exception of the meetings in Brussels in July where agreement had been reached on the 21% haircut, much of the preceding seven months had felt like a preliminary boxing match in which one fighter is not sure he wants to be in the ring and had three managers plus two trainers in his corner. Not that we on the private credit side always knew where we wanted to go; we were at times also groping for a way forward amidst a lot of turbulence.

But finally in December and January a dynamic emerged that began to take the shape of meaningful engagements and negotiations. Greece was front and center in the negotiations, with Papademos at the helm. The dynamic went something like this:

- The Private Creditor-Investor Committee, usually through the Steering Committee, would share a proposal based on considerable internal debate at all levels. The creditors were nervous and increasingly anxious to get something out of their Greek exposure. We increasingly focused not only on the coupon and maturity of the new paper, but two other features: receiving cash or a highly liquid, high-quality alternative for 15% of their holdings (shifting away from a collateral-based approach); and a GDP warrant that offered hope (or wishful thinking?) of a future recovery of claims if the Greek economy recovered more than anticipated by the IMF.

· During this time our legal and financial advisers became actively engaged in supporting us—Allen & Overy and White & Case on legal issues, Blackstone on the financial front. As we dug into the complex details of the negotiation on many matters, such as collective action clauses and warrants, their input became increasingly critical. Of course, on core issues such as net present value calculation based on various discount rates, no one was as quick or as reliable as Mikis. At the eleventh hour, when we were finalizing arrangements in Brussels on February 21, this would become pivotal to the outcome, benefiting the creditors significantly. (The value our advisers added during the December–March period did make me wonder whether we should have brought them on board earlier in the process. Would it have made a difference in the negotiations over the summer? Possibly, but we will never know.)

· Once we had formulated a new proposal, we would formally present it to Papademos or Venizelos, or both (preceded on occasion by communications directly with Merkel's and Sarkozy's offices), which usually took place in two-on-two meetings in Papademos's office involving Papademos, Venizelos, Lemierre, and myself. Papademos and Venizelos would then discuss our proposal with the Troika officials in subsequent meetings as part of their overall program negotiations. As he was dealing with us on the debt negotiations, Papademos also had to deal with the Greek political leader, his cabinet, the parliament, and to continue negotiations with the Troika (primarily the IMF) on further adjustment measures in the midst of the center of an extraordinarily weak economy. I did not envy his job.

· Following discussions with the Troika, Papademos would revert to us on our proposals, giving us concrete feedback on issues pertaining to the debt restructuring. At the same time, he and Venizelos, as well as Jean and I, were maintaining a continuous dialogue with key European officials to reinforce our negotiating position.

· Following their feedback, sometimes reinforced by direct discussions between our staff and the Finance Ministry's team, we would enter into a round of discussions with our creditors to consolidate another response on our side, and the process would move into another cycle. This paradigm, although quite odd in the recent history of sovereign debt restructurings, actually worked much better than the previous one.

In the course of our negotiations, we developed a direct line into the offices of Merkel and Sarkozy through their economic advisers. For example, on December 28, 2011, a week before our letters to Merkel and Sarkozy, Jean and I wrote to Lars-Hendrik Röller, Merkel's Chief Economic Advisor, and Xavier Musca, Sarkozy's Chief Economic Advisor, telegraphing our proposal in advance, and doing so with full agreement with Papademos. This enabled us to leverage not only our own outreach to other officials, but those of Papademos as well. In our letter to each of the advisers, we refer to conversations that Papademos held with Draghi and Rehn, both of whom shared the importance of finalizing an agreement without further delay.

During the holidays, Peixin and I sought a break in Barbados. Although we enjoyed the warm weather, there was little relaxation as the negotiations gathered momentum. Virtually every day involved numerous calls with creditor groups and key officials, including Papademos. It was encouraging to learn that his positions and those of the creditors were broadly aligned on several issues. His commitment to voluntary restructuring was as firm as ours. He also shared our view that the IMF program was excessively focused on fiscal adjustment, with successive tax increases and other measures contributing to further weakness in the economy. Regarding key financial parameters of the restructuring, he relied heavily on Evangelos Venizelos and his team at the Ministry, and of course he had to give weight to the views of the Troika. However, he always listened carefully to our perspectives, asking many questions as he tried to balance the tremendous pressures he faced. Through it all, he remained calm, courteous, and focused.

On January 18, 2012, the EFSF issued its first guaranteed notes in the amount of €27 billion—guaranteed by the Eurozone members with the exception of Greece and Ireland. This was a crucial step toward implementing the October 26 agreement, enabling the Eurozone to raise the capital needed to make the €30 billion loan to Greece—and for Greece to use it to pay down 15% of the debt owed to private creditors.

It was becoming obvious that, unsurprisingly, the Greek economy was far from stabilizing. Industrial production had declined 5.5% from a year earlier, and labor shedding had continued to be aggressive. Detailed data released around the turn of the year showed that 324,000 jobs had disappeared from a year earlier—7% of the entire labor force—mostly from the private sector. The public sector, on the other hand, protecting positions that were too often inefficient, lost only 2% over the same period.

Notwithstanding these depressing data, the IMF was pushing for more austerity. Revenues were weaker than the IMF had expected. Despite a massive correction in the underlying deficit from 2009 to the end of 2011 of over 11% of GDP, the IMF was asking for more in the way of both spending cuts and tax increases.

On the structural reform front, Greece had arguably been its own worst enemy throughout much of 2011. Less than €2 billion of privatization of state assets took place in 2011 despite lofty goals that had been in the IMF program. While some of this may have been due to difficult market conditions, lack of political support for some asset sales by leading PASOK and New Democracy politicians also played a role.[1]

Another issue came to the fore in January, which proved to be one of the thorniest we would face: should the new bonds issued by Greece as part of the debt reduction operation have collective action clauses? These had become an important issue in the debate over sovereign debt restructuring during the first decade of the century. Collective action clauses (CACs) became popular in the early 2000s as a device to limit the extent to which a minority of individual creditors could hold out and either prevent the implementation of a sovereign restructuring that has the support of a supermajority or could obtain special terms. As the Institute was developing the draft set of Principles for sovereign debt restructuring in 2003 and 2004, the use of CACs was developing momentum within the G10, G20, the IMF, and various official circles. The IIF was at the forefront of debating and encouraging their adoption. In the years that followed, the International Capital Markets Association (ICMA) took the lead in guiding the private sector's positions on many issues relating to CACs, such as creditor engagement clauses (ensuring that the debtor engages widely with creditors), pari-passu clauses, etc.

As we began our deliberations on this in 2012, the issues before us were, as usual, complicated. The bulk of the privately held Greek government debt (€177 billion of the €206 billion) had been issued under Greek law without CACs. Most of the remainder was issued under English law, so the crucial question was whether to insert CACs into the new bonds that were under Greek law prior to the exchange. This was, of course, linked to another question: under what law would the new bonds be issued: Greek, English, or other? Our legal counsel advised us that the Greek Parliament could insert CACs, but they would be vulnerable to legal challenge, as the whole idea behind them was to insert them into new-issue bonds rather than ones that were in the process of being restructured. Would their insertions through Greek parliamentary action be consistent with a voluntary approach, to which we were bound? Several of us had serious reservations regarding this. It seemed to depend in large part on whether the other terms of the new bond were settled through a process of negotiations or through a "cram-down" process.

There was also the pivotal question of whether we could achieve a sufficient number of creditors supporting the deal without this device. After all, if the Greek Parliament did insert a collective action clause (CAC), and if a creditor wanted the new paper (the old paper would be worthless), they would have to accept the new CAC on the existing Greek law GGBs. As we approached the meetings in mid-January, this whole issue was very much an open question.

In early January, I made a quick trip to Ottawa to see Mark Carney. I had worked with Mark since his time at Canada's Department of Finance in 2004–2007, during which he served as that country's G7 Deputy. During those years he showed an unusual mix of market awareness and policy savvy, especially with regard to international debt issues. In early 2012, he had just been appointed as the new Chair of the Financial Stability Board, a very important group of central bankers and regulators that had been created in early 2009, institutionalizing the Financial Stability Forum, which itself had been formed in 1999 by the G7 on the recommendation of Hans Tietmeyer.

Forgive me for this digression, one of many, I know, but Hans had been a giant in central banking circles for many years (I introduced him earlier in connection with Greece's entry into the Eurozone). He had served as President of the Bundesbank from 1993 to 1999, and in that capacity he had proposed the creation of the group to supplement the work of the Basel Committee, which consisted only of central bankers and focused on regulatory matters and financial stability. This came in the wake of two crises in 1998—one surrounding the Russian debt default in August 1998, and the subsequent, related collapse of Long-Term Capital Management in the US. Hans and others had seen the need to bring central bankers and finance ministers together in a group that was broader than just the G5 or G7.

It was a prescient move. By the time Carney took over the Financial Stability Board in 2011, the group was helping to build a stronger, more resilient global financial system after the global financial crisis of 2008–2009. Numerous initiatives were under way to strengthen the regulatory framework, especially for banks, including higher capital requirements and stronger risk-management standards. There was no doubt at the time that higher levels of capital were needed in the banking system, but the pace and magnitude of raising capital requirements was being hotly debated between the banks and the regulators. The crisis had caused such a drastic, sharp collapse of the global economy that banks were being pummeled by the media, politicians, and at times, the regulators. Although the discourse between the bankers and regulators was generally civilized and professional, it could also get heated at times. In the fall of 2011, the IIF worked together with our member firms and the Security Industry Association (SIA) to organize a meeting in Washington among the world's leading finance Chairmen/CEOs and Mark Carney. We had numerous committees and working groups engaged in a structured dialogue with the regulators on a host of issues, but occasionally more senior level discussions were useful to get to the bottom of things, more or less.

At the time of the meeting, held in a conference room of the historic US National Archives Museum in Washington, many bankers felt that the new regulatory standards were being applied in such a fashion that they would inhibit economic recovery, since increases in capital requirements were constraining banks' lending capacities. Tensions were running high, and in hindsight perhaps inviting only one senior central banker/regulator to a meeting with twenty or so CEOs was not a brilliant idea. As we went around the room, bankers began to sharpen their criticism of various regulatory initiatives. Carney was, predictably, responding calmly with his own perspectives until one senior US banker released an especially searing and indicting set of broad-based criticisms. Carney listened as the banker unloaded, then firmly responded, "I don't have to tolerate such insults, so I am leaving." He picked up his papers and promptly walked out of the room and into the night. We were all stunned, but there was nothing to be done. Not a high point in our role at the IIF as a bridge between the financial community and the central banking/regulatory community.

I was somewhat concerned that this would affect our dialogue going forward with Mark in his new global position, but fortunately he did not carry a grudge, at least not that I could discern. We had talked informally around the edges of the G30 meeting in early December in New York. And he had brushed off the incident. What he had not brushed off was his concern about the debt crisis in Europe. In fact, a few days later, on December 8, Canada's leading newspaper, *Globe and Mail*, wrote an article titled "Bank of Canada warns of dangerous euro zone ripple effect."[2] The Bank of Canada had issued a report that highlighted the risks to Canada if Europe failed to contain the crisis. The "Financial System Review" in the report set forth the risks in a direct and foreboding passage: "The risks to stability of Canada's financial system are high and have increased significantly over the past six months . . . The main risks are:

- "The spillover associated with a further escalation of the euro-area sovereign debt crisis" [highlighted as risk number one].

- "Dislocations in Euro Area sovereign risk have been amplified by growing doubts over the credibility of the policy response to the crisis."[3] Ouch—that was rather frank language coming from central bankers directed toward European politicians and finance officials. Nevertheless, it was hard to argue the point.

- "Tensions have become acute for a broader range of countries, including Italy, . . . the world's third-largest sovereign bond market. . . . The risk is very high that a further escalation of tensions in the Euro Area could adversely affect domestic financial stability, particularly through a general retrenchment from risk taking, funding pressures, and confidence effects."[4]

The globalization of capital markets over the 1980s, 1990s, and 2000s had substantially increased the tendency of markets to transmit anxiety and deteriorating confidence globally, and to do so at a much faster pace than in the past. The "contagion factor" at the moment was clearly centered around the fates of Italy and Greece, but because Italy had ruled out an IMF program, still had market access (albeit at very high interest rates), and by then had a technocratic government, all eyes turned to Greece.

I had for some years been impressed by the capacity of Canadian officials to see the world clearly through a global lens. Canada is an open economy, especially to trade with the United States and Europe. Although its banking system has very little direct exposure to European sovereign or corporate debt, the indirect exposure through the US financial system is great. As we learned through the painful experiences of the global financial crisis in 2008–2009, the financial system has a myriad of arteries through which to transmit shock and spread contagion.

Because Canada's economy is one of the world's ten largest, Canadian officials have had a keen awareness of how the world at large affects them. During the early 1980s, Finance Minister Michael Wilson became the Chair of the Interim Committee of the IMF, the global ministerial group that provided overall policy guidance to the IMF Board and staff. He handled his responsibilities with great skill and aplomb. He had an experienced finance ministry officer at his side by the name of Don McCutcheon, and between the two of them they provided strong leadership during a challenging period in the world economy.

Our luncheon at the Bank of Canada on January 5 was also attended by Tiff Macklem, then the bank's Deputy Governor and now Governor. I was joined by Phil Suttle, the IIF's Chief Economist. We had a lot of issues to discuss on the regulatory front, especially given Mark's elevation to the Chair of the Financial Stability Board, including cross-border resolution (how to resolve financial institutions with significant cross-border exposures), shadow banking (how to regulate or monitor the parts of the financial system not directly under control of regulators), risk management (a top-line concern after the crisis), and insurance regulation.

But that day at lunch all of this took a backseat to Greece and the European crisis. I briefed Mark and Tiff on my initial round of talks with Lucas Papademos and the precarious outlook for negotiations in January. He and Tiff both strongly supported the need for a voluntary restructuring and expressed deep concern about the potential adverse consequences for the global economy if Greece broke out of the Eurozone or if there was a disorderly, unilateral restructuring. Carney assured me he would use his voice to offer support for us where he could.

The walk back down the hill to the hotel following lunch at the bank was as challenging as ever in the frigid Ottawa air of early January, but I nevertheless was encouraged to know that we had Carney and the Bank of Canada on our side.

That afternoon I also met with David Dodge, Mark's predecessor at the bank. David had been a Deputy Finance Minister in the early 1990s, when Canada was struggling with a burgeoning deficit, declining growth, and a broad economic malaise that threatened to turn into a full-blown crisis. He had played a pivotal role in bringing the deficit under control. From 2001 to 2008, he served as Governor of the Bank of Canada with distinction, his term characterized by steady growth with low inflation in Canada.

As always, David greeted me with a hearty, "Hello, Charlie, it's great to see you!" and a slap on the back. Over the years, David and I had developed a close friendship and I knew I could count on his unvarnished advice and counsel. Direct in his communication (see his recent comment responding to a criticism of the Bank of Canada by one of Canada's leading Conservatives: "That's bullshit."),[5] David was one of the most effective economic policymakers with whom I have ever worked. The IIF had persuaded him to be one of the Co-chairs of the Trustees of the Principles when they were launched in 2004. He joined Jean-Claude Trichet and Henrique Meirelles (President of the Central Bank of Brazil) as the inaugural Co-chairs. They made a great team, leading this group during its first few years of existence as the Trustees established their collective credibility. In early 2012, as we sat down in his new office at Bennett Jones, a law firm where he had become a senior adviser, he asked me bluntly, "Charlie, how bad is it? From here it looks like the euro could break apart if you and your team don't get things under control."

I sketched out the state of play and he started shaking his head. "You are mighty close to an involuntary scenario and better not give much more ground. The euro system has a deep structural problem with a common currency and widely varying fiscal policies and underlying economies. Eventually, this will have to be fixed. But at least you are fortunate to have Lucas there now." I agreed with him and walked out thinking how favored we all were that Canada and the world economy had David Dodge. I wished more officials in Europe were as clear-headed as Dodge was about the situation.

On the night of January 10, it was time to head off to Athens for our first significant round of negotiations since the breakdown in December. We had received considerable informal feedback from our official contacts in Europe, and were looking at various alternative scenarios of coupon, maturity, GDP warrants, etc. Mikis was engaged in virtually endless presentations of these scenarios to us in order that we would know, with each calculation of coupons and maturity structure, the net present value loss. Despite the support of Rehn, Juncker, and others on the official side, it was becoming clear that the IMF once again wanted to reboot the underlying growth estimates. This would inevitably lead to pressure for us to accept a larger haircut, or Greece would be forced to take additional restrictive fiscal measures, or both. The former would not be welcomed among the creditors; the latter would not be welcomed by Greece. We began to develop a sense of solidarity with Greece, for neither of us wanted to see another version of the Troika's "debt sustainability analysis."

Before flying into Greece, I decided to stop in to visit Larry Fink at BlackRock. Larry had built the world's largest asset-management platform and had a remarkably broad horizon over which to observe the world's markets. I wanted to gain a glimpse of how the world looked through his lens. He said that the markets had begun the year on a positive note, based primarily on improving signs out of the US economy, and asked me whether the crisis in Europe had been stanched, expressing concern that while Italy seemed to have stabilized somewhat with a new government, Greece still seemed very much in trouble. I confirmed that indeed that was the case and that we were on a knife's edge.

"The markets have a wary eye toward Europe, but they are not prepared for a disorderly Greek default or exit from the euro, so good luck,

Charles," he told me. "A failure could be very destabilizing for global markets."

I landed in Greece the next night after the briefest stopover in Paris for a conference call with Board Leadership.

Our discussion with Papademos began early the next morning in his office. Jean and I were greeted warmly with a handshake from him and a hug from Venizelos. By this point we had been working with Evangelos for some time and had developed a close relationship despite our differences. Lucas, on the other hand, always had a formal air about him, so I did not dare embrace him. On this occasion, however, he reacted to my cordiality with Venizelos, smiled, and said, "What, I don't get a hug?" Surprised, I immediately moved to embrace him as well before he ushered us into his office.

We brought copies of our January 5 proposal and went over it element by element. But before we dove into it, Lucas brought us up to date on certain aspects of the negotiations with the Troika and more extensively recent economic and financial developments. He was faced with an almost impossible predicament. In November, he had inherited an economy that was steadily declining, and nothing that had happened in the interim had altered that trajectory. Retail trade had shrunk by around 11% over a year earlier in the fourth quarter of 2011, while on the industrial front new orders had declined by 8% in the fourth quarter. By the end of 2011, real GDP had declined by a cumulative 13% since 2009. Despite this, the external balances, as represented by the current account deficit, hovered around 10% of GDP, reflecting weak export performance.[6]

On the market front, spreads on Greek debt had become more volatile. By January 10-year Greek bonds had risen to an astounding spread of 3300 basis points, while credit default swap (CDS) spreads had also ballooned.[7] By this point, Greek banks were also in deep distress. The debt restructuring was shaping up to send a monsoon over the banks' financial health. Depending on the precise nature of the restructuring, the banks were looking at the virtual wiping out of their capital. The restructuring would potentially eliminate €22 billion of their capital, compared to Tier I capital in the entire system of only €23.8 billion. Regulatory capital would be wiped out from four banks representing 44% of assets in the Greek banking system. Consequently, Lucas noted, the required recapitalization of Greek banks in the second adjustment program would be substantial. As if that weren't enough, domestic deposits were fleeing the system, most likely to foreign banks outside Greece and into mattresses inside Greece. The deposit base dropped 18% during 2011, a shocking shrinkage.[8] Meanwhile, on the asset side, non-performing loans continued to increase, reaching over 15% of total outstanding loans by the end of the year.

As a result of these factors, the banks had little choice but to curtail further lending, thus feeding the negative cycle in the economy as "tight credit supply and lack of trade credit became the main concerning factor, generating a negative feedback loop through the economy that put further pressure on the banking system."[9]

It was in this tumultuous economic climate that Papademos was facing growing demands for additional fiscal nuances and further reforms for which he noted that the parliament and the Greek people would have absolutely no appetite. His coalition government consisted of representatives from PASOK; the previous government, New Democracy; and the Popular Orthodox Rally party. It was the first coalition government in Greece in over twenty years. Even in the best of times, it would have been an unwieldy cabinet, consisting of forty-eight individuals: seventeen ministers and a large number of alternate and deputy ministers (thirty-one). Many had served in the previous cabinet, but twelve were new, and importantly, the cabinet included the previous main opposition party, New Democracy.

Despite early polls showing very large support for Papademos and his government among the people (75% support in one poll)[10] when he first stepped in, the coalition was beginning to fray only two months later. Demonstrations were being held on an almost daily basis in Syntagma Square. Papademos was negotiating with the Troika and would have to present to the parliament many measures, including wage cuts, the opening of "closed professions" such as pharmacists and truck drivers, and further retrenchment of pensions. These were long overdue reforms, but the political resistance was likely to remain strong. Lucas talked about these challenges as he sat calmly in his chair, but you could sense the concern with which he was grappling with them.

"The introduction of certain reforms, particularly in the labor markets and pension system, will face real resistance from both politicians and social partners. But reforms in these areas are necessary to enhance competitiveness and remain in the Eurozone. At the same time, the Troika is proposing fiscal and other measures of a magnitude that would further weaken the economy and exacerbate the problems we are facing, both economically and politically. I have discussed this with Christine Lagarde, Jean-Claude Juncker, and Mario Draghi, and I believe they understand the dilemmas and problems we face."

We commiserated with him, as we had witnessed for some time the negative feedback loop (to use the same words the IMF subsequently used in its assessment) to which the IMF was contributing through its approach to fiscal adjustment. Higher taxes and reduced government spending, however necessary they were for medium-term adjustment, were actually increasing the deficit rather than reducing it. I told Lucas, "We call this approach by the Troika chasing a rabbit down a hole. You never catch it."

We then walked him and Venizelos through our January 5 proposal in detail, explaining our thinking on the A/B loan structure, underscoring that use of English law was a deal breaker, and outlining our thinking on the debt sustainability targets of the IMF. We expressed deep skepticism about the IMF approach to debt sustainability and conveyed that clearly to Lucas and Evangelos.

Both Jean and I agreed that there are so many factors that determine a sustainable level of debt for a country that they cannot possibly be captured in one ratio. Markets look at the recent and prospective growth rates, the degree of political stability, the maturity structure and interest rate level of the debt, the attitude of the government toward servicing its debt, the ability of the government to formulate and implement policies that could rein in the debt, and the overall mood of the markets toward risk-taking. These and other factors were part of a constantly evolving mix in determining a country's debt sustainability. Market confidence is such a fickle phenomenon, especially with regard to sovereign debt. If confidence collapses in a country's external position or outlook, debt can be suddenly unsustainable, largely independent of the debt-to-GDP ratio. Despite considerable analysis by both academics and practitioners, sovereign risk assessment remains more of an art than a science. Of course, guidelines are essential, and debt-to-GDP ratios can be one useful benchmark in determining a country's debt sustainability. But as the sole test? Enough to put a country through further wrenching tax increases? We did not think so.

We had explained this to Chancellor Merkel in October, and as we outlined our thoughts to Papademos and Venizelos, they appeared to also agree with the thrust of our arguments. Papademos is, of course, a world-class economist, and he nodded and said, "I share your concerns." Venizelos was an exceptional lawyer and experienced politician. He brought us back to reality after our discourse by saying, "Jean and Charles, you may be right, but the IMF has convinced the European Commission and the Greek government that we have to meet a certain debt-to-GDP ratio to conclude this agreement. We have no choice but to try our best." We assured him that our January 5 proposal could bring the ratio in at 121.5% in 2020. We explained the step-up provisions of our coupon structure:

- 4.0% during 2012–2014
- 4.65% during 2015–2020
- 5.9% after 2020

We stressed that the average coupon rate of 4.4% during 2012 through 2020 would be comparable to the ESFS lending rates to Greece. Looking back upon this, I find that rather remarkable—the private sector offering to extend credit to Greece at the same terms as the official sector after writing off completely more than €100 billion of loans. We also indicated our willingness to include "appropriate collective action clauses" to "help mobilize high participation in the debt exchange." We pointed out that this exchange would provide as much as €180 billion during 2012–2020 in cash flow relief to Greece, which should allow them to lay the basis for recovery and a return to the capital markets. We covered a plethora of other issues that day, such as how to assure high participation, how to deal with the likely triggering of selective default determination by the rating agencies, and CDS contracts.

After a lengthy session, Lucas stood up and informed us that he had to prepare for a cabinet meeting. We wrapped up our meeting and they thanked us for our presentation and forward-looking proposal, saying they would get back to us shortly. Jean and I returned to the Grande Bretagne, where we reviewed our situation with Hung and Mikis.

Papademos called the next morning and asked to meet that night. In the interim, our advisers had met with Greece's advisers, Cleary Gottlieb and Lazard, along with officials from the Greek finance ministry. Despite the breakdown in Paris, it was clear, at least in this small group, that Greece was on the precipice of a disorderly default that could create an unprecedented wave of contagion in Europe. None of us wanted that to be our legacy, so the small technical teams on both sides tried to forge progress as well. On a range of issues—coupon structure (whether fixed or floating), coupon payment rate, payment of accrued interest on existing GGBs (important issue since it amounted to roughly €6 billion), the structuring of the new GDP securities, and many other issues—matters were advanced, and clarifications made.

Over the next days, the process gained some momentum and a rhythm and tone to our talks that was at times tense but with an undercurrent of potential. Papademos was spending much of his mornings in meetings with his cabinet and key members of the parliament discussing and assembling the package of economic reforms and stabilization measures. He was also meeting with the Troika and his economic team to advance negotiation with them over the requirements of the new program. It seemed like Papademos and Venizelos were constantly moving on the dance floor with three different partners: the political leaders and the parliament, the private creditors, and the Troika.

At the end of the January 11 meeting we issued a statement from the IIF: "A range of issues were discussed, and some key areas remain unresolved. Discussions will continue in Athens tomorrow, but time for reaching an agreement is running short. It is essential in order to finalize the voluntary bond swap agreement that support be given by all official parties in the days ahead."[11] A senior Greek government official (most likely Venizelos) stated that talks were "positive" and "constructive."[12] The prior day, Venizelos had been quoted as saying the negotiations "have advanced and are now at a very good point."[13]

I'm not exactly sure why we issued our statement, which admittedly said very little. Three things, however, may have been going through our minds:

1. The markets were very nervous, and a little handholding might do some good and steady the nerves; or

2. To send a message to the IMF, ECB, EU, and national capitals, especially in Berlin and Paris; or

3. The press was hounding our media relations team to death, and they wanted to give them something!

We had an outstanding media relations duo in Frank and Emily Vogl, a husband-and-wife team who were very experienced in global economic and financial matters. Frank had served as a business and economics correspondent at the *Times* of London and then as head of public affairs at the World Bank. They were very capable and managed all our media relations at the IIF. If Frank or Emily recommended that we issue a statement, we usually did.

The Troika was in Athens at the same time we were meeting with Papademos regularly, trying to secure yet another round of adjustment measures in the midst of an economy that continued to be very weak. The third partner was us, the creditor group, struggling to salvage a negotiated restructuring before events took us into the uncharted waters of a hard default and exit from the euro. Papademos and his government were constantly on the dance floor. He had the pressure coming in waves from three sides and one could expect that he might have wanted to walk out of the dance hall. He took a stern approach, when necessary, not only with the parliament but with the public at large. In a public speech to senior parliamentary leaders on January 4, he had stated bluntly that decisions made over the coming weeks would determine whether the country holds on to the euro or reverts to the drachma. "If we want to secure our most significant achievements—participation in the euro and avoidance of a massive, vertical income devaluation that a disorderly bankruptcy and exit from the euro would lead to . . . Then we must accept a short-term income reduction. With the beginning of 2012 we enter the most critical period for the course of the Greek economy. The coming weeks will be extremely crucial."[14]

On the morning of Friday, January 13, we resumed our tense routine. We had a staff meeting in the Churchill Room in the Grande Bretagne, decided on which issues needed technical work, debated various options on interest-rate structures and GDP warrants, and then made phone calls, lots of them, to the usual senior European leaders—Juncker, Rehn, and various key officials, but also to our Committee Board members. There were broadly two views emerging among them: one, that we had given more than enough and there was no more room for further movement that would lead to additional net present value losses; and two, the European economic and financial situation was becoming so precarious that we needed to find a solution, and find it fast.

Juggling the phones as part of the ceaseless effort to find common ground on Greece's debt—and to help keep the Eurozone in one piece. © Pete Ellis

With Juncker, Rehn, and others we were seeking support for the Troika to not re-run the estimate of the financing gap based on the latest data. With the IMF's continued inability to see that their policy prescriptions were undermining their own forecasts, the financing gap was ever widening, putting more pressure on both the Greek government to cut spending further and raise more taxes, and on us to accept a larger haircut on the debt. The IMF's obsession with the 120% debt-to-GDP ratio by 2020 was the proximate goal during all of this. Although we certainly understood the need to reduce the debt levels to something more sustainable, both Jean and I felt strongly that there was no magic to the ratio of 120%. Juncker and Rehn had considerable sympathy for our views, but we were uncertain whether they could prevail on the IMF.

We received a call mid-day inviting us to resume our talks with Papademos and Venizelos at 1:30 p.m. that afternoon. We gathered our papers and headed to his office. Both greeted us warmly, offered us tea, and we sat together to advance discussions. Lucas always sat in a chair near his desk and the phone, with Evangelos in a chair near him. Jean and I sat on the couch. Although finance was not Venizelos's area of expertise, he had quickly grasped the fundamental issues surrounding the negotiations and the broad implications for Greece if we all fell short. Nevertheless, he often did not bring pen, paper, or laptop for the meetings, nor ready access to the endless variations of interest-rate levels and structure options. I noticed the night before that he had not brought notes, so I came prepared with an extra pen and pad, and even another copy of various interest-rate options. As he sat down, I reached over and handed him the pen and paper, and he thanked me profusely as we got under way.

Jean and I asked about the negotiations with the Troika. Lucas responded that they had gone as well as could be reasonably expected; there were clear differences over how much additional adjustment could be expected. He was particularly concerned about the proposal by the Troika for reductions in wages and certain institutional reforms in labor markets, as well as the size of cuts in pensions. We then shared our concern about the pressure on the banks and the limited room for maneuver we had left.

We suggested that he call both Merkel and Lagarde. He said he would consider it, but asked us to consider whether we could secure additional flexibility from the creditors as well.

(Left to right) Prime Minister Lucas Papademos and Finance Minister Evangelos Venizelos greeting Jean Lemierre and me as we resume negotiations on January 13, 2012. A moment of cordiality before getting down to business. AP Photo/Thanassis Stavrakis

"We will try, Lucas," I told him, "but I can't promise anything." As Jean and I left his office, we knew the window for a deal was closing rapidly, and that we would indeed likely have to prepare ourselves for another move.

The next morning was a Saturday, cold but sunny in Athens, and Lucas had told us that he would not be able to meet before late in the evening. I arose early and decided to take a break and go for a walk to the Plaka. I had discovered the Plaka as a young naval officer during my time in Greece in the early 1970s. At that time, it was a sprawling neighborhood at the base of the Acropolis. It is, in fact, "the oldest continuously inhabited part of Athens" according to Bruce Clark, one of the foremost historians on the fabled city.[15] Clark is of the view, in fact, that the Plaka is actually one of the oldest continuously inhabited places in the world. I had little sense of that when I went wandering through the area in the fall of 1970. It was a popular place for sailors (perhaps too popular), and I had been told that one could also get a decent Greek meal for a reasonable price. Along with two fellow officers, we did find excellent Greek salads and moussaka. I also found some souvenirs to take back to family. However, the area as a whole had been somewhat seedy in those days and seemed to have more than its share of bars and nightclubs. That was no surprise, since in virtually every port we visited there was a section of town catering to sailors on shore leave with some money in their pockets. Only later did I learn that the Plaka had quite an important history, sitting at the foot of the Acropolis. It was the original temporary site of the University of Athens, which was formed in 1836, soon after the independent Kingdom of Greece itself was formed. More tragically, it had been the site of some wary hospitality by local Greeks hesitantly welcoming the conquering Venetians in 1687 after their tragic bombardment destroyed much of the Parthenon.

On the morning of January 14, 2012, I was rambling through a Plaka that was entirely different from the one I'd first encountered in 1970. It was clean, with attractive restaurants and shops, and I enjoyed wandering up the street looking for a few souvenirs for my three grandchildren, Oumar, Vanessa, and Alya. I had always enjoyed buying mementos for my children—Stephen, Emily, and Bryan—from the places to which I traveled. Stephen had developed an interest in bronze Greek and marble Roman statues, so I would often try to bring some home for him. Now I was shopping for my grandchildren, and the stores were just opening. As I was browsing in one shop, the owner approached me and asked in broken English if he could help. I told him no, that I was just looking, and then found a small Greek ceramic spoon holder that I thought Vanessa would like. At an early age she was becoming her father's daughter and liked to cook (her father, Stephen, was quite an accomplished chef at home), so I thought she would enjoy it. I also found small items for Oumar and Alya and took them all to the counter. The proprietor suddenly approached, took them from my hands and said, "You're Mr. Dallara, aren't you?" I admitted that I was, and then he surprised me.

"I won't take your money because I believe you are a friend of Greece."

"Yes, I do consider myself a friend of Greece, but I won't take your items without paying for them," I responded. He put up his hands and became very firm.

"No, I insist. You are trying to help us, and I ask you to accept these items as a sign of my appreciation." I hesitated; I could tell it had become a matter of honor to him. Yes, in some inexplicable, perhaps even bizarre fashion, we at the forefront of the negotiations had developed a reputation as supporters of Greece despite our role representing the creditors. Bankers are never popular, especially in a situation in which the citizens of a debtor country are suffering. Perhaps they had exhausted their enmity on Germany and the IMF, and they had little left for the bankers. I thanked the man, shook his hand, and walked back toward the hotel. While it was good to know that he considered me a friend, I knew that the months ahead would be very difficult for him and thousands of other shop owners. I returned to the hotel with a heavy heart, realizing that even if we were able to help keep Greece in the euro, it would take some time for the country to see the benefits. I didn't realize, however, that it would take many years for the full benefits of our collective efforts to bring meaningful improvement to life on the streets of Greece.

CHAPTER 27

ANOTHER TURN
OF THE SCREW

"Character is revealed when pressure is applied."

—Unknown

We met once again on Saturday evening, January 14. Lucas Papademos reported that he had held a constructive call with Lagarde and had a call pending with Merkel. Having always thought of himself as an economist and central banker, he was developing a new image as a head of government—a peer of Merkel and Sarkozy. Although he seemed to be reluctant at first, he now appeared more comfortable in his new role. He indicated that Christine Lagarde seemed sympathetic to his assessment that a further increase in the financing gap was not warranted by the additional information available over the past few months, but he was uncertain about the outcome as that would depend upon the views of the IMF staff.

We then discussed various options for the coupon structure at some length, based on three phases: the first from 2012 through 2014, the second from 2015 through 2020, the third from 2021 through 2041. Not only was the level of the coupon critical, but so was the selection of the discount rate for the calculation. This was a very inexact science in dealing with such an unprecedented restructuring. What was a reasonable expected return on the new bonds? The higher the assumed discount rate, the greater the NVP losses (i.e., haircut) to the creditors. It was very difficult to know what proper discount rate to use. If we used a 9% rate, the NPV losses would be less than they would be with a 12% rate by about 5 percent; if a 15% discount rate were used, the losses grow another 3 or so percent. Certainly 9% was premised on the expectation of a successful exchange, which would bring down Greek sovereign interest rates from their stratospheric levels.

Our meeting went late into the evening as we also discussed the problem of free riders: how to limit the number of debt holders who refused to participate in the exchange but would benefit from a full payout. We were increasingly coming to the view that we would have to insert a retroactive collective action clause into the exchange through Greek legislation. We returned to the Grande Bretagne to debrief our team and got a late bite to eat at the rooftop restaurant. It was a clear evening, and when I went to my room, I made a point of walking to the balcony and staring at the Acropolis. As both the moonlight and artificial lights shone on the Parthenon and the Erechtheion, I reminded myself that if Greece could create something this magnificent, they could get through the current storm. I had admired the audacity of the Parthenon, which was built during the golden era of Pericles under his leadership, since my first encounter with it in 1970. A "sublime work of art and worship," it also reinforced the Athenian democracy by reminding citizens of their common origins. Some architectural aspects of the building remain astonishing even today, such as the fact "that the columns slope inward and bulge in the middle."[1] More than anything else, however, the Parthenon represented the birth of democracy and is as much of a beacon to the world as is the Statue of Liberty to Americans.

On Sunday, January 15, we realized that the IMF was moving the goalposts once again as the weakness of the economy continued to undermine the achievement of budgetary goals. We reluctantly began preparing another offer. After considerable debate and discussions over the ensuing days, we decided to modify our proposal based on input from Papademos and Venizelos as well as from Greece's technical team. Expectations were running high, so we issued another statement noting that talks had resumed. Nothing more. Hung and Mikis met with Petros Christodoulou on the afternoon of January 19 to compare notes on how things looked. Petros had been briefed on the IMF Board meeting that had taken place on January 18. Apparently, the Board had been very critical of Greece's performance and, implicitly, of the IMF's handling, but they did agree that another mission would go to Athens to finalize a program.

Things were beginning to come into focus on January 18, and the outline of a possible deal appeared to be coming into view, floating vaguely on the horizon. But I had a personal problem. I was scheduled to leave the night of January 19 to go to Paris for Peixin's birthday party. It was one of those with a round number at the end of it, and so I had organized a gathering of fifty or so of our friends, mostly European-based, for a dinner. Since Peixin is originally from Beijing, some friends were coming from China as well. The dinner was scheduled for Saturday, but I initially planned to meet her there on Wednesday, January 18. As our negotiations intensified, that plan had gone by the boards, and as our discussions continued to the afternoon of the nineteenth,, I could see that a departure that night was also out of the question. That evening, Jean Lemierre and I sat down with Papademos and Evangelos Venizelos in the Maximos Mansion, the Prime Minister's office, to outline our latest proposal. Key elements remained the same from our January 5 proposal: 50% reduction value of GGBs; 15% upfront cash payment; the remainder, 35%, converted to new government Greek bonds (NGGBs), with a maturity of 30 years and a grace period of 10 years; English law for the new bonds. Other elements had changed: the GDP-linked warrants would give investors an initial NPV value of only 1–2%, instead of 3%; most important, the coupon structure was reduced from 4% (2012–2014), 4.65% (2015–2020), and 5.9% after 2020 to 3.5%, 3.9%, and 4.25% respectively. This would bring the estimated debt-to-GDP ratio for 2020 down from 121.5% to approximately 118%.

This represented a very large concession on the part of the creditors that implied an NPV loss of 66%. Thus, even though the nominal haircut remained at 50%, the lower returns embedded in the coupon structure of the new debt, when combined with the maturity structure and grace period, meant that the banks would have lost two-thirds of the value (NPV calculation) of the old bonds. But the positive side of this was that it would provide cash flow relief to Greece of €180 billion during 2012–2020, providing a basis for Greece to restore growth and capital market access.

Lucas and Evangelos were generally impressed but asked if they could respond in the next day after discussing it with their team. As we walked out of Lucas's office that night, we were mildly optimistic that we were closing in on a deal, but we sensed that there was more ground to be covered. I knew, of course, that I was scheduled to be on the first flight out the next morning for Paris, but I hoped Peixin would understand if I arrived Saturday morning instead. I knew it was cutting it close, but I felt like I could not leave at that moment. I called her as soon as I returned to the room. She wasn't pleased, but many friends were clearly in town, and she was enjoying their company. "As long as you are on the first flight Saturday morning, but make sure." I hung up the phone realizing I had no margin for error.

On Friday afternoon, January 20, we received the now predictable call from Papademos's office inviting Jean and me to meet at 6 p.m. Throughout the course of the week, we had asked senior officers from each of the Steering Committee firms to remain in Athens for what we hoped would be the final round of negotiations. We spent the day with them reviewing our proposal and anticipating Papademos's and Venizelos's response. Having them in town, in the Churchill Room at the Grande Bretagne Hotel, eased the communication burden on the four of us, although we were still constantly on the phone touching base and laying the groundwork for next steps. I made a special point of calling Lars-Hendrik Röller in Merkel's office to let her know that a new proposal may be on the way.

Lucas was obviously fatigued after a long day of meetings with the Troika. We finalized our revised proposal with them and agreed that it would be formally transmitted to Papademos the next day, with copies sent directly to Merkel, Sarkozy, Juncker, and Rehn. "As you may be aware," our letter to them read, "we have made a final offer on behalf of the Private Creditors & Investor Committee for Greece."

At the conclusion of our meeting on January 20, Papademos looked at us and asked, "Charles and Jean, what time shall we meet tomorrow?" I responded, "Lucas, I am afraid we cannot meet tomorrow. I have arranged a long-scheduled birthday party for my wife in Paris tomorrow night and I will be in serious trouble if I do not make it." He graciously replied, "Then you must go, Charles, and we will resume on Sunday upon your return." I was relieved and only hoped that the flight Saturday morning was not delayed. There were many questions by the media, so we decided to issue a statement indicating that I "had a long-standing personal appointment out of Greece and that talks would continue at a technical level." We certainly didn't want rumors that talks had broken down. The statement appeared to quell concerns, but as both Jean and I checked in at the airport we were spotted, and rumors began circulating that we were off to Paris for consultations. A headline in the *Bangkok Post*, of all places, announced "Banks top negotiator quits Greece, but talks go on."[2] The *Bangkok Post*? Really?

Jean was also planning to attend the dinner with his wife, Jeanne-Marie, and I know he welcomed at least one night back home. Thankfully the plane was on time, and I made it to the hotel by 2 p.m. with at least four hours to spare. The party went off without a hitch.

Jean and I had been scheduled to be in Davos the coming week, but clearly it was more important for us to remain focused on the Greek negotiations rather than spend four or five days on the merry-go-round of Davos. Joe Ackermann planned on attending, and he and I stayed in close touch each day as discussions progressed. Joe was also planning to meet German Finance Minister Schäuble in Davos, and we both thought that could be helpful, or at least enlightening.

The next morning, I called Papademos, and we agreed that there was no urgent need to resume negotiations until our latest proposal was evaluated by European and IMF officials. Jean and I then decided to stay in Paris both for consultations with the French government and to meet with our Steering Committee.

On Monday, January 23, we got word that the IMF had in fact updated its DSA on the basis of the latest downward revision of the Greek economy. On that basis, they were once again increasing the financing gap, asking both Greece and the banks for more adjustment and a larger haircut, respectively. Venizelos was off to a Eurogroup meeting in Brussels that day and told me he would find out where things stood with the IMF (Troika) program and let me know. He had reportedly said in a PASOK gathering during the days leading up to the meeting, "It is no exaggeration to say that the next three months will be more challenging than any other period since the Second World War."[3] Although I knew Venizelos to have an occasional flair for the dramatic, I couldn't help but think he was probably correct, certainly for Greece and perhaps for Europe as a whole. While our latest offer was still on the table on January 23, we began to look at variations of interest rate structures that might keep the debt-to-GDP ratio below 120% even with the revised IMF debt sustainability data that took into account the weaker economy. As expected, the latest estimates pointed to the need for even more adjustment by Greece and more "contributions" from the private creditors. One option we considered was to reduce the "second stage" coupon (for 2015–2020) from 3.9% to 3.75% and raise the third stage from 4.25% to 4.34%. This would leave the average coupon rate for the entire period at 4.04% and would also leave the NPV losses virtually unchanged at 66%. The effects of these "twists" would be to provide more cash flow relief and keep the debt-to-GDP ratio down at the "magical" year of 2020. Regrettably, we had, of course, not been provided with details of the calculations or the black box on which the DSA model was based.

As we worked through the bits and pieces of data we had, it increasingly appeared that the latest change could put a deal out of reach. On Tuesday morning, while sitting in the BNPP conference room in Paris, I received the following email from Mikis:

"MH to CD/JL/HT—Tuesday, January 24, 2012: We have a problem. As you can see from Lubo's quick calculation, there does not seem to be any reasonable coupon structure that can deliver debt to GDP ratios below 125% by 2020 under the new DSA."

I dropped my head with a strong sense of foreboding. Had we made it this far only for Greece to be lured into a hard default? I walked over to get another cup of coffee.

Despite all my travels to Europe over the years I had never become a fan of espresso, so I was glad that the bank had finally accommodated my coffee tastes by providing milk with coffee throughout the morning. I returned to my seat and read the memo from Lubomir Mitov, one of several economists in the European Department at the IIF. Lubo was an excellent economist and stepped in to help us with our own attempt at simulating the IMF's calculations. He worked up estimates based on the IMF markdown of expected growth in the out years, thus reducing projected GDP in 2020 and pulling up the debt-to-GDP ratio, ceteris paribus. Unfortunately, it wasn't ceteris paribus—other things were not equal. The fiscal deficit for 2011 had increased to 9.5% of GDP from 9.1%, thereby increasing the projected debt in 2020, with both the numerator and denominator moving in the wrong direction. It was easy for us to see that, once again, we were in trouble. This elevated the debt-to-GDP ratio from 118.5% under our January 21 proposal to 129.5%.

Jean and I met in his office and discussed options. We decided to make some phone calls to express our concerns about the latest turn of events and ask for help with the IMF. I called Treasury Secretary Tim Geithner, and Jean called Lagarde at the IMF. We made calls to other European officials including Juncker, Rehn, Musca, and the new chair of the EcoFin Deputies, Thomas Wieser. I alerted Ackermann, who was meeting with Schäuble in Davos, and asked him to weigh in there. In most cases we were met with sympathy, but not much else. Geithner told me that he had made numerous efforts to persuade the Eurogroup to accelerate solutions to the euro crisis, but his efforts were not always appreciated. I explained the difficulty of the IMF frequently moving the goalposts, to which he commiserated and promised to do what he could.

I also talked to Papademos, who was equally disturbed by the latest development since it pointed to the need for more adjustment by Greece: "Charles, it is clear that the emphasis on more fiscal adjustment will backfire by weakening the economy further. But they appear unwilling to change their approach."

Later that day, I went to see the leadership of CNP Assurances, a major French insurance corporation. Although their exposure to Greece was not as large as that of many of the creditors, it was nevertheless important that we consult with them and keep them involved as the discussions unfolded.

We had a constructive meeting, and as we left their headquarters looking for a taxi I spied a newspaper at the corner newsstand that had a sketch of a vaguely familiar face on the front page. The paper was *Les Echos*, France's old daily paper. As I moved closer, I discovered it was a caricature of me. With its protruding ears, wavy hair, a rather bulbous nose, and a very long face, I did not find it very flattering, but I had to admit that it captured my features, even if exaggerated—as is the case with caricatures! The drawing was accompanied by an article in French about my role in leading the Greek debt negotiations.

I bought a copy of the paper and showed it to my colleagues—who thought it was a precise likeness of me—and threw it in my briefcase. We soon became preoccupied once again with our predicament, and I forgot about the article until I cleaned my briefcase after returning to the States. I showed it to one of my French-speaking colleagues, Abdessatar Ouanes, and he gladly translated it for me. It turned out to be more interesting

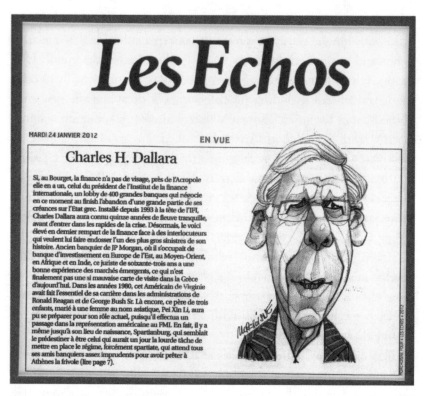

The caricature and article from Les Echos, *January 2012.* © *Jean Claude Morchoisne/*Les Echos

English translation: If, at Le Bourget, finance has no face, near the Acropolis it has one, that of the president of the Institute of International Finance, a lobby of 400 banks that is currently finishing the negotiation on the abandonment of a large part of their claims on the Greek state. Installed since 1993 at the head of the IIF, Charles Dallara will have known fifteen years of smooth sailing, before entering the rapids of the crisis. Now, here he is elevated in the first crest of finance against interlocutors who want to make him endorse one of the biggest claims in its history. Former JP Morgan banker, where he was in charge of investment banking in Eastern Europe, the Middle East, Africa and India, this sixty-three-year-old lawyer has a good experience of emerging markets which is in fact not a bad calling card in today's Greece. In the 1980s, this American from Virginia had spent most of his career in the administrations of Ronald Reagan and George Bush, Sr. Here again this father of three, married to a woman with an Asian name, Pei Xin Li, will have been able to prepare for his current role, since he was also the US representative at the Board of the IMF. In fact, even his birthplace, Spartanburg, seemed to pre-ordain him to be the one who would one day have the heavy task of setting up the regime, inevitably Spartan, which awaits all his banker friends who were imprudent enough to have lent frivolously to Athens.

than I had anticipated, so I have reproduced it with the English version alongside the French original.

On the morning of January 25 I was back in Paris. The meeting of the Steering Committee the next day was a somber affair. On Monday,

January 23, the Eurogroup met at Ministerial level and rejected our offer of January 21. Juncker was quoted by Reuters as saying that "talks would have to resume" to reach a settlement that is "clearly below" the bondholders' existing offer. He asked for a 3.5% coupon for the entire period up to 2020. The IMF had clearly presented an updated but downbeat report on the woeful state of the Greek economy and forecast debt levels for 2020 significantly above 120%. Reportedly, the ECB and the Commission "took a less optimistic view of long-term debt levels than the IMF."[4]

I had felt reasonably confident over the weekend of January 21–22 that a deal was nearly in hand. We had heard from both Papademos and Venizelos that the latest proposal was initially well received and the debt-to-GDP ratio of 118% looked quite impressive, well below the 120% target. At a 9% discount rate, the NPV loss was a massive 66%. I felt that the creditors had gone far enough and stated publicly, "It is clear we are at the limits of a voluntary deal; we are at a crossroads." I knew that the ECB was also under pressure to find some way to contribute to the solution, but we were not directly involved in that dispute. All of this changed when the IMF's latest revisions of the DSA began to emerge the next morning, on January 23. So, it was back to the drawing board.

At our meeting of our Steering Committee in Paris on January 25, we spent hours debating the core issue: the interest rate attached to the new debt. Mikis and Lubo had prepared numerous options for consideration, each of them leading to slightly different losses for the creditors. Any way you looked at it, we would take a bath—it was just a matter of how hot the water was. Somewhat to my surprise, there was an emerging consensus that we should continue to negotiate rather than draw a line in the sand. There was, in fact, a whiff of resignation in the air. We knew that we'd have to move the initial rate down toward 3% from 3.5%, but even with that, the debt-to-GDP ratio target remained around 128%. It appeared that our only hope was that the ECB and the member banks would agree to take at least a modest haircut.

At the end of the meeting, the Committee authorized Jean and me to return to Athens for one last attempt at an agreement. We boarded a plane late that evening in Paris, worn down but with a ray of hope. As we were struggling with these key parameters, our legal and financial advisers were meeting around the clock with Greece's PDMA team and their advisers. A number of key issues remained open, such as the matter of governing law of the new bonds (we continued to insist on English law), a proposal from Greece to allow the future fiscal obligations of Greece to be reduced by buybacks (we were opposed), pari-passu clause (they wanted to be able to subordinate new GGBS to existing official financing as well as existing domestic debt; we were opposed since it would weaken the value of the new claims), collective action clauses (remained a very delicate issue), cross acceleration, and many other issues. Some of these were discussed by the Steering Committee, which provided guidance to the advisers, and they in turn would negotiate many of these points directly with Greece's advisers. Our strong team of lawyers, led by Yannis Manuelidis and Katrina Buckley of Allen & Overy and Mark Glengarry and Ian Clark of White & Case, were stepping up as the legal documentation began to take shape. On the financial side, we had Michael O'Hara and Nicolas Hubert of Blackstone, who did an excellent job of analyzing the financial implications of all the legal and financial twists and turns in the negotiations.

The morning of January 26 was another cold, sunny day in Athens. We were scheduled to see Papademos in the morning, but he was tied up with the Troika, as they were insisting on yet another round of spending cuts and reforms in order to release to Greece up to €30 billion in the months ahead. Meanwhile, the Greek economy continued to slide—nothing new there.

In this depressing environment, Papademos had the unenviable task of mobilizing his coalition, cabinet, and the parliament to support another round of tax increases and spending cuts as well as structural reforms. On the latter it was hard to have much sympathy for Greek politicians. They had, for the better part of two years, dragged their feet on a wide range of structural reforms that would address some of the underlying, deep-seated problems of Greece's weak competitiveness; excessive state ownership of enterprises, a bloated public sector, protections on a whole range of labor activities, and rigid wage structures were only a handful of areas where progress had been meager.

On the former—tax increases and spending cuts—the Greek citizens were paying the price in part for a political structure that had failed them. Yes, they had voted for the two parties time and again since the return of democracy, but were they given other choices? Were they responsible for the brutal civil war that had spawned the political systems of postwar Greece? It is hard to conclude that Greek citizens deserved the crushing depression that enveloped their country in 2010 and had continued throughout 2011 and early 2012. Unemployment was a stratospheric 21.7%, compared to a Eurozone average of 11.8%. The economy shrank 5.5% in 2010, 10.1% in 2011, and eventually contracted another 7.1% in 2012. In all my years I had never seen an economy imploding with such force.

Against this backdrop, the IMF and their Troika brethren were pressing Papademos and Venizelos, once again, to bring the fiscal deficit down further. They were being asked to chase the rabbit down the hole, with the rabbit always seemingly out of reach. Neither we nor the Greeks could catch it.

As the pressure was building on us and the Greek government, a proposal reportedly emerged in the German government that Greece would "cede sovereignty over tax and spending decisions to a Eurozone budget commission" in order to secure disbursements under the new program. Under this proposal, the new commission would be able to veto budget decisions of the Greek government if they were not consistent with targets embedded in the program. "Given the disappointing compliance so far, Greece has to accept shifting budgetary sovereignty to the European level for a certain period of time." As if that were not enough, Athens would be forced to adopt a law permanently committing state revenues to debt service "first and foremost."[5] Even though I was representing the creditors, I blanched when I read this.

This proposal actually made it out of the German Finance Ministry and was circulated to the Euro Working Group chaired by Wieser. Fortunately, from my perspective (we were never consulted on it, although it would clearly have benefited the private as well as the public creditors), this was never put into effect. It did, however, as the *Financial Times* pointed out, "underscore the depths of mistrust between Greece and its European lenders."[6] Indeed, mistrust was very high. When Chancellor Merkel visited Greece later that year, she expressed solidarity with Greece, but that did not satisfy the tens of thousands of Greeks who protested her visit vehemently. An estimated 25,000 people demonstrated as Greece was in the depths of recession with unemployment hitting a new record. Soup kitchens were evident throughout the city, and Merkel did note that Greece was going through a "very difficult phase." It was, to say the least, an understatement. One banner read, "Merkel we are a free nation and not your colony." Another banner referred to the 3,500 Greeks who had committed suicide during the crisis.[7]

CHAPTER 28

A LEGACY OF BAD DEBT AND LOSS OF AUTONOMY

"We live, not as we wish, but as we can."

—Menander, circa 4th century BC

The issue of Greece turning over "budgetary sovereignty" to a European fiscal master was, of course, a dramatic proposal that went nowhere in this instance. However, when I read the proposal, my thoughts went to the question that had been haunting me since the early days of our negotiation in June 2011. Had Greece, in fact, not already surrendered a great deal of its economic sovereignty, a good bit of its autonomy? And what was Greece's history in dealing with external debt issues? Was there a precedent to what we were living through? Was history repeating itself?

Membership in the Eurozone was, in fact, a partial ceding of economic sovereignty. The melding of twelve currencies into one on January 1, 1999, was a huge decision of ceding exchange rate and monetary policy authority from national capitals to the ECB in Frankfurt. This eliminated two key policy instruments used by countries to adjust imbalances, control inflation, slow or stimulate growth in an economy, and more generally manage an economy. The voluntary ceding of these adjustment tools by Greece made the borrowing in international capital markets in the 2000s an especially high-risk process. Of course, membership in the

European Union had already involved the transfer of some important aspects of economic sovereignty—trade policy, competition policy, and regulatory policy among the most relevant.

But in the spring of 2011, I felt something more had been forfeited— Greece's basic right to represent itself with its creditors; to speak for itself, argue for itself, or draw a line where necessary in defense of its national interests. To be fair, certain aspects of this phenomenon were frequent when it came to IMF programs. They often have involved a country being forced to accept policies it would otherwise not have followed. This was the nature of the beast: a country finds itself in economic difficulty, lacking access to either official or private market financing (or both) and engages in discussions with the IMF to help restore sound policies, credibility, and market access.

Over the years, I have seen many countries dragged reluctantly into IMF programs, often in dire circumstances. Countries such as Mexico, Brazil, and Argentina, which became involved in the Latin debt crisis that erupted in 1982, were generally forced into, often abruptly, IMF programs as private credit dried up and they were faced with imminent default without an IMF-supported program. In such cases, an abrupt partial loss of economic control of the country was a common feature, as major decisions on economic policy had to be negotiated with the IMF, and critical aspects of external debt restructuring negotiated with both private and public creditors. In each of these, and many others, there was a short-term sacrifice of a significant degree of economic independence, or economic sovereignty. Fiscal, monetary, exchange rate, regulatory, competition, trade, labor market, and structural policies such as privatization were at times the subject of intense negotiations.

The IMF, however, developed a philosophy that the country must take ownership of a program if it was to succeed. This approach became especially prominent after an infamous photo of Michel Camdessus, Managing Director of the IMF, was pictured standing over Indonesian President Suharto in 1998 while he was signing an agreement with the IMF on an adjustment program. It was an unfortunate photo to say the least. As *Bloomberg* said in an article in 2017, "it's a photo that still haunts the International Monetary Fund."[1] Or as the *Wall Street Journal* noted, "one of the more searing memories of the 1997–1998 financial crisis was the image of IMF Managing Director Camdessus, standing, arms folded, over former Indonesian President Suharto as Suharto signed a bailout deal with international creditors packed with painful austerity measures."[2]

While this was interpreted as indicative of an arrogant IMF seeking to impose its formula of austerity on a poor developing country, the reality was much more complicated. Indonesia had left itself exposed to the Asian financial crisis as a result of years of cronyism and a patronage system that led to monopolies and widespread corruption. As with many other cases of countries seeking IMF support, Indonesia's own economic policies made it highly vulnerable to instability sparked by exogenous forces. The reality is that most cases involving formal IMF lending programs do involve a considerable short-term loss of economic independence. Is this also a loss of economic sovereignty? It depends. Viewed through the lens of the economic and financial interdependence that has increased dramatically since World War II, one can argue that a loss of a substantial degree of economic sovereignty has been the price nations pay for the benefits of globalization. I find this concept somewhat misleading, however, since the decisions to engage in global trade; allow for the mobility of labor and capital; agree to treaties; join organizations such as the World Trade Organization (WTO), the IMF, and the World Bank; engage in bilateral and multilateral investment in trade treaties; and allow both outbound and inbound foreign investment are made by the sovereign. Often those are not just executive decisions; they are also endorsed by legislators. Thus, it's difficult to conclude that the economic interdependence that has grown among nations is synonymous with a loss of sovereignty.

The sacrifice of independent national decision-making is often a product of inappropriate policies at home combined with a dependence on external debt. This is the story of so many sovereign debt sagas of the last fifty years: borrow heavily abroad, allow fiscal and external deficits to balloon and structural problems to fester, and you have a situation ripe for loss of independent national decision-making. This was the story of multiple countries during the Latin debt crisis of the 1980s. The partial loss of independent national decision-making often manifested in IMF programs that generally involved the need for fiscal retrenchment, monetary restraint, a plethora of structural reforms, and balance of payment adjustment. All in an effort to put the economy on a more realistic and competitive path and to restore confidence among the creditors.

It should be noted, however, that not all IMF programs of the last fifty years were forced by debt problems, balance of payments difficulties, or unsustainable deficits. The programs of Poland and Czechoslovakia in the early 1990s after the fall of the Berlin Wall provided opportunities for these countries to leverage the credibility and financing of the IMF and move decisively toward market-oriented economies. The program for the Philippines in 1986–1988 was part of a broader effort to support a fledgling democracy after the fall of Marcos. As the US Executive Director of the IMF at the time as well as a senior Treasury official, I was directly involved in developing that program, working closely with Anoop Singh of the Asian department of the IMF, as well as Peter McPherson as the head of USAID, to assemble a supportive program to bolster the economy. Anoop, a highly skilled economist who subsequently led the Western Hemisphere department at the IMF, designed the program to stabilize the economy and increase the focus on structural reforms, while dismantling restrictions that hindered private sector activity and exports.[3] An IMF Report prepared many years later speculated that "International political factors probably also have their place in explaining the IMF's long program engagement in the Philippines."[4] From my perspective, Singh did an excellent job balancing a need for economic reform with the realization that after two years of a collapsing economy, a 17% contraction in 1984–1985, and a new democratic administration trying to find its footing, stabilization and the beginnings of reform were the goals.

There were other cases in which the national ownership of an IMF program was considerable, and they used the IMF to reinforce credibility for their program with market participants. Hungary comes to mind. In 1996, they agreed to a 264 million SDR program (approximately $387 million) to support the government's economic policies. They had no intention of using any funds from the loan arrangement from the outset, and in the event did not use any. They had a strong economic team led by Finance Minister Lajos Bokros and Central Bank Governor György Surányi, and formulated a credible program of measures to cut the budget and current account deficits, rein in inflation, and tackle long-standing structural problems, such as strengthening the Social Security system, privatizing state-owned enterprises, and liberalizing trade.

The IMF arrangement involved very little, if any, marginalization of economic independence, as it basically endorsed the Hungarian-designed program. At the helm of the IIF at this time, I received a call from Surányi asking if we could organize a presentation to investors and bankers in New York on their program, and we were glad to arrange it. Part of our role was to be a bridge between governments and the private financial community, and we brought Bokros and Surányi together with fifty or so investors in New York in order for the Hungarians to present their program. The IMF staff joined the presentation and confirmed their support, and the presentation by the Hungarian team was convincing. They successfully implemented the program and rebuilt confidence among private investors.

Cases such as that of Hungary in 1996, however, were the exception. In the overwhelming number of circumstances in which IMF-adjusted programs were put into place, there were extensive negotiations between the IMF staff and national authorities. There was clearly a temporary sacrifice of economic independence. Many national authorities may not fully appreciate the fact that dependence on international goods and services can create economic dislocations when such products are no longer available, or when prices change abruptly due to product shortages, supply chain difficulties, or natural disasters. But even if they do have full realization of that risk, they take the risk—as they should—because of the tremendous benefits of international trade.

Dependence on foreign debt capital is a whole different phenomenon. Virtually nothing can sacrifice economic independence like the loss of confidence in a sovereign's economic prospects by its private creditors. If the creditors are official, the effects of a loss of confidence is often gradual, or the economic constraints on independence may be mitigated by political, strategic, or financial considerations. Take Egypt in the mid-to-late 1980s, for example. The bulk of its external debt was to official creditors—the US government, the World Bank, the IMF, etc., and the flow of official credit never completely ceased, no matter how misguided their policies were at various times. Egypt did, however, lose some of its policy independence, as the US decided to link its aid to an IMF program. That didn't sit well with President Mubarak. In a memorable meeting with Treasury Secretary James Baker in September 1986, Mubarak insisted that he was "doing the utmost" (a phrase he and his team used quite frequently). He asked Secretary Baker if he would refuse to support the IMF's insistence on subsidy reductions as part of their

IMF program, which was in the process of negotiation. I had worked closely with the IMF staff, especially their Director of the Middle East Department, Shakour Shaalan, and I was prepared for this request. So was Secretary Baker.

"Mr. President, we strongly support you, as you know, but there are limits to what we can or will do when it comes to IMF programs. Mr. Dallara is in charge of those matters at the Treasury, and so I would ask that you work with him on the issues involved." President Mubarak immediately shifted his gaze to me. But he did much more. He pivoted his whole body in my direction, left his chair, got down on one knee, and pleaded, "Mr. Dallara, I beg you. We are doing the utmost. Do not ask us to reduce the grain subsidies. Bread is the essence of life for most Egyptians, and we do not want another round of riots." I was stunned and somewhat embarrassed—for him, for Secretary Baker, and for myself. Mubarak lifted his hands up in a plaintive motion as if we could absolve him of his economic sins.

I didn't quite know what to do. Baker looked clearly over to me, and I knew I had to say something. Finally, I said, "Mr. President, we realize you have made major strides in economic reform, and of course we share your desire to avoid riots. At the same time, you cannot afford to continue your subsidy program the way it is designed now. Let us sit together with the IMF and work to find a solution." Mubarak slowly got up off his knee and back in his chair, but he did not seem too convinced.

"Mr. Dallara," he said, "you must understand, it is essential that we have stability."

"We fully appreciate the need for stability, Mr. President," I responded, trying to placate him, but again without great success.

In the broader scheme of things, I don't believe Egypt in the end sacrificed a great deal of economic autonomy. Unfortunately, nor were they always persuaded to follow sound policies that could promote growth. The IMF was leery of engaging with Egypt due to its record of failure to embrace adequate economic reforms, but we (the US government) persuaded them to give it another try in this instance. They did, and six months later Egypt was, unsurprisingly, already falling short of the program's objectives.

There were other cases where substantial policy change was needed, but after a period of debate and reflection, difficult decisions were not only made but heartily embraced by national authorities. These are the cases where there was genuine ownership by the country, and where the ownership became an important ingredient in the program's success.

A prime example was Mexico in 1989. The oil market was collapsing when we launched the Brady Plan that spring, and Mexico's budget was under tremendous pressure. As negotiations unfolded it became clear that Mexico would have to make painful cuts to its budget as well as launch a major series of economic reforms including privatization. Pedro Aspe, Mexico's Finance Minister, came to Washington to see Secretary Brady and consider the necessity for severe budget cuts. After discussing the matter with David Mulford and me (we had both been in consultation with Ted Beza, IMF head of the Western Hemisphere department), Secretary Brady felt that Mexico had no choice but to bite the bullet and take drastic action to cut its deficit. We were, after all, launching an entirely new debt strategy, and its success hinged in large part on the underlying strength of Mexico's economic program. The creditors—and citizens of Mexico—needed to be assured that the future really would be different from the previous decade. Pedro Aspe agreed with that, despite the difficulties he would face in implementing the changes, and convinced President Carlos Salinas that the reforms and budget cuts were essential. Together they wholeheartedly embraced the new program. It took some time, but this genuine ownership helped propel Mexico into six years of growth and prosperity supported by the innovations of the Brady Plan.

In the case of Greece, I witnessed something that I had never seen before in more than forty-five years of dealing with sovereign debt matters. I saw a country that was dispirited, that appeared to be disenfranchised. Of course, the decision to join the euro has been a conscious decision to trade off independent monetary and exchange rate policy for price stability and greater economic convergence with the rest of the Eurozone.

When the creditors sat down with Greece for the first time in June 2011, the Greek authorities had already been struggling with a Troika-supported adjustment program for over a year. Greece seemed to be in a tug of war with the IMF, EC, and ECB over a wide range of policies: fiscal (including pensions), labor market structures, and privatization among them. But until June 15, negotiating a debt restructuring had not been on the table. On these various issues, Greece faced considerable pressure for adjusting policies to their new reality, but at least they spoke for themselves, however constrained they were.

But when it came to the debt negotiations, they were not allowed to speak for themselves, at least not with meaningful authority. It was not that the Greek representatives were incapable. Far from it. It was that the Eurogroup Deputies had been designated as our counterparts, and Greece was not in charge of this group. When had Greece actually transferred the authority to negotiate the restructuring of its debt to someone in Brussels? The answer, to my knowledge, was "never."

There was, actually, some degree of logic to this rather twisted situation. By June 2010, Eurozone members and the IMF together had already disbursed a large amount of funds to Greece and were well on their way to being among Greece's major creditors. It was therefore natural that they would want to be involved in negotiations with the private creditors, who at the time were by far Greece's largest creditor group. But to appropriate de facto Greece's authority to represent itself in these negotiations? Unparalleled not only in my experience, but in modern history.

Until mid-December, the authority and the negotiation were purportedly in the hands of the Eurogroup deputies. During that period, Greece's voice was heard at times. George Zanias was taciturn during much of these negotiations. But when he chose to speak, others listened, as he was a highly respected economist, even if his comments were often more analytical than operational. Petros Christodoulou, Head of PDMA in the Greek Ministry, was not shy to voice his perspectives, often focused on specific aspects of the negotiations. At the same time, his comments were often one voice among many. To complicate matters further, Vittorio Grilli, as I have indicated to the point of reader fatigue, professed his own lack of a mandate to negotiate on behalf of Greece or the Eurozone. Discussions with Evangelos Venizelos during this period from mid-June to mid-December were generally of a different nature. Venizelos is a man with a gift of oratory, and he did not hesitate to use it when engaging in discussions with Jean Lemierre and me. But it often did not reflect an authoritative voice for Greece on specific aspects of the debt negotiations.

"Gentlemen, I understand your concern," he was wont to say, "but we are not the masters of our fate. It is our obligation to agree with the Troika as they have the power, and we have little. Our future is with Europe and must always remain so."

Only when Lucas Papademos arrived, and we had the dust-up in Paris with the Eurozone Deputies, did I see Greece reasserting itself in the negotiations. Oh, Greece had still not wrested full control of its fate, but Papademos, the mild-mannered economist, had brought more than a semblance of influence back to the negotiating table that had previously been absent. As we moved through this roller coaster of negotiations, reminiscent of riding the Cyclone (an antique roller coaster) at Coney Island—if you've ridden it, you know how it felt for us at times, Greece gradually gained weight to its views. Over time, as the negotiations progressed with the creditors and the Troika, Greece affected the outcome.

How did Greece end up here? Was there a deeper history of debt problems for Greece that compromised independence well before the current crisis? As Greek historians know, the answer is yes. But like most things Greek, it's complicated.

The birth of modern Greece was tumultuous. With the benefits of what Roderick Beaton refers to as the "Greek Enlightenment," a fertile environment for the circulation of ideas from France, Britain, and German states to Greece arose during the eighteenth and early nineteenth centuries.[5] Trade and travel during the years of the Ottoman Empire expanded Greece's horizons and knowledge of many of the intellectual and scientific advances of Western Europe that had not previously penetrated the area we now know as Greece.

At the same time, Western historians, authors, and artists began to shape the idea that Europe owed a tremendous debt to classical Greece for its many contributions to the Western civilization. Ideas of what would become the Greek nation-state began to emerge in the late eighteenth century. Leveraging the French Revolution and constitution, thoughts of a Hellenic Republic began to emerge, and intellectuals such as Rigas and Korais began to spread thoughts of revolution and independence. In 1821, the Greek revolution broke out under the stewardship of Alexandros Ypsilantis, the new leader of the Filiki Eteria (Friendly Society), a group founded in Odessa in 1814. By 1822, Greece had a provisional constitution. Foreign support began to emerge in 1824, and by 1827, after much blood had been shed, a new Greek nation emerged after the defeat of the Ottoman fleet at the naval Battle of Navarino Bay by a task force of British, French, and Russian ships. Oddly, no Greeks took part in the battle, even though the future of Greece was being determined. What a messy way for a country to be born—by a battle between British, French, and Russian forces on one side and Ottoman and Egyptian forces on the other. Greece's independence was not firmly secured, however, until 1830, when the Protocol of London was signed and decided that "Greece will form an independent state." In a move that is eerily familiar to those of us involved in the resolution of the Greek debt problem, Greece was nowhere in sight when the Protocol was signed.

Independence did not come without its costs. In 1824 and 1825 Greece was able to raise two loans for a total of 2.8 million pounds sterling—rather impressive for a country that did not even formally exist! Then again, bankers and investors have been chasing yield for centuries. Each loan had a 5% coupon and established a sinking fund equal to 1%. Furthermore, the first loan was floated at a discounted price of 59 and the second at 55. Of interest is that both loans were secured by "all the revenues" and "the whole of the national property of Greece," but Greece received little benefit from either loan. Perhaps trying to channel the brilliant strategy of Themistocles, they used the proceeds from the second loan to purchase ships. According to a summary by William H. Wynne, a US Treasury official of the 1940s and 1950s, "vessels which could have been bought, at a moderate price, ready for sea were not purchased. Instead, orders were placed in England and the United States for the construction of new ships . . . Through a series of miscalculations and mishaps, Greece was able to obtain delivery . . . after long and disheartening delays, of less than half the number ordered. One ship burst its boilers on its first passage, another blew up, and two rotted in the Thames River."[6]

Greece was fighting for survival and defaulted on the two loans after two years. It took five decades—five decades—before the defaulted loan was finally extinguished.

Mark Mazower has looked into the British loan to Greece in 1824 and 1825 and explains it as "the sheer abundance of investable capital at that time." In a fascinating possible confluence of events, he stipulates that "the architecture of international finance capital was being built as the Greek revolt began."[7] London had become the center of a new sovereign loan market. British investors had lent to the "Republic of Buenos Aires," Columbia, Mexico, and Peru, all governments in the process of formation. All would end up in default by the end of the decade. Edward

Blaquiere had written a report that apparently excited the British investors. His report "glossed over the political difficulties" of Greece. Lord Byron also became an advocate of Greece and became the representative of the London Greek Committee in Greece. "I did not come here to join a faction but a nation," Byron wrote in September 1823.[8]

Greece's second foray into international borrowing ended on an even more sour note. In 1832, Greece was confirmed as a Kingdom under the protection of Great Britain, France, and Russia, with Prince Otto of Bavaria as the new King. As part of the agreement that brought him to the throne, the three powers guaranteed a loan of 60 million francs. Debt service on this loan took precedent over the loans of 1824 and 1825, much to the chagrin of the first round of creditors. The coupon was again 5% with a 1% sinking fund, but the discount was modest as they were sold at 94% of face value. By 1836 the initial disbursement of 40 million francs was gone and Greece could not even pay the interest. By 1840, the entire loan of 60 million francs was in default and the guarantors had to meet their guaranty.

In 1843, Russian pressure led the three powers to insist that Greece pledge customs and stamp duty supplemented, if necessary, by license fees and land taxes. It was, paradoxically, a time of great admiration of all things Hellenic, especially in the Bavarian court. From *Leander*, the first novel published in the new independent Kingdom, the crowning of the new king was captured by the following statement: "O King of Greece! Old Greece bequeathed the lights of learning to Germany, through you Germany has undertaken to repay the gift with interest, and will be grateful to you, seeing in you the one to resurrect the firstborn people of the Earth."[9]

Germany repay the Greeks? That wasn't quite how it worked out in those first few years of the Kingdom of Greece. In 1843, the pressure put on the King to take measures to service the debts turned into the first financial crisis of modern Greece. The measures that were agreed by King Otto were humiliating, and further austerity equal to 3.5 million francs was to be imposed. According to Beaton, both the circumstances and the conditions were uncannily similar to those of the so-called "third bailout" in July 2011, when once again a Greek government would be obliged to surrender its fiscal autonomy to its European creditors.[10] It should be underscored that these first two episodes of Greek "sovereign" borrowing and default were heavily influenced by political developments and power struggles within Europe. They were by no means solely a reflection of poor economic management by Greece.

The events of 1843 were a rather remarkable example of Greece sacrificing the bulk of its policy independence to foreign powers under the pressure of resolving its external debt. But it had an interesting twist, which ironically helped establish a degree of natural Greek identity and voice. The king maintained his throne, but his concessions to the three powers had so angered the Greeks that both the Greek army and the Greek politicians turned against him. As a result, modern Greece gained its first constitution and reasserted its position as the center of Europe, and Hellas was back.

Thus, in a bizarre fashion, Greece's first financial crisis had gained it some independence. Alas, it was short-lived. By 1856, Greece's external debts came back to haunt them again. The British advised Greece in 1845 and 1846 that they "might feel obliged to interfere in that country's internal affairs if Greece did not service its guaranteed debt."[11] It sounds like a stern warning to me, but by 1854 not a penny of debt service had been paid from the Greek Treasury.

Meanwhile, on another waterfront, so to speak, Greece got itself in a pickle with Britain. Concerns were growing in London about expropriation of the property of British citizens in Greece, and an attack on the house of a Jewish merchant in 1847 who had the protection of the British crown provoked serious action. The port of Piraeus was the site of ignominy when the British Foreign Secretary, Viscount Palmerston, in one of the earliest adventures of "gunboat diplomacy,"[12] ordered it blockaded. This was eventually resolved peacefully, but very soon another naval force arrived in Piraeus, and this time the British were joined by the French. Greek irregular troops had advanced on Ottoman territory as they joined forces with Russia in what eventually became the Crimean War. This war was waged much to the displeasure of London and Paris, both of whom wanted to keep the Ottoman Empire afloat (they aligned themselves with the Ottomans, the French, and others in defeating Russia in that war). On the basis of the misappropriation of revenues that were pledged to service the guaranteed loans, the British and French visited Piraeus, blockading and occupying the port. Once again, an unserviced external debt had brought Greece to its knees. The occupying fleets were only withdrawn in 1857, when a new scheme was developed to impose external financial control. In what appears to be a forerunner of IMF or Troika-imposed requirements in 2010 and 2011, a British/French/Russian Commission was asked to prepare a report on Greek sovereign finances. Issued in 1859 (an early version of an IMF report on a standby arrangement?), the report detailed the "abuses and defects of the fiscal system," proposed specific reforms, and recommended that Greece pay at least 900,000 francs a year in debt service, with the idea of progressive increases in the payments. Once the powers approved the report, Greece agreed to pay the 900,000 francs per year, only one-fourth of the debt service obligation. Greece did in fact make the first payment in 1860.

As Lord Byron had noted, however, "Every loan is not a merely speculative hit, but seats a nation or upsets a throne. Republics also get involved a bit." (*Don Juan*, Canto XII) How true indeed.

In 1862 another change to the loan of 1833 took place. In October of that year, King Otto was deposed by a revolutionary government following his support of Austria against Italy in their war for independence, as well as in protest of his refusal to accept political reforms. The new king was a Dane, and also quite remarkably seventeen years old, as was Otto when he was crowned. The British had selected the new king, despite weak support for him in an election that had been held in Greece to select a new sovereign. So much for home rule. As part of the agreement, the new king was given no authority over the constitution. The new constitution of 1864 gave all adult males the right to vote, a remarkably democratic system at that time.[13] Furthermore, the British decided to cede control over the Ionian Islands to Greece. As part of the treaty that established this, the three powers agreed to ease the annual debt charge by one-third. Astonishingly, Greece apparently never paid additional interest on the debt, but with payments of 900,000 francs a year, completed repayment in 1973—140 years after the original guaranteed loan. That was one hell of a debt restructuring.

Regarding the market loans of 1824 and 1825, the market demonstrated discipline and blocked Greece's access to new loans until they were repaid. In October 1867, forty-three years after the initial loan was disbursed, representatives of Greece and the English bondholder committee met and reached a tentative agreement. But somewhat like our June 21 agreement in 2011, the agreement of October 1867 did not hold together. The bondholders were looking for better terms based on Greece extending its boundaries (we did not think of that in 2011 and 2012), and the Greeks wanted assurances of new money from the creditors, a familiar request of private creditors in the 1980s Latin debt crisis.[14]

Nine years later, however, in contrast to our nine months, agreement was finally reached. New bonds were issued at a face value of £31 (in 1824 bonds) and £310 (in 1825 bonds) for £100 of the original bonds, with the same coupon of 5% that the original bonds had. For each £100 of unpaid coupons, new bonds were issued to the tune of £11.12. It appears that the original bondholders took a bath even greater than what we did in 2012, but they added an interesting twist to the haircut service of the new bonds. They were to be secured by the customs duties of Corfu and by a second change in the stamp duty. Receipts from these revenues were to be paid fortnightly to the National Bank of Greece for the account of the bondholders. And here is where the additional step entered the picture. Greece agreed that the tax collectors would be held criminally responsible if they failed to make the prescribed deposits.[15] It is not clear whether this provision was ever used. No wonder Greek tax collectors reportedly expect "extra bonuses."

By 1878 the nominal amount of debt had grown to approximately £10,00,000, and the debt was reportedly settled by the issuance of bonds with a face value of £1200.00.[16] What a saga. But it was not over—not by any means.

It wasn't long before another chapter in the growing history of troubled Greek debt was opened. With the 1878 settlement, Greece once again had access to the international capital markets. And once again, they rushed headlong into accumulating new foreign debt. It is hard not to shake one's head when reading Beaton's description of how things started: "Faced with the choice early in his premiership, of both building infrastructure and supporting the army, Trikoupis (the Prime Minister at the time) had elected to do both." Apparently the 1880s were a decade of "frenetic borrowing and spending."[17]

Greece secured a series of loans from 1878 to 1893, when it once again fell into debt servicing difficulties. In 1893, the Minister of Finance stated in a rather remarkably frank assessment of Greece's finances, "If indeed one takes the approach of an unbiased historian, honestly studying our economic history independent of the effects our national policies have on our economic situation, they will have to admit that Greece defaulted in 1882."[18] In fact, the Prime Minister announced that Greece was unable to pay its debts. As one contemporary stated, "Greece is not a failed state like Turkey, Peru, Mexico, Honduras..., Greece is the sole nation in the world to exist in a state of fraudulent bankruptcy."[19]

The international loans of the late 1870s and early 1880s came from Paris, as French bankers ignored Greece's past. In 1884, a loan of 170 million francs was contracted with a syndicate of French and Greek bonds, but it was undersubscribed and had to be secured by customs duties. In 1887, another loan was secured by revenues from government monopolies of petroleum, matches, playing cards, cigarette paper, and other items. Other foreign loans ensued. By 1893 the government was desperate and tried to launch a very complicated funding operation. That effort failed, however, as export revenues collapsed with the increase of duties on currants by France, Germany, and Russia. Revenues from currants, comprising two-thirds of Greece's exports, consequently fell by two-thirds. On December 10, 1893, Greece suspended sending full payments on previous loans and reduced interest payments by 70%. Greece was again in default.

This time it was a combination of English, French, and German bondholders. The debt once again became caught up in a war, this time between Greece and the Turks. Greece lost in a rout, but Turkey was forced to cede back to Greece most of the land it had gained during the war. A seventeen-year-old cadet from Turkey watched in dismay as this took place. His name was Mustafa Kemal.[20]

It was a debacle for Greece as the country came under fire. In the summer of 1897, German bondholders, backed by the German government, decided that an international commission of control would be established over Greek finances. One century and fifteen years later, nearly an identical proposal had been put forward by the German government.

In 1898, the proposal was actually adopted by the Greek government. What ignominy Greece suffered. In 2012, the Troika had considerable influence over Greek government finances, but their role mercifully stopped short of the Commission of 1898.

As unwelcome as such a loss of economic sovereignty was, the Greek economy actually recovered strongly between the years 1897 and 1912. "Fiscal discipline had been imposed by the international financial

Commission. Educational opportunities had been expanded towards the end of the nineteenth century and thus began to pay dividends."[21] With the financial commission in place, Britain, France, and Germany once again decided to guarantee Greece's credit in order to allow for funds to be raised to both pay indemnity to Turkey for the damages done during the ill-advised war, as well as make payments to the holders of the defaulted external debt. This time, the three guarantors made the guarantee joint and several, rather than just several as in 1833. Once again, the guarantors secured the collection of various revenues from not only the state monopolies but also from energy and petroleum revenues. The Commission's involvement in revenue collection went deep into the process, even involving the production of the revenue stamps and tobacco wrappers.

The Financial Commission consisted of representatives of not only France, Great Britain, and Germany, where the major creditors resided, but also Russia, Austria, and Italy for political consideration.[22] It is interesting to note that the debt restructuring of 1897 included the entire Greek public debt outstanding, both externally held and internally held. The Commission was struggling to deal with debt originating in 1833 as well as more recent debts, especially those incurred in the 1880s. In reading documents related to this restructuring, one has the impression that sorting out the competing claims, as well as trying to respond to Greece's contemporary needs, was nearly an impossible task. Another interesting note is that throughout the period of default, while interest on external debt had been cut 70%, interest on internal debt had been paid in full.

By 1902, Greece was raising new money—yet again. The first was a 4% loan for the construction of a railroad, secured by surplus receipts from previously assigned revenues as well as a mortgage on the railroad. The work of the Commission had actually contributed to the rehabilitation of Greek credit. This 1902 loan was under the direct control of the Commission.

More loans were issued until 1910, but the Balkan War of 1912–1913 disrupted things once again. Nevertheless, with the Commission again in direct control, and various revenues pledged, one loan of 500 million francs, the largest by far, was contracted.

Over the next forty years, Greece went through continued cycles of economic stress, bankruptcy, restructuring, and renewed access to loans on the international markets. During WWI, Greece was funded by new credits from the Allies. According to the terms of the Peace Treaty of Sèvres (August 1920), Greece was granted important parts of the former Ottoman Empire, including parts of Western Anatolia, virtually doubling the size of the Greek state. This, along with many other political and military machinations, set the stage for the Turkish War of Independence, a humanitarian disaster. The Greek army was roundly defeated by the Turkish army and thousands of Greeks fled the fighting in Anatolia. The worst disaster took place during the Great Fire of Smyrni, where possibly "hundreds of thousands" lost their lives in a massive fire and killings.[23] On the heels of this apocryphal event came the extraordinary decision embodied in the Convention of Lausanne, Switzerland, in July 1923. With an amazing number of signatories, including France, the United Kingdom, and Japan, the convention agreed on a compulsory exchange of Turks and Greeks, based on their respective religions. The human and economic consequences of the war and the Convention led to the relocation of an estimated 1.3 to 1.4 million people into Greece, mounting inflation, and another desperate financial situation.[24] Once again, international support arose, with the League of Nations calling for an international loan as well as a refugee resettlement commission. A loan emerged that was backed by the League, the continued authority of the International Financial Commission, and various monopoly revenues. In 1928, for the first time, the United States stepped up with a large ($12,167,000) twenty-year loan to support refugee resettlement.

As this book was being finalized, Lex Rieffel, a good friend of mine since my days at the US Treasury, handed me an envelope during a luncheon at the Cosmos Club in Washington, DC. The envelope contained five original bonds from Greek debt that was issued in 1924 as part of the effort to raise money to cover the extraordinary cost of the resettlement. Part of the papers of M. Marc-Aurele Rieffel, a French-American banker with Citibank and Lex's father, they were labeled "Refuge Loan of 1924." They were bearer bonds with maturity of "Forty-Year 7% secured sinking fund Gold Bonds" and were accompanied by five coupons entitling the bearer to $35 in gold coins. These bonds apparently went through a series of restructurings in the 1930s as Greece struggled to meet its obligations. Then the German invasion in April 1941 forced both the government and the Bank of Greece to flee from Athens and made further transfers

A 1933 Greek Government Bond issued to refinance a League of Nations–backed Refugee Loan of 1924. Accompanying it is a coupon entitling the holder to $35.00 in gold. Those were the days! Courtesy of Lex Rieffel

impossible. I have no idea whether the bonds currently have value but given my current expectations (July 2023) for Greek sovereign debt to be revised upward soon to investment grade, I believe I should, with the permission of my friend Lex, bequeath them to the Greek Finance Minister before they become too hot to handle!

Under the pressure of the depression that encircled the globe in the early 1930s, Greece fell back into default, which continued through World War II and Greece's Civil War. The formal default in 1932 was followed by a strong economic revival until 1940, after which extreme conditions of war, occupation, and civil war basically wrenched the entire economy.[25] The International Financial Commission established in 1898 actually continued in existence until 1975, an astounding seventy-seven years after its creation. Although it is not at all clear that it played an important role after World War II, the existence of this Commission for such a lengthy period provides a telling lesson on the costs of excessive borrowing by a sovereign nation.

CHAPTER 29

FIRST AND GOAL FROM THE ONE-YARD LINE

"When you've got the momentum in a football game, that is a time to keep going and get it into the end zone."

—Vince Lombardi, 1982

As any American football fan knows, when a team is on the other team's one-yard line with a first and goal, you have four attempts to get the ball into the end zone for a score. Sometimes, that final yard can be excruciatingly difficult to achieve. That was how it was beginning to feel in our negotiations. We knew we were close, but pinning down the final details was proving to be very, very elusive.

We finally met with Papademos late on January 26 and again on the following day, during which we reviewed various options of interest rates on the new bonds. We were also continuing to discuss the issue of a collective action clause (CAC) on the outstanding Greek law bonds and whether it was necessary in order to achieve a successful outcome. Other issues yet to be resolved that day included the GDP warrant, negative pledge clauses, clearing system issues, and cost acceleration. We had daily conference calls with the Steering Committee to keep them fully informed and to secure their agreement on each part in our negotiation as things evolved.

Greek debt talks hit a snag. Jean Lemierre and I leave Prime Minister Lucas Papademos's office as negotiations bog down. January 2012. AP Photo

The press accurately described our talks as inching ahead. "Greece once again appears on the verge of reaching a deal with its private sector creditors," reported Landon Thomas Jr. in the *New York Times*.[1] However, he wisely pointed out that talks had broken down before. Indeed, we were not over the goal line. And the issue of the ECB's handling of its Greek bonds also remained unresolved. Positive comments were beginning to emerge from Davos as well, as even Wolfgang Schäuble and Olli Rehn were reported to have said that "they were confident Greece would avoid default."[2] I had been in touch with Rehn throughout the week and was not surprised to hear of him reported as upbeat. Schäuble was another matter, since he had been so difficult and one of the proponents of a program focused on endless rounds of fiscal adjustment. But Ackermann confirmed that this was indeed the tone of a meeting the two had. Furthermore, Papademos was regularly in touch with Merkel during this period, and that may well have also affected the evolving positions.

The days and nights in Athens seemed to be getting longer, and the lights shining on the Acropolis seemed to be getting dimmer. Although I still looked through the window or walked to the balcony, depending on which room I had, to gaze at the Acropolis, its magic gradually began to lose some of its luster. I had somehow convinced myself that the residue of Greece's distant past glory would reach across the millennia and propel Greece toward a resolution. Did the past still inspire the people of Greece today, or was it a relic that had no bearing on these seemingly overwhelming problems of 2012? I would find no clear answer, but I took some small comfort in knowing that the pressure was building on all sides.

As for the creditors, we were feeling the heat to close the deal and contain the damage to our balance sheets and minimize the risk to the broader exposures in Italy, Spain, and Portugal. Tensions in these three countries had eased somewhat in early February, but we knew that a hard default by Greece threatened to resurrect the market contagion of a few weeks earlier. At the same time, pressure was growing on the official creditors to share a greater part of the adjustment burden. Press reports indicated that discussions were under way between the IMF and the Eurozone, asking all Eurozone countries with outstanding bilateral loans to Greece (totaling €55.6 billion) under the Greek Loan Facility (GLF) to accept a small decline in the interest rate on these loans of 75 basis points. If this were to be agreed, it would lower the debt-to-GDP ratio by 1.5% by 2020. As my colleague Mikis, who was following this issue very closely, said to me in a note, "small but not insignificant." One of our sources on the EU staff confirmed the accuracy of the press reports. At the same time, the IMF had refused to refinance its outstanding disbursements in the standby arrangement of €17.8 billion into a longer-term maturity Extended Fund Facility (EFF) program. This was yet another example of the rigidities of multilateral institutions in the face of overwhelming financial logic. The private sector was extending its maturities up to forty years, including the grace period, and the public sector, whose role is to advance the global public good, refused to extend its maturities beyond five years.

Pressures grew in Greece to strengthen the economic adjustment and reform program. Papademos was caught between an increasingly reluctant parliament on one hand and the Troika on the other hand, pressing for more budget cuts despite the growing evidence that this approach was counterproductive. Once again, rather than closing the budget deficit and financing gap, these measures were increasing them. It appeared, based on the information available to us, the new debt sustainability estimates would require an additional €15 billion in budget cuts to put the country on a more sustainable basis.[3]

Pressure was also building on the ECB to contribute to Greece's widening financing gap. Juncker, Chairman of the Eurozone Finance Ministers, suggested publicly that the ECB should also consider playing a role. The ECB was the single largest holder of GGBs, at roughly €50 billion. Many ECB officials, however, were very resistant to the idea. The IMF and Greece recirculated a proposal for the ECB to consider which would have contributed substantially to solving the problem. It would reduce the government debt by €18.7 billion by 2020, equal to 6.7% of GDP. This would be on the basis of a 15% nominal haircut on the ECB's holdings, along with savings to Greece on interest charges.

With the growing pressure on the euro governments, the ECB, and the Greek government, Jean Lemierre, Lucas Papademos, Evangelos Venizelos, and I decided to take a short break in our talks to allow discussions with the other parties to advance. This was the first time that the focus had shifted to the ECB and Eurozone governments to step up more, and we thought it was a good time to disengage, temporarily, on the private debt restructuring front. Let others do battle for a while. Paul Volcker once told me that it was not always necessary to be at the center of every economic policy dispute. "Let others wear themselves out, Charles," he'd said in discussing the endless disputes between Argentina and the IMF during the debt crises of the 1980s.

The break did not last long. Having returned to the US, I called Papademos on my first day back and he reported renewed pressure for further concessions by the private creditors.

We decided it was far too risky to stay away for too long, so Jean, Hung, Mikis, and I quickly returned to Athens. Upon our return we had another one of our meetings with Papademos and Venizelos. We seemed to agree that the coupon structure on the new bonds had gone about as far as we could take it, and calls to both Juncker and Rehn had reaffirmed that they understood that we had reached our limits. We focused instead on the GDP warrants, and progress was made there. But they had very little time and were preoccupied by negotiations with the IMF and the Greek parliament. Lucas looked weary, and Evangelos looked harried. We indicated that further details could possibly be advanced by our team directly with the Greek PDMA. And that is exactly what happened.

They made significant progress in narrowing the gap and reaching a compromise solution on all but one of the outstanding points. The only outstanding issue appeared to be the starting point of the GDP warrants. Greece's PDMA proposed 2016, and we proposed 2015 in recognition of the significant concessions made by the private creditors on the coupon structure, NPV losses of the private debt restructuring deal, and the prospect of the GDP Security instruments being called by Greece after 2020. We decided to propose the following package:

- Starting point of GDP warrants: 2015
- Cap of 1%
- Multiplier 1.5x
- Starting point of call option: December 31, 2020
- Starting points of cumulative growth over two-year period in case of negative real GDP growth: 2021
- No supplementary payments whenever real GDP growth is negative

Even while the demands temporarily eased on the private creditors, it was continuing to build on Greece. What seemed to be lost on the Troika was that by February 2021, Greece had already accomplished an unprecedented 11% of GDP of reduction of its underlying fiscal deficit adjustment since 2009.

A week later the ECB agreed to significant concessions on its holdings of Greek government bonds. In a complicated arrangement, the ECB would exchange Greek bonds for bonds of the European Financial Stability Facility, who in turn would return them to Greece. The ECB/EFSF transaction would take place below face value, but since the bonds were purchased at a discount, the ECB would not necessarily take a loss. Nevertheless, it would contribute to an easing of Greece's debt problem. While we certainly could take no credit for this development, it was good to see progress not dependent on further private creditor concessions or additional Greek austerity.

We shifted back to Paris for another Steering Committee meeting on February 9. It was a long day during which we reviewed the bidding on key issues as Europe and the IMF quarreled. With the revisions related to the weaker economy, we couldn't figure out how to get the debt-to-GDP ratio below 127.6% with a coupon structure that we could accept. (We were already at 3%/3%/3.75% and a total NPV loss of 65.4% at a discount rate of 9%.) However, the meeting, hosted by AXA, proved to be very useful. We agreed on the creditor priorities. The key finding was that cash at hand was far better than higher coupons or higher value of new bonds. This was perhaps the least costly way for the creditors to contribute further—to accept a higher up-front haircut. Following the Steering Committee meeting we had a meeting of the IIF Board leadership plus CEOs of the largest creditors. After considerable debate, Paco Gonzalez, the Chairman of BBVA, a leading Spanish bank, summed up the views of the majority of Directors: "We are so close. Do everything you can to strike a deal."

From that point onward, however, things began to pull apart once again, or at least it felt that way. Like trying to dock a ship in rough weather when the waves keep increasing, pushing the ship away from the pier despite being so close. Papademos was struggling to secure agreement on a reform package, and German officials were apparently debating whether to separate the debt agreement from the reform package. We knew, however, that this would be politically impossible; would Europe really authorize the €30 billion needed to underpin the deal without a reform program that would close the financing gap and lower the debt-to-GDP ratio close to 120%? Very doubtful. Greek and German officials were starting to bicker publicly. German Deputy Finance Minister Steffen Kampeter reportedly told a group of lawyers in Hamburg on February 16 that "This coming Monday, we will see whether Greece delivers or whether we will be forced to decide on another course of action, one that is not desired."[4]

Minister Schäuble added his own rather unhelpful comment when he suggested that Europe was "better prepared than two years ago to withstand a default."[5] This kind of implied threat was not infrequent during various stages of the negotiations, but it was especially unwelcome with the markets focused on an upcoming March 20 bond redemption of €14.5 billion due. Without a deal, Greece would most assuredly default. Venizelos was quoted as accusing the richer European nations of "playing with fire" by toying with the idea of dismissing Greece from the Eurozone. Papademos, always seeking to calm the waters despite his ever-growing frustration, stated that the economic pain of austerity measures is "contained in comparison to the economic and social catastrophe that will follow if we don't adopt them."[6]

Americans began to add their view to the public debate. Former US Treasury Secretary Hank Paulson spoke about the danger of allowing a systemic institution to fail. I thought it was an unusual comment coming from the Treasury Secretary who allowed Lehman to fail, but nevertheless the point was well taken.

Market commentators were also speculating about the potential that a Greek default would cause others to go. A consultant, analyzing credit default probabilities, suggested that "if Greece defaults, Portugal had a 60 percent chance of following. If that happens, then the odds increase that Ireland, Spain, Italy, and perhaps even France could tumble like dominoes."[7] While I found that rather dramatic, we had known for some time that the risk of a default creating a wave of contagion throughout the continent was quite likely. We became so increasingly concerned at the Institute that certain European leaders were really flirting with the idea of a default that we commissioned our own staff paper titled "Implications of a Disorderly Greek Default and Euro Exit" (see Appendix 6).

Phil Suttle, our Global Chief Economist, took the lead in this exercise, supported by Jeff Anderson, our Chief Economist for Europe, as well as the other staff members. It was painful reading. A few excerpts convey a sense of the potential disaster that our analysis foresaw, for both Greece and Europe. Apart from the chaos that would spread through the Greek economy, some of the less obvious likely ramifications included:

- Sizable potential losses by the ECB; their exposure to Greece was approximately €177 billion, nearly 200% of the ECB's capital base. This would have required urgent recapitalization by the Eurozone countries.

- The likely need for an additional €380 billion in official (Eurozone/IMF) support for Portugal and Ireland to help persuade markets that they were fully insulated from Greece.

- The need for additional official support in the range of €350 billion for Spain and Italy to keep them from being swept into the Greek maelstrom.

· An estimated €160 billion in recapitalization costs for European banks, with private investors probably very reluctant to provide additional equity to European banks.

If these first- and second-order effects were not enough to induce sobriety by the Eurozone leaders, an even broader set of reflections would likely frighten even the most cynical European official. Europe was at that time building a "firewall through the funding" of the EFSF/ESM mechanics. The EFSF lending capacity had been increased to €440 billion. While that was an impressive figure when compared to Greek needs, it paled when matched against a broader collection of troubled Eurozone economies. The reality was actually that Europe's most effective firewall was not the EFSF/ESM, but the ECB itself. And the ECB would most probably be a damaged institution if Greece left the euro. I had to agree with Venizelos that Europe was playing with fire.

Despite the progress that had been made in Ireland, Portugal, Italy, and Spain, none of them were out of the woods and free from the vortex that would surely follow a Greek collapse. And the ECB had become the lifeline for these countries. For example, the Securities Market Program (SMP) was launched May 2010 by Trichet to "ensure depth and liquidity in malfunctioning segments of the debt securities markets and to restore an appropriate functioning of the monetary policy transmission mechanism."[8] SMP purchases of Spanish and Italian debt by the ECB amounted to as much as €100 billion in the six months alone between July 2011 and January 2012. Furthermore, analyst estimates were that Spanish and Italian banks accounted for one-third of the ECB's €416 billion of outstanding LTRO. This program, the long-term refinancing operation (thus LTRO) was announced near the end of 2011 to help ease the effects of the Eurozone crisis on the banks. It was a subsidized loan scheme (1% charge to the banks) enabling the banking systems of Europe to avoid a complete credit crunch throughout the Eurozone economies. Some of this liquidity provided funding into the marketplace, while some went to support national sovereign debts, helping to contain the rise in bond yields for countries such as Spain and Italy.

The ECB balance sheet had expanded by an astounding 9% of Euro Area GDP during the second half of 2011, most of it increasing the central banks' exposure to the weaker, peripheral countries.

It was clear that Europe's vulnerability to a Greek exit ran not just through their economies, which would have been severe enough, but through their banking systems and the ECB itself. We knew it, and most European leaders knew it too. But their words and deeds did not always reflect it. If the capital base of the ECB were substantially reduced, it would be severely wounded in its efforts to stanch the spread of disorder that would inevitably follow a Greek exit. Of course, the Eurozone countries would have been able to recapitalize the ECB. But this stultified, sluggish manner of decision-making in Europe on such matters gave little hope that a full-blown euro crisis could be averted.

We decided to fan copies of the IIF staff note out to key officials throughout Europe. Did it do any good? Who knows. We received high praise for the document, but that was almost uniformly from officials who already agreed with it and needed no convincing.

CHAPTER 30

A DEAL REDUX

"He has the most who is content with the least."

—Diogenes, circa 380 BC

The Greek Parliament gathered in Athens to meet on Sunday, February 12, 2012, to vote on the second adjustment program that had been negotiated with Troika staff and would be presented for approval at the Eurogroup meeting. I called Lucas Papademos that morning to wish him luck, but he was not in a sunny mood.

"Will you get the vote?" I asked.

"It is likely, but not certain," he responded. "I believe we have the necessary votes secure, but there is uncertainty about the number of coalition parliament members who may abstain or vote against it. The economic situation is precarious, and social conditions are of serious concern. You can see it on the streets, and you can see it in the eyes of parliamentarians."

Indeed, the streets were once again full, and the demonstrations became violent as protesters began throwing Molotov cocktails at police. The anger and violence, however, were not just in Athens. There were clashes in Salonika in the north, Volos in central Greece, and on the islands of Crete and Corfu.

The markets were also exhibiting another round of instability. The threat of a disorderly default by Greece had once again rocked global financial markets. As one news outlet put it, "the world is waiting to

Athens in flames as demonstrations turn violent. February 12, 2012.
Photo by Aris Messinis/AFP/Getty Images.

see what happens with the Greek austerity package." Apparently, at least one Eurozone minister was insisting that the fiscal adjustment was not enough, and the Eurogroup asked for an additional €325 million to be cut from "structural expenditures" in 2012.[1] Did it really make sense to ask the Greek government to go to the well one more time? I had my doubts, and so did Papademos: "We thought we had a deal a few days ago, but certain issues have been raised that require further negotiations."

Lucas and Evangelos Venizelos were, however, determined to do everything possible to get this through because they fully understood what was at stake. And they succeeded. The vote was 199 in favor, 74 against, 27 abstentions, despite the violent protests, which left dozens of buildings aflame.[2] It was a tribute to the combined strength of this unlikely two-man tag team.

As fires smoldered in Athens on the morning of February 13, we gathered once again in the Churchill Room at the Grande Bretagne. We had many issues on which to chew, but as we looked at the smoking remains of the violent demonstrations in Syntagma Square, our issues seemed rather petty. Greece was struggling for its life, and we were concerned with how to account for accrued interest??

With the passage of the legislation by Greece, the odds were growing that the Eurozone governments would finally approve the new €130 billion package of official financial support for Greece. If so, would we be ready? As we headed into the week of February 13, many issues remained unresolved. Among them was the rather arbitrary expansion of the bonds that would be included in the debt reduction exercise. The Greek Finance Ministry had agreed with the IMF that certain public sector Greek entities that had the guarantee of the Hellenic Republic would be included. Of course, this shifted the burden ever further on the backs of the Greek banks. They already had an outsized 22% of all GGBs; in this new category, they held 60%! I received a note from Yannis Costopoulos. This would increase the recapitalization costs of the Greek banks by an additional €11 billion, on top of the previous estimate of €23 billion. At the same time, it would augment very modestly the effort to close the financing gap through the debt restructuring.

We had sympathy for the Greek banks' position, and spoke to Venizelos about the matter, but he refused to intervene, even though it would deepen the damage to the Greek banks.

Other issues included how to deal with unpaid accrued interest, the treatment of the ECB's holdings, the exact structure of the GDP securities, and of course, the seemingly perpetual issue of interest rates on the new bonds.

All roads once again were leading to Brussels. But as we prepared for the meetings there, an article emerged in the *Financial Times* on February 15 that reported that the meeting of Finance Ministers scheduled for that night had been canceled. The most troublesome part of the article was the report that Eurozone Finance Ministers had sought advice from the Greek financial and legal advisers on whether the debt restructuring could be aborted after it was launched. A bizarre idea, to be sure. Once a debt restructuring was launched by Greece, it was out there, to succeed or fail on its own merits. The thought of interrupting a bond exchange already offered is mindboggling. It would lead to a plethora of lawsuits and, most important, a disaster for the Eurozone.

The concern reflected the anxiety of the Eurozone Finance Ministers that they may not be able to secure parliamentary approval of the agreement because of concerns that "the increasingly obstinate German, Dutch, and Finnish legislatures—will not know for sure if Greece has lived up to its side of the bargain before they vote."[3] These so-called "prior actions" by Greece would not likely be implemented by the time euro member states needed to start the parliamentary approval process.

When I read the report, I immediately called Juncker and expressed my concern.

"Jean-Claude, you can't be serious about pulling the deal after it is agreed. The markets would react violently."

"But the Germans and the Dutch are being very difficult."

I sensed that even though Cleary Gottlieb reportedly had expressed its view that legally Greece could withdraw the offer, this would be a grave mistake. In his usual assured manner, Juncker responded, "Charles, we will get it done."

"Jean-Claude, I certainly hope so. We cannot afford to let this fall apart when we are so close."

The dilemma reflected the fact that the whole notion of having parliaments vote individually on each new package of support for Greece was absurd. It politicized the entire crisis management of Europe and was a major factor in why the Greek economy was in a depression, and the Eurozone economy in a recession. I thought back to the Latin debt crisis in the 1980s and wondered what would have happened if the US Congress had been required to vote on every tranche of support for Mexico, Argentina, Brazil, Venezuela, Chile, etc., or even vote once on each IMF program. It would have never, ever worked. The IMF was an indispensable instrument to finance the restructuring of Latin debt throughout the 1980s and ultimately to support the Brady Plan, which cleared away the Latin debt problem in 1989–1990. It has been useful in countless other circumstances where sizable funds are disbursed to countries in economic difficulty solely on the basis of the decision of the IMF Executive Board. No legislators in sight. The European architecture was, however, woefully insufficient, and Greece paid the price.

As the meeting on February 20 loomed, we met one more time with Papademos and Venizelos to narrow the list of open issues. It was difficult to do, however, given the quantitative uncertainties surrounding the ECB holdings, so we found ourselves unable to make much progress.

We then all migrated to Brussels, where we agreed to meet the Eurogroup Deputies while the Ministers met to review the reinforced Greek adjustment program. Jean, Hung, Mikis, and I met once again in the European Commission headquarters at the Berlaymont building. At least this time we were not in the bowels of the building, as we had been in July.

When we sat down for negotiations at roughly 4 p.m., however, we were in for a surprise. No, a shock. Although the meeting was chaired by Thomas Wieser, the Austrian finance official who had stepped in to replace Vittorio Grilli, we were surrounded by some faces we had never seen before, at least not in this group. Jens Weidmann showed up for the first time to represent the Bundesbank. Deputy Ministers from the Netherlands and other countries also were present. I surmised that it was perhaps natural that senior officials would attend this meeting, since they had accompanied their Ministers to Brussels. At the same time, I had become accustomed to seeing all the junior representatives from the Eurozone countries, taking notes and leaving the talking to the IMF and/or the European Commission. We were a bit unsettled, but soon we were thrown a serious curveball. The officials explained that the calculated debt-to-GDP ratio was still well above the target level of 120%. Apparently, the measures agreed to by the ECB and the Eurozone central banks, under the strong encouragement of Papademos, had brought the ratio down from an extraordinary 138% of debt to GDP to the range of 128%. Papademos felt that the 138% figure was, in any case, unjustified on the basis of three months of new data. Despite the reduction in the ratio brought about by the ECB's and central banks' actions, the Eurogroup was seeking to reduce the €30 billion support to the debt restructuring that had been committed by Merkel back in July to €20 billion in order to lower the stock of debt to 120% of GDP by 2020.

Jean and I exchanged glances, knowing this would never fly. We knew our creditor base, and we knew that they would never, ever give up this €30 billion voluntarily. Since we had shifted away from the collateral approach the European banks, pension funds, and insurance firms who owned the Greek government debt lived for the thought that they would receive 15 cents on every dollar (so to speak) that they had lent to Greece. At times, it almost seemed as if that was all that mattered. Seeing the commitment for this from Merkel and Sarkozy in July had been the highlight of an otherwise rather miserable negotiation for the creditors. The accountants had assured them that much of the losses on their Greek holdings had already been realized. The payment by Greece of €30 billion, through the potential funding of the Eurozone countries, was tangible, real, and almost taken as a given. For once, we didn't have to call our Board members, our CEOs, or the Steering Committee. We knew it was out of the question.

And we told them so.

"Gentlemen," Jean said in his typically calm, but firm voice, "this is not acceptable. We have made a huge contribution to the solution of Greece's debt problems. But we cannot do this, alas. Others will need to step up more. Eurozone governments and the ECB should be more transparent about how they will contribute."

Despite this, they repeated their assertions that they were no longer in a position to provide the €30 billion. I reminded them that this had been a commitment of Chancellor Merkel, Prime Minister Sarkozy, and all of the Eurozone heads of state. Some of them seemed unaware, as if this was news to them. We began to feel a sense of anger growing and asked for a break. It was getting late, and we had already ruled out further cuts in the interest rates of the new bonds. The four of us asked for a meeting room next door as the night dragged on. The journalists were calling us constantly and we refused to take any calls. Our trusted media adviser was on hand to tell them that we could not have a statement until negotiations were finished.

The public sector was not quite as discreet. The *Guardian* had decided to create a blog of "rolling coverage of the Eurozone debt crisis." It makes for interesting reading. The lead-in for the blog was the "hundreds of thousands of people who took to the streets on Sunday to demonstrate against austerity, spending cuts, and labor reforms."[4] The smell of tear gas reportedly hung over the streets of central Athens for the second straight weekend. Expectations were growing, as "the talk is that this would be a historic day in the country's history, despite the political infighting and public anger."

At the same time, talk was floating around about Europe paying its newly committed funds into an "escrow account," instead of to Greece. Austrian Finance Minister Maria Fekter said, "I would welcome such an account." The lack of confidence in Greece was palpable. A part of me understood this—Greece had fallen short time and again. But did it really make sense to belittle Greece at this moment, with so much at stake for Europe?

French Finance Minister François Baroin also reportedly said he would also support the idea of paying Greece's funds into an escrow account. Then he apparently stated that he would urge Europe to support the bailout package today.[5] The two statements were obviously inconsistent. An escrow account would have required an entirely new structure. Days, if not weeks, of delay would ensue to establish a new structure.

There were many uncertainties also swirling around our position. Would we reach an agreement, and even if we did, would a sufficient number of private creditors take part?

As the four of us gathered in an adjacent room, it was approaching midnight. We were tired and frustrated, and we were seemingly out of good ideas. Jean and I knew that there was no need to consult with anyone else—the four of us were on our own. First I called Papademos, who had exceptionally come to Brussels to participate in the Eurogroup Ministers meeting in order to allow for our negotiations to continue, and asked him to join our meeting. He said he would try, since at that point the Ministers had taken a break. There had been extensive discussion among the Ministers on Greece's second economic adjustment program, which was approved. It turned out that there had also been discussions on the contributions that the ECB and the member central banks would make to reducing Greece's debt, although the details were not revealed to us at the time. Papademos showed up ten minutes after we spoke. We discussed the situation with him, and he agreed that we had gone very far on the coupon rates on the new bonds. But he implored us to find a solution: "We have come this far, and Greece has sacrificed a lot, Charles. If there's anything else you can do, please consider it." Always calm, respectful, and professional.

He left us to our own devices, as they were, walking rather disconsolately out of the room and back to the gathering of the Ministers, where they had apparently finished their work.

At 1:16 a.m., a quote was reported in the running *Guardian* blog, stating that I had said "a 50% cut in nominal value is the IIF's final offer."[6] Actually, it was right around that time that Hung recalled the recent discussions in Paris and came up with an excellent idea. Rather than give any further ground on the coupon rates, or even begin to think about the unthinkable—giving up some of the €30 billion collateral—he suggested, "Jean, Charles, why don't we wipe out completely more than

50% of our holdings, as had been debated at our last Steering Committee meeting? This would eliminate more debt, thereby lowering the debt to GDP ratio significantly toward 120%." Instead of reducing the nominal level of debt by 50%, we began looking at reducing it by 53%.

We called Ackermann and Prot to test the idea out on them, and they both quickly agreed. We knew it would move us substantially toward a solution, but we did not know how far. Mikis, working from our hotel in Brussels, promptly began to crunch the numbers with our Blackstone advisers, coordinating with our colleague Lubo Mitov in Ireland. Mikis was calculating coupon options and NPV losses while Lubo was making an updated debt sustainability analysis. As this rather unorthodox process unfolded, we realized we were on to something, and sent word to Papademos that we would soon need him back in our side room.

This time, we asked Juncker to join us as well. He was in charge of the Ministerial meeting that night, and we had always known him to be a reasonable man within the constraints set for him by the powers who loomed over these negotiations from the start—Germany and the IMF.

They both arrived promptly; it must have been around 2:15 in the morning. We shared our new thinking with them and Thomas Wieser, the Chairman of the Deputies Group. Wieser stepped out to ask the Troika staff to make a new set of debt-to-GDP calculations. By that point, Mikis and Lubo had finished their calculations.

"A 120.5 debt-to-GDP ratio," Mikis said proudly as he sent us their calculations. We all smiled, but there was wariness circulating in the room as we knew better than to take anything for granted. A report came to us that Lagarde accepted the 120.5% debt-to-GDP ratio. But after consulting with Lemierre, we decided to increase the amount of upfront debt reduction to 53.5%, which definitively brought the debt to GDP down to 120%. At that point, Papademos declared, "That is wonderful, Charles and Jean! I know the ministers will accept this. What do you think, Jean-Claude?" Juncker was sitting in the most comfortable chair in the room, one leg sprawled over the side of the chair. "You are right, Lucas, but Thomas, has the IMF confirmed these numbers?" Wieser jumped up and went back to the main room, where a collection of fifteen or so European officials were still gathered, looking every bit as bedraggled as we felt. Wieser emerged from the room after five minutes with a look of displeasure.

"Jean-Claude, the IMF controls the calculations, and the person who does it is based in Washington. Unfortunately, they can't reach him, and no one here can run them."

Juncker muttered a few obscenities in French, looked Wieser squarely in the eye and said, "Track him down wherever he is for Christ's sake! The world is waiting."

As the seconds ticked by, Jean asked if Mikis would double-check his numbers. Mikis was skeptical at the request, knowing that they were correct, but nevertheless went back to his laptop, fired it up, and within three minutes called us back and said, "These are correct. This will bring the rates down to 120.5% debt-to-GDP ratio by 2020, based on the IMF's own assumptions."

Juncker received a call from someone in the Ministerial room, obviously impatiently asking where things stood. "We may have a deal in hand, but we are having trouble verifying it with the IMF," Juncker said gruffly as he hung up the phone. "Thomas, they said you have ten more minutes to have an IMF response." Wieser walked briskly out the door again, looking even more fiercely for an answer from across the Atlantic, his frustration visible.

"Jean-Claude, we are completely confident in Mikis's numbers," I said. "He has not failed us in months of making these calculations." Jean and I were quite proud of our team.

Wieser re-emerged, shaking his head. "Still nothing, Jean-Claude."

Jean-Claude stood up. "Enough is enough. Let's go with the IIF numbers." He walked over and embraced Jean and me, then walked out of the room to reunite with the other Ministers. Papademos joined him after a quick smile and a handshake.

Just after 4 a.m., Juncker convened a press conference to announce the deal. The Eurogroup statement emphasized that the new program provided a "comprehensive blueprint for putting the public finance and the economy of Greece back on a sustainable footing and hence for safeguarding financial stability in Greece and in the Euro Area as a whole."[7] I found these last words especially interesting: "in the Euro Area as a whole." It was the first time that I could recall that in a statement primarily about Greece, the Eurozone had acknowledged that their entire financial stability was heavily dependent upon a successful resolution of the Greek crisis. If this were so, why was Greece paying such a disproportionate social and economic price? Of course, the banks and other creditors were taking a huge hit, but as long as the damage was contained to Greece, it was not fatal except for the Greek banks, who were unfortunately caught in the center of the storm and largely stripped of their capital base. The other northern Eurozone countries? They had suffered through a period of weak economic performance, but it was hardly of crisis proportions. And in any case, it was certainly not an exclusive function of the Greek crisis. As for the budgetary implications of the support provided to Greece, the average increments to their respective budget deficits were miniscule. Again, hardly a crisis.

The Euro Ministers also asked the European Commission to establish a permanent presence on the ground in Greece, in order to coordinate technical assistance and to ensure "the timely and full implementation of the programme."[8] This measure harkened back to the International Financial Commission that operated from 1898 to 1975, although the European team in Athens hardly had the authority of the International Financial Commission. While I understood the case for it, I did not support it. Of course, such actions could, in theory, facilitate implementation. But Greece had already been humiliated enough and if there was ever going to be genuine ownership of the program by Greece, this seemed to be the time. Papademos was planning to step down and pave the way for a new round of elections. It was time for Greece to stand on its own.

The Eurogroup also acknowledged "the common understanding between the Greek authorities and the private sector on the general terms of the PSI exchange offer." The statement went on to say that a "successful PSI operation is a necessary condition for a successful program."[9] And, quite critically, the contributions of the ECB and the national central banks of the Eurozone were finally confirmed. They would both pass on their profits from the interest income earned on their holdings of GGBs. Although it was an imperfect solution, it nevertheless contributed quite crucially to the financing of Greece. We also issued a statement on behalf of the Steering Committee outlining the details of our commitments.

Due to their importance to the final outcome of this tortuous process, I have included the text of both the Eurogroup's and the Steering Committee's press releases. The key features of this historic restructuring were:

- The elimination of $107 billion of Greece's debt, equal to roughly 50% of Greece's GDP;

- A reduction in the amount of maturing debt to be refinanced between 2012 and 2020 of approximately €150 billion;

- Coupon rates on the new debt of 2% for the first three years, 3% for the next five years, and 4.3% for the following 22 years. These were, of course, far, far below market rates;

- A 10-year grace period of all principal repayments with the remaining amortizations stretched out another 30 years to 2042.

There were many other elements of the agreement, some of which were quite important to the creditors, such as the cash payment for 15% of GGB holdings by private creditors (€30 billion financing from the official creditors), the GDP-linked securities, and English law. There would also be a co-financing structure between the EFSF €30 billion loan to Greece and the new Greek loan, bound by a pari-passu clause. In order to ensure we were all on the same page, we immediately wrote separate letters to Papademos and Draghi. The former was quite detailed, setting forth not just the key terms, but every particular item such as the policy of the Call Option, the right to replace the Bond Trustee, and other important minutiae.

We walked out of the building that morning feeling an odd combination of fatigue, satisfaction, and anxiety. Congratulations began to pour in, especially from our bankers and other creditors. Texts and emails from Prot, Ackermann, Marcus Wallenberg, Henri de Castries, and many others came over my BlackBerry. (I know, it's hard to imagine, but I was loath to give up my BlackBerry. I liked the keyboard, and even though I had an iPhone, my primary mobile instrument was still the BlackBerry.)

The note from de Castries of AXA was especially poignant. AXA had never been a member of the Institute, and when I approached him at the early stages of the negotiations, I asked him to join, and committed to refunding the annual membership fees if he was not satisfied with the outcome of the negotiation. I took his note as a signal that I would not have to worry about that again.

There were, however, other things to worry about. The Greek government had submitted a bill to parliament with collective action clauses

(CACs). We had been advised by our attorneys to be very careful about our public comments on the CACs. They were already included in the foreign law bonds but were just being introduced to the Greek law bonds. The effect was to require any holders of Greek bonds who wished to change them for new GGBs to vote for the entire set of amendments. Once a minimum of two-thirds of voting new Greek bond holders voted in favor of the exchange, Greece was able to make the debt exchange binding on all holders. We had historically opposed the introduction of CACs retroactively, but we deemed it necessary to gain sufficient participation in the crucial exchange.

And therein lay the biggest concern: could we receive sufficient yes votes to make the debt exchange successful? Despite our persistent efforts to mobilize support within the creditor community, we knew that more than half of the universe of Greek debt lay outside the direct reach of our committee. Our full Committee represented only €80 billion holdings of the total €253 billion. One strange aspect of the world of sovereign debt is that neither the debtor nor other creditors really knew who held the debt at any point in time. This was the price of the globalization of capital markets. Who was holding the debt that was in the distant corners of the financial universe? Hedge funds, most likely, and also private speculators, banks, and even small investors willing to take a risk for a potentially hefty profit. How many of the creditors would be tempted to challenge the agreement and sue Greece for full payment? No one knew.

We had one very experienced hedge fund manager on our Committee, Hans Humes of Greylock Capital, who believed strongly in the validity of the cooperative negotiating process, and certainly was committed to the exchange. However, it was very hard to predict the intention of other hedge funds, and legal experts suggested that investors that sued could have a case.

The market's reaction to the agreement was decidedly mixed. What should have been a favorable reaction was significantly undermined by a Troika report that implied strongly that Greece would be unlikely to meet its new targets. As in the aftermath of the October 26 agreement, Europe had once again managed to rain on its own parade. What should have been celebrated as a huge success (assuming the creditors voted through the agreement) was greeted with skepticism. Papademos was, nevertheless, right when he said, "It's no exaggeration to say that today is a historic day for the Greek economy."

Papademos, with the vital support of Venizelos, had guided Greece through a remarkably turbulent period. He had been able to manage the incessant demands of the IMF for more and more fiscal adjustment, despite the increasingly deep depression and the growing reluctance of parliament and the Greek people to accept another dose of austerity. The program that was pushed through parliament was, in fact, not all about fiscal adjustment. Papademos had managed to pull together a solid additional set of structural reforms, most of which were woefully needed. Among them were:

- The removal of labor market rigidities. These had been a major factor in feeding a high wage/cost structure and needed radical reform.
- Government restructuring and downsizing. Ripe for reform.
- Tax reform. Does it surprise anyone that better tax collection was a benchmark?
- Recapitalization of the banking system. Absolutely essential.
- A revised plan for privatization, marking down the target to €19 billion from the initial target of €50 billion. Realism sets in.
- Product price liberalization focused on professional services, transportation, and electricity. Greeks had been paying way too much for these—way too much.
- Measures to facilitate investment, both domestic and foreign. Direly needed, but would take time to catalyze new investment until the overall macro and political environment stabilizes.
- Financial reform. Desperately needed.

Papademos and Venizelos secured these reforms, although the IMF and EU deserve credit for also keeping their eye on these critical issues.

On the morning of February 21, I was relieved that we had an agreement in principle, but I was not elated. There had been too many false dawns in this whole saga. Better buckle down a few more weeks, I thought.

CHAPTER 31

THE LAST FEW MILES

"The woods are lovely, dark and deep,
But I have promises to keep,
And miles to go before I sleep,
And miles to go before I sleep."

—Robert Frost, "Stopping by Woods on a Snowy Evening," 1923

In early March, concerns were gathering steam in the market about the prospect of a credit default. We knew that the initial retroactive introduction of CACs on outstanding Greek law GGBs wouldn't trigger the default, but that the credit default swaps would likely be triggered when the CACs were activated. Nevertheless, we thought the CDS credit event, in the end, would not be such an earth-shattering event, and fortunately, we were right.

On March 9, when the restructuring was complete, key Credit Derivatives Determination Committees declared a credit default on Greece and managed to pay out all of the holders who had bought credit protection on Greek loans.

But I'm getting ahead of the story. There was a lot of work remaining to be done to bring the restructuring to closure. Our lead finance advisory staff had prepared a long list of issues that needed review; it was enough to make one's head spin!

- The universe of bonds offered
- Review of the Trust Deed
- Review of Amortization Table
- Review of proposed treatment of index-linked bonds
- Review of the treatment of guaranteed bonds

And on and on. As the work proceeded, I was once again thankful not only for our outstanding small IIF team, but for the expertise and experience of our legal and financial teams. I shook my head and wondered what we were thinking back in July when we had no financial advisers and a very thin team of lawyers.

It was unclear what role the Steering Committee could play in the run-up to the vote scheduled for March 9. We were concerned that Greece would not initiate a "road show" to sell the restructuring to its creditors, and we wrote Venizelos encouraging him to launch a series of road-show meetings with investors. At the same time, Venizelos was concerned that member firms of our Steering Committee were not publicly declaring themselves in support of the agreement. He wrote to us: "Due to the uniform practice of committee endorsement, there is a serious risk that the lack of such endorsement will be understood by the market to reflect rejection of the deal by the Committee itself. It is imperative that we remove any pretense for that interpretation."[1]

I had some sympathy for his concern, but we were constrained by both our attorneys and by the realities of the process. We had, of course, released our statement on the morning of February 21, characterizing the agreement as "a major step forward toward implementing the debt exchange." But we had to be careful not to presume that each bank would automatically support the deal. We stressed that the consensual nature of the agreement was consistent with the "Principles for Stable Capital Flows and Fair Debt Restructuring." But we could not make the decision for each creditor. Given the unprecedented nature of this agreement, each firm needed to be afforded the opportunity to make its own decision, and in many cases, this involved a review by the Board of Directors. I called Venizelos in response to his letter and explained the situation to him. He was not happy. I encouraged patience, which was in short supply for all of us at that point.

In the days leading up to the vote, we talked with individual members of the creditor committee, answering any last questions that they might have. It appeared that every firm was leaning toward supporting the restructuring, but we could not be certain. The lawyers and advisers had done their jobs, and the documents were in good shape. And, somewhat surprisingly, the European parliaments had done their job, voting through the package despite the many reservations. Germany actually approved the package on February 27 by a vote of 496 to 90. Merkel called it, as she did at times, on the money, so to speak. "The risks of turning away from Greece now are incalculable. No one can assume what consequences would arise for the German economy, or Italy, Spain, the Eurozone as a whole, and finally for the whole world of a Greek bankruptcy," Merkel added. When I read her statement, I could not help but think, I wish she had convinced her Finance Minister of that months ago. It could have saved both Greece and Europe a lot of pain.

After spending two weeks finishing up business in Athens and elsewhere in Europe, I went to Brazil, where the IIF was holding an annual Chief Executive gathering for our Latin bankers. The event drew fifty or so top executives from around the region, hosted by my good friend Roberto Setubal of Banco Itaú. The meeting was a success, and I was glad to get my mind off of Greece for a few days. But as we were preparing to leave, my focus returned to Greece. Unfortunately, as I tried to make a call to Athens, the São Paolo airport was chaotic. It was just after midnight, and many flights had been canceled and delayed. People were strewn about everywhere—young families with squalling children, exhausted tourists, businessmen staggering about in a daze looking for a place to plug in their laptops or recharge their cell phones, and masses of students sprawled out over the floor, napping or zoned out on their iPhones. Peixin and I were waiting for our flight home, but first, one last detail. I needed a spot in the vast terminal with quiet and connectivity to make a call.

For this was March 8, 2012, the day before the vote on the restructuring of sovereign Greek debt would finally be completed, and I had been waiting with mounting anticipation. I had no reason to think it would go against us, but in this business, you never know. Uncertainties still abounded. I did know that the restructuring mattered enormously to Greece. A "no" would mean default, as it would lock Greece into the existing debt payments it had no prayer of paying. That would reap drastic consequences in the country, and most likely throughout Europe and beyond as the dominoes started to fall.

But would the creditors come through? They were being asked to take a terrific hit, and no one likes that. There were a vast number of them, over 200, scattered about, but concentrated in major European financial houses like BNP Paribas and Deutsche Bank. Plenty of other banks and investment firms in Europe were also involved, having been attracted by the sweet yields on Greek paper in the early 2000s. And some debt was held by total unknowns, since the loans had ping-ponged around the globe so many times. I'd done my soundings with as many creditors as I could, but samples inevitably are only samples. They are not substitutes for the actual tally. And people can think differently when they have a ballot in front of them, committing them to an outcome that was sure to be unpleasant.

The emails we sent out asked a formal commitment from each firm, registering whether or not they accepted the terms offered by the Greek government in the attached document. It was a lot to go through, with many provisos and contingencies. As explained earlier, in many cases, Boards of Directors had to review the terms of the deal. Responses had initially drifted back slowly, but more heavily as the deadline approached. March 9, however, was the deadline.

While it was after midnight in Brazil on March 8, it was after 6 a.m. on March 9 in Athens. Greece's debt-management office had been open through the night, receiving responses from around the world. After checking in for my flight to Washington, I found a spot next to a pair of students dead asleep on a grimy floor. Once I leaned against the window, my call finally went through. I thought that if I drove my index finger into my other ear, I would hear at least a little bit of what somebody was saying in Athens.

"*Yassou*," said a voice. At least that's what I thought he said.

"*Yassou*," I replied. Alas, that was about as far as my Greek would take me. "Charles Dallara here." There was a kind of scratching on the line. "Dallara," I repeated. "Hello?"

I was pretty sure someone said something back.

"Sorry," I shouted, in mounting frustration. "It's very noisy here, and we have a bad connection." I paused. "Charles Dallara," I repeated. "From the IIF. I'm calling about the results. Hello?"

It was maddening. Could the man hear me? Was he saying something back? No matter how hard I strained to hear, I could not be sure. I called back, hoping for a better line of communication. This time I reached Petros Christodoulou, veteran of our negotiations and head of the Greek PDMA, and magically the connection cleared.

"We aren't quite there yet, Charles," he told me, sighing with fatigue. We need a 'yes' on 75 percent of the ballots."

"How many are in?"

"We are well over 60 percent of all of the creditors," he said. "But many more still to be heard from." He paused. "There is still time, Charles. I am hopeful."

I wanted to wait there, to find out the results. But Peixin was frantically signaling that we needed to hurry to our plane. We dashed to the gates, dragging our suitcases behind us. We were the last to make it inside before the doors shut. I settled into my aisle seat and buckled my seat belt. My mind was spinning: How would the count go? What would it mean? But as preoccupying as all that was, I simply could not think about it anymore. It was approaching 1 a.m., I was exhausted, and my worries left me as I was soon fast asleep, headed home.

CHAPTER 32

THE DEAL IS DONE —MORE OR LESS

"It was thought that this day was the beginning of liberty for Hellas."

—Xenophon, circa 360 BC

As we landed at Dulles Airport on the morning of March 9 after our overnight flight, I was waiting anxiously for my phone battery to turn on. I sighed in relief when I read the numbers in an email from Hung Tran: 83.5% of the outstanding privately held bonds had been tendered for exchange, €172 billion of the total €206 billion of eligible bonds. Once the collective action clauses were activated, the total would be raised to 95.7%. Hung called me as soon as my phone was on to make sure that I had seen the results. We finalized two press releases on the outcome and immediately put them on the wires. The creditors had suffered a massive loss, wiping out roughly 73% of the value embedded in their loans. And yet somehow, virtually every creditor saw this as not only an acceptable outcome, but as a good outcome. Why?

Despite the huge losses on some issues, the creditors achieved some victories; for example, the use of English law for the new bonds and the co-financing structure with the EFSF were both seen as strengthening the underlying value of the new bonds. In addition, the GDP-linked securities held out the potential of higher returns should the Greek economy outperform the weak performance built into the baseline forecast. Finally, there was the €30 billion that was lent by the Eurozone countries to Greece in order that they could buy down 15% of the outstanding privately held debt at par. This had taken on an outsized importance in the eyes of many creditors, and when it was secure it seemed like a small victory in a sea of red ink.

Beyond these specifics, there was the broader context of the outcome. It had been negotiated, not crammed down in a unilateral action by the debtor. All creditors had attached considerable importance to this, despite the reality that we had never been in the strongest negotiating position. But the Principles for Stable Capital Flows and Fair Debt Restructuring had, in the end, been applied, notwithstanding the pressure from various European quarters to have a unilateral solution. This set an important precedent for future sovereign debt negotiations to protect the long-term balance in the system between creditors and debtors, and it also reinforced the credibility of the Principles and their Trustees.

More important than any of these factors, however, was that the Greek restructuring was a crucial step in pulling Greece and the Eurozone back from the brink of disaster. Without the agreement, Greece would have experienced a hard default in March and the Eurozone could have likely fallen into an irreversible crisis and possibly disintegrated.

The creditors with whom I worked, almost to a person, at all levels of seniority, were supportive in the end of the restructuring for one overriding reason—we had made a major step toward saving the Eurozone from economic collapse. As stated earlier, this was not pure altruism. Virtually every bank, and many insurers, had exposure in Italy, as well as in Spain in some cases, that was a multiple of their exposure to Greece. The domino effect of a crisis that took down these economies and their banking systems could have inflicted major damage on each of these lending institutions, perhaps of crippling magnitudes.

But there was something else at work in the minds and moods of many of the European private creditors. They were, by and large, European patriots. They did not want to see the European "project," as it was often referred to, going up in smoke. They had little to no affection for the overbearing bureaucracy of Brussels, but did not want to be a part of the destruction of the most important economic integration Europe had ever launched. I believe this underlay their willpower, at the margins, to tolerate losses that may otherwise have been unacceptable. Cynics may find this a dubious observation, perhaps even lacking plausibility. But I can assure you this was a real sentiment that flowed through the background of these discussions. I sometimes even got the impression that bankers were more concerned about the future of the Eurozone than were some of the politicians. Politics in Europe were often, as in the US and other democracies, of a very nationalistic nature, reflecting local, regional, and national sentiments, but only rarely embracing a Eurowide perspective.

Part of this undoubtedly reflected an understandable fatigue of dealing with Greece. By the spring of 2012, Greece had been in perpetual crisis for almost three years and had failed to follow through on any of its commitments on numerous occasions during this period. Fatigue and exasperation would have risen in the most patient, Hellenic-minded of politicians. This was likely much more than they had bargained for when Greece was invited into the Eurozone in 2001.

But was there something more at work that explains why even after the debt restructuring and reform agreements of February and March 2012, certain European officials continued to berate and threaten Greece? Papademos had done a remarkable job of steering Greece through this. He prepared to step down as new elections were planned for May. For a man who was never cut out to be a politician, he had walked a political tightrope with the skill of a Wallenda. I asked him a number of times if he would consider running in the elections scheduled in May, but he wouldn't even contemplate it.

With the debt restructuring in place, Greece was given breathing space to implement a full range of economic reforms, rebuild its banking system, and stimulate renewed investor interest. The huge decline in the amount of maturing debt that was brought about by the restructuring would also ease the significant pressure on Greece's fiscal accounts. Of course, it should be acknowledged that the huge restructuring and elimination of privately held debt was significantly offset by an increase in debt that Greece owed to the official sector, including the IMF, regional governments, and regional institutions. The needed recapitalization of the Greek banks alone required €41 billion, and there was the €34.6 billion lent to Greece to buy back the 15% of outstanding debt at par.

Despite this, it was clear that Greece was provided a crucial window of opportunity to begin to rebuild its economy and renew the fabric of society. It took quite some years, however, before Greece could seize that opportunity. Before explaining why, let me turn first to the broader environment of the Eurozone in the aftermath of the Greek debt restructuring.

As contagion eased from Greece, another country slipped into the center of a storm: Spain. A banking crisis that had been simmering for some time burst into flames. Bankia, one of Spain's largest banks, declared bankruptcy and urgently needed recapitalization.[1] Meanwhile, the new government in Italy had gained credibility under the leadership of Mario Monti but was still under pressure from the markets.

As the Greek election neared to replace Papademos, Wolfgang Schäuble suggested that perhaps it would be better for the Greeks not to hold elections.[2] "Suspending Greek democracy would allow the key measures to be put through before the voters were given a chance to have their say."[3] A very provocative comment by a senior European official, but he apparently outdid himself a short time later. According to Tim Geithner's memoirs, characterizing his exchange with Schäuble, "letting Greece burn" would "make it easier to build a more credible firewall." An absurd idea, as Geithner also apparently thought: "I found the argument terrifying," he wrote.

Another Eurozone finance minister said, "We are going to convey very clearly to the Greek people that if there is no stable government to implement the conditions of the program, then we are going to have difficulties and are going to adopt Plan B."[4] Even Merkel and Sarkozy apparently got in on the act. After a meeting in Berlin, they were reported as having stated that Greece's election in June would be a referendum on euro membership.

To what end were such stark, threatening comments made? To influence the electorate to vote for a particular candidate? In the first round of voting on May 6 to replace Papademos, PASOK was decimated at the polls, with its vote falling from a 43.9% share to 13.2%. The left-wing movement SYRIZA, together with the Communist KKE party, garnered almost twice as many votes as PASOK. New Democracy fell from 34% to 18%, while Golden Dawn, a neo-fascist group, collected 7%.[5] As Adam Tooze so accurately described it in his book *Crashed*, Greece hung in midair. In the runoff, voters gave enough support to New Democracy in order for its leader, Antonis Samaras, to form a government.

It remains unclear how the not-so-veiled threats to the Greek people affected the outcome. At times, it almost seemed as if the intent of both the policies and the rhetoric of certain European politicians had another dimension woven into it: punish the sinners.

A few weeks after the settlement of the Greek debt exchange, I was in Rome to give a speech at a conference hosted by Partners Group. The night before the conference, the host arranged a marvelous dinner in the Vatican, preceded by a special tour of the Sistine Chapel. No matter how many times I visit the Sistine Chapel, I never fail to marvel at the beauty and audacity of Michelangelo's work. Like most tourists, my focus had always been on the frescoes painted on the ceiling. On the occasion of my visit that evening in May 2012, however, my attention was drawn to the painting behind the altar, the *Last Judgment*.

Painted more than two decades after the frescoes on the ceiling, it has a stark and somewhat terrible air about it. It depicts the second coming of Christ on the Day of Judgment as described in the Gospel of John, often referred to as the Apocalypse of St. John the Divine. To the left are those who are raised from their graves to be judged by Christ, sitting majestically in the center of the painting. To the right are the sinners who have been condemned to hell. The painting became quite controversial soon after its creation because Michelangelo captured the figures in their full "state of nature," completely nude with no effort to hide delicate parts of their anatomy. Although they were subsequently painted over by Daniele da Volterra, now known as the "breeches painter," what captured my interest were the anguished, terrified expressions of the sinners being sent to hell. Many tried to cling to one another or grasp onto a column. Although I was quite familiar with the scene in biblical teachings due to my Southern Baptist "fire and brimstone" upbringing, I was nevertheless taken aback. I wondered whether some in Europe perceived Greece primarily as a sinner, and took the view that sinners need to be punished. This was certainly never explicitly stated, nor is it fair to impugn the integrity of the multilateral and regional institutions who strove to cope with a virtually impossible situation. But some of the officials?

Perhaps they had forgotten the parable of the two sinners. One was a Pharisee, a member of an ancient and revered Jewish sect, known for strict observance of religious traditions. The other was a tax collector, who as we know were among the most reviled people, and certainly considered sinners. Both went to the temple to pray. The Pharisee focused on his good deeds, his religious practices, and his tithing. The tax collector, on the other hand, put his head down, hit himself, and asked for forgiveness. Only the tax collector had pleased God. In Luke 18: 9–14, Jesus concludes, "Everyone who exalts himself will be humbled and he who humbles himself will be exalted."

A more basic interpretation of this parable might be that we are all sinners, and upon reflection it may just be that there were a lot of sinners who contributed to the Greek economic tragedy. Certainly, Greece's governments over the years would have to be put at the top of the list for their legacy of clientelism, a bloated and inefficient bureaucracy, and the sheer irresponsibility of public sector spending under many governments, including the Karamanlis government of 2004–2009.

But Greece was not the only one to violate Europe's Stability and Growth Pact. In 2003, both France and Germany exceeded the 3% of GDP budget-deficit limit. The European Commission considered these "fiscal sins" so serious that they sued Germany and France in the European Court of Justice. Both countries flouted the rules further by refusing—with the support of other Eurozone Finance Ministers—to pay the fines set forth by the Commission.

Looking more broadly, the roots of the crisis that enveloped Europe in 2009–2012 went far beyond Greece—it was clearly systemic in its nature, globally in 2008–2010 and then regionally within the Eurozone. As we have recounted, Ireland preceded Greece into crisis, and Italy, Portugal, and Spain followed.

Of course, any discussion of sinners surrounding the Greek crisis cannot exclude the creditors. As discussed earlier, the virtually complete breakdown in sovereign risk management toward Greece by the private financial community—largely European banks and insurance firms, but even pension funds—cannot be ignored.

The saga of the Greek economy was far from over following the debt restructuring. But before turning to that issue, a dramatic step was taken toward easing the overall European crisis. Nine days after the Greek election, Mario Draghi gave a speech in London to a global investor conference. In between the Greek elections and Draghi's arrival at the conference, Europe had announced a Growth Pact along with a plan to provide support by the ESM for the government debt of all member countries in compliance with the Commission's fiscal rules. Although these were steps in the right direction, they appeared to be irrelevant to helping Spain deal with their mushrooming crisis. A country with a fiscal deficit of 11% was hardly in compliance with the "Commission's fiscal rules."

As Draghi rose to speak, he decided to send a strong message to the markets that the ECB was prepared to take decisive action to stabilize the euro: "Within our mandate, the ECB is ready to do whatever it takes to preserve the euro." He added, "And believe me, it will be enough."[6]

Although Draghi had few concrete tools at that stage to back up his bold assertion, the speech proved to be a critical step toward rebuilding confidence in the euro and, eventually, toward easing the European debt crisis. Soon after the conference, my staff arranged for me to discuss Draghi's initiative with ECB Vice President Vítor Constâncio. We were excited about the statement and wanted to know what lay behind it. Vítor's response was, "I am not certain, Charles. There is considerable uncertainty about exactly what we do, and, frankly, some degree of surprise. Knowing Mario, however, we will develop some meaningful instruments."

Vítor was right, as in September the ECB announced its new policy of Outright Monetary Transactions (OMT). Unfortunately, this bond-buying program was quite constrained, applying only to countries that had agreed on an adjustment and aid program approved by the ESM. The specifics were a bit disappointing, but nevertheless, Draghi's commitment and follow-through had helped calm the markets.

Many factors contributed to the somewhat erratic but gradual decline in the yields on Spanish and Italian debt after the Draghi speech. Among the factors were the new Growth Pact and the strengthening of the ESM's powers. But the two most powerful in changing the course of the crisis were, in addition to the Greek restructuring, the Draghi speech and the ensuing policy changes by the ECB. The speech proved to be a convincing statement of an unwavering commitment by a senior European official to ensure that the euro survived the crisis intact. After the repeated comments by other officials hinting at—or even threatening—a breakup of the euro through a Greek exit, the statement was like a balm to the markets.

The Greek restructuring, on the other hand, had removed the uncertainty of this tortuous negotiating process from the Greek and pan-European landscape. No more would there be doubts—at least in the near term—about whether Greece would resolve its huge overhang of private sector debt with a hard default. The cash flow relief provided by the restructuring enabled Greece to meet its deficit reduction targets without relying exclusively on painful tax increases and budget cuts. Yes, the debt to the official sector had grown, but fortunately it was also at subsidized rates, shielding Greece from the still very high cost of its credit in the markets.

Perhaps more important, the debt restructuring had removed Greece as a source of contagion to other vulnerable European countries, especially Italy and Spain. Although these countries were still beset by their own serious difficulties, with Spain especially struggling to stabilize its economy at that time, the threat of Greek default that had been the epicenter of the crisis for two years was removed.

At a luncheon in the summer of 2022, Joe Ackermann pointed out to me one other factor that also contributed to the easing of the crisis: the fact that markets became convinced that Greece would be the only Eurozone country to restructure its debt. None of us involved wanted to go through this again, and neither did the Italians, the Spanish, or the Portuguese. We at the IIF made this clear, as did key European officials, including Dutch Finance Minister Jeroen Dijsselbloem, who would succeed Juncker as President of the Eurogroup. Gradually, the markets became convinced that the Eurozone crisis, as a regional phenomenon, was over.

And yet not all was well with Greece. The full benefits of Greece's restructuring and reform measures would not emerge for another seven years. An eternity for the citizens of Greece.

CHAPTER 33

THIS GREEK TRAGEDY HAS ANOTHER ACT

"Oh, it is easy for the one who stands outside the prison wall of pain to exhort and teach the one who suffers."

—Aeschylus, *Prometheus Bound*, circa 463 BC

For those of us who anticipated that the restructuring would lead to a period of restoration and recovery, there were initially some encouraging signs. Prime Minister Samaras chafed at some of the restrictions in the program, but he did his best to implement them anyway. He had been a skeptic of the reform program during the George Papandreou and Papademos eras. He had a degree in economics from Amherst College and an MBA from Harvard. But he was a political animal, and it was not difficult to surmise that his opposition was largely political in nature. I met with him in mid-November 2012 in his office. It was my first time in the Prime Minister's office since Papademos had stepped down, and it brought back many memories of the long nights with Papademos, Venizelos, and Lemierre. I felt a sense of satisfaction that since those long nights we had closed the debt restructuring, but also some anxiety that things in Greece were not, after all, much better. Samaras was cordial but his brow was deeply furrowed. He was alone, without his finance minister, while I was joined by Jeff Anderson, the head of our European department.

I was not sure what to expect. He began the meeting, however, by thanking me profusely for our support throughout the debt restructuring. I thanked him for his kind words but wanted to move on. "How are things now?" I inquired.

"I have done virtually everything they asked, and yet there is no relief of the pressure on us," he replied. I listened as he recounted the challenges he had faced since taking office in June. In fact, he had done a lot. He had just passed another substantial set of reform measures through parliament, along with another significant set of budgetary cuts that would further consolidate the budget,[1] but euro/IMF funds had not been released.

Things on the ground in Greece were even worse than when I was last there in early March. Strikes and mass demonstrations were once again taking place and the unemployment rate had ballooned to a new record high of 27 percent The fact was, as Adam Tooze so accurately captured it, "the Greek economy had crash landed. Greek society had been battered beyond recognition."[2]

As I walked out of Samaras's office, he took out two pieces of paper and wrote his cell number on both of them, handing one to me and one to my colleague Jeff Anderson. "I really need your help, so let me know if you can weigh in on our behalf. Greece is really struggling." I assured him I would do what I could, knowing that there would be very little that I could do in the circumstances.

An air of despair seemed to hang over the country, and I found it difficult not to absorb some of it. After this huge restructuring, where was their daylight? Yes, the spreads were declining on Greek debt, as well as on Spanish and Italian debt. Except for a period between the unsuccessful first round of elections in May and the elections of June, which brought Samaras to power, spreads of Greek debt had steadily declined from the date of the debt restructuring throughout the remainder of 2012—and in fact 2013, as well. The Spanish and Italian spreads had spiked in the spring as anxieties about Spanish banks and Italian debt grew, but they all followed a broad downward trend throughout the remainder of these two years. The external market dimension of the Eurozone crisis had been addressed, if not fully resolved. One way to look at the situation at that time was that the euro itself was safe from being torn asunder, but some of the economies within the Eurozone were, in fact, decimated. Youth unemployment in Greece was an astounding 55 percent, while in the US, still recovering from the global financial crisis, it was down to 16.8 percent. Spain's youth unemployment was almost on par with that of Greece at 53 percent. Overall unemployment in Spain was a record 24.6 percent. Over 250,000 people in Greece were fed daily by church-sponsored food banks. As one author said, "stripped of the belief that the future will be better, hope can all too easily fade."[3] Or, as one banner that was hung over a statue read, "You got the disease, we got the solution. Revolution."[4]

Crime was up dramatically in Greece, as was drug use. At the same time, in May 2012 reports spread that the government was failing to reimburse pharmacies for prescription medications as the system was intended to do, to the tune of arrears that totaled over €500 million. That had shifted the burden to individual consumers to make up the difference or lose their access to medicine.[5]

The crisis also led to a sharp jump in the rate of suicides. One study pointed toward a 40 percent rise in suicides in the first half of 2011, with a predictable close association between suicide and unemployment.[6] As the economy collapsed, outbound emigration also accelerated. A scientific study estimated that 240,000 Greeks left the country between 2010 and the end of 2015.[7] For a country with only 11 million citizens, this represented a serious loss of talent.

The day after my meeting with Prime Minister Samaras, I made a presentation at the Hellenic Bank Association in Athens. Titled "Adjusting Course: A Strategy for Greece and Europe to Emerge from the Crisis," I sketched out some ideas about how both Greece and Europe should respond to the crisis that still hung over not only Greece, but Europe as a whole. Alas, my hopeful ideas were not to be. The threads of Greece's democracy—the world's oldest democracy—had been stretched too thin. In just over two years, SYRIZA was elected, as the Greek people decided they had suffered enough under traditional political parties and chose a maverick party. The result, however, was another period of turmoil, which once again set back the Greek economy and the Greek people.

Could those lost years in Greece have been avoided? Perhaps so.

CHAPTER 34

FOUR LOST YEARS

"Lost time is never found again."

—Benjamin Franklin, circa 1760

It became increasingly clear during the course of 2013 and 2014 that neither the IMF nor the European authorities had realized that their austerity-focused approach toward Greece seriously needed change. As Tooze explains, "Not only was Greece experiencing a social crisis, it was doing so at the behest of the Troika."[1] The insistent demands for more austerity, when the evidence was profound that it was not working, fed support in Greece for the racist far-right party Golden Dawn, but more powerfully stimulated the support for the radical left in the form of SYRIZA. Appeals by Samaras for economic concessions from the Troika went unheeded, despite the fact that he had successfully led Greece back to the international capital markets with a €3billion bond issue in April 2014. On January 25, 2015, SYRIZA was elected. They had only 36 percent of the vote, but they formed a coalition with right-wing ANEL, and Alexis Tsipras of SYRIZA became the Prime Minister.

The next four years were, in many respects, lost years in Greece. A question that remains unanswered is why it took the Troika so long to recognize the need to shift course during the period 2011–2014. It was obvious in late 2011 that their strategy was backfiring; rather than reducing the debt-to-GDP ratio, it was increasing it. There were various indicators along the way that the IMF realized it had to adjust its approach. According to an article in the *Guardian,* the IMF was said to have admitted, in a report jointly produced by the IMF, the EC, and the ECB, that it had failed to realize the damage that austerity would do to Greece.[2]

Another press report from around the same time stated that clashes between the EU and the IMF had occurred over mistakes in handling the Greek situation. It was, unfortunately, not surprising that some finger-pointing between the two institutions would arise. Each of the Troika members had its own roles and perspectives. I observed that on the program design issues, the ECB generally kept its head down and deferred to the IMF and EC. In this case, apparently the IMF was complaining that the EU had missed an opportunity to restructure the private debt in 2010.

"An upfront debt restructuring would have been better for Greece although this was not acceptable to the euro partners," the IMF stated. A Commission spokesperson told a news briefing, "We fundamentally disagree."[3]

While an earlier restructuring would have captured more private finance in the restructuring, it was not clear until after the rather infamous Deauville gathering of October 2010 and the slackening of Greece's reform efforts near the end of that year that a restructuring was essential. After all, no one had contemplated that a member of the Eurozone would possibly need a sovereign debt restructuring, notwithstanding the high levels of debt in some member countries. The very idea of restructuring was anathema to the ECB, and most other European officials were either opposed or highly reluctant due to the potential contagion effects.

Of greater relevance in the reported disputes between the IMF and the EC was that an IMF statement referred only to the unacceptability of the "euro partners" of an upfront debt restructuring, not the unacceptability to Greece. What was their view? And did it matter? Even the IMF seemed implicitly to disregard the perspective of the country at the center of the storm.

It was much more notable, however, that the IMF publicly acknowledged that it had made "overly optimistic forecasts for the Greek economy." But it wasn't until 2016, while the Greek economy was still in the depths of a deep recession (unemployment remained at 24.4 percent, with 52 percent of youth still unemployed), that the IMF issued a report that acknowledged more explicitly the fundamental mistakes that had been made. "We have acknowledged our mistake, which had to do with the fiscal multipliers," Christine Lagarde was quoted as having told *Bloomberg Markets* on April 11, 2016. She went on to say that "we—all of us, the IMF, Europeans, the ECB—underestimated the contracting impact of some of the measures that we recommended. We overestimated the ability of Greece to actually endorse and take ownership of measures that were needed, because we moved from one government to another to another to another, and it was always 'it's not really our program, it's not really our reforms, it's not really our measures, it's imposed by the Troika.'"[4] It was certainly true that the revolving governments made it difficult to hold any government accountable, but sadly it was also true that the programs were largely imposed by the Troika.

Three months later, the IMF issued yet another "mea culpa" of sorts. A report issued by the Office of Independent Evaluations (OIE) of the Fund leveled withering institutional self-criticism that went to the heart of the difficulties with program design in Greece. The assessment covered IMF programs in the Euro Area, concentrating on Greece and Portugal. I have selected five excerpts from the report, all of which shed light on what transpired in Greece:

- Perhaps the most conspicuous weakness of the IMF-supported programs in the Euro Area was their lack of sufficient flexibility . . . The appearance of persevering with a failing program can damage market confidence.

- As a result, an increasingly unworkable strategy was maintained for too long a period in Portugal as well as Greece. When GDP contracted more than anticipated, the nominal deficit ceiling was routinely tightened in order to achieve the original targets (which were set in relation to GDP) . . .

  - Much has been said about the fiscal multiplier used by the IMF staff, which turned out to be too small in Greece and Portugal. The staff explained that the .5 multiplier was the average value that had been assumed for advanced economies in the past. But the assumption was inappropriate for the Euro Area programs, given the countries' inability to ease monetary policy let alone decide the currency.

- Likewise, the assessment of public debt sustainability for Greece was based on a highly optimistic set of assumptions. This decision reflected both a strong optimistic bias and an unwillingness to consider substantially less favorable outcomes.

- Some officials in Europe stated to the OIE that, in their view, the Troika programs, including the one applied in Greece, were a success because they averted a breakdown of the Euro Area and a widely feared exit of Greece from the single currency.[5]

This remarkably frank assessment contained a lot of core truths, but the two most important were these:

· The program was poorly designed for Greece with the economy's structural weaknesses, and with Greece's lack of an independent monetary- or exchange-rate policy. Despite numerous opportunities—and growing evidence of the need for change—the Troika failed to adapt the program to the weakness of the Greek economy at various stages, especially in late 2011 and throughout 2012, and therefore continued to push the economy into deeper recession.

· This put growing pressure on both the Greek government and the creditors (primarily the private creditors but eventually the public sector creditors) to take measures that would fill the growing gaps in the fiscal balance and the debt sustainability targets.

The end result was that fiscal and debt sustainability, as crucial as they were, put far too much pressure on social and political—one might even say democratic—sustainability. These factors certainly did not solely beget the chaotic reign of SYRIZA —decades of statist economic management had done a lot to undermine the credibility of the political class in Greece—but they were certainly more than inconsequential. At the same time, they helped deprive Greece of many of the benefits of both the Draghi "put" and the historic Greek debt restructuring, at least until a new government arrived. During the years 2014–2019, the crisis for the whole of the Eurozone had passed, but the Greek economy continued to struggle.

The SYRIZA-led coalition of extreme left- and right-wing parties developed a radical and incoherent economic program and a strong resistance to Troika-led programs. Greece was increasingly running out of financial resources during the first half of 2015 as discussions with the IMF and European institutions dragged on.

The SYRIZA government, and especially its brazen finance minister Yanis Varoufakis, essentially called for no new economic memoranda (Troika-led programs) and for European financial support with no conditionality. After a bizarre series of confrontational tactics by SYRIZA, a new three-year program was eventually put into place in August 2015.

Developments after the end of the program in August 2018, however, demonstrated again the fragility of the program ownership and the populist pressures facing the SYRIZA government ahead of the July 2019 parliamentary elections. During this period, to appease the electorate, several important program reforms were either delayed (e.g., structural fiscal reforms), canceled (the pre-legislated pension and personal income tax reform packages), or reversed (e.g., key elements of the 2011–2013 labor market reforms that enhanced labor market flexibility). Despite that, SYRIZA lost the elections and the New Democracy party came to power with a large majority this time under Kyriakos Mitsotakis.

The new government quickly reversed some of the policy slippages by the previous government and launched a broadly ambitious reform program to boost output growth through lower taxes, a better business environment, a more flexible labor market, and higher public investment, including through a reactivation of the privatization program. In addition, Mitsotakis reaffirmed his commitment to meet the fiscal and structural policy commitments to the Euro Area under Enhanced Surveillance, while also indicating his desire to secure Eurogroup support for lower targets for the primary budget balance if its policies generated higher-than-expected growth. These declarations and early policy decisions by the new government enhanced Greece's credibility in capital markets.

Before assessing developments under the Mitsotakis government, it is important to take stock of the overall effects of Greece's adjustment efforts in the period 2010–2018. First, it should be pointed out that despite its uneven policy implementation during the entire program period, Greece did succeed in establishing fiscal discipline and restoring fiscal balance. Furthermore, Greece made significant progress in narrowing its external current account deficit through a lowering of its cost structures and an improvement in its competitive position vis-à-vis its Euro Area partners. As I have outlined in great detail, Greece also gained significant concessions from its external creditors—initially private creditors, and eventually official creditors—that allowed it to reach a more sustainable public debt position. Finally, Greece regained market access at reduced yields and improved its sovereign ratings from default levels to a level that is very respectable, although still one step below investment grade, in May 2023.

As pointed out earlier, however, Greece sustained a deeper economic dislocation and pain from its reform programs than any of the other Euro Area countries that came under duress during the crisis. This was due in part to the gravity and large size of the initial economic imbalances and distortions. Unfortunately, the adverse impact was greatly aggravated by mistakes in policy design and the decisions of the Eurozone and the IMF to limit the available official external financing.

As a consequence, Greece's real GDP declined by a cumulative 25% during the initial years of the program, exceeding significantly initial program expectations. Greece only returned to positive growth during 2017 (1.4%) and 2018–2019 (1.9%), thanks largely to a recovery of tourism, at a time when growth in the Euro Area and the global economy was also recovering. Greece's per capita income by 2019 was 20% lower than its level in 2009 and 42% lower than the average in the Euro Area. Greece's average unemployment rate rose steeply to a peak of 27.5% by 2013, easing gradually thereafter to 19.3% by 2018 and 17.3% in 2019, but remained substantially higher than in other Euro Area countries. The economic contraction has affected particularly the young, has lengthened the duration of unemployment, and has induced a large-scale emigration of skilled workers. By February 2020, according to Eurostat data, the unemployment rate for those younger than age twenty-five (youth unemployment), while significantly down from its peak of 60% in 2013, was still very high, 37% compared with the 15.2% average in the Euro Area. At the same time, 70% of the unemployed were out of work for more than 12 months, compared with an average of 43.6% in the Euro Area. Despite a temporary increase in 2020 due to the pandemic, the unemployment rate fell to 15% in 2021 and is projected by the IMF to fall significantly further to 12.8% in 2022.

The growth recovery attained by Greece during 2017–2019 was rather modest, especially in view of the initial steep output contraction. By 2019, Greece still had a slow recovery in its potential output and a negative output gap (actual real GDP was below its potential level) of around 3%. The experienced low growth was due to under-execution of public investment during the crisis, and a limited recovery of private investment. The weak private sector demand reflected, inter alia, the remaining impediments to growth, such as high direct taxes and social security contributions, but also high indebtedness and liquidity constraints, which were hangovers of crisis. The poor recovery of private investment reflected the destruction of many private enterprises and much private capital during the extended crisis and of the dampening of entrepreneurial spirit.

Greece's real GDP per capita is estimated by the IMF in its July 2022 surveillance report to still be 20% below its pre-crisis level. Astoundingly, it is now estimated that it will take another twelve years, until 2034, to return to pre-crisis levels. This is a shocking statistic, and indicative of the excessive social and economic pain that Greece has experienced. It is also reflective of the gravity of the program design mistakes that were made by the Troika. Various estimates indicate that in 2018 almost a third of Greek households lived in poverty. To put things in perspective, based on IMF data, the United States took only eight years to recover from the 25% output loss during the Great Depression of the 1930s, whereas Greece, with a similar decline in output, would need twenty-four years to recover.

At the same time, Greece was successful in reducing its external imbalances. The current account deficit was reduced sharply from an initial high level of around 12% of GDP in 2009 to 3.5% in 2018 and 2.2% in 2019. The narrowing of the external imbalance was primarily the result of the compression of domestic demand and imports, but also in part the result of an improvement in Greece's competitiveness. The labor market reforms in the early years of the program introduced some labor market flexibility that facilitated a reduction in Greece's wage and non-wage cost structures, with Greece's real effective exchange rate declining (competitiveness improved) by about 20% during 2009–2019.

Any changes in competitiveness are fraught with technical difficulties and can be subject to large margins of error. Developments in Greece's competitiveness were at the heart of the adjustment challenges facing a country such as Greece that is a member of a currency union. As we have seen, the absence of the exchange rate instrument places major emphasis on achieving flexible domestic cost structures as a way of correcting competitiveness gaps and ensuring sustainable external positions. Cost reductions have been extremely difficult to achieve in both Greece and other Euro Area countries that have external current account imbalances due to the rigidities in their labor and product markets as well as the associated lower productivity levels relative to their main trading partners.

On the fiscal front, the improvement in the budget deficit during the crisis was not only impressive, but was excessive and unprecedented. The general government balance switched from an initial deficit of the order of over 15% of GDP in 2009 to surpluses ranging from 0.5% to 1.5% of GDP during 2016–2019. More impressively, the primary general government budget balance, which is often considered the preferred indicator of the stance of fiscal policy, switched from an initial deficit of about 10% of GDP in 2009 to large surpluses of 3.7%–4.4% of GDP during 2016–2019.

However, the way this impressive turnaround in the overall budget balance was achieved was inefficient, and the associated quality of fiscal adjustment was rather low, on both the revenue and expenditure sides. Greece made commendable progress during the program period in enhancing its tax and expenditure administration and in attaining fiscal discipline, but relied more on tax rate increases rather than expenditure cuts. Frequent underspending on budgeted capital expenditure and occasionally, increases in domestic arrears made it possible to achieve the fiscal targets. Steep increases in direct tax rates, social security contributions, property taxes, and VAT rates, along with a modest expansion of the tax base, compensated for revenue collection difficulties (given Greece's poor tax payment culture) in order to achieve the overall revenue targets. This came at the cost of distorting economic incentives, discouraging private investment, and destroying jobs.

Greece's outstanding public debt was at €331 billion, or 181% of GDP at end-2019, the last year before the pandemic. This was a far cry from the goals set in 2012. Recall the target of 120% debt-to-GDP that had been enshrined in the debt restructuring agreement in 2012? Yet, thanks to changes in the terms of this debt, sustainability concerns have actually eased, as indicated in several updated IMF Debt Sustainability Analyses (the most recent in August 2019, before COVID-19), as the debt-to-GDP ratio was projected to decline over the years ahead and, importantly, the annual gross financing need had declined sharply.

What made this dramatic change possible, and why did Greece's debt increase so much? Why, despite the much larger-than-targeted debt-to-GDP ratio, is Greece's public debt considered broadly sustainable, and even safe under some extreme macro scenarios? The answer lies in part in actual developments on the ground in Greece and on performance under its program. But it also reflects to a substantial extent changes in the policies of Greece's official creditors, in particular the IMF. They were belated changes, but changes nevertheless. The details of these developments are outlined in Appendix 7. In sum, the IMF developed a much more pragmatic way to evaluate debt sustainability than had been used, misguidedly, during the crisis period of 2010–2012. Rather than just focusing on one ratio, the debt-to-GDP ratio, the IMF decided to supplement that ratio with an alternative measure, which takes into account the much lower interest rates that Greece pays on its rescheduled and below market debt.

Greece's record of implementation of structural reforms during the period 2010–2018 is rather uneven and disappointing in many ways. Many reforms were either partially completed or poorly implemented, despite some periods of solid implementation, like those under Papademos and the early term of Samaras. The reasons for that were manifold. The reforms covered the whole spectrum of policy areas, most of which were politically and socially sensitive and highly resisted by vested interests and major constituencies of the political parties that had enjoyed enormous benefits under the original structural and institutional setup. These factors, and the associated overly-optimistic assumptions by the Troika about the likely supply response from the reforms, resulted in an excessive burden being placed on labor, contributing to a sense of unfairness and an attendant loss of public support for the program.

The structural reform policies were intended to address, inter alia, the bloated civil service, the generous public pension schemes, the weak tax administration and tax collection, the poor payment culture, the high tax arrears, the inefficiencies in the legal system, the poor state of public enterprise finances, the strong resistance to privatization, the complex and inefficient labor market structures (including major rigidities in collective agreement coverage, and in labor hiring and firing procedures), restrictive product market structures with high barriers to market entry, the high exposure of the banking system to public debt and the associated negative feedback loops, etc. As pointed out in Chapter 30, meaningful progress in many of these areas was initiated under Papademos and even in some areas during 2010 under Papandreou. However, progress needed to be sustained over a period of years, and alas, that was generally not the case. The limited progress achieved in removing these impediments to growth was reflected in the very modest recovery in output growth, and the still rather low overall productivity of the Greek economy.

CHAPTER 35

SHAPING THE FUTURE

"Reinventing democracy to fit the challenges of the twenty-first century may sound like a tall order. But this is the mission of our generation and I'm certain we will accomplish it."

—Kyriakos Mitsotakis, Washington, DC, May 17, 2022

The European debt crisis revealed a plethora of shortcomings in the European superstructure, severe weaknesses in the Greek economy and political system, and flaws in the global financial architecture. A detailed analysis of these multiple lacunae would require another book. Many books have, in fact, already been largely written about the Eurozone crisis, with a multitude of proposals of how to strengthen the fabric of the EU and the Eurozone. Others have addressed the global financial crisis, its roots, and in some cases, provided proposed solutions. Still others look to the particular frailties of the Greek economy (and often the other Mediterranean members of the Eurozone as well). In each area, much more needs to be done. As the previous chapter indicates, a number of important measures have already been taken since the early days of the Greek and European crisis to strengthen the functionality and coherence of Europe. Many steps have also been taken to enhance the competitiveness and efficiency of the Greek economy. On the global landscape, improvements in the architecture have been made to address some of the weaknesses that led to the global financial crisis of 2008 and 2009, as well as the European crisis. In each area, however, the unfinished business is quite substantial. This chapter touches upon some of these issues involved in an integrated approach, addressing some of the key factors that influenced each part of the complex set of interrelated forces that fed the euro crisis.

STRENGTHENING THE GLOBAL ARCHITECTURE

The forces that led to the global financial crisis in 2008 and 2009 have been thoroughly dissected, and much has in fact been done to strengthen the global financial system and prevent a recurrence of a crisis of such magnitude. In particular, capital and liquidity requirements for banks have been strengthened dramatically, resolution plans are in place to resolve a failing institution without taxpayer support, and risk-management systems have been substantially reinforced by the industry. Governance weaknesses of global financial institutions have also been the focus of a lot of endeavor. Recent developments surrounding US regional banks and the collapse of Credit Suisse have, however, raised questions about the adequacy of improvements in risk management, in supervision (in the US, especially), in governance, and in resolution plans. The rest of this section focuses on other areas, in my view, that still need more attention: housing markets, sovereign risk management, reform of the IMF, and sovereign debt management.

Housing Markets

This may seem like a strange point on which to begin, since housing markets were not central to the Greek crisis, but they were at the heart of the global financial crisis of 2008–2009, which measurably weakened the Eurozone and made it vulnerable to the regional crisis that swept over Europe in 2010 and 2011. In addition, both the Irish and Spanish crises were significantly centered on the collapse of bubbles in the housing sector. As we enter a period with the growing risk of another global recession, real estate is once again front and center. Although the current focus is on commercial real estate, residential housing will likely emerge as a problem as the recession unfolds. The Federal Reserve has provided enormous artificial stimulation to the housing market through its quantitative easing policy, which went on for too long. By buying large amounts of mortgage-backed securities (MBS) issued by government sponsored enterprises (GSEs), the Federal Reserve provided non-market support to housing prices. The inevitable decline in housing prices as the Federal Reserve now shrinks its balance sheet risks and raises interest rates at an unprecedented pace could contribute once again to a global recession. For once and for all, governments, legislatures, central banks, and Treasuries should withdraw from interference in housing markets—it often ends badly for those it is intended to help.

Sovereign Risk Management

For much of the period since the opening of the euro markets in the 1960s, national governments of advanced economies have been able to access global markets quite easily to finance their funding requirements. Of course, the history of sovereign borrowing goes back centuries, but funding was mostly done through banks in the past. From the 1960s onward, however, capital markets became a source of sovereign funding, available only to advanced economies at first, then to emerging markets after the Brady Plan. Despite large advances in various aspects of risk management, sovereign risk management remains much more of an art than science. Perhaps that is to a certain extent inevitable, given the difficulty of gauging not only a country's ability to pay, but willingness to pay. However, it is an area of glaring weakness, and should be a priority area for action. This is, of course, only one part of the ongoing efforts to strengthen crisis prevention measures, but it is one of the keys to avoiding future sovereign debt crises.

Evaluating sovereign risk by a potential creditor—or a rating agency—involves analyzing, and weighing, a myriad of factors—macroeconomic, structural, financial, political, and geopolitical, to name a few. It also involves assessing vulnerability to global trends and forces, whether of an economic, political, natural (hurricanes, drought, typhoons, global warming, etc.), or military variety. Since my first days at the US Treasury in 1976, I have been involved in trying to analyze sovereign risks. Within a month of joining the Treasury, I was asked by a wizened old Treasury economist, George Willis, to develop a set of economic indicators that could be used to monitor sovereign risk in a country, with color coding for different levels of key variables such as fiscal and current account deficits, inflation, debt levels, employment rates, reserves, consumer confidence, inter alia. Looking back, we developed a rather simplistic approach, focusing on stock levels and not flows, and with little to no coverage of structural factors such as tariffs, regulation, labor markets, and state ownership. Nevertheless, I was quite impressed that we had developed an "early warning system" of systemic risk. When George looked it over, however, he said, "Not a bad start, Charles, but don't ever believe that any mix of ratios will ever give you the answer. Remember, these numbers are only indicative, not definitive. It is merely a beginning to understanding sovereign risk." I thought of old George years later when the Troika became fixed on the 120% debt-to-GDP ratio. He was a wise man.

Over the years, sovereign risk analysis became somewhat of an extension of corporate risk assessments in many financial institutions. The Institute of International Finance became a repository of expertise in sovereign risk analysis for the global banking community in the 1980s and 1990s, although some firms began to use our analysis less frequently as the Latin American debt problem faded into the background. Many leading banks and investment firms subsequently developed their own macro research departments focusing on sovereign risk, but much of that was prepared for their "sales side" customers (hedge fund/large asset managers, etc.) rather than on their internal risk management processes. In addition, both the IMF and the IIF had put a great deal of emphasis on crisis prevention throughout the 1980s and '90s and continuing in the 2000s, with a focus on sovereign risk management. A Special Committee on Crisis Prevention and Crisis Management formed by the IIF had developed numerous measures that could help prevent sovereign debt crises. In fact, Lemierre, not coincidentally, was Co-chair of that committee with Bill Rhodes when the Euro Area crisis erupted. Such measures as enhancing data and policy transparency, strengthening investor relations, and early corrective action by policymakers were developed by the committee.

Unfortunately, despite these efforts, the almost complete lack of quality sovereign risk analysis in lending to the Greek economy that was revealed by the debt crisis was appalling. But it was not that surprising. Many creditors, especially those based in Europe, had apparently concluded that Germany and other strong members of the Eurozone would "guarantee" Greece's debt. It was a classic case of moral hazard.

As mentioned above, in the wake of the global financial crisis, many aspects of overall risk management were strengthened by the global banking community. Credit risks, market risks, operational risks, compliance risks, and reputation risks were among them. Regulatory standards were toughened, but many firms also moved of their own volition. Perhaps not surprisingly, since sovereign risk mismanagement was not seen as a prime factor in the global crisis, sovereign risk was not high among those new standards and practices. More surprisingly, even after the Eurozone crisis, which involved case after case of misjudgments by investors in the sovereign risks they were taking, there was no major initiative to strengthen sovereign risk management systems. Why? Most likely because it was too easy to see fault in the Eurozone in general and Greece in particular. A key issue here is the asymmetrical cost of sovereign risk mismanaged by the creditor versus the debtor. In Greece, the creditor firms paid an unprecedentedly large price for their mistakes; nearly three-quarters of the value of their claims were squandered. Despite this, even among Greece's largest creditors, the cost was less than one calendar quarter of their earnings. Damaged, yes, but not "below the water line," to use a nautical analogy. For the citizens of Greece, the price of poor risk management by both the creditors and their own officials was incalculable.

As this book is going to print, the dimensions of sovereign risk are expanding to include environmentally related sovereign risk, sanctions-related sovereign risk, supply chain realignment sovereign risk, deglobalization risk, and even armed conflict as part of the larger picture. It is a propitious moment for creditors, ratings agencies, and regulators to up their game in evaluating and managing sovereign risk; the consequences of inaction could be severe.

Alongside such efforts, sovereigns themselves must enhance their understanding of the risks of borrowing in foreign currency. Globalized capital markets have enabled countries of all kinds to access global markets, often at seemingly absurd terms. In June 2017, just over a year after emerging from its latest default, Argentina sold $2.75 billion of a "hotly demanded 100-year bond in US dollars."[1]

Need anything more be said? The IMF should strengthen its monitoring of foreign borrowing by countries, and politicians should be warned by the professionals in their debt management departments of the risks involved. It can seem like dancing with the queen when the markets are humming, but it can turn viciously toward dancing with the devil when they turn cold. The officials in debt management offices and departments should not be allowed to access global markets without having passed, at a minimum, a three-month course on the risk and opportunities in global capital markets offered by a qualified entity or a rating agency.

But the issue goes deeper than that. On the borrowing side, politicians sometimes use foreign debt to finance consumption, short-term political goals, and patronage. The IMF should consider not just intensified monitoring, but specific guidelines on overall borrowing limits by the government. Such guidelines could be featured in both regular IMF surveillance and in any program operations. Much greater stress should be laid on promoting borrowing by the private sector, not the public sector.

On the creditor side, dealing effectively with the moral hazard involved in typical IMF lending operations is difficult enough, but the moral hazard in lending to Greece was even greater. Some creditors apparently have assumed that the Eurozone would find a way to bail them out, despite the statements by Germany and other Eurozone countries to the contrary. More disciplined risk management systems by the creditors will help, but more effective and substantial compensation drawback mechanisms focused on lending officers to sovereigns should also be seriously considered.

Reform of the IMF

The International Monetary Fund (IMF) has been a cornerstone of the global financial system since its formation at Bretton Woods in July 1944. It has played a vital role in preserving or restoring stability in the world economy throughout much of its nearly eighty-year history. But the global financial crisis of 2008–2009 and the Eurozone crisis that followed have revealed some anachronisms and weaknesses that call for substantial changes in the way in which the IMF performs its role as a stabilizer and problem-solver in the global economy.

Some of these are straightforward and long overdue, such as the abolition of the de facto system that has operated for the entirety of their history, which determines that the IMF should be run by a European, and the World Bank by an American. Really, in 2023? Weighted voting—which both organizations employ—geared to the size of each economy should provide more than enough protections for the US and Europe and their interests. If they need to hold top posts to ensure that their interests are advanced, the US and European Executive Directors are not doing their jobs. The US has a voting share of 16 percent, giving it a veto over some key decisions that require an 85 percent supermajority. The Euro area voting share is over 20 percent. During my time as US Director and Alternate Director in the 1980s, I learned quickly that building consensus among like-minded Directors is the key to being effective in representing US interests—not insisting on having key posts held by Americans. Meritocracy is preached in the corridors of these organizations and through them in governments around the world, but these organizations are not important enough to benefit from the principle? So, Tharman Shanmugaratnam (now President of Singapore) and Agustín Carstens end up leading the G30 and the BIS, respectively. Important organizations to be sure, but not quite as vital to the health of the world economy as the IMF and the World Bank.

One of the more complex issues relates to the staffing of the IMF and the lack of diversity in the academic strengths of the staff. Why is this a problem? It can, and often does, lead to the lack of solutions tailored to the particular complex economic problems of an individual member country. Too often, the IMF will bring standardized solutions to unique problems. In the case of Greece, this proved very costly, with an estimate for the fiscal multiplier that was ill-suited for the Greek economy—even according to the IMF's own postmortems—contributing to a considerably more severe contraction than needed. In fact, the IMF's approach actually worsened the fiscal deficit as revenues collapsed. There was also the apparent lack of an in-depth understanding by the IMF and EC of the institutional weaknesses and limitations of Greece and of the capacity to implement structural reform. One would have thought that the European Commission would have compensated for that shortcoming of the IMF in the case of Greece, but it was not obvious that that was the case.

But Greece is only one example among others. The IMF is a global institution that has developed a fairly rigid orthodoxy in its approach to IMF program design. This is based in large part on the economic work of

J. J. Polak, a brilliant Dutch economist who served as economic counselor at the IMF from 1966 to 1979 and played a leading role in developing the IMF's monetary approach to balance of payments adjustment. It became the framework that guided IMF program negotiation for many years, and still influences the IMF's approach to program design today. It is centered around the relationship between the creation of bank credit and the balance of payments. It is not a model to promote and preserve growth, but to address a balance of payment deficit. The IMF culture rewards staff for adherence to certain principles of negotiations. Although there have been adaptations over the years, adhering to standardized formulae for program design is often what gets you promoted.

How to address this orthodoxy, which may not fit every situation? A difficult question, for there is value in this approach because countries will often do anything to avoid painful measures of economic adjustment. One approach, which I proposed during my six years on the IMF Board, was to diversify the talent base. Well-trained macroeconomists are central to the IMF's function, and should continue to be the core of the IMF's staff. However, complementing each region with a few experts on structural reforms, political factors, and even history could have enabled the IMF to avoid the cost of disastrous mistakes made in the Greek program. It was not just the fiscal multiplier that was misunderstood; how could the IMF have embraced the target in the first adjustment program of a privatization program that could privatize $50 billion in assets in only three years? IMF management knows full well that institutional capacity of any government needs to be understood by the IMF if success is to be achieved over time.

There are other aspects of the IMF that also need reforms. Perhaps few are more pressing for the future of the Eurozone than the scale of IMF lending arrangements and the question of how to approach an adjustment problem of a member of a currency union.

IMF lending is geared to "quotas," based roughly on the size of a country's economy. These ratios are, however, very crude, as they consistently lag behind relative changes in the world economy. The point here, however, is more fundamental. This crisis was never just about Greece. It was about the survival of the Eurozone. Why should IMF support have been limited to the size of the Greek economy? Over lunch in Washington during three negotiations, David Lipton, First Deputy

Managing Director of the IMF at the time, told me that consideration had been given to developing an approach to the Eurozone crisis based on the whole of the Eurozone. I had not considered it, but the more I reflected upon it, the more economic logic there was to it. Based on traditional IMF methodology, the IMF lending to Greece had been an unusually large amount relative to Greece's quota. There had, in fact, been a significant amount of grumbling about the extent of the IMF lending in the IMF Board, especially by Latin American Directors. I found this rather myopic, as throughout the 1980s, Europe has supported seemingly endless sizable programs from many Latin American countries. Apparently, bankers aren't the only ones with short memories.

Had the IMF lent on the basis of the quota of the entire Eurozone, the magnitude of IMF programs for Greece would have been approximately twenty times larger. This would have significantly eased the adjustment for Greece and likely mitigated the sizable contraction of Greece's economy during the critical period of adjustment in 2010–2012. This would, you may say, be inconsistent with the IMF Articles of Agreement, which determine access to IMF programs based on each country's quota. But what happens when the realities of a currency zone in crisis—where a country has given up its currency and independent monetary policy for the collective benefits of a common currency—run head-on into the rigidities of the global architecture? Rigidities win; country and region lose. When a member of a common currency zone runs into difficulty, what is the responsibility of the other members? And what is the responsibility of the IMF to support not just the troubled country, but the entire currency zone? Should the surplus countries of the Eurozone have been part of the IMF adjustment program? These are not just rhetorical questions. Admittedly, they are very difficult ones, and easy answers are not available. But that is no reason not to grapple with them as a high priority. The question of IMF lending policies should have been addressed when the currency union was formed. It was not, but it had better be before the next crisis happens in the Eurozone.

Sovereign Debt Management

Another aspect of the global architecture that sorely needs attention is the strategy for resolving sovereign debt problems. During my years at

THE DAILY PAPER FOR THE IMF/WORLD BANK MEETING
WASHINGTON DC, SUNDAY 29 SEPTEMBER 2002

EmergingMarkets

www.emergingmarkets.org

A US court awarded Taiwan a $72 million judgment against us, while I'm only due to get $50 million from HIPC over three years

– Ali Badjo Gamatie

finance minister of Niger

See page 7 news

Inside

Daggers drawn

Debating the best strategy for resolving sovereign debt crises with Anne Krueger, First Deputy Managing Director of the IMF. September 2002. ©2002 Emerging Markets via Global Capital

the IMF and the IIF, many efforts were made to prevent sovereign debt crises. As discussed earlier, the IMF and the IIF both promoted greater transparency of sovereign data and early course correction of wayward policies through IMF surveillance. After the successful launch of the Brady Plan in 1989, there was a window of relative calm in the sovereign debt world as successive countries worked their way through Brady Plan restructurings. But then Mexico hit a wall with the tequila crisis of 1995, and it became apparent that sovereign debt problems were alive and well. This was followed by the Asian crisis of 1997–1998, centered around Thailand, Korea, and Indonesia, and then the Russian crisis of 1998.

Despite the efforts of both the IMF and the IIF, debt crises kept rolling in, seemingly as regular as ocean waves. In April 2002, Anne Krueger, First Deputy Managing Director of the IMF, outlined a new approach to the sovereign debt restructuring (the Sovereign Debt Restructuring Mechanism, or SDRM) that would place the IMF front and center in deciding when and how a debt restructuring would be initiated and managed. It was met with considerable concern by the private financial community as well as emerging market officials. In the fall of 2003, at the IMF Annual Meeting in Washington, Jean-Claude Trichet, Governor of the Banque de France at the time, proposed an alternative to Krueger's: a code of good conduct that would outline best practices and guidelines between debtor countries and creditors.[2] Having heard Jean-Claude's speech—and having been an ardent opponent to Krueger's ideas—I called him as he was on his way to the airport to ask if he would work with us to develop a code of conduct for debt restructuring that was balanced between the interests of debtors and creditors, in contrast to the dirigiste IMF's top-down approach of the SDRM. He said he would, and we immediately began to develop such a code under the leadership of Bill Rhodes and Jacques de Larosiere. The IIF developed a core set of principles to provide a new framework for avoiding sovereign debt crisis and resolving a crisis when it arose. The code took the form of the "Principles for Stable Capital Flows and Fair Debt Restructuring." It was—and remains—a unique endeavor in the modern annals of global finance because it was eventually shaped by a combination of leaders from the private creditor community, the sovereign debtor community, and a few key officials from the G7 and the IMF. This was breaking new ground in the development of the international financial architecture. Until this point, innovations from the private sector were occasionally woven into the global architecture, but only upon the approval of the official sector. This time it was different. We had reached out to debtor countries who were concerned that the SDRM could damage their access to capital markets. It was a remarkable process that brought together a mix of officials from debtor countries, creditor countries, and private financiers. When the Managing Director of the IMF endorsed our initiative in 2005, we had gained some momentum, and then credible officials such as the Finance Ministers of Turkey, Mexico, South Africa, and China, as well as G7 leaders such as Trichet, former US Treasury Secretary Brady, and former Federal Reserve Chairman Paul Volcker, expressed their support for the initiative. A group of "Trustees of the Principles" was formed, which was an unprecedented group combining public and private sector financial leaders.

The initial Principles contained some very broad language which, when addressing the issue of restructuring, called for "negotiations" between the debtor and creditors and a "voluntary restructuring" where needed.

The historic document provided a few basic guidelines for how to handle sovereign debt restructuring. It was a surprise to the IMF and to many other observers that it was strongly supported by both the creditors and the debtors. Trichet stated, "I congratulate both the official and private sector leaders who have transformed this into reality. The Principles address significant remaining gaps in the architecture of global finance."[3] Francisco Gil Díaz, Mexico's Minister of Finance, stated that, "These Principles provide an excellent counterpart to collective action clauses in utilizing market-based approaches to promoting stability and growth in emerging markets."[4]

As these Principles were gaining credibility, a process was under way that was undermining them—Argentinian debt negotiations. Argentina had defaulted on their external bond debt in 2001, and instead of negotiating a restructuring consistent with the new Principles, they decided to pursue a restructuring without direct negotiations with their private creditors, based on their own sense of the market. The US Treasury and the IMF surprisingly supported this approach, but Argentina's strategy proved to be a disaster for that country, isolating them from the global capital markets for well over a decade. Unfortunately, it also set back the efforts to put in place a cooperative debt strategy. By the time of the Greek debt crisis a clear framework for debt restructuring was still not firmly in place, despite the progress made in institutionalizing the Principles. The Principles have been amended and updated over the years, and the Trustees currently still include an impressive mix of public and private sector officials. It is chaired by the Governor of the Banque de France, Francois Villeroy de Galhau; Axel Weber, the former chairman of UBS; and Yi Gang, Governor of the People's Bank of China.

Over the years, many improvements have been made to the process of debt restructuring, including aggregated CACs. Many of these emanated from work done by an IIF/IMF Working Group in 2014, one in which ICMA also played a prominent and constructive role. These constituted major improvements in the architecture and a move away from the "top down" approach that had been followed at times by the IMF. Nevertheless, the framework has not been consistently followed, and key issues such as the issue of "creditor engagement"—voluntary negotiation between the debtor and the main creditors—have not been fully embraced, even though it is clearly part of the Principles. During our negotiations on Greek debt, some of Greece's legal and financial advisers apparently chafed under the yoke of voluntary negotiations, and there were occasional efforts to "cram down" a deal. The lack of an agreed framework for sovereign debt restructuring remains a major hole in the global financial architecture. It feeds uncertainty in markets and prolongs orderly debt negotiations with a cost to the underlying economy.

During the COVID-19 crisis, the World Bank led an effort to create a common framework for addressing debt problems of sovereigns. It has proven to be somewhat useful, but is focused on low-income countries and official creditors. In order for it to be useful for higher-income countries and advanced economies, there will need to be much more input from the private sector. The multilateral institutions should understand that simply telling the private creditors that there must be "compatibility of treatment" with decisions made by official creditors—decisions over which they have virtually no input—will not work.

Another difficulty in resolving sovereign debt problems has arisen in recent years regarding the role of China as a bilateral official creditor. For decades, official bilateral creditors have managed their portion of sovereign debt problems through the Paris Club. With French leadership this has worked quite well, because all the major official creditors participated. No more. China has become the world's largest bilateral creditor, holding more than one-third of the external debt to the obligations of the lowest-income countries. It is imperative that China participate in the Paris Club process if that is to continue to provide a meaningful framework for restructuring official bilateral debt.

Recently the Bretton Woods Committee has launched an initiative to forge progress on this front, searching for a bilateral approach for both creditors and debtors. This holds promise, but there is a need for a concerted effort, building on the IIF Principles and subsequent joint endeavors involving all the key players—the IMF, the IIF, the Bretton Woods Committee, ICMA, and the Emerging Markets Trading Association (EMTA). With regard to the overall challenge of clarifying and codifying a framework for all sovereign debt issues, including middle income and advanced economies, the answer could be for the IMF and IIF, with support from ICMA and the EMTA, to organize a special conference to sort out those issues. It is long overdue.

The saga of the debt-to-GDP ratio for Greece is another example of IMF orthodoxy winning over common sense. Fortunately, this area has undergone dramatic change since the Greek debt negotiations of 2010–2011, as discussed in Chapter 34 and elaborated upon in Appendix 7, but the matter still requires serious systemic attention. During the years preceding the Greek crisis, the IMF had "sharpened," so to speak, its focus on debt sustainability. The key test of any IMF program has always been "balance of payments sustainability." However, the IMF had begun to focus on one aspect of balance of payment sustainability: debt sustainability. During the negotiations with Greece, concerns had grown—understandably—over the scale of Greek debt. At some point, however, this became one of the focal points of the negotiations. It almost seemed to override the other "performance criteria" (target variables to gauge performance under the program) and took on a life of its own. Suddenly, not only were staff members of the Troika speaking of the need for Greece to hit a certain debt-to-GDP ratio in 2020; it became a mantra among key European officials. This became "the" target, overwhelming a more nuanced and analytical judgment about the Greek reform program. It was, frankly, IMF orthodoxy gone wild. Even IMF management became preoccupied with it, as evidenced by the meeting on October 26 with Merkel, Sarkozy, Lagarde, et al.

This was not, of course, just a creation of the IMF, but of the European Commission and the ECB as well. Nevertheless, the IMF should take the lead in finding solutions to these aberrations, which can be very costly to IMF member countries. The Exchange & Trade Relations Department used to be the "conscience" of the IMF. They need to find a new one. At the same time, the European Commission should have taken a stronger lead in determining the "debt sustainability" calculations in the Greek program and will need to take more ownership in the future should the need arise.

REFORMING THE EUROZONE

As important as these measures would be to improvements in the IMF and the structure of global finance, nothing is more urgent to avoid a future sovereign debt crisis in the Eurozone than is action by the Eurozone itself. Much has already been written about this, so I will home in on the critical measures required.

The Eurozone is a grand project. It has been an aspiration of Europe since at least as far back as the late 1960s, when the Werner Report, a report issued by the Prime Minister of Luxembourg, outlined a path to economic and monetary union. The course to achieving monetary union has often been tortuous, but in January 1999, eleven countries—not including Greece—became founding members of the euro. This took place despite enormous economic, financial, and political turbulence during the 1970s and 1980s. Germany had always insisted that some form of political union would accompany monetary union. They saw this as a framework to generate strict monetary policies.[5] Both Germany and France saw "political union" as a means of coordinating economic and monetary policies, but the two had very different visions of how that would work. The French saw a central bank, subservient to political direction, while the Germans foresaw a dominant central bank.

In the end, neither vision prevailed for reasons that are rather obscured in the endless machinations over the launch of the euro. Kohl and the Germans eventually dropped their insistence on "political union." It appears that broad macroeconomic convergence became a rough substitute for greater economic and political integration. A Eurogroup of Finance Ministers was formed to provide a distant form of political supervision over the ECB, as well as make decisions regarding exchange rate policy, although from what I can tell, the ministers have ceded much of that responsibility to the ECB. And if our experience with the Eurogroup of Finance Ministers during the Greek crisis is indicative, the Eurogroup in reality seemed to exercise little power over the ECB.

But this is not the essence of the difficulty that the Eurozone faces. European leaders saw monetary union as a matter of destiny. Even Helmut Schlesinger, former Bundesbank President, said in 2007, "The overall political theatre in Europe made monetary union both necessary and desirable. If the political will was there, it would have been worse —and impossible for the Bundesbank to oppose it."[6] Yes, the political will was there for monetary union, but not for the key ingredient that would make monetary union work for all of its members: a fiscal union. Without a greater willingness to create an integrated fiscal policy, individual members that have serious underlying economic imbalances will struggle to resolve them, especially given that they have virtually no independent control over their monetary policy and no national exchange rate at all to facilitate the adjustment process. These difficulties are compounded by the fact that internal devaluation—through compression of real wages— is exceedingly difficult in so many of the Euro Area countries, some of which—including Greece—still have rigid labor markets. Policies will be vulnerable to market pressures—without countries being able to respond either through their own exchange rate or monetary policies. The structural differences among Eurozone economies remain vast, and the common tools that Europe has created to deal with those circumstances, although expanding, remain limited. The ECB's attempt in 2022 to handle both the need for tighter monetary policy in the face of high inflation while creating an anti-fragmentation policy to assist countries facing higher interest rates in the markets that face disorderly conditions demonstrates the inadequacy of the current institutional arrangements in the Eurozone. With rising base rates and widening spreads, debt sustainability issues may rise again, especially for Italy, with a high level of debt and without the benefit of significant concessional rates on its debt, such as is the case with Greece.

In reality, the ECB's primary mandate is price stability. At a time when prices have raced ahead, the ECB should be focused on the task of reining in inflation, not trying to perform a balancing act by also supporting vulnerable countries in the bond markets. A fiscal union should be put into place to address these difficulties, leveraging the consolidated strength of the Eurozone as a whole. This would require risk-sharing among the Eurozone members, a step that Germany and other countries have been very reluctant to take. In the absence of it, however, the Eurozone will likely prove unsustainable in the long term, a reality that would present a huge setback for Europe and the world. The euro came very close to being ripped apart by the Greek crisis; it would be highly unlikely to survive a similar crisis in Italy. A fiscal union could be, in fact, an essential element in Europe taking greater ownership of its own structure. In the case of Greece, Europe proved unwilling or incapable of doing this. With the expansion of the funding available to the ESM, would the Eurozone be able to handle a major crisis in one of its largest member countries without the IMF? It remains doubtful.

Other changes in the structure of the Eurozone are also sorely needed. In particular, the process of completing a so-called "banking union" has been under way far too long. There is an urgent need for area-wide deposit insurance and a commonly funded backstop to the Single Resolution Fund.

There remains the nettlesome issue of what to do about the Stability and Growth Pact. The pact was put on hold in 2020 due to the pandemic.

Perhaps it is time to recognize that as important as fiscal discipline is, the keys to stability must be managed with a sufficient degree of flexibility, with a broader perspective on what really matters. Do macro imbalances matter, and if so, how to approach and sanction, if necessary, members as well as deficit countries? Should more room be allowed for the "investment component" of national budgets? George Papaconstantinou's recent book *Whatever It Takes* provides some interesting ideas on these and related issues.[7]

There are two more steps that I would consider essential to building a durable Eurozone. The first is mutual respect of each member. It may seem like a naive and elusive goal. And perhaps it is, but a minimum measure of comity would go a long way to paving the way for a stronger, more cohesive, and more powerful European Union. Yes, Germany is the strongest economy in Europe, and its dominant political force, but it sometimes fails to recognize the co-dependencies that are running through the Eurozone. German exports to the rest of Europe account for more than two-thirds of Germany's total exports, with almost one-third of German jobs linked to exports.

This codependency was certainly recognized by key German officials in the preparation of the euro. Otmar Issing, a brilliant Bundesbank economist who later became the Chief Economist at the ECB, stated, "I would not have previously forecast that the European currency would start during the 1990s. The decisive moment came with the currency crisis of 1992–93. The status quo was not tenable. We found a 30 percent devaluation of the lira. Some companies in southern Germany competing with Italy went bankrupt. There was a danger of controls on movements of goods. I and others came to the conclusion that the common market would not survive another crisis of these dimensions."[8] German Finance Minister Theo Waigel voiced similar concerns.

When you read or hear condescending comments directed at other Eurozone countries, you wonder about the awareness of those facts. More important, the mutual support that should arise from mutual respect could go a long way to reinforcing the concept of a united Europe. During both the COVID-19 crisis and the current energy crisis, and even more recently the Russian invasion of Ukraine, Europe has shown considerable solidarity. It is now time to capitalize on that solidarity and reinforce it on a more permanent basis.

Something also has to be done about bureaucracy and the spread of its influence over so many aspects of European life. The President of the European Commission, Ursula von der Leyen, should appoint a special commissioner to streamline the bloated bureaucracy of the Commission and eliminate the many unnecessary, intrusive, and homogenizing rules and regulations that stifle the individuality and creativity of Europe's citizens. The economic diversity of Europe makes for a powerful economic block, with a GDP of almost €17 trillion, close to the size of the US economy. It is a tourist mecca, with more than six times the number of inbound tourists as the United States. Germany and northern Italy constitute one of the most powerful industrial centers in the world. France is the cultural wine and cuisine envy of the world. The Greek islands are rival to none. Italy is not just the design capital of the world but captivates us with its history and engineering prowess. I could go on and on, but the point is that Europe is, in many respects, an unrealized aspiration that is far from realizing its full potential. Every culture, every language, and indeed, every economy contains its own strengths, its own comparative advantage. Yes, there are many weaknesses, but collectively the countries of Europe can compensate for one another. Compensate, not condescend. Underpin, not undermine. Reinforce, not remake.

If the European project is to succeed, nationalist attitudes will have to be subjugated to the broader interests of the citizens of Europe. The COVID-19 crisis, the flood of refugees, the global supply chain difficulties, and particularly, the Russian invasion of Ukraine have presented not only new challenges for Europe, but new opportunities. And, in fact, Europe has seized the opportunities in some respects: New facilities to support countries under duress from COVID-19 and the new energy crisis. The temporary suspension of the Maastricht criteria. The rise of a historic form of brutal despotism in Russia has given Europe a new raison d'etre. It has brought back memories of Nazism and fascism, and Europe has responded on many issues with a degree of cohesion that has not been visible for decades. Will that cohesion recede once the war is over, only to retreat to petty nationalistic squabbles that characterized the European crisis of 2010–2012? Europe can harness the power that is inherent in its member states by recognizing, embracing, and strengthening the diverse strengths of each country. Greece, Italy, Spain, and Portugal will never be remade in the image of Germany or the Netherlands. But they can be competitive, efficient economies that thrive in a more flexible, dynamic framework of a new European Union—even a new Eurozone.

Much of Europe's success in dealing with these issues will revolve around Germany. My good friend and former colleague on the Board of the IIF, Stephen Green (Baron Green of Hurstpierpoint), wrote a book in 2014 about the "Reluctant Meister," as he characterizes Germany.[9] A lifelong student of Germany, Green lived there and studied Germany's culture and history at great length. He takes the view that even Germany could become part of a broader European identity, a more blended concept of what it means to be European based on a deep sense of shared history, values, interests, and geography; an identity that values and respects economic and cultural diversity but also is empowered by the commonality of those values and interests. If this is to come to pass, it will likely require a Germany that has the humility of Konrad Adenauer and not the bluster of some officials during the crisis. Henry Kissinger's recent remarkable book on leadership provides some valuable historical lessons on the unique strengths of Adenauer.[10] The times are very, very different today, but a Germany led by a combination of humility and a sense of destiny would be a powerful leader of Europe in the twenty-first century.

TRANSFORMING GREECE

And what about Greece, you may ask? If the global financial architecture is strengthened, if IMF practices are better aligned with the realities of a currency zone, if fiscal union is finally realized and the Eurozone builds a durable framework for greater cohesion among the member countries—will Greece then be out of danger and able to avoid another devastating debt crisis? That answer will, ultimately, rest on Greece's shoulders.

For over half of Greece's history as a modern nation, it has been in the midst of debt problems: defaults, reschedulings, and financing arrangements that compromised its independence. Like other European nations that came of age during the nineteenth and twentieth centuries, such as Italy, France, and Spain, it has gone through cycles of political instability as it struggled to establish a functional framework of democracy. During some of these periods, Greece was engaged in various wars that drained its finances and contributed to the debt difficulties. Furthermore, Greece's four-and-a-half-century subjugation to the Ottoman Empire deprived it of many of the benefits of the Enlightenment as well as the first phase of the industrial revolution. It not only experienced two destructive world wars, but a civil war that both overlapped with and followed World War II. During the postwar era, the military seized power for seven years, which once again set back the country's economic and democratic development. And for much of the period since democracy returned in 1975, the political elite created a largely self-serving system that brought corruption into various layers of government and eroded the capacity of the government to deliver basic services to its citizens. Throughout a considerable portion of the last half-century the economy has been poorly managed. Joining the euro has not brought lasting price stability, as had been anticipated, but it has deprived Greece of having its own monetary policy and exchange rate as tools with which to help manage the economy. And, over the last decade, Greece has undergone the worst economic crisis of modern Europe, destroying jobs and much of the country's capital stock.

Despite these waves of adversity, Greece has demonstrated remarkable resilience. At a time when the security of Europe is once again under threat, Greece has established itself as a stable presence on the eastern flank of NATO, despite having troublesome neighbors. After being pushed to the brink of becoming a dysfunctional democracy during the height of the crisis, it has reestablished its democratic credentials by persevering through multiple national elections without completely succumbing to extreme populism of either the political left or the right. Greece has also restored its economic independence with the conclusion of the Troika economic adjustment program, and even moved past the special EU monitoring arrangements of its economy. In addition, Greece established a new rapport with Germany, as epitomized by the cordiality and mutual respect exhibited all around during Chancellor Merkel's final official visit to Athens in October 2021.

The election of Mitsotakis in mid-2019 brought in a government that understands the importance of stimulating investment as one of the keys to restoring economic vitality. Taxes have been reduced, albeit cautiously to avoid rekindling unmanageable fiscal deficits. The wage compression of the crisis years has helped restore competitiveness to many sectors, although much more needs to be done to build on the improvements in the flexibility of labor markets accomplished under the Papademos

Prime Minister Kyriakos Mitsotakis welcomes German Chancellor Angela Merkel on her last official visit to Greece, October 29, 2021. Capturing the change in mood, she noted the "heavy price" that Greece was called on to pay during the crisis. Mitsotakis spoke of Merkel being "the voice of reason and stability." A new day dawns. Photo by Marios Lolos/Xinhua/Alamy Live News.

government. Barriers to entry in product markets have been eased, but a further push needs to be made here as well.

The government has launched not only an impressive program to promote investment but has begun to cut away at the tangle of government regulations and policies that have stifled private investment for many years. The digitalization of the government services has been accompanied by digital innovations across many sectors of the economy. Core sectors have been revived, such as tourism, and an array of European leaders such as pharmaceuticals, scientific research, and renewable energy have been established.

These hopeful developments notwithstanding, Greece still has a long path ahead to build a strong competitive economy on a sustainable basis. Despite the unprecedented reduction in debt and debt service obligations, Greece's debt remains high and needs to be monitored carefully. Decades of political patronage and clientelism have led to a steady erosion in the capacity of government that can only be corrected by sustained assertion of a meritocracy, accompanied by the steady downsizing of government. Segments of the economy that are now being opened to greater competition, including many service sectors such as pharmacists and trucking, need to be placed on an accelerated path to create greater job opportunities.

The government has already taken a number of initiatives to improve the handling of business licensing, but Greece still ranks near the bottom among European countries in terms of being "business friendly." Deregulation across a range of industries is sorely needed. Privatization also needs acceleration—it has taken far too long to remove state-owned enterprises from the government's balance sheet.

The Greek banking system has recovered substantially from its near-death experience in 2011 and 2012. The "trifecta" of heavy exposure to Greek government bonds, the collapse of the economy, and the withdrawal of funds from the banking system, put tremendous liquidity stress on the banks and weakened dramatically the quality of their loan portfolio while also destroying capital. The sovereign debt restructuring of 2012 decimated much of what was left of the capital in the Greek banking system.

A decade later, the picture has dramatically improved. Capital has been restored through the Hellenic Financial Stability Fund (HFSF) while at the same time preserving private sector control of the banks, thus minimizing the interference of government; profitability is on the way back; non-performing loans (NPLs) have declined to single-digit percentage levels of loan portfolios; and liquidity has risen to acceptable levels. Two measures introduced by the government in 2020 have accelerated the process of resolving NPLs, including a new bankruptcy code.

Nevertheless, challenges remain for the banking system. Measures are needed to stimulate credit to small and medium-size enterprises, and the private sector is only gradually regaining creditworthiness on a broad basis. Nevertheless, the finance system has momentum that it has not had for over a decade and a half.

One other area that requires further action is the inefficient judicial system. It is in need of major reform, still plagued by lengthy and costly dispute resolution procedures and shortage of judges.

While these reforms are under way, it will be vital to maintain fiscal discipline. The key will be continued restraint on government spending and steady economic recovery, as tax rates remain much too high despite reductions put into place by Mitsotakis.

The structural challenges that lie ahead are not ones that can be addressed in one political cycle; some are multi-generational and will, as already suggested, require a new version of the social contract between the Greek government and its citizens. Structural weaknesses of the Greek economy are deep seated and are woven into the fabric of Greek society. The resounding victory of Mitsotakis in the June 2023 elections has given him a mandate to continue—and even accelerate—his reform agenda. It will be critical that he seize the opportunity to capitalize on this opening and advance with determination on some of the more difficult areas.

As the government moves to address these challenges, the citizenry will need to adapt their expectations. Rather than having a government with inflated salaries that offers jobs to their cousins, citizens may fairly expect a more efficient set of government services and a government that manages the economy with prudence and a determination to strengthen competitiveness. A key part of this should involve repatriation of Greeks who left the country during the crisis; the government has initiated a program toward that end, but its success will depend largely on the willingness of the Greek diaspora scattered from Canada to Australia and many other parts of the world to heed the call of their home country. A national movement to strengthen tax compliance could also be a key ingredient to Greece breaking free of the past. Greece's escape from the cycles of mismanagement and financial stress can be inspired by the still-dazzling accomplishments of the classical Greeks, but it will only be realized by the will, ingenuity, and creativity of today's Greeks, with enlightened leadership restoring Greece to a place of leadership in Europe and the world. Greece has displayed remarkable tenacity and fortitude during the travails of the last decade, and a path to revitalizing growth and creating jobs has begun. Now the challenge is to sustain it. If it does, the dividends for the Greek people could be tremendous.

CHAPTER 36

GREECE TEN YEARS AFTER THE RESTRUCTURING

"No man ever steps in the same river twice, for it's not the same river and he's not the same man."

—Heraclitus, circa 500 BC

It was an inviting early spring afternoon on April 5, 2022, when Peixin and I landed at Athens airport. I had anticipated this trip for some time, and found myself excited to be back in Greece, but uncertain what would lie ahead. It had been almost three years since I had set foot in Greece, and almost exactly a decade since the debtors and creditors closed the chapter on the largest debt restructuring in history. After the four years of SYRIZA, Greece had elected a new face: Kyriakos Mitsotakis. Of course, New Democracy was not new, and neither was the Mitsotakis name in Greek politics. His father, Constantine Mitsotakis, had served as Prime Minister from 1990 to 1993, and his sister was a former foreign minister and mayor of Athens.

His father had been quite a successful premier. He had steered the New Democracy party away from a close association with the pre-dicta-torship right.[1] He promoted economic neo-liberalism rather than social-ism, and advanced a brand of conservatism that was fully consistent with the trends globally—with George H. W. Bush in America and the fall of the Iron Curtain in Europe. However, he was not always popular with his own party.

Nevertheless, he pursued strong economic policies to reduce the public deficit and control debt while also advancing structural and administrative reforms designed to strengthen the capacities of government. Unfortunately, his government didn't last long, and we didn't get to see what might have come if he had served for five or six years.

Kyriakos Mitsotakis's election in 2019 was considered a landslide in terms of Greek politics, with New Democracy winning 40 percent of the votes and securing a majority of 158 seats in the 300-member parliament. I had not been in Greece since his election, and I was looking forward to meeting him again after some years. I had been with Partners Group since 2013, when I left the IIF and became Executive Vice Chairman of the Board and also Chairman of the Americas for Europe's largest private markets investment firm. I shifted gears in 2019 to become Chairman of the US Board and an Advisory Partner of the firm and was still involved with the firm on a global basis when I arrived in Athens. We had recently made a €1 billion investment in a Greek pharmaceutical firm named Pharmathen, and I was looking forward to introducing the Chairman (Lead Director as we call them) and the CEO of the firm to Mitsotakis.

When we arrived at our hotel—we stayed at the Grande Bretagne once again—I had a quick meeting, then met my wife for a drink at the rooftop bar. I found that my admiration for the Acropolis, the Parthenon, and the Erechtheion had not dimmed. Just as the Greek economy had been battered over the last decade, so the Acropolis had been battered over the centuries. Worse than battered, of course, since, as mentioned earlier, much of the Parthenon had been blown sky high by the Venetians with the support of German mercenaries in 1687. The Parthenon has, in fact, suffered many other indignities, including plunder by Germanic tribes or Visigoths in 396 AD, the removal of some of its most precious sculptures by Lord Elgin in 1801, and occupation by the Germans during World War II. Its use has also evolved over the ages, from its initial purpose as a temple honoring Athena and site of the Delian League's treasury to its use as a Christian Church under Roman Emperor Theodosius between 389 and 391 AD. It yet again shifted from a Greek Orthodox cathedral to a Roman Catholic church after the Fourth Crusade of 1204, and even became a mosque under the Ottoman Turks soon after 1458.

None of this has changed the fact that, as Joan Breton Connelly has written, the Parthenon serves as "both magnet and mirror. We are drawn to it. We see ourselves in it, and we appropriate it in our own terms . . . What is clear is that the Parthenon matters. Across cultures and centuries, its enduring aura has elicited awe, adulation, and superlatives." An Irish artist once described the Parthenon as "the most unrivaled triumph of sculpture and architecture."[2] While I am certainly in no position to validate such claims, what I do know is that it is an architectural wonder. As has only recently been grasped, the technical excellence was astounding. Bruce Clark can describe this better than I can: "All the lines look perfectly straight because of cleverly executed illusions. The floor of the temple appears flat but in fact it swells upwards. The columns slope inwards and they bulge in the middle."[3]

All that, and we haven't even gotten to the brightly colored friezes, many of which now reside, regrettably, in the British Museum. They apparently capture highlights of a Panathenaic festival that was carried out every four years. What exactly was in the mind of Pericles, the mastermind behind the Parthenon, and the sculptor Phidias? Although the Parthenon was only part of a larger construction plan involving many new buildings in Athens, it is the Parthenon that captured the imagination of Athens when it was completed in 432 BC, the entire Delian League soon thereafter, and the Western world over the ensuing centuries.

During my weeklong visit to Greece, Peixin and I were celebrating our nineteenth wedding anniversary. As we looked out over the Plaka to the Acropolis and Parthenon on April 5, we decided we would go to the site on the twelfth, the day of our anniversary. It was the first time we had been on the rock in many years, and we wanted to revisit it with the benefit of a professional tour guide. During my first visit there in 1970, one was able to scamper around the site with no constraints. One could climb on any part of the Parthenon, hoist oneself into the Erechtheion and wander wherever our gaze and our feet would take us. I toured it with two fellow naval officers, Bob Casteel and David Eckstrom, and we thoroughly enjoyed and exhausted ourselves that day. Only a few years later, rails and other protections were installed, sensibly so. But I can still recall the joy of touching the columns as we

Peixin on our anniversary in Athens on April 12, 2022, with the luminous backdrop of the Acropolis at sunset. Photo courtesy of the author.

inspected them and putting our hands on the feet of the Caryatids, the beautiful "Maidens of Athens."

My visit with Peixin on April 12 was quite different. We yearned to understand better how this creation came about, and we first visited the

Acropolis Museum, the beautiful museum designed to protect the rock's most precious art and sculptures (there had been museums there as far back as 1874, but this one was only opened in 2009).

From a distance, the Acropolis is awe-inspiring. Up close, it is jaw-dropping. Are the Acropolis and its wondrous architectural gems still somehow relevant for sorting through Greece's sovereign debt problem of the early twenty-first century? Although I had no clear answer to that question, it bears reflection. It resonates across the ages that democracy is embedded in our Western culture; democracy is deep in not only our shared history, but in our DNA. On a regional basis, the European Community today, supplemented by NATO, is a modern variation of the Delian League, which operated during the golden era of Greece. On a global scale, the Western alliance and the institutions built out of the destruction wrought by two world wars in the twentieth century—especially the UN, the IMF, the World Bank, and world trade organizations—are instruments to preserve the fabric of modern democracy and economic opportunity. We should not forget that Athens during the time of Pericles was not just an unprecedented democracy; it was a very successful, thriving, prosperous economy. As Azoulay recounted, "the fact is, in the fifth century, the democratic city experienced a phase of extraordinary prosperity."[4] Piraeus became a major seaport, and Greece's coins became the coin of the Greek world. Athens had a system of well-enforced laws, and, as Clark describes it, "an inner moral compass."[5] Remarkably, Pericles took a certain attitude toward family finance, which pervaded his approach toward managing Athens—no debt. Imagine!

Of course, we know that Athens of the fifth century BC was not just a thriving democracy and an expanding economy; it was a time of literature, theater, historians, philosophers, and remarkable naval prowess. Socrates, Plato, and Aristotle all came onto the scene in the fifth and fourth centuries BC and left their indelible mark, not only on philosophy, but on how we see ourselves. The older I become, the more I realize the wisdom in Socrates's famous statement "The only true wisdom is in knowing you know nothing." Or "education is the kindling of a flame, not the filling of a vessel."

The playwrights of Athens in the fifth and fourth centuries BC were no slouches either. Aeschylus founded the concept of theatrical tragedy, and the dramatists Sophocles and Euripides wrote plays that are still performed today. On the military front, the battles of Marathon, Thermopylae, and Salamis were arguably among the most consequential military battles in history—certainly for the preservation of democracy, which has never been a favored form of government for the Persians of old or the Iranians of today. Nineteenth-century philosopher John Stuart Mill characterized the importance of Marathon as follows: "The Battle of Marathon, even as an event in English history, is more important than the Battle of Hastings (which of course led to the Norman conquest of England). If the issue of that day had been different, the Britons and the Saxons might still have been wandering in the woods."[6] Coming from one of Britain's most highly regarded thinkers (a statue of him adorns Victoria Embankment), you would have thought this could have helped convince the British to return the Elgin marbles. Still, they have not been—at least not yet.

None of this would have happened, of course, without the military genius and courage of Leonidas and Themistocles. And finally, one cannot fail to mention the great Greek historians of this very rare era— Herodotus, Thucydides, and Xenophon. It is through Herodotus, considered by some to be the Father of History, that we know so much about the Greco-Persian wars, since he too made his contributions to Western culture during the fifth century. Thucydides came along soon after Herodotus and laid his claim as the Father of Scientific (or impartial) History. There followed Xenophon's accounts of his military adventures (he had one of the largest armies of his time, "The 10,000"), along with his dialogues with Socrates.

In fact, it is rather astounding to realize that many of these exceptional leaders of Greece in the fifth century BC made diverse contributions to their society. Historians cannot quite figure out, for example, whether Xenophon should be considered a general, or historian, or a philosopher. All of the above? Socrates himself was a hoplite, one of the many citizen soldiers of Athens. Bettany Hughes, in her fascinating book *The Hemlock Cup*, states, rather astoundingly to me, "Socrates' skill with a stabbing sword and an outsize hoplon shield would have been as important to his fellow citizens as any cleverness with philosophical words."[7] Think about that for a moment.

Pericles, one of the great statesman of his time, was a highly skilled orator and remarkable politician who was elected and reelected at least fifteen times to the Greek "strategos," the council that commanded the Athenian army (perhaps vaguely analogous to the National Security Council in the US today, except with more authority, since there was no standing commander-in-chief). The concept of the Renaissance man seems to have been developed in Italy during the Renaissance, but somehow the Greeks seemed to personify it some two millennia earlier.

The fact is that when we reflect on Greece's history, we are left with two competing narratives: the wondrous history of Periclean Greece, and the disorderly instability and ongoing travails that have characterized much of Greece's modern history. These narratives are not just competing; they are in many aspects contradictory and puzzling. How do we reconcile the two, and what do we do about the Ottoman period, which David Brewer refers to as "the hidden centuries?"[8]

At this point the reader may politely ask, fine, we appreciate the brief tour of classical Greece, but what does this have to do with modern Greece's debt problems? Only the most distinguished historians could try to answer that question, but it is certainly not irrelevant to argue that the world has never seen a century as impactful on today's modern culture and systems of governance as fifth-century Greece. Does that not earn Greece at least a small benefit of the doubt when coping with a problem that was only partly of their making? Did the leaders of Europe ever for a moment consider this?

My first reaction when I arrived in Athens on April 5, 2022, was decidedly mixed. On the way in from the airport, I noticed much more activity on the streets than I recalled from my visit a few years prior. Did this signal that the economy was on the mend? I also noticed, unfortunately, that the explosion of graffiti from the crisis period was still evident on many walls and sidewalks. It rarely looked artistic, but instead served as an ugly reminder of what Greece had gone through.

The room in the Grande Bretagne brought back memories: the dark wooden furniture, the elegant mirrors, the old-fashioned television, the sketch on the wall of a Greek urn, the ancient chandelier. The view from the window brought back two other memories: the permanence of the Acropolis, always reassuring, and the surprisingly perpetual state of demonstrations in Syntagma Square. Perhaps they have never stopped since 2012. This time, however, it was a rather small crowd, trying to rally the troops with a very loud megaphone. I soon realized that at another part of the square there was a competing demonstration, with an equally loud megaphone. And someone, somewhere, on the square was playing Greek music. None of it seemed terribly menacing, especially compared to the demonstrations I'd witnessed a decade ago. A good sign? Too early to tell.

That night Peixin and I had dinner with George Papandreou. He had chosen a neighborhood seafood restaurant named Little Kitty, not far from his home. A casual seafood restaurant with a large window at the counter displaying fresh fish, common in Greek taverns, it had an inviting atmosphere. The proprietor immediately recognized that we were George's guests and quickly ushered us to a quiet corner table away from other guests. Peixin warned me when we left the hotel that I could be overdressed in my suit and tie, and when George arrived in his casual sweater, her look confirmed it.

George was, as always, courtly and urbane. I had always considered him a composed person, even in the midst of pressure. It had been quite some time since we'd met, and we began to reminisce. He recalled the moment in late spring 2010 when he presented a keynote address to the IIF Spring Membership Meeting in Vienna, Austria. I had, at first, some difficulty taking my mind back to that moment. While it had only been a dozen years, it seemed like a lifetime ago. Then it gradually came into view: George standing at the podium, speaking convincingly of the economic reforms he was putting into place. Joe Ackermann, Chairman of the Board of the IIF, stating that he had been skeptical, but he was now inclined to believe that Greece would, in fact, turn the corner. All of us in the audience standing and applauding Papandreou, sharing Joe's optimism. "Charles, it was probably the best moment of my time as Prime Minister," he said with a wistful look on his face.

Alas, Greece was not able to turn the corner. This was before Deauville, before things slipped on the reform program. It was simply not to be.

But George is not a bitter man. He has lost his hair, but has a beard to compensate, and he still has a warm smile, a warmth Peixin and I both reciprocated. I had a question that had been lurking in my mind for a decade. I decided to broach the topic.

"George, I have never fully understood why you launched the referendum. We had just reached agreement on a historic restructuring and reduction of your debt. Why take that action?"

"I had no choice, Charles. The reaction to the agreement throughout Greece was intense—full of anger. We had a very thin majority in parliament, and I thought we could win and strengthen our position."

I looked at my glass of wine and wondered how the world of Greece would have been if he had not launched a referendum.

We moved on. A colleague of his had joined us for dinner, and I was impressed with his expertise on the internet. He had served in the government during the Papandreou administration to bring the IT structure of the government into the twenty-first century. A tough job.

I had two more questions that had been haunting me since I read *Democracy at Gunpoint*, the autobiographical book written by George's father, Andreas, about the coup of 1967 in Greece.

"Was the US involved in the coup that overthrew the government?"

"I'm afraid so, Charles," he responded resignedly, without the anger that his father would have likely displayed. "The evidence is quite clear that the CIA was involved." I did not want to believe it. When does idealism become naivety? Naive at my age? It happens. As a young naval officer serving in Greece in 1972, I could not conceive of it. As an older American citizen working to support a restoration of the Greek economy, I still did not want to believe it.

"Were you on the balcony when your father was captured by the junta?"

"Yes, I was fifteen and trying to hide in the dark corner of the balcony. But they spotted me and put a gun to my head. I think it is the only reason my father surrendered."

George spoke of it rather casually over dinner, but I imagine he was far from relaxed at the time. It was a moment that drew the curtain on democracy in Greece for seven years. The family was eventually exiled to Canada, where his father wrote his book. The coup also provided some of the impetus that would later propel Andreas Papandreou to the role of Prime Minister in 1981, a post he was to hold for eleven out of the next fifteen years. In the process, PASOK did a lot of damage to the fabric of Greek governance and ossified the private economy further.

We started talking about our times working together and agreed that Deauville had been a costly mistake.

Finally, we turned to Greece today. He told me that he had a new partner, a lady from the Netherlands, and a new party, Movement for

Change, which had brought him back to the parliament. Finally, we talked about the Mitsotakis government.

"How do you think he is doing, George?" I asked. "It certainly looks encouraging to me."

"I agree," he replied, somewhat to my surprise. "He has done a good job with the economy so far and is in a relatively strong position politically after those disastrous years of SYRIZA."

It seemed like a good note on which to conclude our dinner. As we walked out, his bodyguards reappeared, and George walked slowly into the night. He seemed like a man at peace, perhaps happy not to be carrying the burden of leading anymore.

The next day was full of business meetings with companies my firm was considering as possible acquisition targets as well as with bankers, some of whom I had worked closely with during the height of the crisis. Two of my closest associates during those dark days, Fokion Karavias of Eurobank and Paul Mylonas of the National Bank of Greece, had ascended to the helm of their respective banks, and I was pleased for them. Even in the midst of the turmoil of 2011 and 2012, it was evident that they were very competent bankers. They both were in buoyant spirits despite the difficulties that continued to bedevil aspects of the financial sector. The consensus was that the economy was recovering, and that the Mitsotakis government had brought a sorely needed boost of confidence. Investment capital was slowly returning to the economy, both from domestic sources as well as foreign. Most importantly, economic reforms were being put into place by a committed government. Karavias and Mylonas offered that while the overall government debt-to-GDP ratio was around 190%, miles above the target of 120% that the IMF had insisted upon in 2011, the markets were taking a relatively benign view of this, as was the IMF. The dramatic interest rate reductions on the rescheduled debt agreed as part of our final package in 2012 were now finally beginning to have their positive effect on Greek creditworthiness and the Greek economy as a whole. Greek bond yields had dropped dramatically since the height of the crisis—when they were near 30%—and had further dropped sharply on the election of Mitsotakis in July 2019. At the end of 2021 they were all the way down to 1% before inflationary pressures in the Eurozone began to push up interest rates in 2022.

The bankers were concerned, however, about the lack of resolution of NPLs on the books of many companies, both private and publicly owned. The NPLs had been largely cleared off the banks' balance sheets, but in many cases the debtors were still saddled with the debt, both undermining their capacity to participate in the economic recovery and to clear their own balance sheets. Furthermore, one view that I heard in regard to some of the state-owned enterprises was that the government did not want to put them through bankruptcy and deal with the subsequent job losses.

It appeared that finally the credit was flowing from the banking system to the real economy, but mainly to the top quality borrowers in the system. Unfortunately, many small- and medium-size enterprises (SME) were generally still not in a position to obtain credit, a common problem throughout much of the Eurozone. Finally, even though the banks have been recapitalized, there remained issues regarding the quality of the capital. Despite all of these questions and concerns, I had not seen the bankers in such an overall positive frame of mind since the early 2000s.

I also had an insightful exchange over dinner with Spyros Filaretos, one of the most capable bankers I had ever met in Greece. Like the others, he had been intimately involved in the debt restructuring, always speaking on behalf of the Greek bankers but also acutely aware of the regional and global realities. The former Chairman of Alpha Bank, Yannis Costopoulos, who passed away in 2021, had relied heavily on Spyros, who had become the general manager at Alpha responsible for growth and innovation, and was now leading the bank's charge into the digital world. Spyros was equally bullish on both the government and the economic outlook, but when I pressed him about the SME credit problem, he had a story to share. While on vacation in the summer of 2021, he was approached by a restaurateur. It was a very successful taverna, but the owner had not been able to get a loan from Alpha Bank. Spyros assured the businessman that he would look into it. When he got back to the office, he asked for the loan application. It took no time to spot the problem: the taverna owner had reported only €1000 as income during the preceding year. Some habits obviously die hard in Greece.

During my visit I studied the economic data to see if it validated the improved economic indications. For the most part, it did. Growth had been an impressive 8.3 percent in 2021 as exports, capital formation, and private consumption all surged following the COVID-19–induced contraction of 9% in 2020. Tourism rebounded, as did investments in machinery and equipment, one of the keys to sustained growth. The unemployment rate fell to 12.7%, the lowest since early 2011. Even though this was well above the Euro Area average of 6.6%, it had dramatically improved from the 25% level of 2012. Furthermore, as mentioned earlier, Greece also managed to reestablish access to the global capital markets. While this had actually begun toward the end of the SYRIZA regime, the access was very fragile at that time. In July 2017, Greece raised €3 billion in a five-year bond issue. But roughly half of that issue involved the swap of previously issued debt with holders who were enticed by an extra €40 in payment to make the exchange. The bonds were priced at a yield of 4.625. The markets were then quite hesitant following the damage done to Greece's credibility in 2015 and 2016 by the brinkmanship of Prime Minister Tsipras and his Finance Minister, Yanis Varoufakis.[9] But by April 2021, Greece had firmly reestablished itself in global bond markets, and after a sovereign credit rating upgrade by Standard and Poor's to BB+ from BB, only one notch below investment grade, Greece was able to raise €1.5 billion 7-year money at a yield of 2.4%. Despite Greece's continued high debt-to-GDP ratio hovering at 193%, the tone of the IMF's assessment of debt sustainability was light years away from the assessments of 2011 and 2012. What a difference a decade can make. Instead of the rigid orthodoxy that a certain ratio eight years into the future deficit was the alpha and omega of debt sustainability analysis, the IMF Staff Report of May 23, 2022, took a much more pragmatic and analytical view: "Public debt is expected to decline and roll over risks are manageable over the medium-term. The debt-to-GDP ratio is expected to drop below the pre-pandemic levels by 2022, reflecting robust growth, fiscal adjustment, and higher inflation."

On the fiscal front, Mitsotakis's government had consolidated the deficit in 2022, after the unwinding of pandemic-related fiscal exposure, and appeared to be on track for a major reduction in the primary deficit from 5% in 2021, to 2% in 2022. This is also a reflection of Greece's upward economic growth: it is always easier to trim a deficit in a growing economy. The IMF staff's largely sensible recommendations for fiscal policy included a "gradual, growth friendly but credible fiscal adjustment over the medium term."[10]

On the structural front, as mentioned in the previous chapter, the Mitsotakis government has implemented a slew of measures to increase the competitiveness of the economy. One of the most impressive—and most far reaching—has been the digitalization of government service. Mitsotakis had served for two years in the cabinet of Antonis Samaras as the Minister of Administrative Reform, and in that capacity may well have had a taste of the depth of inefficiency in some parts of Greece's bureaucracy. Even before his election, he apparently planned a major digitalization initiative. The day following his election, he announced the creation of a Ministry of Digital Governance and appointed an MIT-educated computer and political scientist as the Minister. As Minister of State and Digital Governance, Kyriakos Pierrakakis has made a real difference in the lives of ordinary Greek citizens by digitalizing citizen access to government services and creating a platform for digital transactions with the government. Throughout my weeklong visit to Greece, I heard positive comments about the new system from the taxi driver in Delphi to the businessman in Athens. It has the potential to assist in the transformation of Greece's historically weak, corrupt, and inefficient provisions of public services, but it is still much too early to declare victory.

Structural progress has been made in many other areas over the last three years. Greece launched its Recovery and Resilience Plan in the summer of 2021 and took advantage of over €18 billion of EU loans and grants to fund numerous reform projects. Some were aimed at decarbonization; some at modernizing the labor market with vocational training and investment in healthcare. Others were directed at the sorely needed area of improving the business environment and streamlining the regulatory framework.

As with the digital initiative, it is premature to draw conclusions. It will most likely take at least a full generation of consistent reform and stabilization to put Greece on a path for sustainable economic competitiveness and recovery from the lost decade of 2008–2018.

I also had the occasion during my stay in Athens to review the economic situation with Lucas Papademos. We had lunch early in my visit, and I found him nearly fully absorbed in his work at the Academy of Athens, a prestigious organization dedicated to scientific research and the cultivation of the humanities and fine arts. The Academy was founded only a century ago, but its roots go back to Plato's Academy. Around 386 BC, Plato established a sanctuary for study, discourse, and a lively exchange of views on thorny issues.[11] Astonishingly, Plato's Academy lasted nearly 1,000 years until it was shut down by the Christians. The approach of Plato—centered around civilized dialogue to debate various issues—actually seemed rather well suited for Lucas. Perhaps had he been born two and a half millennia ago, he would have been a philosopher rather than an economist and central banker.

Papademos had become President of the Academy and was involved in guiding the research and other key activities there. Still, he found time for his economic analysis, which he continues to enjoy. Lucas considered that the ECB was trying to do "too much," and consequently allowed inflation to persist at very high levels as supply chain problems and energy prices put considerable momentum into rising prices. On the home front, he was encouraged by the government's policy thrust and overall orientation to attracting foreign investment and enhancing the role of the private sector. He was also complimentary of the digital initiative. However, he cautioned on four fronts: the financial sector still needed strengthening to ensure that credit moved more readily into the economy, and in order for that to happen, non-performing loans needed more complete resolution; despite solid fiscal performance anticipated this year, the deficit and debt still needed continual discipline; it will be imperative that all parties let go of their old habits of clientelism and corruption; and the Greek people must visibly see new standards by the politicians. I listened carefully to him, as always, but said that while I fully understood his concerns, I had not seen this much economic momentum in a decade, and policies were clearly driving in the right direction.

We reminisced about the intense period during which we had worked together and with others to negotiate the debt restructuring. He was, understandably, quite pleased of having secured agreement both on the debt and on key structural reforms. Some of the latter, he noted, are now paying dividends, such as labor market reforms.

"However," he added, "I was somewhat disappointed, Charles, that the Troika did not give more emphasis to the structural reforms, but rather were focused very heavily on the fiscal agenda."

A few days later I was being interviewed in Delphi as part of the Delphi Economic Programs. I was asked what the keys to solving the

Greek debt crisis had been. I noticed that sitting in the audience in front of me was Papademos. I immediately answered, "Lucas Papademos." Of course, there were many other factors—the willingness of the banks to accept huge losses, the continued financial support of Europe for Greece despite growing misgivings, the willingness of the Greek people to put themselves through an extraordinarily long and deep depression in order to remain in the European Union—these were some of them. But in my view, Papademos was the key final ingredient that enabled Greece to persevere through this tragedy and eventually emerge from it—bloodied but standing. His seven months in office provided the window for the largest debt restructuring in history to be agreed, for crucial reforms to be put in place, and for Greece to transition to another popularly elected government. If Europe had a Citizen of the Year award, it should have been unanimously awarded in 2012 to Dr. Lucas Papademos. Even 2023 or 2024 would not be too late, Brussels.

On one of our last nights in Athens, Lucas and his wife, Shanna Ingram, an accomplished artist from the Netherlands, invited Peixin and me to a restaurant in Piraeus. It brought back memories of pleasant evenings at waterfront tavernas in Piraeus during my Navy days. The area had changed drastically, with sleek modern restaurants serving world-class cuisine. The restaurant Lucas chose was, of course, one of the best in the area and right on the harbor. We discovered that one thing had not changed in the five decades since my first visits to Piraeus—the quality of the seafood. In accordance with Greek custom, we went to the counter and chose our fish from among many choices. It was delicious, and we lingered over dinner as we became engrossed in further conversations regarding the Greek and European economies. I knew that Papademos had become a target of some of the protests during his term in office, as he became the face of austerity to many. What I did not realize was how personal it had been. Both Lucas and Shanna opened up about the reign of terror they faced during those seven months, including frequent death threats. And of course, there was the assassination attempt. On May 25, 2017, a letter bomb sent to him went off in his car, wounding him and his driver. Although the wounds weren't life threatening, Papademos was seriously injured and required surgery. It was shocking to all of us who knew Lucas, a man who had done so much to heal the divides of Greece during the peak of the crisis.

No Greek Prime Minister had been targeted in such a fashion since two attempts on the life of Eleftherios Venizelos in 1920 and 1933. Unsurprisingly, the divisiveness and anger born out of the crisis had apparently not dissipated much five years later, and still one can see and feel signs of it. Talking with someone during my visit about the improved economic outlook, I found a simmering resentment at the severe disruption to his previously successful career. "Yes, things are getting better, but many of us have lost a decade in our lives."

Our dinner with Lucas and Shanna went very late, as we had not yet solved all the problems of Greece and the Eurozone. Nevertheless, Lucas insisted that on our way back to the hotel we go to see the Stavros Niarchos Cultural Center, the relatively new (2017) center funded by the famous shipping magnate's foundation and designed by renowned Italian architect Renzo Piano.

When we arrived, it was cold and windy, with only the moonlight to guide us. Nonetheless, Lucas bounded out of the car with surprising enthusiasm. We walked the length of the canal as he proudly gave us a tour of the exterior of the Center, the Opera Hall, and the new National Library. It was inspiring to see that, despite what he and his fellow Greeks had gone through, Lucas had limitless pride in his country.

During my visit I also had the opportunity to have dinner with Evangelos Venizelos. Over the course of the crisis we occasionally had a challenging relationship. He was not steeped in finance, having been trained as an attorney and served in a remarkable number of ministerial positions in the Greek government. His inclination, therefore, was to see things in geopolitical terms, and when we were negotiating key elements of the restructuring, as described in earlier chapters, he would often respond with florid descriptions of the difficulty of dealing with a German-centric Eurozone. It was frustrating for us at times, receiving that kind of response when we were looking for something like, "Charles, we need a 2% coupon for the first eight years."

Over time, however, we came to respect each other's strengths and perspectives. His expressive oratory often captured the rather absurd diplomatic and political realities of Europe and Greece. Once Papademos arrived on the scene, Venizelos seemed to bear down on the tasks at hand and was a strong partner to Papademos in securing parliamentary support for the reform program, overcoming strong popular and legislative resistance.

Over dinner, we exchanged views about the state of the Greek economy (definitely improving) and the Greek political system—"Mitsotakis is strong, but the next government may have to be a coalition." We discussed the developments in Cannes in November of 2011 when Papandreou arrived with his referendum proposal on the table. "I could not support the call for a referendum, because I could not contemplate leaving the euro," he said with a shake of his head. "This is why I took the position I did when we landed in Athens," referring to his statement that the package approved in Brussels must not be approved. On this, he was absolutely correct—it made no sense to backtrack on the package of support from Europe as well as private creditors, and certainly a decision to leave the euro would have been disastrous for Greece and Europe.

"I became physically sick as a result of Papandreou's call for a referendum," Venizelos said slowly, looking at his plate of food. "At the same time, Charles, Sarkozy's conduct in Cannes was brutal. It was uncivilized. It was atavistic," he said solemnly, choosing his words carefully.

The trip to Delphi by Peixin and me the next day brought back a flood of memories. Who cannot be captured by the mystical history of Delphi? The modern town of Delphi is actually quite dilapidated, the infrastructure primitive, with roads and hotels having missed out on the modernization that swept over much of Greece's touristic areas. As far as I could tell, there were only a few restaurants, and walking the roads or the sidewalks was a hazardous activity.

None of this mattered. The ancient site was as mesmerizing as ever. I had not visited in fifty years, but it all came back. On a beautiful sunny spring day, we took a tour of the ancient site situated in the crevices of the Parnassian mountains, overlooking a sweeping valley. It is not difficult to judge why the ancient Greeks determined this to be the center of their world. Supposedly founded by the god Apollo, Delphi became the site of divine guidance from the Greek gods, as expressed by the Pythia, the women selected to convey the guidance, as "translated by local priests." Under the influence of gaseous vapors emanating from the rocks, the Pythia would often respond to questions with considerable ambiguity, leaving it up to the questioner to make their own interpretation of the divine guidance. A millennium of oracular statements has given us many examples of how the Pythia operated. One of the most famous—and one especially renowned among naval officers—concerns the naval Battle of

Salamis. After having won the Battle of Marathon against the Persians, Athens now had to face them again in the Bay of Salamis. Seeking guidance on how to win yet another battle against the mighty Persians, Athens approached the oracle again. After an apparently unhelpful initial response—"Give up and escape"—the Pythia responded the second time with, "Trust in your wooden walls." There was, predictably, much dispute about what this meant. Some Athenian leaders argued for building a wooden wall around the Acropolis. But Themistocles, who had earlier persuaded Athens to use its silver proceeds to build a fleet of wooden triremes, won the day again with the argument that the oracle's guidance meant they should take to the sea and fight from their wooden triremes. This led to a spectacular victory for Athens, which sent the Persians packing for good.

As we walked through the ruins in 2022, the remains of the temple of Apollo and the Athenian treasury stood out. Both built to honor the gods for the Athenian victory at Marathon, they demonstrate the degree to which fifth-century BC Greece was still enthralled with its Greek gods despite the emergence of philosophers such as Aristotle, Plato, and Socrates. As participants gathered for this Economic Forum in April 2022, I reflected on mankind's continuing search for guidance and wisdom from a power that lies beyond our human capacities.

At this writing in fall of 2022, Europe struggles to find a clear path forward on how to manage the energy crisis that is sweeping over the continent, I wondered how the oracle would respond today. "Gather your wool together" or "search for peace in the east" could be two among many possibilities. One thing is certain—the oracle would have responded with her hallmark ambiguity. In the end, true leaders must figure out a path forward themselves, with or without the benefit of divine guidance. The Delphi Economic Forum, organized impressively by Symeon Tsomokos, an accomplished Greek businessman, was very robust, spanning a wide range of topics regarding the future of the Greek and European economies. I was encouraged to see the commitment of European government, business, and academic leaders debating key issues of the day, all with a sense of optimism about the future of Greece.

The program also had a few global leaders, such as General David Petraeus and Tony Blair, spread among a strong cast of European and Greek leaders. The agenda was heavily focused on strengthening the Greek economy, and there was a sense of momentum in the corridors. It would have been hard to imagine anything like this only a few years earlier.

The key moment of the conference was an interview of Prime Minister Mitsotakis alongside the new head of the OECD, Mr. Mathias Cormann. Although the latter acquitted himself very well (a Belgian-born Aussie who was quite skillful in handling his questions), Mitsotakis stole the show. I have been present for hundreds of speeches and presentations by heads of state and government, but rarely have I seen a leader as knowledgeable about the key economic challenges facing his country. Of course, oratorical skills are no substitute for action, especially in a situation like that of Greece, with so much ground to make up and so many challenges still to be faced. But it was, nevertheless, very impressive, especially when combined with the actions he had already put in place.

Two days earlier I had met Mitsotakis in his office. It was my first time in that office since Antonis Samaras was Prime Minister in 2014. I hardly recognized the waiting room. The drab and dark furniture had been replaced by bright sleek couches, surrounded by modern Greek art. I was joined by two of my colleagues from Partners Group, the Chairman and the CEO of Pharmathen. As mentioned earlier, in July 2021, we had made an investment of €1 billion to take a controlling share of the company. Partners Group has a highly disciplined and conservative investment committee, with a huge amount of due diligence taking place before an investment decision is made. In this case, our investment represented a crucial judgment that with the right opportunity, Greece was becoming an attractive location for foreign investment. The particular strength of this company, which is one of Europe's leading generic pharmaceutical firms, drove the investment, along with the potential to expand and transform the company. The healthcare industry, influenced by demographics in many countries, has been a thematic area of investment focus for Partners Group for some years. We had a successful investment in a US pharmaceutical supply chain solutions firm and were open to other opportunities in the pharmaceutical field. Pharmathen is a leader in research and development in "sustained release" technologies such as slow-release drugs. Finally, the macroeconomic and political environment in Greece had become an asset instead of a hindrance. The Pharmathen CEO is a dynamic group executive named Dimitris Kadis. We were joined in the meeting by Thomas Werner, an experienced German businessman who chairs the Board.

Mitsotakis bounded into the meeting wearing a mask, as was common during the pandemic, but took it off swiftly as he walked toward me. It had been some years since we had last met, when he had served in the cabinet of Samaras, but he did not look any worse for wear. We met in a conference room rather than his private office, since his team wanted to make a presentation. When we greeted one another, I recalled that my first-ever visit to Europe was as a young naval officer setting foot in Soudha Bay, Crete, described in Chapter 2. I had been at sea for over thirty days—two weeks transiting the Atlantic and two and a half weeks more keeping Soviets from interfering in the Jordanian civil war. Soudha Bay is only fifteen minutes from Mitsotakis's hometown of Chania. "I was never so happy in my life to set my feet on land, Kyriakos," I said. He smiled and spoke fondly of Soudha Bay and the surrounding countryside.

Then we quickly got down to business.

"What a pleasure it is to be in this office and not be talking about rescheduling debt, but instead focusing on investments," I said. I introduced my two colleagues and Pharmathen. Mitsotakis was familiar with the company and was pleased to meet the leadership. We discussed Partners Group's plans to make an additional €50 million investment to further deepen Pharmathen's research capacities.

"I would like to ask my colleagues to make a presentation on the investment environment in Greece today, gentlemen," the Prime Minister said. He turned to two senior officials, who took us through an impressive slide deck on the opportunities to invest in Greece, emphasizing the skillful and "cost efficient workforce," the business-friendly environment (still a work in progress), and fast-track procedures for new licensing. They summarized the new development law, which leverages the country's digital transformation. We then discussed the more troublesome macro implications of the Russian invasion of Ukraine, including the energy price surge, as well as the overall inflationary pressures. Despite these looming challenges, Mitsotakis was optimistic. I underscored the need, in this difficult environment, to monitor the fiscal and debt outlook carefully.

"After what we have been through, Charles, I am well aware of the dangers which lurk in these areas," he assured me. We discussed another investment opportunity that Partners Group was considering, and then wrapped up our meeting. As we walked back to our car, Dimitris turned and said, "I was impressed by the Prime Minister's grasp of the need for an attractive investment environment." Thomas Werner, a savvy German businessman with a rather stern countenance, looked back admiringly toward the Prime Minister's office and said, "I wish we had more politicians like that in Germany." I could not help but smile and reflect on the irony of that statement after what Greece had been through over the last decade. I felt like Greece was on the right track, and there was something vaguely floating in the air that made me feel that Europe might at last be coming together.

APPENDICES

BACKGROUND INFORMATION ON THE BRADY PLAN AND ITS POTENTIAL RELEVANCE FOR GREECE

This appendix contains two documents focused on the Brady Plan prepared during the Greek debt negotiations by the Private Sector negotiating team. The first document ("Experience Under the Brady Plan") provides core information on the countries which engaged in Brady Plan debt restructurings, outlines the key financial elements of the Plan, and highlights two cases: Mexico and Brazil.

The second document ("Greece—Debt Buyback Scheme: Co-Financing Experience under the Brady Plan and Possible Sources of Financing for Greece") explores in more detail how the credit enhancements for the Brady bonds operated and how they were financed. It also contains a brief section speculating on how similar arrangements could be financed for Greece.

EXPERIENCE UNDER THE BRADY PLAN

Overview[1]

As outlined in Chapter 14, the Brady Plan was developed by the US Treasury Department, entailing essentially:

- a restructuring of the outstanding stock of debt with a view to restoring debt sustainability;

- upfront stock of debt and debt service reduction (haircuts);

- the exchange of the remaining debt with new 30-year bonds with credit enhancements in the form of

- rolling interest payment guarantees; and
- the collateralization of the principal repayment at maturity with zero-coupon 30-year US bonds.

It was applied initially to Mexico in 1989, after long negotiations. But once creditors and debtors realized the mutual benefits that could result from Brady Bond deals, similar deals were concluded subsequently in 17 other countries during the period to 1998 (see list of countries below).

Mexico	Sep-89	Ecuador	May-93
Philippines	Aug-89	Jordan	Jun-93
Costa Rica	Nov-89	Bulgaria	Nov-93
Venezuela	Jun-90	Poland	Mar-94
Uruguay	Nov-90	Brazil	Apr-94
Nigeria	Mar-91	Panama	May-95
Argentina	Apr-92	Peru	Oct-95
Bolivia	Mar-93	Vietnam	Mar-98
Dominican Republic	May-93	Cote d'Ivoire	Mar-98

Approximately US$200 billion of Brady Bonds were issued during 1989–98, with more than two-thirds by Mexico, Brazil, Venezuela, and Argentina, with a total debt reduction amounting to around US$60–70 billion, entailing average haircuts of the order of 30–35 percent.

A typical Brady bond debt restructuring agreement included:

- A 30-year discount bond (after the haircut), supported by a zero-coupon bond collateral for principal and a rolling guarantee of 12–18 months of interest and market rates.

- A par bond (with no haircuts) with a below-market interest rate of about 6 percent, with similar collateral.

- A debt-buy-back/or new-money option.

The rationale of offering a menu of options was to accommodate the different needs and preferences of the various creditor banks, given the differentiated legal, regulatory, accounting, and balance sheet exposure circumstances of each creditor. The various options were carefully designed to ensure a comparable treatment/burden sharing by each creditor, while the overall debt relief package provided sufficient debt reduction to the debtor to facilitate the restoration of a sustainable external debt position.

The option of new money was very important in the context of the circumstances faced by debtor countries at the time, whereby there was a need to ensure the full covering of the country's external financing needs consistent with the growth objectives under the adjustment programs pursued by the debtors. The new loans extended by creditors who chose this option did not enjoy any credit enhancements and thus had a greater credit risk than the discount bonds and the par bonds, and, together with a judicious choice of the coupon on these loans, insured broadly comparable treatment (contribution) with other creditors.

Mexico (1989)

After lengthy negotiations, the debt reduction deal among the authorities and their bank creditors (with long-term claims amounting to $48.5 billion) included the following menu of options:

- · An exchange of outstanding debt with a new 30-year bond denominated in US dollars after a 35% reduction (haircut) in face value (discount bond), at market related interest rates, with two forms of credit enhancements. The repayment of the principal was collateralized with a zero-coupon 30-year US Treasury bond purchased by Mexico. Interest payments were also collateralized through a rolling 18-month rolling guarantee with cash US dollar deposits at the New York Fed.

- · An exchange of outstanding debt with a 30-year par bond with no principal reduction (no haircuts) at a fixed rate of 6.25 percent (below the prevailing market rate of 10 percent)—implying a NPV reduction of 35 percent—with the same collateral as the discount bond.

- · Provision of new loan financing to Mexico equivalent to 25 percent of the outstanding creditor claims (with no upfront haircut) over three years, with half to be provided during the first year, with no interest or principal collateral and at appropriate interest rates to help ensure comparable treatment.

The financing of the purchase of the US Treasury bonds (with an estimated price of only 5.7 or a discount of 94.3 percent, given the 10 percent market rates) was provided primarily by the IMF, the World Bank, and Japan, in the context of structural adjustment programs supported by the IMF and the World Bank. In parallel, Paris Club official bilateral creditors provided a debt rescheduling.

The debt deal included also a "value recovery mechanism": after the first 7 years, 30 percent of any increase in oil prices (Mexico was a significant oil exporter) above $14 per barrel was to be distributed to bondholders, but if oil prices fell below $10 per barrel, the banks and official lenders were to provide an additional $800 million in lending.

From the menu options, 41 percent of commercial bank creditors selected the discount bond option, 47 percent for the par bond option, and 12 percent the new money option. What made the Mexico Brady bond deal for Mexico possible?

- After a sequence of debt reschedulings —with no debt reduction— and debt equity swaps, the outstanding debt burden remained high and pressure was building for a more definitive solution;

- A limited number of creditors, especially large commercial banks, that by then had made provisions in the balance sheets for possible debt losses (in a major break with past practices and strongly held perceptions that sovereign debtors do not default);

- An innovative US Treasury Secretary who saw the need for change; and

- Major pressures on both bank creditors and the Mexican authorities behind the scenes by the US authorities, the IMF Managing Director, bank regulators, and the willingness of Japan to provide additional financing.

Brazil (1994)

Brazil concluded a Brady bond debt restructuring deal in April 1994, covering $44 billion of obligations to bank creditors. The menu of options included the following instruments:

- Par bond;

- Discount bond;
- Front-loaded interest reduction bond;
- Front-loaded interest reduction with capitalization bond ("C" bond);
- Debt conversion bond; and
- New money

Brazil was able to finance the purchase of the zero-coupon US Treasury bonds and provide interest payment credit enhancement from its own resources, benefiting from a wave of net private capital inflows to Latin America during 1991–93.

Special positive/attractive features of Brady Bonds:

- The broad uniformity of their maturities, terms, and currency denomination made them fairly marketable, allowing creditors to unload their holdings in secondary markets and debtors to buy these claims back at attractive prices over time, well before maturity (and thus avoiding a bunch of maturities).

- The alleviation of the debt burden and the parallel improvement in fundamentals thanks to the successful implementation of structural reform programs have allowed debtor countries to enhance their economic performance and lower the credit risk on their securities. Most debtor countries actually started issuing their own bonds, moving away from the until then traditional syndicated bank loans.

- As a consequence, secondary market prices of Brady Bonds rose quickly after the conclusion of debt reduction operations; by late 1993, Brady Bond prices had risen by 128 percent for Mexico, 109 percent for Venezuela and Brazil, and 408 percent for Argentina, virtually eliminating the country risk premium.

Can Brady Bond debt reduction deals be used by current highly indebted countries?

In principle, yes, but as we learned during the Greek debt negotiations, there are more constraints to overcome:

- With the shift to bond issuance rather than bank loans, the number of bondholders is currently fairly large, which makes it more difficult to forge Brady Bond–like agreements with creditors, especially if account is taken of the complications that could rise from holdout creditors and the absence of collective action clauses.

- Mark-to-market accounting rules and the different accounting treatment of claims held to maturity or available for sale can complicate the impact of any debt deal on the balance sheet of bank and other creditors.

- With the low market interest rates which prevailed until recently, the cost of purchasing zero-coupon 30-year bonds for collateral purposes was substantially higher than at the time of the Brady Plan.

On the positive side, the widely accepted market-friendly and cooperative guidelines which underpin the "Principles for Stable Capital Flows and Fair Debt Restructuring"—emphasizing open dialogue with creditors, transparency, good faith negotiations and non-discrimination among creditors—could facilitate a debt restructuring deal that entails credit enhancements based on a Brady Bond scheme or other schemes.

GREECE—DEBT BUYBACK SCHEME: CO-FINANCING EXPERIENCE UNDER THE BRADY PLAN AND POSSIBLE SOURCES OF FINANCING FOR GREECE

This note summarizes the experience with co-financing of the debt restructuring operations under the Brady Plan.

Brady Bond Experience

As the attached table indicates, the total cost of providing the collateral (credit enhancements for the Brady bonds issued by the 18 countries that restructured their external public debt under the Brady Plan during 1989–98) amounted to $24.3 billion. The bulk of this cost was financed from the countries' own resources (40 percent) and direct earmarked financing from the IMF (20 percent) and the World Bank (18 percent). The remainder was covered mainly by financing from Japan through the

Export-Import Bank (17 percent), and in part by the Inter-American Development Bank (4 percent) and other external sources (2 percent).

COSTS OF FINANCING ENHANCEMENTS FOR BRADY BONDS
millions of US dollars

Country (year of agreement)	IMF	World Bank	Japan EXIM	IDB	Other external	Own resources	Total	Notes
Mexico (1989)	1688.5	2010.0	2050.0	0.0	0.0	1373.6	7122.1	
Philippines (1989 & 1992)	320.0	300.0	500.0	0.0	0.0	346.0	1466.0	(1)
Costa Rica (1989)	0.0	0.0	0.0	0.0	183.0	43.0	226.0	
Venezuela (1990)	880.0	500.0	600.0	0.0	0.0	-306.0	1674.0	
Uruguay (1990)	35.0	65.0	0.0	58.0	0.0	340.0	498.0	(2)
Nigeria (1991)	0.0	0.0	0.0	0.0	0.0	1681.0	1681.0	
Argentina (1992)	986.0	625.0	800.0	475.0	0.0	173.0	3059.0	(3)
Brazil (1992)	0.0	0.0	0.0	0.0	0.0	3447.0	3447.0	
Jordan (1993)	0.0	0.0	0.0	0.0	0.0	147.0	147.0	
Bulgaria (1993)	101.0	125.0	0.0	0.0	0.0	0.0	234.6	(4)
Dominican Republic (1993)	0.0	0.0	0.0	0.0	0.0	201.0	201.0	
Poland (1994)	400.0	400.0	0.0	0.0	0.0	1293.0	2093.0	
Ecuador (1994)	85.0	130.0	73.0	134.0	200.0	116.0	738.0	(5)
Panama (1996)	29.7	30.0	0.0	30.0	0.0	134.0	223.7	
Peru (1997)	223.0	183.0	100.0	233.0	0.0	688.0	1427.0	
Vietnam (1998)	0.0	35.0	0.0	0.0	0.0	19.0	54.0	(6)
Total	**4,748**	**4,403**	**4,123**	**930**	**392**	**9,696**	**24,291**	
(share in total)	*19.5%*	*18.1%*	*17.0%*	*3.8%*	*1.6%*	*39.9%*	*100%*	

(1) Numbers combined from 2 Brady deals
(2) $25mm IMF facility not used
(3) Excludes $700 downpayment from country reserves on past due interest (PDI)
(4) "Other external" funding from Govt. of the Netherlands
(5) "Other external" funding from Andean Reserve Fund (CAF)
(6) $35mm from World Bank were credits under the IDA program

Japan's contribution was instrumental for the success of the Brady Bond debt restructuring by the first country—Mexico—that applied the Brady Plan. This contribution amounted to $2 billion, or 28.2 percent of Mexico's total debt restructuring cost, and was provided in the form of co-financing roughly equally divided under the IMF- and World Bank–supported programs. The terms of this co-financing, according to information provided by the Mexican authorities, went beyond the normal financing terms under IMF and World Bank adjustment programs. In particular, the Japanese co-financing with the IMF amounted to $1 billion and had more generous repayment terms than the standard IMF terms under the EFF (10-year maturity with 4½ years of grace at floating interest rates based on the SDR rate plus a small margin). In particular, the financing from Japan had a 13-year maturity with 3 years of grace, and an interest rate linked to the Japanese Long-Term Prime Lending

Rate (LTPLR) minus 20 basis points (LTPLR in November 1989, when the loan was extended, amounted to 6.2 percent). The Japanese co-financing with the World Bank involved three separate loans for a total sum of about $1 billion and had a maturity of 17 years with 5 years of grace, at a fixed, slightly concessional (relative to market rates at that time) interest rate of 5.8 percent. No information is available at this stage on the financing terms of the co-financing by Japan and the other cases of Brady Bond countries, but the amounts involved were fairly modest in comparison to Mexico.

STRATEGIC STATEMENTS BY THE PRIVATE CREDITORS AND THE OFFICIAL SECTOR ON GREECE

This appendix contains two documents prepared as the first phase of negotiations gathered momentum. The first document, "IIF Task Force on Greece White Paper," outlines our overall perspective on the challenges faced by Greece, the private creditors, and the official creditors in early June 2011. It underscores the commitment that was developing among the private creditors to find a balanced approach that took account of the needs of all parties.

The second document, "Statement by the Eurogroup of July 11, 2011," was, in effect, the official sector's response to the White Paper.

IIF TASK FORCE ON GREECE
White Paper
July 10, 2011

Recent market developments have complicated the policy challenges of addressing Greece's debt problem. European government bond markets have reacted negatively to the lack of firm and comprehensive commitments by Euro Area member states to addressing the expanding crisis. Potential impairment losses on Greek government bonds increase the risk of contagion to other peripheral government bond holdings and the urgent need for a comprehensive and credible program to restore market confidence.

Financial markets are now expecting a comprehensive approach consisting of:

i. a clear and jointly endorsed commitment by Euro Area member States and the IMF to provide adequate liquidity with the voluntary support of the private sector for a sufficient period of time to allow reforms to take hold and the fiscal adjustment to deliver results; and

ii. a more comprehensive and durable solution to improve Greek debt sustainability and growth prospects while mitigating spillover effects on other countries and possible financial markets disruptions.

Market deterioration in the last few days underscores the fact that a comprehensive approach is needed immediately to contain contagion and avoid a global financial crisis.

Recent adverse developments

The key recent adverse developments include:

· Mounting concern following the public announcement by S&P that an assignment of Selective Default (SD) for Greece was fairly likely with any restructuring transaction. The concern focuses not so much on the rating itself, but on the implications of an SD rating for the ECB's collateral policies with regards to Greek government bonds;

· A growing sense (while not final) in the accounting and auditing community that holdings of Greek government bonds by banks, insurance companies and other investors at end-June 2011 may be wholly or partially impaired in the financial statements scheduled to be issued starting the third week of July for a number of financial institutions reporting under IFRS. Such impairment would require them to recognize losses in their second-quarter income statements. In many European jurisdictions these losses would impact such institutions' regulatory capital position which is intrinsically based on the IFRS accounting results. This in itself could lead to contagion depending on how markets assess the overall approach to Greece. The decision on impairments will need to be taken very soon;

- Escalating market concerns about the possible impact on exposures to Greece and other Euro Area peripheral countries have disrupted access to short-term funding and the ability of European banks to raise new capital. For example, recently several capital-raising exercises have been postponed. The longer this lasts, the more severe will be the risk of funding difficulty, which could negatively impact global markets;

- Increasing anxiety by non-European investors about the inability of Euro Area member states to act swiftly and comprehensively to resolve the Greek sovereign debt crisis has led to decisions not to continue rolling over maturing positions in Euro Area government bonds as well as maturing loans to EU financial institutions;

- The release of the results of the EBA bank stress test, scheduled for July 15, may exacerbate market concerns about potential losses on other Euro Area sovereign bonds.

Commitment of the private sector

Against this background, the private sector financial community confirms its commitment to work closely with the Euro Area public sector, the IMF, and other international financial institutions as well as the Greek authorities in the context of a comprehensive approach to contribute on a voluntary basis with broad-based creditor participation in order to help cover Greece's short-term funding gap and address the underlying debt sustainability concerns over the long term. These initiatives would need to be combined with the reinforced efforts by the Greek authorities to implement effectively the broad range of fiscal and structural reforms envisaged under their adjustment program so as to achieve the targeted further improvements in the primary budget balance and improve the underlying efficiency of the economy.

Addressing immediate contagion risk

It is crucial that the Euro Area member states and the IMF clearly commit to sufficient funding for Greece, with the voluntary support of the private sector, to cover its refinancing needs for the next three years. Equally important is a commitment to work with the private sector to reduce Greece's debt burden. There needs to be a credible statement by the Euro Area authorities, alongside that from the private sector, squarely addressing both aspects of Greece's debt problem. Otherwise, contagion impacts will likely accelerate for Euro Area government bond markets as well as financing and capital raising for European banks.

To complement these funding commitments, it is essential that the ECB clarifies as soon as possible its response to the potential assignment of Selective Default by credit rating agencies and its approach toward ensuring the funding needs of affected financial institutions, especially in Greece. The absence of such clarity is clearly contributing to market anxiety and contagion. It is critical to remove all uncertainties about the ECB collateral policy so as to help reduce the existing fragility in the Euro Area banking system and foster financial stability.

In addition, public and private sector efforts should firmly aid to avoid a Credit Event as divined by ISDA, which would have damaging effects on confidence and financial stability across the Euro Area. It is our understanding that the various options outlined in this paper, if implemented on a voluntary basis, would not trigger a Credit Event as defined by ISDA.

Comprehensive and credible program

The early announcement of a comprehensive and credible program to address not only Greece's short-term funding needs but also long-term debt sustainability would go some way to alleviate the pressures in bank funding and ease the contagion risks for other Euro Area countries. This could allow the ECB to consider using its Securities Markets Program as needed—this would be very reassuring to market participants as the new Greek program takes hold. In addition, this could set the stage for increased participation in European sovereign and private sector financial debt markets by non-European central banks, Sovereign Wealth Funds, and other investors. This is very important as a very large portion of Euro Area sovereign debt is held by these investors.

The plan would need to be large and meaningful, reducing Greece's debt burden and returning it to cost-effective market funding as well as improving its long-term sustainability. This could in turn alleviate the burden on Euro Area public sector financing for Greece. Plans focused solely on covering Greece's financing needs without debt reduction will not work at this stage to stabilize markets and reverse contagion.

The early adoption of such a comprehensive and credible program would reassure investors, rating agencies, accountants, and regulators of the prospects for a timely discharge of Greece's debt service obligations in the years ahead. It would help to resolve some of the uncertainties around accounting judgements, although there can be no guarantee that any program will be able to provide sufficient justification to avoid the recognition of impairment losses entirely. Whatever the outcome of the accounting judgements on Greek bonds, such a comprehensive plan would help contain contagion to other Euro Area sovereign bond markets.

Public Sector/Private Sector Partnership

To address these objectives, the private investor community is committed to exploring, on an urgent basis and in close collaboration with the official sector, a menu of options for voluntary private sector involvement that would allow for the mobilization of significant financing support for Greece over the coming years, while simultaneously helping to lower Greece's public debt burden to more sustainable levels.

Here we would like to stress that this menu of options need not involve additional European taxpayer resources over and above the levels which otherwise could be required under the present official strategy in the years ahead. Instead, these options would leverage public resources through a more efficient and flexible use of EU/IMF funds, possibly complemented by other international official sources, to help catalyze private resources and promote Greece's early renewed capital market access, thereby reducing the need for official funding in the medium term.

More concretely, the integrated approach will need to offer multiple options in order to encourage maximum private sector involvement. We are currently developing structures for a debt extension, a debt exchange, and a tender offer which should be considered with options for pure Greek risk and credit-enhanced alternatives (please see the Annex for more details). These transactions, taken together, will provide funding at interest rates that are below current market levels in order to reduce the debt service burden and will entail a significant extension of maturities to promote a more sustainable debt profile for Greece.

To balance the competing objectives of interest rates that Greece could afford with the need to obtain extensive voluntary investor participation that does not trigger a CDS Credit Event or increase the likelihood of impairment means that credit enhancements are essential for the new instruments. Credit enhancements, such as the collateralization of principal and possibly interest payments, could be funded through a combination of sources, including re-programmed official support (perhaps channeled through the EFSF). Contingent and other funding techniques could be explored to make the use of credit enhancement more effective.

Credit enhancement can also provide some degree of "leverage" of the resources placed at the EU/IMF disposal as opposed to upfront disbursements of cash to redeem maturing bonds at par. Further leverage can be gained through the use of partial credit enhancements by EFSF and other public bodies issuing collateral without Lisbon Treaty implications.

Well-structured credit enhancements could allow private investors to remain engaged in Greece long term. As an illustration, if we target the 2011-2019 maturities (involving about €180 billion of outstanding bonds) with transactions outlined above, there is a potential of spontaneous private sector financing perhaps early in this time frame, with an amount much greater than that expected by the official sector from the private sector debt restructuring. In other words, credit enhancements will likely lead to greater levels of private sector commitment. There is a multiplier effect with this commitment which compares favorably to current public sector thinking.

Debt reduction schemes

These options will need to be complemented with other approaches that allow for a reduction in Greece's nominal stock of debt—without such reduction there would be no alleviation of its debt burden and potential calls for additional support from European taxpayers. Actions to this end would include a menu of debt reduction options—not only involving the exchange at a discount of outstanding bonds with credit-enhanced new instruments but also cash buybacks.

A Debt Buyback Facility (DBF) could be established by the Greek authorities with the objective of taking advantage of the existing large discounts on Greek debt in the secondary market. Under the DBF, Greece could target the buyback on a voluntary basis of individual bond issues with large secondary market discounts (ranging at present from 10 percent for near term maturities to over 50 percent for longer-dated paper) using various techniques, such as open-market purchases, special tenders and negotiated deals with individual investors at market-related prices.

The debt buyback operations could achieve a meaningful amount, comprising privatization proceeds over and above the needs of the revised program for the period ahead, earmarked IMF resources and co-financing under the IMF-supported program by non-European countries on standard low interest and 10-year IMF repayment terms. Depending on the average discount, the net debt reduction from such buyback and discounted exchanges could be significant.

The various options outlined above are still under review and could be structured under broadly equivalent economic terms such that different private sector investors voluntarily participate in one or more of the options according to their own individual preferences while maintaining a level playing field taking into account types of investors, accounting constraints, and regulatory issues. Options will be developed that are workable for the Greek banks.

Conclusion

In conclusion, the private financial community is committed to working closely with the Euro Area official sector and the Greek authorities to develop an appropriate and convincing strategy for addressing Greece's debt difficulties and mitigating contagion risks.

As regards timing, while recognizing that a fully articulated new EU/IMF-supported 3-year program for Greece would not be finalized before end-September, it is essential that Euro Area member states and the IMF act in the coming days to avoid market developments spinning out of control and risk contagion accelerating. Concretely, while a definitive and comprehensive plan may take some weeks to develop and implement, an announcement following the July 11 Euro Area Finance Ministers' meeting of an approach outlined above followed by intensive technical discussion would calm markets and lay the basis for market stability and recovery.

We look forward to a positive response to this need by the Euro Area Finance Ministers as well as a timely clarification of the ECB policy approach to the acceptance of Greek government bonds as collateral should a Selective Default rating be announced by a rating agency. The private sector financial community stands ready to play its part.

Such actions as outlined above would go some distance toward mitigating the adverse impact on financial institutions and preserving the financial stability in the Euro Area, while at the same time minimizing the possible need for additional public sector support for Greece and affected financial institutions.

ANNEX
Potential Transaction Structures

The IIF has organized a large number of financial markets participants to work on developing a number of structural alternatives to be included in any voluntary restructuring program. The working groups on all aspects of a future restructuring program are fully staffed by a broad group of private sector bank and insurance investors, legal specialists and accounting consultants.

The transaction structure being considered falls into three main categories:

1) Transactions which preserve principal value at par – these transactions can be structured as a debt exchange at par, debt extension, or debt substitution (along the lines of the initial French proposal). Investors will retain the principal value of their debt at par but will significantly extend their maturity (30 years) while reducing the interest rate on the new debt. In order to increase investor participation in this type of structure, different forms of credit enhancements, through the collateralization of principal and possibly interest payments, can be used. This credit enhancement would be accompanied by an additional reduction in interest rate on the new debt. The funding of this collateralization could be secured through a combination of sources, including re-programmed official support (perhaps channeled through the EFSF).

2) Transaction which reduces the principal value of Greek debt – these transactions can be structured as a debt exchange below par or debt substitution. Investors will accept a reduction in the principal value of their debt but will receive an interest rate closer to current market levels and will extend their maturity for a shorter period (10-30 years). In order to increase investor participation in this type of structure, different forms of credit enhancements, through the collateralization of principal and possibly interest payments, can be used. This credit enhancement would be accompanied by an additional reduction in principal value on the new debt.

3) Tender offers and other discounted repurchase transactions – the objective of these transactions would be to capture and crystallize the discounted trading prices of outstanding Greek government bonds. By repurchasing this debt at prices below par, Greece will be able to reduce the volume of its outstanding debt and improve, over time, its debt solvency position. Financing for these types of transactions can come from private sector investors, re-programmed official support, IMF resources, and non-European countries through co-financing under IMF-supported programs.

The proposals referenced above are, in most cases, applications of earlier public finance experiences. As a result, technical issues can be addressed promptly and their proposals refined into concrete and actionable exercises in a very short time frame. We look forward to working with your technical teams to further these developments and finalize potential structures for a public-private partnership.

Statement by the Eurogroup of 11 July 2011

Ministers reaffirmed their absolute commitment to safeguard financial stability in the euro area. To this end, Ministers stand ready to adopt further measures that will improve the euro area's systemic capacity to resist contagion risk, including enhancing the flexibility and the scope of the EFSF, lengthening the maturities of the loans, and lowering the interest rates, including through collateral arrangement where appropriate. Proposals to this effect will be presented to Ministers shortly.

Ministers discussed the main parameters of a new multi-annual adjustment program for Greece, which will build on strong commitments to fiscal consolidation, ambitious growth enhancing structural reforms, and a substantial privatization of state assets. Ministers welcomed the reinforcement of monitoring mechanisms of the program of Greece, the nomination of the board of the privatization agency, which comprises two observers representing euro area Member States and the European Commission, and agreed to provide extended technical assistance to Greece. They called upon the Greek government to sustain its ongoing efforts to meet these commitments in full and on time.

Ministers welcomed the decision by the IMF to disburse the latest tranche of financial assistance to Greece, as well as the proposals from the private sector to voluntarily contribute to the financing of a second program, building on the work already underway. The ECB confirmed its position, reaffirmed by its Governing Council last Thursday, that a credit event or selective default should be avoided.

While the responsibility for resolving the crisis in Greece lies primarily with Greece, Ministers recognized the need for a broader and more forward-looking policy response to assist the government in its efforts to bolster debt sustainability and thereby safeguard financial stability in the euro area.

In this context, Ministers have tasked the Eurogroup Working Group to propose measures to reinforce the current policy response to the crisis in Greece. The Eurogroup Working Group will notably explore the modalities for financing a new multi-annual adjustment program, steps to reduce the cost of debt servicing, and means to improve the sustainability of Greek public debt. This reinforced strategy should provide the basis for an agreement in the Eurogroup on the main elements and financing of a second adjustment program for Greece shortly.

Ministers commit to continue negotiating with the European Parliament the legislative proposals to reinforce economic governance in the European Union in order to agree on an ambitious reform as soon as possible. The reinforced governance should be fully operational without delay.

KEY DOCUMENTS FROM THE JULY 21, 2011, AGREEMENT ON GREEK DEBT RESTRUCTURING

This appendix contains two documents that formed the initial agreement between the private sector and the public sector on restructuring Greece's debt. After negotiations early in the morning of July 21, 2011, the IIF presented a "financing offer" which was then embraced by the Council of the European Union and embedded in their statement issued later that day. The following is the full text of the IIF Financing Offer and key paragraphs excerpted from the Council's statement. (The full text of the Council's statement can be found at https://www.consilium.europa.eu/media/21426/20110721-statement-by-the-heads-of-state-or-government-of-the-euro-area-and-eu-institutions-en.pdf.)

Thursday, July 21, 2011
IIF Financing Offer

The members of the IIF and other major financial institutions extend a financing offer to Greece. We welcome the intention of the EU to improve the terms of its financial assistance to Greece, including lower interest rates, extended maturities, and a more flexible and a broader scope of operations for the EFSF. As part of a comprehensive plan, including additional support by the IMF and the redoubling of adjustment efforts by Greece, we are prepared to participate in a voluntary program of debt exchange and a buyback plan developed by the Greek government. In summary, the program involves an exchange of existing Greek government bonds into a combination of four instruments together with the Greek Debt Buyback Facility.

Four Instruments: (Refer to the Term Sheet for Details)

1) A Par Bond Exchange into a 30-year instrument

2) A Par Bond offer involving rolling-over maturing Greek government bonds into 30-year instruments

3) A Discount Bond Exchange into a 30-year instrument

4) A Discount Bond Exchange into a 15-year instrument

For instruments 1, 2, and 3, the principal is fully collateralized by 30-year zero coupon AAA bonds. For instrument 4, the principal is partially collateralized through funds held in an escrow account.

It is assumed that investors will select among the four instruments in equal proportions of 25% of total participation.

All instruments will be priced to produce a 21% Net Present Value (NPV) loss based on an assumed discount rate of 9%. The terms outlined in the Term Sheet are broadly comparable to those of the official sector. The interest rates are structured to maximize the benefits to Greece in the early years of the program as Greece regains access to global capital markets. For example, the coupon on the Par Bond will be 4% during the first five years, 4.5% during the next five years, and 5% for the years 2011–2030. Based on a target participation rate of 90%, the private sector investors through this program will contribute €54 billion from mid-2011 through mid-2014 and a total of €135 billion to the financing of Greece from mid-2011 to end-2020. In addition to this assured financing, this program will also improve significantly the maturity profile of Greece's debt, increasing the average maturity from an average of 6 years to 11 years.

The size of the Buyback Facility will be determined after having further discussions involving the official sector. It is expected to be of sufficient scale that when combined with the €13.5 billion debt reduction through the discount bond exchange, there will be a meaningful reduction in the stock of Greece's debt relative to GDP. This will be reinforced by Greece's new privatization program and prospects for higher growth which should emerge as the program takes hold.

We consider this offer to be unique given the exceptional circumstances of Greece. Notwithstanding the progress made by Greece during the last one and a half years, the scale of Greece's economic imbalances and the inefficiencies that have been embedded in its economic structures require a special approach that can enhance debt sustainability and restore confidence in the future of the Greek economy.

The offer is already supported by the financial institutions listed in Annex 2, and we expect support to build as the offer and the comprehensive program surrounding it is more widely disseminated.

Our offer is conditioned on the comprehensive economic reform program of Greece, the strong support of the EU, which has just been reinforced, and additional support by the IMF.

Annex 1 – Term Sheet
Instruments and Technical Aspects

1. A **Par Bond Exchange** into a new 30-year instrument with the principal collateralized by 30-year zero-coupon AAA rated bonds. The zero-coupon bonds are purchased using EFSF funds. Greece pays the funding cost to the EFSF. The principal is repaid to the investor using the proceeds of the maturity of the zero-coupon bonds.

   The coupon paid to the investor has the following structure:

Period	Coupon
Years 1–5	4%
Years 6–10	4.5%
Years 11–30	5%

   This is equivalent to a 4.5% fixed coupon rate.

   Assumed *participation rate*: 25% of total exchange.

2. A **Par Bond offered at par value** as a Committed Financing Facility to roll into new 30-year par bond at the time the current claim matures. The principal is collateralized using the same mechanism as for instrument 1.

The coupon paid to the investor has the following structure:

Period	Coupon
Years 1–5	4%
Years 6–10	4.5%
Years 11–30	5%

This is equivalent to a 4.5% fixed coupon rate.

Assumed *participation rate*: 25% of total exchange.

3. A **Discount Bond Exchange** offered at 80% of par into a new **30-year** instrument. The principal is collateralized using the same mechanism as for instrument 1.

The coupon paid to the investor has the following structure:

Period	Coupon
Years 1–5	6%
Years 6–10	6.5%
Years 11–30	6.8%

This is equivalent to a 6.42% fixed coupon rate.

Assumed *participation rate*: 25% of total exchange.

4. A **Discount Bond Exchange** offered at 80% for a 15-year instrument. The principal is partially collateralized with 80% of losses being covered up to a maximum of 40% of the notional value of the new instrument. The collateral is provided by funds held in escrow. These funds are borrowed by Greece from the EFSF. The EFSF funding costs are covered by the interest earned on the funds in the escrow account so there is no funding cost to Greece of this collateral. The funds in escrow are returned to the EFSF upon maturity, if not used, and the principal on the bond is repaid by Greece.

The coupon paid to the Investor is 5.9%.

Assumed *participation rate*: 25% of total exchange.

The rates presented here are indicative only based on today's market conditions. Final pricing will be based on a fixed margin over the relevant euro mid-swap rate at the time of execution.

All instruments will be priced to be economically equivalent at 21% NPV discount calculated at a discount rate of 9.

Coupons quoted are fixed, annual rates.

Council of the European Union, Brussels, 21 July 2011 Excerpts from the Statement by the Heads of State or Government of the Euro Area and EU Institutions

5. The financial sector has indicated its willingness to support Greece on a voluntary basis through a menu of options further strengthening overall sustainability. The net contribution of the private sector is estimated at 37 billion euro.¶ Credit enhancement will be provided to underpin the quality of collateral so as to allow its continued use for access to Eurosystem liquidity operations by Greek banks. We will provide adequate resources to recapitalise Greek banks if needed.

Private sector involvement:

6. As far as our general approach to private sector involvement in the euro area is concerned, we would like to make it clear that Greece requires an exceptional and unique solution.

7. All other euro countries solemnly reaffirm their inflexible determination to honour fully their own individual sovereign signature and all their commitments to sustainable fiscal conditions and structural reforms. The euro area Heads of State or Government fully support this determination as the credibility of all their sovereign signatures is a decisive element for ensuring financial stability in the euro area as a whole.

¶ Taking into account the cost of credit enhancement for the period 2011-2014. In addition, a debt buy back programme will contribute to 12.6 billion euro, bringing the total to 50 billion euro. For the period 2011-2019, the total net contribution of the private sector involvement is estimated at 106 billion euro.

(The following is an attachment issued with the Statement by the European Council on July 21, 2011)

IIF offer + Debt Buy Back

Participation rate 90

PSI contribution 2011–2020

Gross	135
Cost of credit enhancement	42
PSI net of credit enhancement	93

PSI contribution 2011–2014

Gross	54
Cost of credit enhancement *of which €16,8 bn for bonds maturing 2014*	35
PSI net of credit enhancement *of which €18,4 bn for bonds maturing 2020*	19

Debt reduction from PSI	13.5
As % of GDP	6,0%

NPV loss	21%
Official contribution from EA for DBB	20
Debt reduction from DBB (*)	12,6
As % of GDP	5,6%

Total debt reduction PSI + DBB	26,1
As % of GDP	11,6%

Financing for Greece without PSI	88

Additional financing for Greece after PSI 2011–2014	34
Cost of credit enhancement	35

Cost of DBB	20
Cost for bank recapitalisation	20
Total additional official contribution EA/IMF	109
Total net PSI contribution including DBB - 2014	31
Total net PSI contribution including DBB - 2020	106

(*) Average Debt Buy Back Price: 61.43%

(**) Does not include about €45 billion still to be disbursed under the current Greek programme

EXCERPTS FROM THE EURO SUMMIT STATEMENT –OCTOBER 26, 2011

EURO SUMMIT STATEMENT, BRUSSELS, 26 OCTOBER 2011

(Full text can be found at https://www.consilium.europa.eu/uedocs/cms_data/docs/pressdata/en/ec/125644.pdf)

9. We welcome the decision by the Eurogroup on the disbursement of the 6th tranche of the EU-IMF support programme for Greece. We look forward to the conclusion of a sustainable and credible new EU-IMF multiannual programme by the end of the year.

10. The mechanisms for the monitoring of implementation of the Greek programme must be strengthened, as requested by the Greek government. The ownership of the programme is Greek and its implementation is the responsibility of the Greek authorities. In the context of the new programme, the Commission, in cooperation with the other Troika partners, will establish for the duration of the programme a monitoring capacity on the ground, including with the involvement of national experts, to work in close and continuous cooperation with the Greek government and the Troika to advise and offer assistance in order to ensure the timely and full implementation of the reforms. It will assist the Troika in assessing

the conformity of measures which will be taken by the Greek government within the commitments of the programme. This new role will be laid down in the Memorandum of Understanding. To facilitate the efficient use of the sizeable official loans for the recapitalization of Greek banks, the governance of the Hellenic Financial Stability Fund (HFSF) will be strengthened in agreement with the Greek government and the Troika.

11. We fully support the Task Force on technical assistance set up by the Commission.

12. The Private Sector Involvement (PSI) has a vital role in establishing the sustainability of the Greek debt. Therefore, we welcome the current discussion between Greece and its private investors to find a solution for a deeper PSI. Together with an ambitious reform programme for the Greek economy, the PSI should secure the decline of the Greek debt to GDP ratio with an objective of reaching 120% by 2020. To this end we invite Greece, private investors and all parties concerned to develop a voluntary bond exchange with a nominal discount of 50% on notional Greek debt held by private investors. The Eurozone Member States would contribute to the PSI package up to 30 bn euro. On that basis, the official sector stands ready to provide additional programme financing of up to 100 bn euro until 2014, including the required recapitalisation of Greek banks. The new programme should be agreed by the end of 2011 and the exchange of bonds should be implemented at the beginning of 2012. We call on the IMF to continue to contribute to the financing of the new Greek programme.

13. Greece commits future cash flows from project Helios or other privatisation revenue in excess of those already included in the adjustment programme to further reduce indebtedness of the Hellenic Republic by up to 15 billion euros with the aim of restoring the lending capacity of the EFSF.

14. Credit enhancement will be provided to underpin the quality of collateral so as to allow its continued use for access to Eurosystem liquidity operations by Greek banks.

15. As far as our general approach to private sector involvement in the euro area is concerned, we reiterate our decision taken on 21 July 2011 that Greece requires an exceptional and unique solution.

16. All other euro area Member States solemnly reaffirm their inflexible determination to honour fully their own individual sovereign signature and all their commitments to sustainable fiscal conditions and structural reforms. The euro area Heads of State or Government fully support this determination as the credibility of all their sovereign signatures is a decisive element for ensuring financial stability in the euro area as a whole.

BREAKDOWN OF GREEK GENERAL DEBT END-2011

BREAKDOWN OF GREEK GENERAL GOVERNMENT DEBT END-2011 (ESTIMATED)
(Based on IMF data, estimates by Alpha Bank, and IIF estimates)

	(In billions of euros)	Share in total (in %)
Total Central Government Debt	373	106.3
GGB Holdings by social security funds	22	6.3
TOTAL General Government debt	351	100.0
Short-term	9	2.6
Medium- and long-term	342	97.4
Holders of MLT debt by holder		
Official sector (IMF/EA)	73.4	20.9
IMF	17.8	5.1
EA bilateral	55.6	15.8
ECB	46.4	13.2
Loans (Public enterprises)	17	4.8
GGB holdings by the Bank of Greece	5	1.4

GGB holdings by foreign central banks	12	3.4
Other (EIB and other)	4.2	1.2
Private sector	184	52.4
Foreign	141	40.2
Banks	56	16.0
Institutional investors/Hedge funds	81	23.1
Insurance companies	20	5.7
Pension funds	10	2.8
Other/Hedge funds	51	14.5
Individual investors	4	1.1
Domestic	43	12.3
Banks	42	12.0
Individual investors	1	0.3
Memorandum item: Total privately held GGBs (including Greek social security funds)	206	58.7

IIF STAFF NOTE: IMPLICATIONS OF A DISORDERLY GREEK DEFAULT AND EURO EXIT

February 18, 2012

Dear Colleagues,

As you are aware, questions have been raised about the potential impact of a hard Greek default on Greece, Europe and the world economy.

Although it is obviously not possible to forecast with any precision the likely impact of a Greek default, I think you might find the attached IIF staff note of interest. It has been pulled together under the direction of Phil Suttle, our Chief Economist, and Hung Tran, Deputy Management Director, with the benefit of input from a number of other IIF colleagues.

The conclusions are necessarily quite tentative, but the analysis points clearly to the high risk of a Greek default, setting in motion developments which could seriously damage not only the Greek economy but the ECB and the Eurozone more widely. In addition, the potential impact on global markets should not be underestimated.

Please do not hesitate to contact Phil or Hung if you have questions regarding this work.

Best regards.

Sincerely,

Charles H. Dallara

IMPLICATIONS OF A DISORDERLY GREEK DEFAULT AND EURO EXIT

Summary

There are very damaging ramifications that would result from a disorderly default on Greek government debt. Most directly, it would impose significant further damage on an already beleaguered Greek economy raising serious social costs.

The most obvious immediate spillover is that it would put a major question mark against the quality of a sizeable amount of Greek private sector liabilities.

For the official sector in the rest of the Euro Area, however, the contingent liabilities that could result would seem to be:

- Direct losses on Greek debt holdings (€73 billion) that would probably result from a generalized default on Greek debt (owed to both private and public sector creditors);

- Sizeable potential losses by the ECB: we estimate that ECB exposure to Greece (€177 billion) is over 200% of the ECB's capital base;

- The likely need to provide substantial additional support to both Portugal and Ireland (government as well as banks) to convince market participants that these countries were indeed fully insulated from Greece (possibly a combined €380 billion over a 5-year horizon);

- The likely need to provide substantial support to Spain and Italy to stem contagion there (possibly another €350 billion of combined support from the EFSF/ESM and IMF);

- The ECB would be directly damaged by a Greek default, but would come under pressure to significantly expand its SMP (currently €219 billion) to support sovereign debt markets;

- There would be sizeable bank recapitalization costs, which could easily be €160 billion. Private investors would be very leery to provide additional equity, thus leaving governments with the choice of either funding the equity themselves, or seeing banks achieve improved ratios through even sharper deleveraging;

- There would be lost tax revenues from weaker Euro Area growth and higher interest payments from higher debt levels implied in providing additional lending;

- There would be lower tax revenues resulting from lower global growth. The global growth implications of a disorderly default are, ex ante, hard to quantify. Lehman Brothers was far smaller than Greece and its demise was supposedly well anticipated. It is very hard to be confident about how producers and consumers in the Euro Area and beyond will respond when such an extreme event as a disorderly sovereign default occurs.

It is difficult to add all these contingent liabilities up with any degree of precision, although it is hard to see how they would not exceed €1 trillion.

There is a more profound issue, however. The increased involvement of the ECB in supporting the Euro Area financial system has been such that a disorderly Greek default would lead to significant losses and strains on the ECB itself. When combined with the strong likelihood that a disorderly Greek default would lead to the hurried exit of Greece from the Euro Area, this financial shock to the ECB could raise significant stability issues about the monetary union.

---

1.   A Disorderly Greek Default

This note does not address the circumstances triggering a disorderly default by Greece on its public debt obligations, but rather the consequences of such a development, especially for creditors outside of Greece. It also does not address the social and human cost of a disorderly default on the Greek population, which would be sizeable and come against a backdrop of four years of pain and adjustment. While these costs are not quantified here, they could be among the most meaningful that result from a disorderly default.

A disorderly default will begin with the failure of the Greek authorities, a Troika, and Greece's private sector creditors to agree on a package of measures that would permit the disbursement of new official funds, and the debt exchange of existing private sector claims on Greece for a new debt at a deep discount. It would most likely have the following characteristics:

- The impact effect would be that Greece would default (not honor interest payment and principal repayment obligations within the due deadlines) on its public debt by the time of the next redemption payment for Greek Government Bonds (March 20). This default would not be limited only to claims by the private creditors but would probably apply also to all outstanding claims by the official sector (including the IMF). General government debt at end-2011 amounted to €368 billion, of which some €73 billion were due to Euro Area countries and the IMF.

- This default would trigger a wave of further financial dislocations. It would most likely cause a collapse in the Greek banking system, and put at jeopardy:

  - €91 billion (as of end-2011) owed by Greek banks to foreign lenders and depositors (€28 billion of which are owed to Euro Area lenders, the bulk of which are banks);

  - €247 billion owed by Greek companies and households to Greek banks, 15 percent of which are already nonperforming. (Relative to GDP, this amounts to 115 percent.) The balance sheet impact of a redenomination of claims (in the event that Greece leaves the euro) would lead to a wave of bankruptcies among financial institutions and households, thus exacerbating the recession.

  - It would cause significant financial stress in the Greek non-financial corporate sector and put much of the €21 billion owed by resident Greek corporations to foreign lenders at risk.

  - Perhaps most significantly, a disorderly default by Greece would have substantial consequences for the ECB, which has an exposure to Greece possibly amounting to €177 billion comprising:

    › €43 billion of holdings of Greek government bonds under the SMP;

    › €110 billion of collateral in the form of GGB's and other eligible securities (mainly in the form of Greek government guaranteed bank bonds) provided by Greek banks under the ECB's refinancing facility;

> A potential €24 billion of ELA loans to Greek banks that would presumably be drawn down fully in a period of severe stress.

Given these financial traumas, it is difficult to conceive that Greece can remain a functioning member of the Euro Area in the event of a disorderly default. The Greek authorities would have little option but to regain monetary policy independence by exiting from the Euro Area and introducing a new national currency.

The practical difficulties, costs (both for the government and the private businesses in terms of switching to a new payment system) and implications of such a rushed decision would be substantial. Practical difficulties in day-to-day transactions would be serious as there would be no easy way to separate the euro notes circulating in Greece from those circulating in other Euro Area countries, with the potential for further capital flight. There would also be major difficulties/challenges in sorting out the appropriate re-denomination and valuation of existing financial assets and liabilities in current private and public sector balance sheets, in different jurisdictions.

In the circumstances, the Greek authorities would be forced to resort to borrowing from the Bank of Greece to cover budget spending, recapitalize the Greek commercial banks (which would be de facto nationalized) and put in place minimum facilities for the provision of credit to the private sector. The risk of embarking on a vicious circle of inflation and devaluation would be significant. Draconian capital controls would almost certainly be re-introduced.

The issue of whether Greece can remain in the European Union after defaulting and leaving the Euro Area is not clear cut. In principle, Greece could remain in the EU. However, the likely imposition of capital controls and possible inability to honor other EU laws and directives would raise important questions. The Lisbon Treaty, in force since 2009, introduced an EU exit clause, but does not provide for an exit from the Euro Area. The European Commission has confirmed that there was no provision under EU treaties to exit the euro without also leaving the EU. In any event, leaving the EA/EU would mean renegotiating Treaty changes—essentially negotiating Greece's disengagement from a vast web of privileges and obligations with all other Treaty members who will have to agree with the changes. This would be a lengthy and messy process, during which financial markets will be driven by panic capital flight spreading contagion to the rest of Europe and the global economy.

2.   Contagion to Other Periphery Countries

Investors experiencing a traumatic loss in value on their Greek holdings are far more likely to be conservative in their assessment about whether such things might occur in the case of other countries.

Problems in Greece spread to Ireland and Portugal in 2010–11, leading the European authorities to assemble large programs to take all three countries out of the market through 2012. The obvious focus will be on whether a second round of contagion might spread.[1]

One issue that should be emphasized is that in the circumstances of a disorderly default, the problem of contagion results not so much from the breakdown in trust that creditors have about debtors, *so much as the breakdown and trust that creditors have about each other*. Greece has delivered on many fronts, but has failed on others; other peripheral countries started with fewer problems and have delivered more on a broader array of fronts, including those of key structural adjustments. These efforts are liable to be overwhelmed, however, in an environment where investors become once more focused not so much *on* the return on their investment, as the return *of* their investment.

Despite bold efforts by the government, contagion would likely be most acute in the case of Portugal, which lost financial market access in early 2011, and is already rated well below investment grade by the major agencies. Its debt currently trades at distressed yield levels. Contagion might then quickly spread to Ireland, Italy, and Spain (the latter two continue to roll over their debt in financial markets but have seen their yields remain elevated despite some decline). Italian and Spanish banks have become far more dependent on ECB funding in recent months.

These contagion risks would no doubt increase sharply if Greece were to withdraw from the Euro Area. The very fact that such a withdrawal occurred for one country would set up fears that it *could* happen for others.

In order to address these contagion worries in a credible manner, Euro Area governments will need to carry through on promises to meet the financing needs of the governments that have lost market access for a period of time that could turn out to be far longer than originally planned.

Both Portugal and Ireland have shown strong political resolve and made substantial progress in implementing their adjustment programs, but are likely to suffer strong adverse effects from expectations—prompted by Greece's effective exit from the Eurozone—that they would be hard pressed to avoid severe pressures.

The adverse shock for **Portugal**, which has to implement a particularly ambitious fiscal adjustment this year against the backdrop of a much weaker growth outlook, will be particularly strong. Indeed, the recent sharp increase in government bond spreads suggests that markets are already concerned about possible fallout from Greece. A disorderly Greek default is likely to prevent Portuguese borrowers from returning to capital markets anytime soon. If, by way of illustration, it is assumed that Portugal is unable to access markets through 2016, then official lenders would be required to:

- Provide €16 billion annually in financing to the government from 2013 through 2016, or €65 billion in total;
- Help assure that €77 billion of term funding is available through 2016, or about €15 billion a year from 2012 through 2016, together with the refinancing for some €86 billion in short-term credit to fulfill the obligations of Portuguese banks and corporates to foreign lenders;
- Help assure financing sufficient to manage some €330 billion in debt owed by Portuguese corporates and households to domestic banks, 7 percent of which are nonperforming, and some €220 billion owed by Portuguese banks and corporates to foreign lenders. (Relative to GDP, these exposures amount to 194 percent and 129 percent, respectively.)

Substantial additional official support could well be needed for **Ireland**, too, despite its strong implementation record and an improvement to date and market sentiment that may well have already brought the Irish sovereign close to regaining significant financial market access. A Greek default, however, would be likely to increase risk aversion anew, undercutting prospects for an early return to capital markets later this year or next. A return to market access for Irish borrowers could well end up being delayed for years to come. Official lenders, then, could find themselves needing to:

- Provide €18 billion annually on average in financing to the government from 2013 through 2016, or roughly €70 billion in total, that markets may now be disinclined to provide;

- Help assure that perhaps €28 billion of term funding is available through 2016, or about €7.5 billion a year, together with refinancing for most of €95 billion in short-term credit obligations of Irish banks (domestic and foreign owned) to foreign lenders;

- Help assure that perhaps €56 billion of term funding is available from 2012 through 2016, or about €11 billion a year, together with the refinancing of some €104 billion in short-term credit to fulfill the obligations of Irish corporates to foreign lenders;

- Help assure financing sufficient to manage €295 billion in debt owed by Irish corporates and households to Irish banks (domestic and foreign owned), 11 percent of which are performing, and some €250 billion owed by Irish banks and corporates to foreign lenders. (Relative to GDP, these exposures amount to about 190 percent and 160 percent, respectively.)

Borrowing costs paid by **Spain** and **Italy** could be expected to increase as financial market participants begin to price in potential exits from the Euro Area which would no longer be unthinkable following a Greek exit, and because growth outlooks for both countries are clouded by the need for sizable procyclical fiscal adjustments to reassure rattled financial markets.

Were borrowing costs for both countries on new borrowing to rise by 300 basis points from the average on their outstanding debt (roughly tracking the pre-Deauville average/post-Deauville peak), then:

- Spain might see an increase in its annual interest payments equal to as much as 1 percent of GDP, depending on the pace of deficit reduction and the course of nominal GDP. This would equal €10 billion a year for Spain, cumulating by 2016 to €150 billion more in interest payments over 2012–2016 than had Spanish borrowing costs returned to their pre-Deauville lows. On average over the same period, interest costs might prove to be 2.5-3 percent of GDP a year larger than would otherwise have been the case.

- Italy, with a larger debt than a smaller deficit relative to GDP, might see an increase in its annual interest payments equal to as much as 0.7 percent of GDP. Interest payments would increase by €13 billion a year more, or nearly €200 billion accumulatively over 2012–2016, averaging about 2 percent more than might have been expected if borrowing costs declined again to pre-Deauville lows.

Under Europe's tightened fiscal rules, these increases in interest payments would have to be offset with tax increases or cuts in noninterest outlays, draining equivalent amounts from private incomes and demand. The broader effects of this additional tightening could be expected to weaken demand for exports from the northern half of the Euro Area.

Taken together, indeed, Spain and Italy account for 8 percent of exports for the Euro Area members as a whole, compared with just 2 percent for Greece, Portugal and Ireland. Comparable numbers for Germany are 7.5 percent and 1.5 percent for the two sets of countries. France, by contrast, sends 12 percent of its exports to Spain and Italy, compared with just 1.7 percent to Greece, Portugal, and Ireland.

Follow-on effects of weaker import demand in Spain and Italy should be expected to have significant effects on output, employment, and tax revenues in those countries and the northern half of the Euro Area, including Germany, France, the Netherlands, and Belgium, for which Spain and Italy are important markets.

3. Spillover to the Euro Area Banking System and the ECB

Prominent among the broader implications of this disorderly group default and Euro Area exit would be the additional capital requirements that markets and supervisors could be expected to place on European banks as a result of both actual and potential losses resulting from the asset price declines and credit losses that would follow from a disorderly default.

Rough calculations assuming the need to offset increases in yields of 300 basis points on Spanish and Italian debt would indicate a need for an additional €100–€110 billion of capital for the larger banks covered by EBA stress tests. Factoring in the effects of further/renewed declines in Portuguese and Irish bond prices (to 20 percent of par) would add another €25–€30 billion in capital needs. Taking these together, the additional sovereign buffer requirement could total nearly €160 billion. This would be four times the roughly €40 billion in a sovereign exposure buffers the EBA required in its October 2011 recapitalization exercise.

Leaving aside the considerable additional capital that would be needed to provide for the increase in nonperforming loans that could be expected to result from a renewed weakening of activity across the Euro Area, these more expensive sovereign buffers would need to be met either by raising additional capital of this magnitude from private markets or from additional capital injections by Euro Area governments.

The latter would add directly further to government debt and potentially to the deficit, depending on the precise form of capital support. If, on the other hand, the bulk is to be raised in private markets, then recent evidence suggests that this would likely result in accelerated credit deleveraging, which would have a substantial further adverse effect on Euro Area economic activity. In turn, this would further weaken government revenue in a vicious circle.

The EFSF and its soon-to-be successor, the ESM, have been promoted as the key "firewalls" to prevent contagion. They would presumably be responsible for much of the extra financing that might be required for the periphery, as discussed above. Market sentiment was positively affected by revisions to these European financial support mechanisms since the July EU summit. These revisions have undone some of the damage done by the Deauville Summit. EFSF landing premia were cut to nil and maturities extended in principle to 30 years. Euro Area heads of state and government pledged that the rescheduling treatment accorded Greece would be "unique and exceptional" and that other member states with programs would have their financing needs met until they were able to restore market access. Language was rescinded from the Treaty establishing the ESM-required debt sustainability assessments and private sector involvement before new programs of official financing can be agreed. The effective lending capacity of the EFSF was boosted to €440 billion from roughly €260 billion earlier and utilization expanded to include primary and secondary purchases of sovereign debt, the lending for bank recapitalization, and agreement for "precautionary, contingent financing." The startup date for the ESM was brought forward to mid-2012 from mid-2013.

The German government, finally, was rumored to be prepared to agree in March that the EFSF should be allowed to run alongside the ESM through mid-2013, boosting EU support facilities to €1 trillion for one year only, potentially alongside additional IMF funds of another

€0.5 trillion, funded partly by the €150 billion pledged by the Euro Area Heads from the ECB reserves.

Disorderly default by Greece, however, would immediately unwind what positive sentiment market remains about the adequacy of the financial support mechanisms that Europe has put in place. Expectations would harden that the Euro Area governments would choose to cap combined EFSF/ESM lending at €500 billion. More significantly, hopes would fade that lendable IMF resources could be increased significantly from €280 billion at present.

That all said, the most effective "firewall" to date has been provided by the ECB, in the form of its willingness to refinance the Euro Area banking system. This has allowed banks to reduce the extent to which they have had to trim lending to the private sector and, crucially, has allowed banks in periphery countries to maintain holdings of government debt on their balance sheets. This refinancing support has been accompanied by the ongoing support from direct bond purchases under the SMP:

- SMP purchases of Spanish and Italian debt by the ECB are understood to have amounted to as much as €100 billion since July 2011;

- Analyst estimates suggest that Spanish and Italian banks may have accounted for one-third of the take-up of the ECB's €486 billion December LTRO, or €160 billion. To the extent that the latter was used to fund buying of the bonds of their respective sovereigns, this suggests funding needs (filled since last summer by the ECB) at an annual pace of roughly €0.5 trillion. These have been sufficient to reverse only two-thirds of the 300 basis point post-Deauville run-up in Spanish bond yields and only one-third of a similar-size run-up in Italian bond yields.

One proxy for how much the ECB has become involved as the key "firewall" is supporting weaker Euro Area government debt and banking markets in recent months the size of the ECB's balance sheet, which has risen by a stunning 9 percentage points of Euro Area GDP, to 30% of GDP, since the middle of 2011. The exposure of the ECB has been increasingly directed to weaker Euro Area periphery countries, and this exposure would be clearly put at considerable risk by rising turmoil in the Euro Area resulting from a disorderly Greek default.

4.   Wider Macroeconomic Implications

A significant disruption from Greece to the broader Euro Area would have significant and global macroeconomic ramifications.

Each percentage point that a disorderly Greek default might clip off the level of Euro Area GDP would amount to annual income forgone of about €100 billion. In turn, this would lower annual government tax revenue by about €100 billion.

The Euro Area accounts for about 19% of the world economy. If the loss in Euro Area GDP were to have a multiplier effect on the rest of the world of a similar proportion, then each percentage point lost in Euro Area GDP would translate into an income loss elsewhere of about €90 billion.

These ripples would spread beyond the Euro Area through two key transmission mechanisms:

- There would be a direct hit to global aggregate demand and trade flows. The Euro Area accounts for about 26% of world trade. Countries closer to the Euro Area—including Eastern and Central Europe, the United Kingdom, and the Nordic countries—would be most affected, but the ripples would be far more widespread than that. Importantly, it should be noted that exports to the Euro Area account for about 4% of China's GDP and about 2% of GDP for both India and Brazil. The US and Japan are less exposed to this direct trade channel (exports to the Euro Area account for about 1% of GDP in both cases).

- Financial linkages are potentially more powerful, especially since market developments since the onset of crisis in 2007 have highlighted a propensity for "runs" to occur on a scale and at a pace that had previously been unimagined. Many policymakers incorrectly believed that the fallout from a Lehman bankruptcy would be contained, since markets had been apparently pricing in a significant default risk well ahead of the actual event.

5.   Broader Institutional Consideration

Deliberations now about providing the additional official funding needed to facilitate an orderly restructuring of Greek debt are understandable given the large upfront outlays—€60 billion for bank recapitalization and credit enhancements—needed to secure €100 billion of nominal debt reduction, the large interest savings—on the order of €7–8 billion a year initially—that would result from the proposed bond exchange with private sector creditors. Together with this large effective interest subsidy, the reprofiling and lengthening of maturities on the new bonds to 30 years would help lay the basis for renewed growth.

Catastrophic bankruptcy, however, would put at grave risk much of what has been achieved by Greece since 2009. Social strains would intensify as the economy reeled and unemployment surged from an elevated level already in excess of 20 percent. Living standards would collapse with economic activity and the further diminution of the Greek state's ability to provide basic social services and support. Against this backdrop, it would become more difficult—not less—to build the political consensus needed to free the economy, the government, and the society from vested interests that deeper crisis would more firmly entrench. Whatever its economic benefits, a sharply depreciated "new" drachma under these circumstances would assure that the costs of adjustment, now greatly increased, would be distributed even more unevenly than at present.

Europe, too, would take a considerable step backwards, not just because of the considerable additional financial costs that look likely to result from intensified contagion and inadequate firewalls. Europe's governments and its core institutions, the ECB in particular, would incur enormous financial losses not four years removed from the large but more limited ones incurred in the wake of the Lehman crisis. Tightened fiscal rules would provide still more constraining to growth, employment, and living standards under the strains of the additional resources needed to recapitalize banks and the ECB and as a result of the revenue forgone as activity contracts. Sitting governments would be hard pressed to convince electorates that their mandates should be extended.

Greece's effective expulsion from the EU would represent the first failure of European integration since the founding of the coal and steel community in 1951. This would have lasting ramifications. Successive extensions of Community and then Union institutions, accompanied by successive accessions, have transformed Western Europe and now central Europe, economically, politically, and socially.

Similar success in Greece will take time, patience, and resources from both the private and public sectors. Overcoming setbacks, recognizing what has been achieved, and sustaining the commitment needed assure that what has yet to be done gets done would sustain the powerful example Europe holds for the remainder of eastern Europe and the southern and eastern rims of the Mediterranean. Perseverance now would keep Europe on course to assume more of the greater global role that remains commensurate with its size, wealth, and potential.

THE EVOLUTION OF GREEK PUBLIC DEBT AND DEBT SUSTAINABILITY 2012–2018, BY MIKIS HADJIMICHAEL

The main text of this book provides considerable background on developments in Greek public debt and debt sustainability leading up to the crisis and during the period of negotiations in 2011 and 2012. This appendix provides additional background on how those key parameters unfolded following the period of negotiations on the sovereign debt.

Greece's general government debt amounted to €356b (177% of GDP) at end 2011 but declined markedly to €305b (162% of GDP) by end-2012 as a result of the restructuring. It rose somewhat again in subsequent years, fluctuating within a narrow range of €312b–€321b during 2013–17, and peaked at €335b (186% of GDP) at end-2018 toward the end of the SYRIZA-led government, easing to €331b (181% of GDP) at end-2019 before the COVID-19 pandemic. Greece's central government debt is actually higher by some €20b per year, reflecting debt holdings by official entities in Greece that are netted out on consolidation at the general government level. Debt stock levels were higher than expected or targeted at the time of the restructuring in 2012 as the result of over-optimistic program projections, policy design mistakes, and slippages under program implementation, as well as the associated need for more exceptional financial support from Greece's official partners. In fact, Greece was not expected to have a third three-year adjustment program at the time of the restructuring. The higher debt-to-GDP ratios also reflect developments in the denominator. The nominal GDP trajectory since 2012 has remained below expected levels as a result of real growth shortfalls as well as lower-than-expected increases in the GDP deflator.

Naturally, the higher-than-expected debt ratios raised sustainability concerns. The response by Greece and its official creditors was twofold. First, these efforts entailed intensified policy commitments and an extension of the program period, with primarily more ambitious fiscal targets. The latter included increased primary budget surplus targets during the third program period and beyond. Second, more debt relief became necessary. However, as the share of Greece's public debt due to private creditors had declined to about 18% after the restructuring, the needed additional debt relief had to come from official creditors, namely Greece's Euro Area member countries.

In fact, the IMF, based on its new policy framework for lending to market access countries with unsustainable public debt positions, called on Greece's official creditors in 2015 to provide an upfront nominal debt reduction (haircut)—as the private sector creditors did with the private debt restructuring. But the Euro Area strongly resisted such requests. It would have been very difficult to reward Greece's SYRIZA government with an upfront debt haircut so soon after the developments and renewed "Grexit" risks in the first half of 2015, and the EU constitution does not allow support to a member country in the form of outright debt reduction from other member countries. In the face of this impasse, the IMF opted out from any additional formal engagement and new financial support under the third three-year adjustment program for Greece. In addition, it called, unsuccessfully, on Euro Area creditors to ease their requirement for annual primary budget surpluses of 3.5% of GDP by Greece so as to facilitate a more pro-growth fiscal stance.

However, Greece's Euro Area official partners eventually agreed to other forms of debt relief during the period after 2013 that were quite beneficial to Greece. They substantially eased the borrowing terms on both Greece's outstanding official debt as well as on new adjustment lending, resulting in a steep reduction in Greece's annual debt service payments. This debt relief included a significant lengthening of the maturities of old debt and new lending, lowering the interest rate on Greek debt to the EFSF and the ESM to a fixed level just above the ESM borrowing cost in capital markets (AAA terms), and the granting of lengthy (in excess of 10 years) grace periods on capital and sometimes on interest payments on EFSF and ESM debt.

The end result of these debt relief measures, combined with the historic restructuring of privately held debt in 2012 as well as effective liability management by Greece, is that Greece's public debt has become highly concessional and broadly sustainable. Until 2019, the share of public debt to official creditors remained fairly stable in recent years at 82%. Among official creditors, the bulk of Greece's obligations at end-2019 were to the EFSF (37%), the ESM (17%) and the Greek Loan Facility (bilateral loans from Euro Area states, 15%)—for a total of 69%—all with very long maturities. The repayment schedule of the outstanding debt due to these entities is stretched out to 2070, 2060, and 2041, respectively. Debt to the IMF, which is relatively more expensive with high interest rates and only maximum 15-year maturities, declined to only 1.5% of total debt by 2019, following the early repayment in September 2019 (with ESM agreement) of one-third of the total outstanding IMF debt that carried a surcharge of 300 basis points. The average maturity of Greece's public debt rose from 6.3 years at end-2011, prior to the private debt restructuring, to 20.5 years by end-2019.

At the end of June 2020, 96.5% of the debt was on fixed interest rates, with an average time of almost 20 years to the next re-fixing date. Almost all (99%) of Greece's public debt is denominated in euros, and while new issuance of bonds increased during 2019–21, the share of tradable debt remains very low at 23%. At the same time, the effective average interest on Greece's public debt declined from 4.5% in 2011 to a narrow range of 1.6%–1.9% during 2013–19. On this basis, Greece's public debt is clearly highly concessional, and the ratio of total debt to GDP is not very meaningful, if not misleading, as an indicator of Greece's public debt burden.

Based on its experience with Greece and other Euro Area sovereign debt crisis countries, as well as developments in other countries and pressures from private creditors, the IMF revised its methodology for assessing debt sustainability in 2013 for countries relying on market financing. The effect was to downplay the exclusive reliance on nominal stock of debt-to-GDP ratios, which was the key obsession at the time of the restructuring in 2012. Instead, the IMF now includes the ratio of annual general government gross financing need (GFN) to GDP as an alternative and complementary indicator, which is more reflective of the degree of concessionality of the stock of debt and the urgency and pressure of accessing new market financing to cover both interest payments and the rolling over of maturing debt. Under the new methodology for its Debt Sustainability Analysis (DSA), GFNs as ratios to GDP below a threshold of 15% are considered as consistent with debt sustainability by the IMF.

Based on this methodology, the IMF assessed the Greek public debt as sustainable, both in its pre–COVID-19 DSA in August 2019 and in its updated DSA in November 2020, which was the last post-program monitoring report (taking into account the initial COVID-19 effects). In particular, the August 2019 DSA indicated that Greece's public debt would decline steadily to 145% of GDP by 2028, and that GFNs would average 7.9% of GDP during 2019–28, well below the threshold of 15% of GDP.

The November 2020 assessment indicated that Greece's public debt remained sustainable over the medium term, although downside risks had increased. The assessment also indicated that both the debt level and GFN trajectories would be somewhat higher than before COVID-19 but would still be declining after a jump in 2020. In particular, the debt-to-GDP ratio would rise to 208% in 2020 before gradually falling to 153% by 2029. The ratio of GFN to GDP would, after a one-off marginal breach of the 15% threshold in 2020, average 10% over the next ten years, only two percentage points of GDP higher than before the pandemic.

Greece has, as indicated, also experienced a major turnaround in its ability to access capital markets. As explained in the book, at the onset of the financial crisis in 2010, Greece had effectively lost access to capital markets at affordable borrowing terms. But by 2014, following the restructuring and some progress in effectively implementing its program, Greece tapped capital markets, issuing €2.1b of 3-year bonds and €4.0b of 5-year bonds at coupons of 3.5% and 4.75%, respectively. Although relatively high compared to other European bonds and the funding cost from the EFSF, these coupons were surprisingly low, certainly in comparison to the pre-restructuring market yields for Greek bonds, but also for a country in a crisis and with a doubtful debt sustainability outlook. The fact that the new bonds had fairly short maturities in relation to Greece's increasing official creditor debt helped a lot, as these bonds were de facto first in line to be repaid. The new issuance was oversubscribed by interested investors.

Greece tapped capital markets again in 2017 and 2018 at a modest amount, issuing €3b in each year, but more intensively in 2019 (€9b) and especially during 2020 (€12b) and 2021 (€14b) at increasingly longer maturity paper and at sharply narrowing coupons. This reflected the growing confidence that markets had in the Mitsotakis government policies. The inclusion of Greece in the ECB's quantitative easing program, the prevailing very easy monetary conditions (with zero ECB policy interest rates during 2018–July 2022), the substantial excess liquidity in capital markets and the associated search for yield (with negative yields for German bonds for up to 10-year maturities) also contributed to Greece's improved terms in the capital markets. As a result, the yields on new GGBs issued in 2020 fell sharply to 2% for 7-year bonds, 1-2%–1.6% for 10-year bonds, and 1.2% for 30-year bonds. The yields fell even more for 5-year and 10-year new bonds to 0% and 0.9%, respectively, during 2021, but rose to 1.7%–2.0% for 30-year bonds.

In parallel, Greece stepped up its early repayments of high interest rate debt to the IMF and individual EU states under the Greek Loan Facility, as well as the voluntary exchange in December 2021 of the bulk of outstanding expensive private debt restructuring bonds of 1-year to 20-year maturities issued to private creditors under the debt restructuring arrangements in 2012. As a consequence, the share of private creditors in total Greek public debt rose to 23% by end-2021, and the average interest rate fell further to 1.6%. Greek public debt rose to €341b (206.3% of GDP) by end-2020 and €353.4b (193.3% of GDP) by end-2021, according to PDMA data. In its latest reports, the IMF has revised these estimates upward for some 4 percentage points of GDP (to 212.4% of GDP and 199.4% of GDP, respectively) as a result of revisions to historical GDP data and the inclusion of deferred interest payments on EFSF loans.

However, the easy financial market conditions have begun to unwind, with the tightening of the ECB monetary policy stance in July 2022 and into 2023, as well as expected further increases in policy interest rates. Greece's gradual increasing reliance on market borrowing as official debt matures over the longer term have also been a factor, with the yields on new Greek market borrowing expected to reflect financial market conditions more fully. The spreads on 10-year GGBs widened to over

2 percentage points over German bonds by July 2022. In this context, Greece is eligible to benefit from the new ECB policy instrument (the Transmission Protection Instrument, announced in July 2022), which aims to guard against excessive spread widening on Eurozone member states' bonds.

The inherent risks for the sustainability of Greek public debt are substantially mitigated by the long debt maturities to both private and official creditors and the associated exceptionally long average maturity of Greek public debt at over 20 years by end-2021. Furthermore, the renewed access to capital markets at very reasonable costs and drawings from the ESM before the expiration of the third program allowed Greece, according to PDMA data, to build a substantial cushion of cash reserves of €26.8b by end-2018 (equivalent to 14.9% of GDP), which eased to €23.5b by end-2019 and €17.3b by end-2021. The IMF estimates the cash cushion at end-2021 to be much larger (at €31.6b or 11 months of Greece's gross financing need), once account is taken of Greece's SDR holdings and cash deposits of public entities with Greek commercial banks.

These mitigating factors, as well as the improved growth performance and medium-term prospects for the Greek economy, are expected to still allow a sustainable outlook for Greek public debt. This is confirmed by the debt sustainability assessments for Greece included in the Article IV Consultation Reports of July 2021 and June 2022. The July 2021 DSA indicated that Greece's public debt remained sustainable over the medium term, and that, while a feasible set of policies and interest rate trajectories could deliver sustainable debt dynamics over the longer term, uncertainty was too large to reach a firm conclusion. The DSA projections suggested a firmly downward path for public debt as a ratio to GDP of 169.5% by 2030 and low levels of gross financing need, averaging 12% of GDP over the 10-year projection period, well below the benchmark of 15% of GDP for debt sustainability.

By the time of the June 2022 report, Greece had recorded a strong growth performance in 2021, fully repaid the IMF, exited its post-program monitoring status, and was graduated to a surveillance country by IMF norms. Furthermore, the IMF revised its DSA methodology yet again, adopting a more sophisticated probability-based framework for assessing sovereign stress risk (partly based on machine-learning models), a concept considered to be wider and more encompassing than debt sustainability risk. In this context, the IMF considered that Greece had a moderate risk of sovereign stress in its June 2022 report, with public debt on a declining path as a ratio to GDP and with manageable rollover risks over the medium term.

However, there was significant uncertainty over longer-term developments. Greek public debt ratio was projected to decline steadily to 142% of GDP by 2032, based on conservative assumptions on real GDP growth (1.2%) and primary budget surpluses (1.5% of GDP) during 2028–2032. The gross financing needs were also projected to remain modest after 2022, amounting on average to 8.3% of GDP, lower than estimated in earlier years. Greek authorities agreed with these assessments, recognizing that the medium-term and longer-term outlooks depended on the likely risk premia on Greek debt, as well as on the likely success in implementing growth-oriented structural reform policies and the authorities' ability to realize primary budget surpluses. The authorities felt confident that they would, in fact, be able to achieve both primary surpluses of 2.2% of GDP and stronger growth than assumed by the IMF, resulting in even lower debt ratios over the projection period.

Not surprisingly, Greece's assessments by the major credit rating agencies have improved significantly since 2012 and 2013H1, and the renewed low ratings in 2015 and 2016, when SYRIZA came to power and "Grexit" concerns re-emerged. More specifically, Moody's raised its rating from C in 2012 to BB- at present (July 2022). Fitch was relatively less critical of Greece, raising its rating from CCC in 2012 (and CC in early 2015) to BB in July 2022. S&P was in between, raising its rating from CC in 2012 to BB- until 2021, but upgraded Greece to BB+ in April 2022.

SPEECH—THE GREEK DEBT EXCHANGE: LESSONS FOR EUROPE AND THE GLOBAL FINANCIAL SYSTEM

"THE GREEK DEBT EXCHANGE: LESSONS FOR EUROPE AND THE GLOBAL FINANCIAL SYSTEM"
Luncheon Presentation in Dublin, Ireland, by Charles H. Dallara, Managing Director, Institute of International Finance, Institute of International and European Affairs (IIEA)—May 16, 2012

Speaking Notes

1. **Introduction**

   · An unprecedented voluntary debt exchange for Greece was concluded during mid-March to early May 2012

   · This is a historic event in many ways:

     - The first debt restructuring by a mature country in decades

     - The first debt restructuring by a Euro Area country

     - The largest debt restructuring in history

     - The first debt restructuring that has had such a major impact on regional economic and financial developments, market sentiment and financial stability in the euro area, global output growth, and global financial market developments—all from a country of 11 million people and an output equivalent to only 2% of activity in the Euro Area

· We will discuss why this is the case and what the debt exchange entails, what is novel, and why it is so important.

· We will also discuss briefly the broader sovereign debt crisis management challenges in the Euro Area, remaining contagion risks and implications for the Euro Area banking system.

· But first, a broad indication of the global setting.

  - We are currently going through a period of concern about global output and employment growth. Global economic prospects have regrettably deteriorated. World growth is expected to slow this year, including in Asia.

  - Many Asian and other emerging markets, while still experiencing solid growth, have been affected by the debt crisis in Europe and the increasing deleveraging by banks, which have resulted in an eased global export demand and reduced European bank exposure to Asia.

  - A strengthened framework for international policy coordination among the G20 countries is sorely needed:

    › Emphasizing

      » Increased accountability and deeper commitment from key economies,

      » As well as a fuller and more active participation of leading emerging markets, including from Asia

      » Aimed inter alia at correcting both global and regional imbalances between surplus and deficit countries.

  - A successful strategy should focus on:

    › Addressing strains in the Euro Area and fiscal imbalances in mature countries in general, and on

    › Balancing the often competing objectives of regulatory reforms for financial stability and sustaining credit growth in the current environment (avoiding unintended consequences).

2.   What does the voluntary debt exchange for Greece entail?

· This is a voluntary debt exchange between domestic and foreign private creditors and the Greek government. This does not affect the Greek government's obligations to the official sector—including Euro Area countries, the IMF, the ECB, NCBs and the EIB. This is a voluntary private sector debt restructuring.

The key terms of the deal are as follows:

· An upfront nominal debt reduction of 53.5%, going beyond the 50% haircut envisaged in the October 26/27 Agreement with the Euro Area leaders, with 15% paid in the form of European Financial Stability Facility (EFSF) notes of 1-2 years maturity, and the remaining 31.5% exchanged with new GGBs of maturities up to 30 years.

· Cash-equivalent payments to private creditors financed by a special contribution of €30 billion by the official sector through the EFSF as a loan to Greece.

· Annual coupons on the new GGBs kept at very low levels (2% during the three-year period to 2014, 3% during the five-year period to February 2020, 3.65% during the year to February 2021, and 4.3% thereafter), well below the prevailing market levels and the coupons on the existing bonds.

· Accrued interest payments of some €5.5 billion paid with six-month short-term EFSF notes.

· Other special features of the debt exchange, designed to help enhance the credit quality of the new GGBs, include a co-financing (A/B loan) scheme with the EFSF €30 billion and the use of English law as the governing legal framework. Under the co-financing scheme, all interest and principal repayments for the EFSF loan and the new GBBs will be channeled through a common paying agent and shared on a pro-rata basis.

· In addition, the restructuring deal includes GDP-linked securities based on the face value of the new GGBs, which offer the potential of supplementary coupon payments after 2014 (subject to a cap of 1% per year) in the event that Greece's actual nominal GDP and the actual real GDP growth exceed the baseline levels envisaged under the new 3-year program supported by the troika (thus in case of Greece's improved ability to pay).

3. **Why is it so special or novel and why is it historic?**

- It covers €206 billion of Greek government debt, the largest ever in history.

- Despite some occasional tensions and pressures for a unilateral restructuring by Greece, it has been agreed in a voluntary, cooperative process of good faith negotiations between a Steering Committee of private creditors and the Greek authorities and the Euro Area authorities (comprising, besides the national governments, the ECB, the European Commission and the European Financial Stability Facility—EFSF) and the IMF—quite a handful of counterparties.

- This is a major achievement, as it underscores the validity of resolving even the most difficult sovereign debt problems through cooperation and good faith negotiations, consistent with the G20 endorsed Code of Conduct for sovereign debtors and their private creditors—the *"Principles for Stable Capital Flows and Fair Debt Restructuring,"* which emphasize open dialogue, data transparency, good faith negotiations, and the avoidance of discrimination among creditors.

- The alternative of unilateral action would have had major adverse consequences for Greece itself, the Euro Area, and the international financial architecture.

- The debt restructuring entailed a very high initial voluntary private creditor participation rate of 83.5%; with the use of CACs, the eventual participation rate as of early May rose to almost 97%, leaving some €7 billion or 3% of the total eligible debt as holdouts.

- It had several novel features:
    - An upfront haircut of 53.5%, lowering Greece's debt by about €106 billion or almost 50% of GDP on day one.

- The use of a co-financing structure with the EFSF loan to Greece and of English law as the governing legal framework for the new Greek bonds, providing some degree of protection/credit enhancement for creditors.

- The use of GDP-linked securities in the event of higher Greek growth than anticipated in the economic program.

. The cost of the debt exchange for private creditors is itself unprecedented and exceptional. While it would depend on their specific accounting circumstances and regulatory environment, it is estimated to go well beyond the initial 53.5% haircut and could well exceed 74% in net present value terms at an assumed discount rate of 12%.

. The Euro Area authorities have declared that Greece is an exceptional case and essentially that the debt restructuring that was needed for dealing with Greece's debt problems would not be a feature that would be expected to be repeated in other Euro Area countries.

4. What would the Debt Restructuring Deal do for Greece?

There will be several interrelated benefits to Greece:

. The debt exchange results will catalyze the strong financial official sector support of €130 billion for Greece's new three-year reform program, including sizable funds to recapitalize the Greek banking system and facilitate the financial intermediation process and bank credit expansion to the private sector.

. The deal is an integral part of Greece's reinforced economic reform program. Greece's updated reform program incorporates stepped-up policy commitments by Greece itself, additional large financing commitments by the official sector for the period to 2014 and beyond (official financial support would continue until Greece regains market access, provided the program remains on track), and the contribution by private creditors.

. Greece's new three-year program builds on the important, albeit uneven, progress achieved over the past two years in lowering fiscal imbalances and introducing structural reforms to improve competitiveness and unblock the productive potential of the economy.

- This took place against the backdrop of deepening economic contraction for the fifth year in a row, rapidly rising unemployment to over 21% of the labor force, weakening consumer and investor confidence, and a deteriorating growth outlook for the Euro Area as a whole.

- The new program incorporates additional deep cuts in public spending and public employment, strengthened institutional arrangements for tax collection, additional cuts and pension benefits, a sharp lowering of the minimum wage, further labor market liberalization, a reinvigorated privatization program, and a broad range of stepped-up structural reforms to enhance productivity and improve competitiveness.

- Overall, the program envisages a shift from a primary budget deficit equivalent to 2.4% of GDP in 2011 to primary budget surpluses of about 4.5% of GDP during 2014–2017, and the resumption of positive economic growth from 2014 onwards.

· The program objectives are admittedly fairly ambitious and the envisaged new measures quite substantive, especially against the background of social tensions, political instability and adjustment fatigue experienced in Greece over the past year. The attainment of these targets would require strengthened and sustained political commitment to reform, including by the new Greek government that hopefully will be formed after the May 6 elections to succeed the current cooperative government headed by technocratic Prime Minister Lucas Papademos. Understandably, downside risks are elevated, particularly in view of the results of the May 6 elections, as the two main political parties that support the commitments undertaken under the new three-year program did not win a majority of seats, and the progress of forming a coalition government remain uncertain. The deadline for forming a new government or calling for new elections is May 17.

· The voluntary restructuring will offer Greece a steep upfront debt reduction and large cash flow benefits through the replacement of all remaining privately held debt with new Greek debt at extremely low interest rates and very long maturities.

· Through these direct benefits, and as an integral part of the combined support package for Greece, the voluntary debt exchange will help provide Greece the necessary breathing space to effectively implement the broad range of reforms needed to achieve fiscal consolidation, lower public debt, enhance competitiveness, regain market confidence and market access, restore economic growth, and thus pave the way for debt sustainability.

· It is estimated that, on this basis, Greece's public debt as a ratio to GDP would decline steadily after 2014 and reach 116.5% by 2020, admittedly still a fairly high level. But, as the downward trend would continue in subsequent years with a projected steady GDP growth and a favorable debt maturity structure, Greece's public debt would be on a clear trajectory toward achieving debt sustainability.

5. What explains the large spillover effects and contagion risks to the Euro Area and beyond?

· Other Euro Area countries facing large budget deficits, large outstanding public debt, and competitiveness gaps have encountered difficulties in accessing capital markets at different degrees in the aftermath of the deepening of Greece's financial difficulties.

· Ireland faced a collapse of its housing market boom that precipitated large financing requirements for its overexposed banking system and had to resort to financial support from the Euro Area and the IMF to secure adequate financing, as access to market financing dried up.

· Portugal had similar public sector funding difficulties as Greece and it, too, embarked on a troika-assisted reform program.

· Spain and Italy have faced at times major liquidity problems in their sovereign debt markets. Spain has experienced a housing market crisis, while Italy has been confronted with large refinancing needs for its maturing public debt, as well as perennial structural problems and weakening competitiveness.

· The sovereign debt markets and many Euro Area countries have faced pressures over the past year or so in the face of increasing risk aversion by investors.

· Commercial banks themselves in the Euro Area have come under pressure as concerns about their exposure to Greece and other peripheral Euro Area countries have disrupted their access to the interbank funding market and in funding equity increases, precipitating large declines in their equity prices. The deleveraging pressures on banks have been aggravated by the EBA request to all European banks to essentially mark sovereign debt holdings to market and to achieve a Core Tier 1 ratio of 9% by mid-2012, well beyond the new Basel III regulatory requirements (7% by 2019).

· The sovereign debt crisis in the Euro Area peripheral countries, irrespective of the underlying causes, have given rise to strong negative feedback loops with the European banking system, reversing sharply earlier progress in fostering financial integration. The inter-linkages between sovereign bond market developments in the crisis countries and the European banking system, combined with additional Core Tier 1 capital requirements imposed by the European Banking Authority (going beyond the current Basel III levels), have resulted in:

  - A fragmentation of the bank funding and sovereign debt markets along national lines;

  - A disruption in the functioning of the interbank market in Europe;

  - Exacerbated bank deleveraging pressures:

  - A breakdown of the monetary transmission mechanism; and

  - A sharp slowdown in bank credit expansion.

· The combined effects from weakening market confidence, contractionary fiscal policies in several countries and weak bank credit expansion have contributed to negative output growth in the Euro Area and have undermined the global growth prospects.

  - The April IIF GEM Projections indicate that real GDP in the Euro Area declined by 1.2% in Q4 2011, and that it would decline further during the first half of 2012 and remain flat in Q3—for 2012 as a whole, real GDP would decline by 0.4% and recover by only 0.9% in 2013.

- The recession in the Euro Area is putting a drag on global output growth and the growth of emerging market exports—it remains one of the major downside risks to global growth.

6. Potential implications from a Greek default

The political impasse after the May 6 elections in Greece has raised the risk of non-implementation of the commitments undertaken under the new three-year program supported by the official sector and has elevated the risk of a potential exit from the Euro Area. While we very much hope that political leaders in Greece would soon fully recognize the benefits of staying the course within the Euro Area, it may be useful to highlight the potential consequences for the Euro Area itself of a Greek default on all its creditors and an exit from the Euro.

The impact on Greece itself would be even more declines in output and employment, a collapse of the banking system, lack of access to any external financing, high inflation, and high unemployment.

There are some very important and damaging ramifications that would result from a disorderly default on Greek government debt. The most obvious immediate spillover is that it would put a major question mark against the quality of a sizable amount of Greek private sector liabilities.

For the official sector in the rest of the Euro Area, however, the contingent liabilities that could result would seem to be:

· Direct losses on Greek debt holdings (about €140 billion after the March 2012 disbursements) that would probably result from a generalized default on Greek debt (home to both private and public sector creditors);

· Sizable potential losses by the ECB: we estimate that ECB exposure to Greece (€177 billion) is over 200% of the ECB's capital base;

- The likely need to provide substantial additional support to both Portugal and Ireland (government as well as banks) to convince market participants that these countries were indeed fully insulated from Greece (possibly a combined €380 billion over a 5-year horizon);

- The likely need to provide substantial support to Spain and Italy to still contagion there (possibly another €350 billion of combined support from the EFSF/ESM, IMF and ECB);

- Bank recapitalization costs;

- Lost tax revenues from weaker growth and higher interest payments from higher debt levels implied and providing additional lending;

- Lower tax revenues resulting from lower global growth.

- It is hard to add all these contingent liabilities up with any degree of precision, although it is hard to see how they would not exceed €1 trillion.

- There is a more profound issue, however. The increased involvement of the ECB in supporting the Euro Area financial system has been such that a disorderly Greek default would lead to significant losses and strains on the ECB itself. When combined with the strong likelihood that a disorderly Greek default would lead to the (disorderly) exit of Greece from the Euro Area, this financial shock to the ECB could raise significant stability issues about the monetary union.

7. **Policy changes in the Euro Area**

   In a nutshell, the policy priorities for the Euro Area and the period ahead encompass the following key actions:

- A rebalancing of fiscal policy to avoid generalized fiscal austerity and accommodate a more differentiated fiscal policy that allows for

  - More room for maneuver for the program countries to ease the output and employment losses; and

  - Less stringent fiscal policies and other domestic policies (such as higher wages) and surplus countries such as Germany to help stimulate regional demand growth.

- Adoption of credible medium-term fiscal consolidation plans, based on the circumstances facing individual countries.

· To complement these measures, as well as helping to credibly break up the existing entrenched negative feedback loop between sovereign debt markets and the European banking system, Euro Area leaders need to commit to implementing a well-articulated road map for (a) the establishment of a Euro Area–wide financial stability framework; and (b) the establishment of fiscal sharing and transfer arrangements, leading eventually to a centralized fiscal authority (fiscal union) and political union.

  - The absence at present of a common Euro Area–wide framework for bank supervision and resolution as well as bank deposit insurance has contributed to the fragmentation of the banking system along national lines, the emergence of large counterparty risks, and the limited expansion of cross-border bank credit. The regional financial integration process needs to be given a major boost with an enhancement of both the institutional environment and the improvement in the economic outlook. The two aspects will be mutually reinforcing and would be greatly facilitated by parallel moves toward fiscal and political integration.

  - Greater fiscal risk sharing, conditional on more centralized fiscal governance, is the most effective way to instill credibility in regional fiscal discipline and the attainment of the articulated objectives for the size of budget deficits over the cycle and the attainment of sustainable debt positions. Ex-ante fiscal risk sharing or mutualization of fiscal risk is an essential ingredient of an effectively functioning monetary union. It would entail a further strengthening of economic governance and the transfer of fiscal sovereignty from member states to a centralized fiscal authority.

  - Fiscal risk sharing can initially take the form of common bond issuance (Eurobonds), with appropriate safeguards to contain moral hazard risk—complementing the fiscal compact and other measures already adopted to reinforce fiscal discipline.

Ultimately, it would involve the establishment of a fiscal union with the centralized federal budget. The benefits of such reforms would include risk sharing and resilience to exogenous shocks, a reversal of the sovereign banking sector negative feedback loop, and the development of a deep, liquid, low premium Euro Area–wide bond market. The concerns about moral hazard or with rewarding policy slippages are understandable under current conditions, but not so relevant if one recognizes that the pressures for resource transfers have already materialized and would likely increase further in the future at a pace that may very well be higher under current institutional arrangements and under fiscal risk sharing arrangements. This is so because under the latter arrangements there would be more effective control of fiscal policy and stronger and more credible fiscal discipline.

· Higher financial firewall resources for the EFSF/ESM and the granting of more flexibility to the EFSF/ESM to borrow from the ECB and lend directly to European banks to help meet the recapitalization needs.

· As a complement, not a substitute to these policies, continued implementation of activist policies for the ECB to help preserve financial stability in the euro area through additional injections of liquidity under the LTRO program, stabilization support under the SMP, and further reductions in policy interest rates.

8. **Conclusion**
   Overall, while the Euro Area countries have faced the most serious policy challenge since the introduction of the euro and despite the limited progress achieved so far, one cannot avoid noting the strong political commitment of all the leading countries in the Euro Area (especially Germany and France) to, as they have declared on a number of occasions, do whatever it takes to ensure the preservation of the Euro Area and the stability of the euro. While the process may be slow and at times painful, I remain optimistic that they will achieve their objective for the simple reason that it is in their best interest.

ACKNOWLEDGMENTS

Writing this book has been a lengthy process, stretching nearly a decade. Throughout these many years numerous people have contributed to the final product.

Foremost among them has been my friend and former colleague Mikis Hadjimichael. Mikis has been a partner from the inception through final edits. He provided detailed comments and critiques on the manuscript as it unfolded, working through many variations of the text. Because he was directly involved in the negotiations, his memory and records filled gaps in the story on numerous occasions and provided for corrections along the way. His considerable expertise in economic analysis was also a valuable resource as I wrote about the travails of the Greek economy and the effects of various policy measures. In addition, Mikis assisted in the drafting of a number of chapters, authored Appendix 7, and was the lead drafter of the speech contained in Appendix 8. Mikis has been an indispensable part of the process of bringing *Euroshock* to life, and I am deeply indebted to him for that.

Once I had assembled the core elements of the manuscript, I sent it to a number of colleagues for review and comments. Jean Lemierre, my fellow leader of the private sector throughout the negotiations, kindly provided extremely helpful commentary. Jacques de Larosiere, Peter Wallison, and Mario Teijeiro all reviewed the draft and shared highly constructive feedback. Jacques was also a valued advisor at several stages in the negotiations. Rodney Beaton was kind enough to review the sections related to Greek history and provided invaluable assistance in my efforts to comprehend and capture aspects of both Classical and Modern Greece. Nicholas Gage also reviewed the manuscript and shared strategic advice that proved most valuable. Charlotte Jones provided very useful critique of the chapter addressing accounting issues that surfaced during the negotiations. To all who took the time to share their expertise and insights, I am highly appreciative. Of course, I bear full responsibility for any and all errors, omissions, and faulty analysis that may remain.

I benefited greatly from the efficient and accurate work of two research assistants: Ted Liu and Han Yang. Both of them provided in-depth research and sound analysis of critical data as I sought to monitor and understand key economic and financial variables during the negotiations, as well as over other relevant periods in Greek and European history. I thank them for their professionalism and dedication.

Kelly Guerra signed on nearly a decade ago to translate my hand-written text into intelligible type. She has done a superb job throughout, turning my nearly indecipherable writing into coherent English. Kelly has also been very valuable in the many edits of the manuscript, helping to ensure that my changes were properly captured while also contributing to the overall quality of the product.

My executive assistants have also facilitated the process of creating this book. Karen Dozier was critical in supporting me during the negotiations—always available and always efficient. Carissa Sahli, Geri Weiss, Theresa Gawlik, and Irina Katz all ensured a smooth and timely flow of material during these long years.

Others have been willing to review special sections of the book. A close friend, Sam Foster II, and his father, Sam Foster Sr., both kindly reviewed the section on my service with Admiral Samuel Lee Gravely Jr., the Navy's first African American Admiral, providing valuable insights.

Bob Lange served with me on the USS *Sampson* (DDG-10) and we have been fast friends ever since. He reviewed the sections recounting my experience on the *Sampson* to ensure that my memory of that distant past was accurate, and for that I am very thankful.

My dear friend and former colleague David Mulford assiduously reviewed the chapter on the Brady Plan and brought key events in the development of the plan into the picture that I had not recalled. Chapter 14 is noticeably better as a result of his input.

My longtime friend Bruce Wells, a professional editor, was willing to lend his services to the many challenging tasks relating to the endnotes—double- and triple-checking sources, accuracy, formatting, and all other necessary details. He maintained a cooperative and professional spirit throughout that rather laborious process and added considerable value.

John Sedgwick also played a role in the creation of this book. A best-selling author himself, John joined hands with me as a ghostwriter in the very first phase of conceiving and drafting this book. Although we parted company early in the process, some of John's unique skills with the English language remain in the final manuscript, for which I am indebted. Similarly, Gail Ross served as my agent during that initial phase and provided timely support in getting the project off the ground.

Over the course of drafting the book I often met with Joe Ackermann, who for many years has been my close friend. We would recall our experiences together during the negotiations, and his observations and reflections invariably sparked new ideas, which have proven valuable in writing key elements of this lengthy saga.

I am also indebted to a number of institutions for their support of this endeavor. Steffen Meister and our colleagues of Partners Group were kind enough to distribute Advanced Reader Copies (ARCs) of the book at our Annual General Meeting in Vienna, Austria, in March 2023. They also allowed me to take sufficient time, especially during the summer of 2022, to finally assemble a full manuscript. Symeon Tsomokos and the Delphi Economic Forum were also willing to make advanced copies available at their gathering in Delphi in April 2023.

The book and the entire experience would not have been possible without the strong support of the Institute of International Finance (IIF). I am indebted to the members of the Board of Directors who allowed the IIF management to go against the grain of history and initiate discussions to restructure Greece's debt, as well as to their virtually continuous feedback and direction during the negotiations themselves. Likewise, none of this would have been possible without the Heraclean support of the IIF staff. The names of the key collaborators are captured in the book, but many others devoted valuable time and resources to this endeavor—or smoothly filled the frequent gaps created by my absence—and for that I thank them profusely. In addition, my reliable former colleague Barrie

Orellana provided timely assistance in locating photos in the digital files of the IIF as well as obtaining approvals for their use.

I also would like to thank the entire team at Rodin Books. Arthur Klebanoff, the founder, has been the consummate professional during this journey, teaching me a great deal about the business of publishing and the process (occasionally painful) of writing a book. David Wilk has done an outstanding job as the orchestra conductor of this multi-dimensional process, coordinating every aspect of the editing, assembly, and production. With great skill the copy editor, Kate Petrella, has been invaluable in keeping me on the straight and narrow when my grammar or punctuation fell short of standards, or when I failed to carry the story forward in an elegant and clear fashion. Melissa Totten has been an excellent collaborator in the challenging task of selecting, processing, and obtaining approvals for the use of many of the photos and caricatures that helped illuminate the story. Alexia Garaventa, the book designer, has helped ensure the quality of the photos and played a pivotal role in bringing the book together in its final form.

My good friend Abdessatar Ouanes and his sister Mounira Fontaine-Ouanes played a creative and essential role in obtaining the permission of the artist Jean Claude Morchoisne to use his caricature from *Les Echos*. I am very thankful for their resourcefulness. Similarly, my close friends at Alpha Bank, Spryos Filaretos and Conny Kallieri, went to extraordinary lengths to locate a caricature used in the Greek newspaper *Kathimerini* and obtain permission from the Greek artist Andreas Petroulakis to use it. Of course, I am also indebted to the artists themselves for allowing me to reproduce their creations. Liz Alderman, a senior correspondent with the *New York Times*, was most helpful in navigating the "morgue" at the *Times* to locate and obtain permissions for the photos published in that newspaper. Another accomplished journalist, Despina Syriopoulou, who covered the debt negotiations on behalf of Greek media, followed my work on the book with great interest and never failed to ensure that I had a clear picture of life on the ground in Greece during those extraordinary years of economic hardship. To all these individuals, I extend my deep gratitude.

I would also like to acknowledge the remarkable qualities of the Greek people, which came to the fore during this crisis. It can be argued, of course, that the Greeks contributed to—or indirectly facilitated—the plight in which they found themselves. Certainly, many did during the decades of clientelism and the growth of a bloated government.

However, very few countries have been subjected to the punishing depression, dislocation, and chaos that descended upon Greece in 2010 and only lifted toward the end of the decade. Despite this, the people of Greece demonstrated a remarkable amount of fortitude, resilience, and ultimately, sound judgment. They flirted with populism and false solutions for a period of time, and they had moments of extreme anger. However, as Professor Roderick Beaton pointed out in his latest book, *The Greeks*, they refused to walk away from democracy, determined to remain faithful to this fundamental approach to governance, which their forefathers had conceived many centuries ago and which continues to have a profound positive effect on the world. On the occasions when fatigue was setting in during the negotiations on the Greek debt, I found myself inspired and re-energized by the perseverance, determination, and wisdom of the Greek people.

Throughout the negotiations and the decade-long undertaking to create this book, my wife, Peixin, was a tower of strength. During the lengthy periods in 2011 and 2012 when the negotiations practically swallowed me, she was always there for a late-night word of advice or solace—and often both. During the creation of this book, she has without hesitation provided criticism and inspiration, sharing ideas and observations at each step of the way, which contributed immensely to the final product. She played the quintessential role in this long journey, which would not have been accomplished without her.

My children Stephen, Emily, and Bryan were tolerant of my peripatetic lifestyle—a trait that became aggravated during the long absences of the negotiations. They also were understanding of the extended period during which the book was taking shape and absorbing my time. For that I am deeply grateful. My only regret is that Stephen did not live to see the book come to fruition.

My grandchildren, Oumar, Vanessa, and Alya, have increasingly shown an interest in the undertaking, although more than once I have had to answer the question, "Grandad, when is the book going to be finished?"

At last, it is!

NOTES

CHAPTER 1—Late Night with Merkel and Sarkozy

1. Peter Spiegel and Gerrit Wiesmann, "Europe on edge as rescue talks stall," *Financial Times*, October 21, 2011.
2. Maureen Farrell, "Stocks plunge 3% on fear factor," *CNN Money*, September 23, 2011.
3. Hibah Yousuf, "Stocks stumble as Europe clouds the market," *CNN Money*, October 25, 2011.
4. Peter Siani-Davies, with the assistance of Mary Siani-Davies, *Crisis in Greece* (Oxford: Oxford University Press, 2017), 179.
5. Siani-Davies, 178.
6. Fiona Ehlers, "On Cine International," *Der Spiegel*, November 1, 2011, 1.

CHAPTER 2—Navigating to Greece

(no endnotes)

CHAPTER 3—Living in Greece and Sailing the Mediterranean During the Cold War

1. Andreas Papandreou, *Democracy at Gunpoint: The Greek Front* (Garden City, NY: Doubleday, 1971).
2. Brendan Simms, *Europe: The Struggle for Supremacy, 1453 to the Present* (New York: Basic Books, 2013), 468.
3. Richard Clogg, *A Concise History of Greece*, 2nd ed. (Cambridge: Cambridge University Press, 2013), 162.

4. Marisol Garcia and Neovi Karakatsanis, "Social Policy Democracy and Citizenship in Southern Europe," in Richard Gunther, P. Nikiforos Diamandouros, and Dimitri A. Sotiropoulos, eds., *Democracy and the State in the New Southern Europe* (Oxford: Oxford University Press, 2006), 127.

5. Organization for Economic Cooperation and Development, *Government at a Glance, Country Note: Greece* (Paris: OECD, June 24, 20011). https:search.oecd.org/gov/48214177.pdf.

6. Federic Holm-Hadulla et al., "Public Wages in the Euro Area: Towards Securing Stability and Competitiveness," Occasional Paper no. 112 (European Central Bank, 2010).

7. Clogg, *Concise History*, 174.

8. Clogg, 3.

9. Francis Fukuyama, *Political Order and Political Decay: From the Industrial Revolution to the Globalization of Democracy* (New York: Farrar, Straus and Giroux, 2015), 96.

10. Clogg, *Concise History*, 3.

CHAPTER 4—Back Across the Atlantic and Serving as an Admiral's Aide

1. "Guardian of the Pacific," *Ebony*, September 1977, p. 70.

CHAPTER 5—Postwar Greece and the Quest for Stability and a Capable Democracy

1. Frances Collins, *The Language of God* (New York: Free Press, 2006).

2. Roderick Beaton, *Greece: Biography of a Modern Nation* (Chicago: University of Chicago Press, 2019), 302.

3. Nicholas Gage, *Eleni* (New York: Random House, 1983).

4. George Papaconstantinou, *Game Over: The Inside Story of the Greek Crisis* (self pub., 2016), 72.

5. Papaconstantinou, 74.

6. Kostas Kostis, *History's Spoiled Children: The Story of Modern Greece* (Oxford: Oxford University Press, 2018), 357.

7. Kostis, 376.

8. Kostis, 325.

9. Kostis, 346.

10. Kostis, 326–27.

11. Kostis, 329.

12. Beaton, *Greece*, 318.

13. Kostis, *History's Spoiled Children*, 372.

14. Kostis, 373.

15. Papandreou, *Democracy at Gunpoint*, 97.

16. Papandreou, 97.

17. Beaton, *Greece*, 318.

18. Beaton, 348.

19. Kristin Tate, "The sheer size of our government workforce is an alarming problem," *The Hill*, April 14, 2019.

20. Kostis, *History's Spoiled Children*, 325.

21. Peter Siani-Davies, with the assistance of Mary Siani-Davies, *Crisis in Greece* (Oxford: Oxford University Press, 2017), 23.

22. Siani-Davies, 30.

23. Siani-Davies, 30.

24. Siani-Davies, 31.

25. Siani-Davies, 32.

26. International Monetary Fund, "Article IV Consultation, Greece," IMF Staff Report, April 23, 1985.

27. IMF, "Article IV Consultation, Greece," 1985, 21.

28. Siani-Davies, *Crisis in Greece*, 35.

29. Siani-Davies, 38.

30. Siani-Davies, 39.

31. Siani-Davies, 42.

32. Beaton, *Greece*, 348.

33. Beaton, 46.

34. Siani-Davies, *Crisis in Greece*, 50.

CHAPTER 6—The Fletcher School of Law and Diplomacy
(no endnotes)

CHAPTER 7—The United States Treasury and the Institute of International Finance

(no endnotes)

CHAPTER 8—Sarkozy on Stage

1. John W. Gordon, *South Carolina and the American Revolution: A Battlefield History* (Columbia, SC: University of South Carolina Press, 2003), 135.

CHAPTER 9—1999–2009: A Decade of Delusion

1. Tom Buerkel, "Italy's Chances for Euro Improve: Creative Accounting Gets EU's Approval," *New York Times*, February 22, 1997, http://www.nytimes.com/1997/02/22/business/worldbusiness/22lht-taxit_2.html.

2. Louise Story, Landon Thomas Jr., and Nelson Schwartz, "Wall St. Helped to Mask Debt Fueling Europe's Crisis," *New York Times*, February 13, 2010, http://www.nytimes.com/2010/02/14/business/global/14debt.html?pagewanted=all.

3. European Commission, *Report by Eurostat on the Revision of the Greek Government Deficit and Debt Figures*, November 22, 2004, 6.

4. "Papandreou Again," *Financial Times*, January 9, 2004.

5. George Provopolous, "The Greek Economy and Banking System: Recent Developments and the Way Forward" (paper presented at the Bank of Greece's social conference, "The Crisis in the Euro Area," May 23–24, 2011), 4.

6. Dawn Kawamoto, "TheGlobe.com's IPO One for the Books," CNET, January 2, 2002, http://www.cnet.com/news/theglobe-coms-ipo-one-for-the-books/.

7. Michael Sokolove, "How to Lose $850 Million—and Not Really Care," *New York Times*, June 9, 2002, http://www.nytimes.com/2002/06/09/magazine/09LENK.html?pagewanted=all.

8. Carolyn Said, "Webvan Runs Out of Gas/Online Grocer Closes It [*sic*] Doors, Laying Off 2,000," SFGATE, July 2,2001, http://www.sfgate.com/news/article/Webvan-runs-out-of-gas-Online-grocer-closes-it-2901363.php.

9. David Marsh, *Europe's Deadlock: How the Euro Crisis Could Be Solved—and Why It Won't Happen* (New Haven, CT: Yale University Press, 2013), 35.

10. John Authers, *Europe's Financial Crisis a Short Guide to How the West Fell into Crisis and the Consequences for the World* (Upper Saddle River, NJ: FT Press, 2014), 138.

11. International Monetary Fund, "Article IV Consultation, Italy," Staff Report, IMF Country Report no. 10/157, May 2010.

12. Martin Eichenbaum, Sergio Rebelo, and Carlos de Resende, *The Portuguese Crisis and the IMF*, IMF Background Paper BPP/16-02/05, July 8, 2016.

13. Siani-Davies, *Crisis in Greece*, 59.

14. Roderick Beaton, *Greece: Biography of a Modern Nation* (Chicago: University of Chicago Press, 2019), 345.

15. International Monetary Fund, "Article IV Consultation, Greece," Staff Report, Executive Summary, IMF Country Report 06/5, December 18, 2006, 3.

16. International Monetary Fund, "Article IV Consultation, Greece," Staff Report, Executive Summary, IMF Country Report 2007/026, January 25, 2007.

17. Alan S. Blinder, *After the Music Stopped: The Financial Crisis, the Response, and the Work Ahead* (New York: Penguin Books, 2013), 87.

18. Terrence Checki, "Reflections on Progress and Prospects in the Emerging Markets" (speech, IMF Spring Membership Meeting, May 31, 2007).

19. Blinder, *After the Music Stopped*, 377.

20. International Monetary Fund, "Article IV Consultation, Greece, 2009," 11.

21. George Papaconstantinou, *Game Over: The Inside Story of the Greek Crisis* (self pub., 2016), 35.

22. IMF, "Article IV Consultation, Greece, 2009," 5.

23. Blinder, *After the Music Stopped*, 799.

CHAPTER 10—Europe and the IMF Step Up

1. Ahsoka Mody, *EuroTragedy: A Drama in Nine Acts* (Oxford: Oxford University Press, 2018), 242.
2. Mody, 252.

CHAPTER 11—Austerity, Then Deauville

1. Siani-Davies, *Crisis in Greece*, 140.
2. "Russia Woos France, Germany at Security Summit," *Kyiv Post*, October 18, 2020.
3. Franco-German Declaration, Deauville, France, October 18, 2010.
4. Mody, *EuroTragedy*, 276.
5. George Papaconstantinou, *Game Over: The Inside Story of the Greek Crisis* (self pub., 2016), 169.

CHAPTER 12—Debt Restructuring Looms

1. George Papaconstantinou, *Game Over: The Inside Story of the Greek Crisis* (self pub., 2016), 194.
2. This and the preceding quotations in this paragraph are from "Moody's Downgrades Greece to B1 from Ba1," Moody's Investor Service, March 7, 2011.

CHAPTER 13—Descent into the Maelstrom

1. European Commission, "Statement by the Eurogroup," June 20, 2011.
2. Steven Fidler, "Debt Calculations Weigh on Restructuring Decisions," *Wall Street Journal*, May 20, 2011.
3. Matthew Saltmarsh, "German Plan for Greek Bailout Would Enlist Private Investors," boston.com: reprinted from *International Herald Tribune*, June 9, 2011.
4. Fidler, "Debt Calculations."
5. Landon Thomas, Jr., "Money Troubles Take Personal Toll in Greece," *New York Times*, May 15, 2011.
6. Costas Paris, Alkman Granitsas, and Bruce Orwall, "Fresh Greek Shock Waves," Wall Street Journal, June 16, 2011.

7. Neil Irwin, *The Alchemists: The Three Central Bankers and a World of Fire* (New York: Penguin Books, 2014).

8. Federal Ministry of Finance of Germany, "Chronology of the Stabilization of the Economic and Monetary Union," November 28, 2012.

9. Bank for International Settlements, *Consolidated Banking Statistics.*

10. *Financial Times*, June 28, 2011.

11. Institute of International Finance, "Highlights of Past Episodes of Debt Restructuring Experiences Under the Brady Plan," May 16, 2011.

12. BBC News, 27 June 2011.

13. Julian Schumacher, Christoph Trebesch, and Henrik Enderlein, *Sovereign Defaults in Court*, ECB Working Paper 235, February 2018, 28.

14. Schumacher et al., 21.

15. Quentin Peel and Daniel Schäfer, "German Banks Support Greek Debt Rollover," *Financial Times*, June 30, 2011.

16. Peel and Schäfer.

CHAPTER 14—The Brady Plan

1. Joseph Kraft, *The Mexican Rescue* (Group of Thirty, 1984), 54.

2. Tim Merrill and Ramon Miro, eds., *Mexico, A Country Study* (Washington, DC: Library of Congress, 1996).

3. Richard Frank, *The History of the Brady Plan* (Washington, DC: Darby Private Equity, September 2010), 19.

4. Frank, 22.

5. Frank, cover notes.

6. Frank, cover notes.

7. Frank, 35.

8. Frank, 35.

9. Nicholas F. Brady, *A Way of Going* (self pub., March 2008), 222.

10. Tim Golden, "Chief of Staff to Salinas Resigns Post," *New York Times*, March 31, 1994.

11. "Excerpts From the News Conference Given by Bush in Paris," *New York Times*, July 17, 1989.

CHAPTER 15—Moving Toward Restructuring Greece's Debt

1. Bloomberg, "Banks Signal Move on Greek Crisis," *Financial Times*, July 1, 2011.

2. Ted Liu research document, September 22, 2015, based on Bloomberg data.

3. Henning Meyer, "At Last, Germany Is Making the Right Noise About the Eurozone," *The Guardian,* June 17, 2011, https://www.theguardian.com/business/debt-crisis?page=278.

4. Nicole Itano and Maria Petrakis, "Greek Banks Ready for Rollover as Investors Discuss New Aid," Bloomberg, July 6, 2011.

5. Anastassios Gagales, Marco Rossi, and Marialuz Moreno Badia, *Greece: Selected Issues*, IMF Country Report 07/27, January 2007.

6. International Monetary Fund, "Greece—2007 Article IV Consultation Preliminary Conclusions of the Mission," December 11, 2007, http://www.imf.org/en/News/Articles/2015/09/28/04/52/mcs121007a.

7. International Monetary Fund, "IMF Executive Board Concludes 2007 Article IV Consultation with Greece," IMF Public Information Notice 08/49, April 30, 2008, http://www.imf.org/en/News/Articles/2015/09/28/04/53/pn0849.

8. National Bank of Greece et al., Letter to the IIF Board, July 10, 2011.

CHAPTER 16—The Deal Is Done (Or Is It?)

1. Bloomberg, "Copper falls further as euro crisis expected to spread beyond Greece," July 13, 2011.

2. Associated Press, "Greece seeking new bailout deal by late August," July 12, 2011.

CHAPTER 17—The Greek Economy Implodes

1. Landon Thomas Jr. and Stephen Castle, "Heads of Europe Back Broad Plan to Rescue Greece," *New York Times*, July 21, 2011.

2. Thomas Jr. and Castle.

3. Rebecca Christie, "Banks Agree to Participate in Greek Bond Exchange, Buyback," Bloomberg, July 22, 2011.

4.   Tim Devaney, "Greek Minister Confident of Program," *Washington Times*, July 26, 2011.

5.   Amy Li, Dow Jones, July 23, 2011.

6.   Wolfgang Munchau, *Financial Times*, July 25, 2011.

7.   "Lex" column, *Financial Times*, July 26, 2011.

8.   Reuters, July 26, 2011.

9.   Richard Milne and Megan Murphy, *Financial Times*, July 26, 2011.

10.   Abigail Moses, "Greece Leads Drop in Sovereign Default Risk on Rescue Package," Bloomberg, July 22, 2011.

11.   Pavan Wadhwa, Aditya Chordia, and Kedran Panagea, *JP Morgan, Exchange Rates Strategy*, July 25, 2011.

12.   Barclays Capital, "Euro Themes: Greece—Assuring the New Debt Proposal," Economics Research Note, July 26, 2011.

13.   Jack Ewing, "In Greek Debt Deal, Clear Benefits for the Banks," *New York Times*, July 25, 2011.

14.   European Commission, Directorate-General for Economic & Financial Affairs, *The Economic Adjustment Programme for Greece*, Fifth Review (Frankfurt: 2011), 9.

15.   Ted Liu, data assembled from various reports of the Bank of Greece issued in 2011 and 2012, Athens.

16.   Simone Foxman, "Finland Demands a Steep Price for Bailing Out Greece," *Business Insider*, August 16, 2011.

17.   Julia Kollewe, "ECB Raises Interest Rates Despite Debt Crisis," *The Guardian* quoting Bloomberg News, July 7, 2011.

18.   Jack Ewing, "European Bank Raises Rate for First Time Since 2008," *New York Times*, April 7, 2011.

CHAPTER 18—The Accounting Conundrum

1.   Adam Jones and Jennifer Thompson, "IASB Criticizes Greek Debt Writedown," *Financial Times*, August 30, 2011.

CHAPTER 19—Adjusting The Sails

1.   Andreas Becker, "Europe Worried Over Potential Fallout of Greek Bankruptcy," Deutsche Welle, September 13, 2011.

2. Mark Rutte and Jan Kees de Jager, "Expulsion from the Eurozone Has to be the Final Penalty," *Financial Times*, September 7, 2011.

3. "Euro-Zone Exit Strategies: Germany Plans for Possible Greek Default," *SPIEGEL International*, September 12, 2011, spiegel.de/ eurozoneexitscenarios, 785690.

4. European Commission, Directorate-General for Economic & Financial Affairs, *The Economic Adjustment Programme for Greece*, Fourth Review (Frankfurt, July 2011), 87.

5. International Monetary Fund, *Greece: Second Review Under the Stand-By Arrangement: Staff Report; Press Release on the Executive Board Discussion; and Statement by the Executive Director for Greece*, IMF Country Report No. 10/372, December 2010.

6. International Monetary Fund, *Greece: Third Review Under the Stand-By Arrangement: Staff Report*, February 28, 2011.

7. Foundation for Economic and Industrial Research, *The Greek Economy 4/11*, Quarterly Bulletin no. 66, December 2011, 12.

8. Peter Spiegel and Kerin Hope, "Greek Bail-out: A Pillar in Peril," *Financial Times*, September 12, 2011.

9. Alkman Granitsas, "Greece Announces New Tax as Unrest Flows," *Wall Street Journal*, September 13, 2011.

10. Peter Spiegel, Alan Beattie, and Joshua Chaffin, "IMF Threatens to Withhold Greek loan," *Financial Times*, September 15, 2011.

11. Harry Papachristou and Lefteris Papadimas, "Greek State Workers Disrupt Audit Talks Again," Reuters, September 30, 2011.

12. Lefteris Papadimas and Renee Maltezou, "Greece Says Not Seeking New Way Out of Crisis," Reuters, September 23, 2011.

13. Papadimas and Maltezou.

14. Landon Thomas Jr., "Investors Ask if Anything Can Save Greece From Default," *New York Times*, September 23, 2011.

15. Foundation for Economic and Industrial Research, *The Greek Economy*, 13.

16. "The Euro Crisis: Is Anyone in Charge?" *Economist*, October 2, 2011.

17. "The Euro Crisis."

18. "The Euro Crisis."

19. Mody, *Euro Tragedy*, 283.

20. Mody, 287.

21. International Monetary Fund, Independent Evaluation Office, *The IMF and the Crisis in Greece, Ireland, and Portugal*, Evaluation Report, June 2016, 25.

22. IMF, *Crisis in Greece, Ireland, Portugal*, 29.

23. Olivier Blanchard and Daniel Leigh, *Growth Forecast Errors and Fiscal Multipliers*, IMF Working Paper WP/13/1 (2013), 41–43.

24. Howard Schneider, "An Amazing Mea Culpa from the IMF's Chief Economist on Austerity," *Washington Post*, January 3, 2013.

25. Binoy Kampmark, "The Errors of Austerity: The Blanchard Prescription," *International Policy Digest*, January 9, 2013.

26. Larry Elliott, Phillip Inman, and Helena Smith, "IMF Admits: We Failed to Realise the Damage Austerity Would Do to Greece," *The Guardian*, June 5, 2013.

27. IMF, *Crisis in Greece, Ireland, Portugal*, 16–23.

28. Jan Strupczewski, "Exclusive: New Greek PSI Haircut Around 30–50 Percent," Reuters Business News, October 12, 2011.

29. James G. Neuger, "EU Said to Weigh One-Time 50% Greek Writedown, Bank Backstop," Bloomberg, October 14, 2011.

30. Neuger.

31. Homer, *Odyssey*, Book IV, line 636, https://owd.tcnj.edu/~odyssey/augustine.html.

CHAPTER 20—The Adventures of Tintin in Europe

1. Simon Kuper, "Tintin and the War," *Financial Times*, October 21, 2011.

2. Laura Steven, Eyk Henning, and Brian Blackstone, "German Bankers Argue Against Capital Plans," *Wall Street Journal*, October 14, 2011.

3. Paul Dobson and Emma Charlton, "Greek Investors Brace for Bigger Loss to Stop Rot: Euro Credit," Bloomberg, October 14, 2011.

4. Aaron Kirchfeld, "Bankers Back at EU Push for Higher Greek Losses, Capital," Bloomberg, October 17, 2011.

5. Dobson and Charlton, "Greek Investors."

6. Liam Vaughan, Gavin Finch, and Ben Moshinsky, "Stress Test Puts Pressure on 24 European Banks to Raise [. . .]" Bloomberg, July 15, 2012.

7. Derek Gatopoulos, "Violence Breaks Out Anti-Austerity Demo," *Salt Lake City Tribune*, October 20, 2011.

8. Rachel Donadio and Niki Kitsantonis, "Thousands in Greece Protest Austerity Bill," *New York Times*, October 19, 2011.

9. Donadio and Kitsantonis.

10. Pete Spiegel, "EU Looks at 60% Haircuts for Greek Debt," *Financial Times*, October 21, 2011.

11. Steve McMorran, "New Zealand Wins Rugby World Cup," *The Independent*, October 23, 2011.

CHAPTER 21—Debt Sustainability, IMF Style

1. International Monetary Fund, "Greece, Staff Report on Request for Stand-by Arrangement," IMF Country Report 10/110, May 2010.

2. International Monetary Fund, "Greece, Staff Report on Fourth Review for Stand-by Arrangement," July 13, 2011.

CHAPTER 22—Sarkozy Sits and Merkel Speaks

1. Stephen Erlanger and Stephe Castle, "Europe Agrees to Basics of Plan to Resolve Euro Crisis" *New York Times*, October 26, 2011, https://www.nytimes.com/2011/10/27/world/europe/german-vote-backs-bailout-fund-as-rifts-remain-in-talks.html.

2. Maureen Farrell, "Global Debt Markets Giddy with Excitement," *CNN Money*, October 27, 2011.

CHAPTER 23—Greece Fractures

1. Kostas Kostis, *History's Spoiled Children: The Story of Modern Greece* (Oxford: Oxford University Press, 2018), 293–98.

2. Paul Blustein, *Laid Low: Inside the Crisis That Overwhelmed Europe and the IMF* (Waterloo, ON: Center for International Governance Innovation, 2016), 267.

3. Peter Spiegel, "How the Euro Was Saved," *Financial Times*, May 11, 2014.

4. Blustein, *Laid Low*, 27.

5. Spiegel, "How the Euro Was Saved."

6. Siani-Davies, *Crisis in Greece*, 181.

7. Spiegel, "How the Euro Was Saved."

8. "IMF's Lagarde says Italian reforms lack credibility," BBC, November 4, 2011.

9. Toby Vogel, "Venizelos vote should not decide Greece's euro role," *Politico*, November 3, 2011.

10. Keith Bradsher, "China, Driver of World Economy, May Be Slowing," *New York Times*, September 23, 2011.

11. Langi Chiang, Alan Wheatley, and Ken Willis, "China [Central] Bank Chief Says Get Ready for the Worst," Reuters Business News, December 4, 2008.

CHAPTER 24—Struggling to Close the Deal

1. William R. Rhodes, *Banker to the World* (New York, McGraw-Hill, 2011).

CHAPTER 25—Rounding Second Base

(no endnotes)

CHAPTER 26—Papademos Steps Front and Center

1. Institute of International Finance, "Greece's Recent Economic, Fiscal, and Reform Developments," IIF Report, January 17, 2012.

2. Jeremy Tobin, "Bank of Canada Warns of Dangerous Euro Zone Ripple Effect," *Globe and Mail*, December 8, 2011.

3. Bank of Canada, Financial System Review, December 2011, 7.

4. Bank of Canada, 7.

5. Stephanie Hughes "'That's Bull ****:' David Dodge fires back at Poilevre's criticism of the Bank of Canada," *Financial Post*, May 9, 2022.

6. International Monetary Fund, *Greece: Request for Extended Arrangement*, Staff Report, IMF Country Report 12/57, March 2012, 5.

7. Fernando M. Martin and Christopher J. Waller, "Sovereign Debt: A Modern Greek Tragedy," Federal Reserve Bank of St. Louis Review, Sept/Oct 2012, 334, https://www.stlouisfed.org/-/media/project/

frbstl/stlouisfed/files/pdfs/publications/pub_assets/pdf/ar/2011/essay.pdf.

8. European Commission, Directorate-General for Economic & Finance Affairs, *The Second Economic Adjustment Programme for Greece* (Occasional Papers 94, March 2012).

9. IMF, *Greece: Extended Arrangement*, 7.

10. Renee Maltezou, "Greek Protest to Test Support for New PM Papademos," Reuters, November 15, 2011.

11. Institute of International Finance, press statement, January 11, 2012.

12. Associated Press, "Greece Convenes Crucial Debt Talks," January 12, 2012.

13. Associated Press, "Greece Crisis Bond Talks Enter Crucial Phase," NDTV (India), January 12, 2012.

14. Associated Press, "Greek PM Warns of Disorder in March Without Loan Deal," CTV News, January 4, 2012.

15. Bruce Clark, *Athens, City of Wisdom* (New York: Pegasus Books, 2022), 52.

CHAPTER 27—Another Turn of the Screw

1. Clark, *Athens*, 78.

2. "Banks' top negotiators quits Greece, but talks go on," *Bangkok Post*, January 22, 2012.

3. Helena Smith, "Greece to Resume Debt Talks," *The Guardian*, January 15, 2012.

4. This and all preceding quotes in this paragraph are from "EU's Juncker Talks Must Resume on Coupon on New Greek Bonds," Reuters, January 23, 2012.

5. This and all preceding quotes in this paragraph are from Peter Spiegel and Kerin Hope, "Call for EU to Control Greek Budget," *Financial Times*, January 27, 2012.

6. Spiegel and Hope.

7. Matthew Chance and Oliver Joy, "Protestors Rally as Merkel Voices Support for Austerity-hit Greece," CNN, October 9, 2012.

CHAPTER 28—A Legacy of Bad Debt and Loss of Autonomy

1. Edna Curran, "IMF Struggle to Shake Off Stigma 20 Years After Asia Crisis," Bloomberg, July 6, 2017.

2. *Wall Street Journal*, "Grand Central: Greece's Debt Restructuring, Like Others, Is No Morality Tale," Economics Blog posted July 7, 2015.

3. International Monetary Fund, Independent Evaluation Office, *Evaluation of Prolonged Use of IMF Resources*, Evaluation Report (IMF, 2002), 147.

4. International Money Fund, 158.

5. Roderick Beaton, *Greece: Biography of a Modern Nation* (Chicago: University of Chicago Press, 2019), 21.

6. William H. Wynne, *State Insolvency and Foreign Bondholders*, vol. 2 (New Haven, CT: Yale University Press, 1981), 285.

7. Mark Mazower, *The Greek Revolution: 1821 and the Making of Modern Europe* (New York: Penguin Press, 2021), 253.

8. *Lapham's Quarterly*, Archive, "Miscellany," https://www.laphamsquarterly.org/politics/miscellany/never-was-such-incapacity-veracity-shown-eve-lived-paradise.

9. Beaton, *Greece*, 126.

10. Beaton, 126.

11. Wynne, *State Insolvency*, 288.

12. Beaton, *Greece*, 134.

13. Beaton, 144.

14. Wynne, *State* Insolvency, 292–93.

15. Wynne, 293.

16. Wynne, 294.

17. Beaton, *Greece*, 161.

18. Kostis, *History's Spoiled Children*, 207

19. Kostis, 210.

20. Beaton, *Greece*, 168.

21. Beaton, 176.

22. Wynne, *State Insolvency*, 324.

23. Beaton, *Greece*, 225-26.

24. Wynne, *State Insolvency*, 349.

25. Roderick Beaton, email to author, January 6, 2023.

CHAPTER 29—First and Goal from the One-Yard Line

1. Landon Thomas Jr., "Greek Debt Talks Again Seem on the Verge of a Deal," *New York Times*, January 28, 2012.
2. Thomas.
3. Costas Paris, Alkman Granitsas, and Stephen Fiddler. "Athens, Creditors Close in On Debt Deal," *Wall Street Journal*, January 28, 2012.
4. Brian Parkin and James G. Neuger, "Europe Prepares for Greek Aid Vote," Bloomberg News, February 17, 2012.
5. Parkin and Neuger.
6. Sandrine Rastello and Simon Kennedy, "Lehman Crisis Veterans Say Europe Shouldn't Push Greece Too Far," Bloomberg News, February 17, 2012.
7. Rastello and Kennedy.
8. European Central Bank, *ECB Bulletin*, June 2010, https://www.ecb.europa.eu/pub/pdf/other/mb201006_focus01.en.pdf.

CHAPTER 30—A Deal Redux

1. "The Market," Fox Business, February 10, 2012.
2. Niki Kitsantonis and Rachel Donadio, "Greek Parliament Passes Austerity Plan After Riots Rage," *New York Times*, February 12, 2012.
3. Peter Spiegel, "More on Leaked Greek Debt Deal Documents," *Financial Times*, February 15, 2012.
4. Graeme Wearden, "Eurozone Crisis Live: Deal Reached on Greece after All-night Talks—as It Happened," *The Guardian*, 20 February 2012.
5. Wearden.
6. Wearden.
7. Eurogroup, "Full Eurogroup Statement on Greek Package," Reuters, February 21, 2012.
8. Eurogroup.
9. Eurogroup.

CHAPTER 31—The Last Few Miles

1. Evangelos Venizelos, letter to author and Jean Lemierre, February 29, 2012.

CHAPTER 32—The Deal Is Done—More or Less

1. Adam Tooze, *Crashed: How a Decade of Financial Crises Changed the World* (New York: Viking Penguin Random House, 2018), 431.

2. Tooze, 440.

3. Tooze, 440.

4. Peter Spiegel, "Greeks Urged to Run Poll as Vote on Euro," *Financial Times*, May 17, 2012.

5. Tooze, *Crashed*, 429.

6. Tooze, *Crashed*, 438.

CHAPTER 33—This Greek Tragedy Has Another Act

1. Peter Siani-Davies, with the assistance of Mary Siani-Davies, *Crisis in Greece* (Oxford: Oxford University Press, 2017), 306.

2. Adam Tooze, *Crashed: How a Decade of Financial Crises Changed the World* (New York: Viking Penguin Random House, 2018), 428.

3. Siani-Davies, *Crisis in Greece*, 301.

4. Siani-Davies, 294.

5. Masa Serdarevic, "Greece: When the Drugs Run Out," *Financial Times*, May 17, 2012.

6. Maria Basta et al., "Suicide Rates in Crete and Greece During the Economic Crisis: The Effect of Age, Gender, Unemployment and Mental Health Service Provision," *BMC Psychiatry*, November 1, 2018.

7. Lois Labrianidis and Manolis Pratsinakis, "Outward Migration from Greece During the Crisis: Final Report," London School of Economics, Study funded by the National Bank of Greece, 2014.

CHAPTER 34—Four Lost Years

1. Adam Tooze, *Crashed: How a Decade of Financial Crises Changed the World* (New York: Viking Penguin Random House, 2018), 516.

2. Larry Elliott and Helena Smith, "IMF to Admit Mistakes in Handling Debt and Bailout," *The Guardian*, June 5, 2013.

3. Jan Strupczewski, "EU, IMF Clash Over 'Mistakes' in Handling Greek Bailout," Reuters, June 6, 2013.

4. John Micklethwait, "Q & A with Christine Lagarde": Finance's Firefighter Wants to Be Its Architect," *Bloomberg Markets*, April 11, 2016.

5. International Monetary Fund, Independent Evaluation Office, *The IMF and the Crisis in Greece, Ireland, and Portugal*, Evaluation Report, June 2016, 28.

CHAPTER 35—Shaping the Future

1. Luc Chone and Dion Rabouin, "Argentina Raises Eyebrows with Surprise 100-year Bond Sale," *Reuters*, June 19, 2017.

2. Jean-Claude Trichet, "Statement by the Honorable Jean-Claude Trichet, Alternate Governor of the Fund for France," (IMF annual meeting, Washington, DC, September 23–24, 2003).

3. Trichet.

4. Institute of International Finance, "IIF Report on Implementation by the Principles Consultative Group," Washington, DC, September 2006.

5. David Marsh, *The Euro: The Politics of the New Global Currency* (New Haven, CT: Yale University Press, 2009), 189.

6. Marsh, 177.

7. George Papaconstantinou, *Whatever It Takes: The Battle for Post-Crisis Europe* (Newcastle Upon Tyne, UK: Agenda Publishing, 2020).

8. Marsh, *The Euro*, 185.

9. Stephen Green, *Reluctant Meister: How Germany's Past Is Shaping Its European Future* (London: Hans Publishing, 2014).

10. Henry Kissinger, *Leadership: Six Studies in World Strategy* (New York: Penguin Press, 2022).

CHAPTER 36—Greece Ten Years After the Restructuring

1. Kostas Kostis, *History's Spoiled Children: The Story of Modern Greece* (Oxford: Oxford University Press, 2018), 381.

2. Joan Breton Connelly, *The Parthenon Enigma* (New York: Vintage Books, 2014), xiv–xv.

3. Bruce Clark, *Athens, City of Wisdom* (New York: Pegasus Books, 2022), 79.

4. Vincent Azoulay, *Pericles of Athens*, trans. Janet Lloyd (Princeton, NJ: Princeton University Press, 2014), 67.

5. Clark, *Athens*, 89.

6. John Stuart Mill, "Review of G. Grote's *History of Greece*, I-II," *Edinburgh Review*, 1846, 343.

7. Bettany Hughes, *The Hemlock Cup* (New York: Vintage Books, 2011), 129.

8. David Brewer, *Greece, The Hidden Centuries: Turkish Rule from the Fall of Constantinople to Greek Independence* (n.p.: I.B. Tauris, 2012).

9. Kerin Hope and Kate Allen, "Greece to Tap Market for 7 Year Debt," *Financial Times*, January 29, 2018.

10. International Monetary Fund, *Greece: Staff Report for the 2022 Article IV Consultation*, May 23, 2022, 12.

11. Charles Freeman, *The Greek Achievement* (New York: Penguin Books, 1999), 269.

APPENDIX 1: Background Information on the Brady Plan and Its Potential Relevance for Greece

1. This section draws heavily on the analysis in *The History of the Brady Plan*, 2010; IIF reports; and in part William R. Cline, *International Debt Reexamined*, Washington, D.C., Institute for International Economics, 1995.

APPENDIX 2: Strategic Statements by the Private Creditors and the Official Sector on Greece

(no endnotes)

APPENDIX 3: Key Documents from the July 21, 2011, Agreement on Greek Debt

(no endnotes)

APPENDIX 4: Excerpts from the Euro Summit Statement – October 26, 2011

(no endnotes)

APPENDIX 5: Breakdown of Greek General Debt End-2011
(no endnotes)

APPENDIX 6: IIF Staff Note: Implications of a Disorderly Greek Default and Euro Exit

1. Taken together, the three Euro Area countries with EU-IMF programs have collective external obligations currently of roughly €1.4 trillion:

    · EU and IMF exposures amount to about €150 billion;

    · Lending by the ECB to the banks of each country, via their national central banks, amounts to about €250 billion;

    · Measuring sovereign exposures at market prices, BIS data suggests that foreign banks account for perhaps €0.5 trillion in loans to the three countries.

    Nonbank private lenders, including insurance companies, corporations, direct investors, and other financial institutions account for the remaining €0.5 trillion of exposure.

APPENDIX 7: The Evolution of Greek Public Debt and Debt Sustainability 2012–2018, by Mikis Hadjimichael
(no endnotes)

APPENDIX 8: Speech—The Greek Debt Exchange: Lessons for Europe and the Global Financial System
(no endnotes)

INDEX